Global Histories of Work

Work in Global and Historical Perspective

―

Edited by
Andreas Eckert, Sidney Chalhoub, Mahua Sarkar,
Dmitri van den Bersselaar, Christian G. De Vito

Volume 1

Global Histories of Work

Edited by
Andreas Eckert

DE GRUYTER
OLDENBOURG

ISBN: 978-3-11-061047-5
e-ISBN (PDF): 978-32-11-043720-1
e-ISBN (ePUB): 978-3-11-043446-0
ISSN: 2509-8861

Library of Congress Cataloging-in-Publication Data
A CIP catalog record for this book has been applied for at the Library of Congress.

Bibliographic information published by the Deutsche Nationalbibliothek
The Deutsche Nationalbibliothek lists this publication in the Deutsche Nationalbibliografie; detailed bibliographic data are available in the Internet at http://dnb.dnb.de.

© 2018 Walter de Gruyter GmbH, Berlin/Boston
This volume is text- and page-identical with the hardback published in 2016.
Titelbild: Deutsches Historisches Museum, Berlin
Typesetting: Michael Peschke, Berlin
Printing: CPI books GmbH, Leck

♾ Printed on acid free paper
Printed in Germany

www.degruyter.com

Inhalt

Introduction

Andreas Eckert
Why all the fuss about Global Labour History? —— 3

The Globalization of Labour History

Marcel van der Linden
The Promise and Challenges of Global Labor History —— 25

Christian G. De Vito / Alex Lichtenstein
Writing a Global History of Convict Labour —— 49

Philip Bonner, Jonathan Hyslop and Lucien van der Walt
Rethinking Worlds of Labour
Southern African Labour History in International Context —— 90

Varieties of Work

G. Balachandran
Workers in the World
Indian Seafarers, c. 1870s–1940s —— 125

Alf Lüdtke
Soldiering and Working: Almost the Same?
Reviewing Practices in Industry and the Military in Twentieth-Century Contexts —— 146

Gerd Spittler
Work – Transformation of Objects or Interaction Between Subjects? —— 169

Dynamics of Labour Relations

Sidney Chalhoub
The Politics of Ambiguity
Conditional Manumission, Labor Contracts, and Slave Emancipation in Brazil (1850s–1888) —— **183**

Prabhu P. Mohapatra
Regulated Informality
Legal Constructions of Labour Relations in Colonial India 1814–1926 —— **215**

Alessandro Stanziani
The Legal Status of Labour from the Seventeenth to the Nineteenth Century
Russia in a Comparative European Perspective —— **239**

The End of Wage Labour?

Michael Denning
Wageless Life —— **273**

Kathie Weeks
The Problem with Work —— **291**

Rina Agarwala
Reshaping the social contract
Emerging relations between the state and informal labor in India —— **327**

About authors —— **368**

Introduction

Andreas Eckert
Why all the fuss about Global Labour History?[1]

The New Obscurity

> In my opinion it's a shame that there is so much work in
> the world. One of the saddest things is that the only thing
> that a man can do for eight hours a day, day after day, is
> work. You can't eat eight hours a day nor drink for eight
> hours a day nor make love for eight hours –
> all you can do for eight hours is work.[2]

This insight by literary Nobel Prize winner William Faulkner refers to the central role of work in human existence. Only very few terms summarize such manifold and at the same time such fundamental issues as the concept linked with the word 'work'. What is widely understood by this term today is still very much determined by the conditions that industrial development and the labour movement imprinted on modern societies. Work is regarded as one of the key issues in the political discourse of most industrialized countries. It is sometimes even suggested that once this problem has been solved, all other problems will be solved much more easily. Success and failure, both personal and professional, are closely linked to the concept of work. Work defines status. The supposed unambiguity of the term easily leads us to ignore the fact that 'work' covers an enormous range of activities and concepts which are linked with very different horizons of experience in time and space.[3] Often, debates in industrialized countries continue to use one very limited concept of work, namely, gainful employment, which is more or less clearly separated from the domestic sphere – although this distinction no longer corresponds to the experiences of many people.

Work has been repeatedly subjected to fundamental change, and its form has often differed considerably depending on the region in which it has been under-

---

1 Some sections of this introduction draw from Andreas Eckert/Marcel van der Linden, New Perspectives on Workers and the History of Work: Global Labour History, in: Sven Beckert/Dominic Sachsenmaier (eds.), *Global History Globally*, London (forthcoming). I would like to thank Mahua Sarkar and Marcel van der Linden for comments and suggestions.
2 Quoted in Gerd Spittler, *Anthropologie der Arbeit Ein ethnographischer Vergleich*, Wiesbaden 2016, 85.
3 See Jörn Leonhard/Willibald Steinmetz (eds.), *Semantiken von Arbeit: Diachrone und vergleichende Perspektiven*, Cologne 2016.

taken. After a long period of 'baisse' and a number of academic obituaries, there is a recurrent interest in themes related to work. The constantly growing number of conferences and research projects in this area is telling of this trend in the humanities and social sciences. In this context, reference has been frequently made to on-going debates on social change, including change that could be summarized under headings such as 'financial crisis and global capitalism', 'labour and generational conflict', 'the rise of precarious and informal work', and 'transformations of the working world' through new technologies. Both in scholarly and political debates, 'informal labour', in particular, is very much *en vogue*.[4] Although some Africanists insist that "African economies are the most informalized in the world", non-waged economic activities, unregulated by law and unprotected by social regulations or services, have become increasingly visible in many parts of the world, including the North Atlantic region.[5] 'Precarity' has also become a fashionable new concept in labour studies.[6] It seems to imply that whereas in the past, capital was striving to systematically extract surplus value from a large and growing workforce that at the same time had to be tamed, today more and more workers seem to have become unnecessary. However, some scholars have drawn attention to the fact that precarity does not represent a particular phase of capitalism but that it is an inherent characteristic of capitalist labour.[7]

The discovery of the 'informal' and 'precarity' went in pair with the observation that full-time wage labour with relatively good social benefits over the course of an entire career was not a global norm, but rather the exception in many parts of the world, the contingent product of a particular conjuncture in 20th century world history.[8] This, in turn, led to the insight that the male proletarian does not

---

4 As James Ferguson in *Give a Man a Fish. Reflections on the New Politics of Distribution*, Durham/NC 2015, 93 aptly observes, a critical literature seems to agree on the inadequacy of the term 'informal' but has failed to produce alternative terminology. For a useful review of the literature see Kate Meagher, *Identity Economics. Social Networks and the Informal Economy in Nigeria*, Oxford 2010, 11-26. For critical reflection of the concept, see Jan Breman, A Bogus Concept?, in: *New Left Review* 84 (2013), 130–138.
5 Kate Meagher, The Scramble for Africans: Demography, Globalization and Africa's Informal Labor Markets, in: *Journal of Development Studies* 52 (2016), 483–497, here: 485. For a powerful argument about the global importance of informal labour relations see Jan Breman/Marcel van der Linden, Informalizing the economy: the return of the social question at a global level, in: *Development and Change* 45, 5 (2014), 920–940.
6 A widely discussed intervention is Guy Standing, *The Precariat: The New Dangerous Class*, London 2011.
7 Marcel van der Linden, San Precario: A New Inspiration for Labor Historians, in: *Labor* 11 (2014), 9–21.
8 See Ruth Pearson, Re-Assessing Paid Work and Women's Empowerment: Lessons from the Global Economy, in: Andrea Cornwall et al. (eds.), *Feminisms in Development: Contradictions,*

represent the quintessential worker but is rather one among a number of categories of workers whose histories are connected.⁹ Analysing work 'beyond wage labour' became increasingly important as it allowed for marginalized groups and their activities to form part of labour history – e.g. 'guestwork', housework, care work, children's work, sex work, surrogacy, prison and convict labour, but also non-manual work by employees and civil servants or the work of the police and soldiers.¹⁰ This extension is regarded as crucial in better capturing processes of accumulation and the production of inequality through work. On the other hand, warnings have been articulated against the tendency to dilute the concept of work ("everything is work") and to 'depoliticize' it; that is, to ignore or to play

---

Contestations and Challenges, London 1987, 201–213; Alejandro Portes/Saskia Sassen-Kooh, Making it Underground. Comparative Material on the Informal Sector in Western Market Economies, in: *American Journal of Sociology* 93,1 (1987), 30–61.

9 This is one of the major points made by Marcel van der Linden in *Workers of the World: Essays toward a Global Labor History*, Leiden 2008.

10 On guestworkers see: Stephen Castles, Guestworkers in Europe: A Resurrection, in: *International Migration Review* 40,4 (2006), 741–766; Cindy Hahamovitch, Creating Perfect Immigrants: Guestworkers of the World in Historical Perspective, in: *Labor History* 44,1 (2003), 69–94 (on labour migration see also below); On care work now: Erdmute Alber/Heike Drotbohm (eds.), *Anthropological Perspectives on Care. Work, Kinship, and the Life Course*, London 2015; Dirk Hoerder et al. (eds.), *Towards a Global History of Domestic and Caregiving Workers*, Leiden 2015. For the highly controversial theme of children's work and the ideologically charged issue of child labour, see (mostly from an anthropological perspective) Gerd Spittler/Michael Bourdillon (eds.), *African Children at Work. Working and Learning in Growing Up for Life*, Münster 2012. On sex work: Christine B. N. Chin, *Cosmopolitan Sex Workers in a Global City*, New York 2013; Lin L. Lim (ed.), *The Sex Sector. The Economic and Social Basis of Prostitution in Southeast Asia*, Geneva 1998; On surrogacy: Amrita Pande, *Transnational Commercial Surrogacy in India*, New York 2014; Mahua Sarkar, When Maternity is Paid Work. Commercial Gestational Surrogacy as a New Transnational Industry, in: Eileen Boris et al. (eds.), *Women's ILO: Transnational Networks, Working Conditions, and Gender Equality*, London (in press). On prison/convict labour: Christian de Vito/Alex Lichtenstein, Writing a Global History of Convict Labour, in: *International Review of Social History* 58,2 (2013), 285-325 (reprinted in this volume); Robert P. Weiss, "Repatriating" Low-Wage Work: The Political Economy of Prison Labor Reprivatization in the Post-Industrial United States", in: *Criminology* 39,2 (2001), 253–292; Anand A. Young, Indian Convict Workers in Southeast Asia in the Late Eighteenth and Early Nineteenth Centuries, in: *Journal of World History* 14,2 (2003), 179–208; Florence Bernault (ed.), *A History of Prison and Confinement in Africa*, Portsmouth 2003. On military labour see Erik Zürcher (ed.), *Fighting for a Living. A Comparative History of Military Labour 1500–2000*, Amsterdam 2013. For an influential article on this topic see Alf Lüdtke, Soldiering and Working: Almost the Same? Reviewing Practices in Industry and the Military in Twentieth-Century Contexts, in: Jürgen Kocka (ed.), *Work in a Modern Society. The German Historical Experience in Comparative Perspective*, New York 2010, 109–130 (reprinted in this reader); for an example from a colonial context see: Michelle Moyd, Making the Household, Making the State; Colonial Military Communities and Labor in German East Africa, in: *International Journal of Labor and Working-Class History* 80,1 (2011), 53–76.

down aspects such as violence, suppression, exploitation and political struggles about work.[11]

Be this as it may, the new interest in the theme of 'work and non-work' is highly political. Not only are definitions of what constitutes work and what is excluded from it of central importance; so are the practices and policies surrounding them. Just take the example of the *Code du Travail* in colonial French West Africa from 1952: it was the result of intense debates between French officials and African trade unions and accompanied by numerous strikes. The code placed the kind of tasks that women most often did outside the law's conception of work. The fact that women were crucial to the commerce of West African cities or that they performed a great variety of income-generating activities did not enter into the discussion of any aspect of the law.[12] What is legitimate work and what is illegal has long been a matter of state policy. The line of demarcation between labour and crime has always been fuzzy, and it has shifted and adjusted according to the needs of state and market regulatory regimes. In the same manner, the demarcation of work and leisure, so starkly contrasted in the modern period, is becoming blurred as new forms of work acquire shades of leisure while leisure itself has been industrialized.[13] The other great division linked to this topic is that between paid and unpaid work, the work outside as opposed to inside households or between men's work and women's work. A number of studies suggest that the home and the domestic sphere have always been hothouses where the regimes of discipline and the deployment of labour have evolved. These divisions are being invented, abolished and resurrected regularly, but the question remains to what extent these are rather recent or long-standing phenomena.[14] At the same time, work and non-work are increasingly understood as having culturally specific meanings. In essence, the on-going debates about notions of work triggered a substantial revision and re-evaluation of this concept. There is the danger of

---

11 See Ravi Ahuja, Preface, in: Idem (ed.), *Working Lives & Worker Militancy. The Politics of Labour in Colonial India*, New Delhi 2013. Also: Laurent Bazin, Le travail: un phénomène politique complexe et ses mutations conjoncturelles, in: *Politique Africaine* 133 (2014), 7–23.
12 Frederick Cooper, *Decolonization and African Society. The Labour Question in French and British Africa*, Cambridge 1996, 277–321.
13 Leisure is already a long-standing topic in historiography, especially in British history. See e.g. Peter Borsay, *A History of Leisure. The British Experience since 1500*, Basingstoke 2006. For the African context: Phyllis M. Martin, *Leisure and Society in Colonial Brazzaville*, Cambridge 1995.
14 There is a huge literature on this topic, ranging from Meg Luxton, *More than a Labour of Love: Three Generations of Women's Work in the Home*, Toronto 1987, and Jeanne Boydston, *Home and Work: Housework, Wages, and the Ideology of Labor in the Early Republic*, Oxford 1994, to Karen Tranberg Hansen, *Distant Companions. Servants and Employers in Zambia, 1900–1985*, Ithaca/London 1989.

watering down the concept, but by and large these debates have opened new, exciting (and often explicitly political) perspectives since the often-declared 'end of labour history'.

Thus while labour history and the history of work as a field of research are currently thriving, it has also become a very diverse field, covering a wide array of themes and approaches from ethnographic studies of the shop-floor to transnational strike movements. According to Jürgen Kocka, "it is not yet clear what the leading questions and viewpoints structuring the history of work as a general field of research might be";[15] and in a recent review article, Kim Christian Priemel made the shrewd observation that "the state of the art suggests [...] that labour history as a field of research might thrive even without labour history as a discipline."[16] Another important aspect currently discussed is related to questions of scale: One of the virtues of labour history in recent decades has been its micro-historical focus on workers and work in relation to the range of social processes in a particular milieu – race, gender and ethnicity, for instance. If we increasingly look beyond both locality and region toward wider spatial relationships, what do we learn besides the insight that we are confronted with fuzzy categories and fuzzy constellations? Labour historians face the difficulty of focusing on the necessarily specific historical trajectories in certain localities in Europa or Asia or Africa and across specific patterns of regional migration, without losing sight of the wider context. A growing number of labour historians attempt to write a history of labour and work infused with both specificity and comparison, which sees shared entanglements as bi- or multi-directional rather than unidirectional, and that does not impose a model from one period, nation, or region onto another. These efforts have been subsumed under the rubric of Global Labour History. The following pages present some of the contours of this field but without claiming to be comprehensive. Some important aspects are ignored, for instance, transformations in the historiography of labour movements and workers' resistance.[17] Moreover, the time frame of this essay is more or less restricted to the last 200 years and does not pay tribute to the numerous efforts aimed at systematically developing a long-term perspective of Global Labour History that includes the Early Modern period.

---

15 Jürgen Kocka, Work as a Problem in European History, in: Idem (ed.), *Work*, 1–15, here:1.
16 Kim Christian Priemel, Heaps of Work. The ways of labour history, in: *H-Soz-Kult*, 23 January 2014 http://www.hsozkult.de/literaturereview/id/forschungsberichte-1223 (5 May 2016). See also, Lex Heerma van Voss, Whither Labour History? Histories of Labour: National and International Perspectives, in: *International Review of Social* History 58, 1 (2013), 97–106.
17 See the infuential study by Beverly Silver, *Forces of Labor. Workers' Movements and Globalization since 1870*, Cambridge 2003.

The Emergence of a Global Perspective

Global labour history has become one of the main approaches representing new directions in the field of labour history.[18] Although rather peripheral in most relevant texts that provide introductions or overviews, it is also an important part of the fast-growing branch of 'Global history'. According to Sebastian Conrad, the core concerns of this field are "with mobility and exchange, with processes that transcend borders and boundaries. It takes the interconnected world as its point of departure, and the circulation and exchange of things, people, ideas, and institutions are among its key subjects. A preliminary and rather broad definition of global history might describe it as a form of historical analysis in which phenomena, events, and processes are placed in global contexts."[19] A meteoric rise of Global History has been noted for the Americas, Europe, and Asia, but not for Africa.[20] Although some protagonists of Global History tend to act like missionaries, most representatives of this field would agree that it is not the only acceptable approach but one perspective among others. Moreover, it is common sense that any claims by global historians of radical newness would be misleading. In numerous fields – the history of imperialism and colonialism, migration history, and environmental history among them – historians have long since begun crossing boundaries and challenging the prevailing compartmentalization of the world.[21]

---

18 The key text is still Van der Linden, *Workers of the World*. He also produced numerous essays to map the field, most notably: The Promise and Challenges of Global Labor History, in: *International Labor and Working-Class History* 82 (2012), 57–76 (reprinted in this reader). For another effort in mapping see: Andreas Eckert, What is Global Labour History Good For?, in: Kocka, *Work*, 169-181. More recently: Leo Lucassen, Working Together: New Directions in Global Labour History, in: *Journal of Global History* 11,1 (2016), 66–87. Indian historians gathered under the umbrella of the Association on Indian Labour Historians have been particularly active contributors to the framing of the field. See Marcel van der Linden/Prabhu P. Mohapatra (eds.), *Labour Matters. Towards Global Histories*, New Delhi 2009; Sabyasachi Bhattacharya (ed.), *Towards a New History of Work*, New Delhi 2014. For other efforts see Rana Behal et al. (eds.), *Rethinking Work. Global Historical and Sociological Perspectives*, New Delhi 2011; Babacar Fall et al. (eds.), *Travail et culture dans un monde globalisé. De l'Afrique à l'Amérique latine*, Paris 2015.
19 Sebastian Conrad, *What is Global History?* Princeton 2016, 5.
20 Dominic Sachsenmeier, *Global Perspectives on Global History. Theories and Approaches in a Connected World*, New York 2011. Global History has become the subject of many introductory texts and collective volumes. See, among many, James Belich et al. (eds.), *The Prospect of Global History*, Oxford 2016; Maxine Berg (ed.), *Writing the History of the Global: Challenges for the Twenty-First Century*, Oxford 2013; Sebastian Conrad et al. (eds.), *Globalgeschichte. Theorien, Ansätze, Methoden*, Frankfurt/M. 2007.
21 Conrad, Global History, 37.

This also applies to Global Labour History.[22] As far as its methodological status is concerned, it is more of an 'area of interest' than a theory or school to which everyone must subscribe. It is not "a vertical organization, but a network continuously assembling and breaking up in relation to specific research projects; it does not aim for a new 'grand narrative', but rather to partial syntheses based on multiple empirical research and various intellectual interpretations."[23] One of its main concerns so far has been to integrate more systematically the 'global south' into labour historiography, both at the intellectual and institutional level. The International Institute of Social History (IISH) in Amsterdam was crucial to the development of the field. Since the institution was founded in 1935, it has been one of the most important research and documentation centres for the history of the labour movement and other social movements. In the late 1990s, under the leadership of Jan Lucassen and Marcel van der Linden, the IISH established itself as a worldwide operating platform for Global Labour History. In what almost amounts to a manifesto, Lucassen and van der Linden stressed the importance of "study[ing] the global development of labour throughout history without implicitly using (a particular interpretation of part of) European history as a model."[24] With almost military precision, the IISH's members and associates started a large research initiative which involved numerous conferences and projects in order to explore the empirical and methodological dimensions of this new field.[25] The IISH also supported initiatives and activities in a number of non-European countries to address and discuss Global Labour History and has contributed to the development of a global network of scholars and institutions interested in this field of historical study.[26]

---

[22] The prehistory of Global Labor History is presented in detail by Marcel van der Linden, Labour History Beyond Borders, in: Joan Allen et al. (eds.), *Histories of Labour. National and International Perspectives*, Pontypool 2010, 353–383.

[23] Christian G. De Vito, New Perspectives on Global Labour History. Introduction, in: *Workers of the World* 1,3 (2013), 7–31, here: 12.

[24] Marcel van der Linden/Jan Lucassen, *Prolegomena for a Global Labour History*, Amsterdam 1999, 7.

[25] Some of the projects are listed on www.iisg.nl. See also De Vito, New perspectives. The first undertakings were mainly conceived in a comparative perspective, involving case studies on numerous non-European countries and increasingly attempting to explain similarities, differences and entanglements. See e.g. Sam Davies et al. (eds.), *Dock Workers 1790–1970. International explorations in Comparative Labour History*, 2 vols, Aldershot 2000. For a first attempt to present the state of the art in the field on the basis of both regionally and thematically focused articles see Jan Lucassen (ed.), *Global Labour History. A State of the Art*, Berne 2006. See also this article below.

[26] See the list in Van der Linden, Promise, 59f.; idem, Speaking Globally, in: *International Labor and Working-Class History* 75 (2009), 184–188.

These more recent efforts, however, should not lead us to ignore the fact that, for instance, Latin American historians, like their colleagues in North America and Europe, have been studying the particularities of labour in their regions for decades.[27] African and Indian historians began more recently, but with a focus either on an area or on specific types of labour, for example, plantation labour.[28] For a long time European and Western labour historians tended to 'universalize' their views based on often rather specific examples. They ignored, for instance, Caribbean specialists for whom the relationship of plantation labour and global capitalism has been central since the work of C.L.R. James and Eric Williams in the 1930s and 1940s.[29] Perspectives in the context of (post-)colonialism have been central in many attempts to globalize historical studies.[30] This appears to be true as well with regard to labour history. In this field, the mutual relationship between social change with the colonizing countries and the colonized territories continues to be of interest. The crucial question that remains open is how colonization shapes labour history. One important reference here is the slave plantation as a formative experience in developing large-scale, closely supervised enterprises.[31] How did this experience shape ideas, organization and labour practices in the world? Another is the point Karl Marx made: the availability of land and the possibility of migration are obstacles to original accumulation. Why did this problem remain even after relatively long-term and intense colonization efforts? In fact, there is some reason to argue that Marx's concept of "original accumulation" might gain new importance in the African context, given for example the rush for land in Africa and the political and economic conflicts this entails.[32]

---

27 See James P. Brennan, Latin American Labor History, in: José C. Moya (ed.), *The Oxford Handbook of Latin American History*, Oxford 2011, 342–366.
28 Rana Behal, *One Hundred Years of Servitude: Political Economy of Tea Plantations in Colonial Assam*, New Delhi 2014; Abdul Sheriff, *Slaves, Spices and Ivory in Zanzibar*, London 1987. Much of the literature on plantation labour in Africa has been produced by North American scholars. See e.g. Frederick Cooper, *From Slaves to Squatters. Plantation Labor and Agriculture in Zanzibar and Colonial Kenya, 1890–1925*, New Haven 1980.
29 Eric Williams, *Capitalism and Slavery*, Chapel Hill 1944; C. L. R. James, *The Black Jacobins. Toussaint L'Ouverture and the San Domingo Revolution*, New York 1938.
30 Conrad, Global History, 53–57.
31 Sidney Mintz, *Sweetness and Power. The Place of Sugar in Modern History*, Harmondsworth 1985.
32 Catherine Boone, *Property and Political Order. Land Rights and the Structure of Conflict in Africa*, New York 2014.

Themes, Concepts, Approaches

Global Labour History emphasizes interaction and entanglements between different world regions while taking for granted that the growing circulation of goods, people and ideas not only produced common ground, but disassociations and differences, the search for particularities and the hypostatization of dichotomous structures. The encounters between Europe and the non-European world between the fifteenth and mid-twentieth centuries had been largely within the context of overseas colonialism, and hence, largely hierarchical and repressive.[33] The transfer of work patterns (including juridical concepts, concepts of labour, work ethics, training and discipline) from the West to the colonies was thus not innocent of the highly uneven power relations that marked colonial domination. What did these complex entanglements look like? Even before the subcontinent came under direct colonial rule by the British in the late eighteenth century, the Dutch East India Company was already transferring enslaved labour from parts of India to the colonies further east.[34] During the seventeenth and eighteenth centuries both the trading and the agrarian sectors commercialized further and labour relations were at least partly based on contracts.[35] Indeed, as Ravi Ahuja has argued, there was no need to import European terms in order to express the phenomenon of wage labour. In the Tamil language a wage labourer was (and is) called a 'Kuliyal' or 'Kuli'. Indian workers were also conscious about the difference between free and unfree labour: a Kuli was regarded as nobody's servant. On the other hand, this term had a negative connotation and was linked to subordination and lower caste background. During the nineteenth century, the British used 'Kuli' to denominate an 'unfree' labourer and from this colonial context the term entered European languages, but not as a synonym for wage labourer, but as a symbol for the unlimited subordination of the labour force.[36]

---

33 Stuart Hall, The West and the Rest: Discourse and Power, in: idem et al. (eds.), *Modernity. An Introduction to Modern Societies*, Oxford 1996, 184–228; Robert Miles, *Racism*, London 2003.
34 Marcus Vink, "The World's Oldest Trade": Dutch Slavery and Slave Trade in the Indian Ocean in the Seventeenth Century, in: *Journal of World History* 14,2 (2003), 131–177.
35 See David Washbrook, Progress and Problems. South Asian Economic and Social History, c.1720-1860, in: *Modern Asian Studies* 22,1 (1998), 57–96, here: 72; Ravi Ahuja, Geschichte der Arbeit jenseits des kulturalistischen Paradigmas. Vier Anregungen aus der Südasienforschung, in Jürgen Kocka/Claus Offe (eds.), *Geschichte und Zukunft der Arbeit*, Frankfurt/Main 2000, 121–134, here: 124. For a case study see Ravi Ahuja, *Die Erzeugung kolonialer Staatlichkeit und das Problem der Arbeit. Eine Studie zur Sozialgeschichte der Stadt Madras und ihres Hinterlandes zwischen 1750 und 1800*, Stuttgart 1999; idem, Labor Relations in an Early Colonial Context: Madras, 1750–1800, in: *Modern Asian Studies* 32,4 (2002), 793–826.
36 Ahuja, Geschichte der Arbeit, 125. Sucheng Chan echoes this shift in meaning when she notes that whereas in Asian languages – including in Chinese where *ku li* stands for bitter labour – the

Another interesting aspect of entanglement, although still not systematically researched, is the way in which the practice of colonial labour regulations in the British Empire affected the situation in the metropole. Master and servant acts, the cornerstone of English employment law for more than four hundred years, gave largely unsupervised, inferior magistrates wide discretion over employment relations, including the power to whip, fine and imprison men, women and children for breach of private contracts with their employers. The English model was adopted, modified and reinvented in more than a thousand colonial statutes and ordinances regulating the recruitment, retention, and discipline of workers in shops, mines, and factories, on farms, in forests, on plantations and at sea.[37] The claim that the British colonies were used as laboratories of institutional reforms still needs further evaluation. It is evident, however, that the 'globalization' of English employment law did not lead to the levelling of difference. The most repressive and inegalitarian elements of this law and related legal practices survived much longer in the colonies than in England and were even developed further and tightened. The system of indentured labour is a case in point: Indenture (an apprentice contract or contract of employment) stands for a specifically colonial legal form which was not restricted to South Asia. For the period of the contract (which the worker could not terminate), the plantation owner had nearly unlimited rights of disposal over 'his' workers. This practice beyond 'free wage labour', which goes back to the North American colonies in the sixteenth century, was justified with the cynical argument that indenture was 'a school for Indian workers' to teach them how to conclude and to keep to a contract.[38]

The indentured labour system was one aspect of the long and complex history of (labour) migration, which is itself a well-established theme in historiography that received new impulses from the emergence of global perspectives.[39] During

---

word "signifies the nature of the work that a person does", in North America, where the term was introduced by the British, *kuli* or *coolie* "references the innate attributes of a person occupying the negative pole of the binary 'free' versus 'unfree' labor." See Sucheng Chan, Asian American Economic and Labor History, in: David K. Yoo/Eiichiro Azuma (eds.), *Oxford Handbook of Asian American History*, Oxford 2016, 299–330, here: 302.

37 Douglas Hay / Paul Cravan (eds.), *Masters, Servants, and Magistrates in Britain and the Empire, 1582–1955*, Chapel Hill and London 2004.

38 See Ravi Ahuja, Arbeit und Kolonialherrschaft im neuzeitlichen Südasien. Eine Einführung, in: Dietmar Rothermund/Karin Preisendanz (eds.), *Südasien in der Neuzeit*, Vienna 2003, 199–211, here: 200; Ranajit Das Gupta, *Labor and Working Class in Eastern India. Studies in Colonial History*, Calcutta 1994; Marina Carter, *Voices from Indenture. Experiences of Indian Migrants in the British Empire*, London/New York 1996.

39 Jan Lucassen/Leo Lucassen (eds.), *Globalizing Migration History. The Eurasian Experience (16th–21st Centuries)*, Leiden 2014; Jan Lucassen et al. (eds.), *Migration History in World History. Multidisciplinary Approaches*, Leiden 2010.

the Early Modern period, the links between Europe and the rest of the world in terms of work and labour were already apparent in the context of slavery and the slave trade.⁴⁰ For example, labour has always played a central role in the long history of relations between Europe and Africa. The creation of a world economy by European capitalists and the reordering of economic relations in nearly every part of the world was followed by a huge need for human labour, which could only be satisfied by various forms of force and coercion.⁴¹ The slave trade completely transformed labour regimes in most parts of the 'New World', but also in Africa, where in many regions slaves not only became a crucial commodity, but also the main resource for labour.⁴² The mobility of large numbers of people, most of them unskilled workers, therefore, was one of the defining characteristics of the late nineteenth and early twentieth centuries. Between 1840 and the 1930s, more than 150 million people left their countries of origin, in many cases to settle elsewhere permanently. While earlier research mainly focused on the 60 million Europeans who had left their homes in order to begin a new life in the 'New World', recent studies refer to the crucial importance of the large flows of people from India and Southern China to areas in Southeast Asia and the Indian Ocean, as well as to large transborder migrations in Northeast Asia. They also refer to the paradox that these global movements were accompanied by the erection of global walls.⁴³ One central focus of Global Labour History has been the group of seamen who travelled between different continents, and represented mobility and connection.⁴⁴

It became apparent that 'freedom' and 'free labour' stand as central concepts through which the world of labour has been thought about and interpreted, at

---

40 See David Eltis (ed.), *Coerced and Free Migrations. Global Perspectives*, Stanford 2002.
41 See, among many others, Paul E. Lovejoy / Nicolas Rogers (eds.), *Unfree Labor in the Development of the Atlantic World*, London 1994.
42 Paul E. Lovejoy, *Transformations in Slavery. A History of Slavery in Africa*, 2ⁿᵈ ed., Cambridge 2000.
43 See especially the highly influential work of Adam McKeown, Melancholy Order. Asian Migration and the Globalization of Borders, New York 2008; idem., Global Migration, 1846–1940, in: *Journal of World History* 15,3 (2004), 155–190. Also: Wang Gungwu (ed.), *Global History and Migrations*, Boulder 1997. For an analysis of current South-South labour migration that addresses the unfree/free divide and other themes central to Global Labour History see Mahua Sarkar, Producing Precariousness: the Un-Freedom of Bangladeshi Transnational Circular Migrants as an Instituted Process, in: *European Journal for Sociology* (forthcoming).
44 See Leon Fink, *Sweatshops at Sea. Merchant Seamen in the World's First Globalized Industry, from 1812 to the Present*, Chapel Hill/NC 2011; Gopalan Balanchandran, *Globalizing Labour? Indian Seafarers and World Shipping*, c.1870–1945, Delhi/Oxford 2012. For a broader perspective see Roland Wenzlhuemer, The Ship, the Media, and the World: Conceptualizing Connections in Global History, in: *Journal of Global History* 11,2 (2016), 163–186.

least for the last two centuries. Considering relations and labour policies in the world of work, the binomial 'free' and 'un-free' is of particular importance, especially given the centrality of the ideology of 'free labour' from the nineteenth century on, in slave, post-emancipation and colonial contexts. Indeed, the idea of modern 'freedom' helped to shape contemporary political language and provided a set of standards through which the social experience could be read. First, it created a master narrative that constructed the history of Western societies as a progressive path towards 'freedom' and 'emancipation', and embedded in particular forms of social relations, institutions and values. Second, it set this narrative as the model towards which institutions and values developing in different cultural and social contexts should progress and against which they therefore ought to be evaluated.[45]

Recent global historical research, often building on area-based studies, has drawn out numerous hybrid constellations, for example, when slaves were ordered by their owners to leave the mansion or the plantation and work for wages, but bring back part of their earnings.[46] Other combinations of slave and wage labour or serfdom and capitalism (such as in Russia around 1900) would seem to relativize Karl Marx's and other classical writers' theses of the outstanding importance of contractually free wage labour as a defining element of capitalism.[47] Comparing Russia and England between 1780 and 1850, Alessandro Stanziani highlights: "Servants, wage earners, the poor, criminals, slaves, and serfs all had to respond to common general principles of utility and efficiency."[48] In societies where slavery was crucial – as in parts of the Americas, Africa and elsewhere – the distinction between 'free' and 'unfree' became essential, especially

---

45 See Robert J. Steinfeld, *The Invention of Free Labour: The Employment Relation in English and American Law and Culture, 1350–1870*, Chapel Hill/NC 1991; idem, *Coercion, Contract and Free Labor in the Nineteenth Century*, Cambridge 2001; Tom Brass/Marcel van der Linden (eds.), *Free and Unfree Labour: The Debate Continues*, Bern 1997. See also the articles of the thematic issue "Shifting Boundaries between Free and Unfree Labor" of the *International Journal of Labor and Working-Class History* 78,1 (2010), ed. by Carolyn Brown/Marcel van der Linden. The following paragraph owes a lot to discussions with Henrique Espada Lima and Sidney Chaloub.
46 João José Reis, The Revolution of the Ganhadores: Urban Labor, Ethnicity and the African Strike of 1857 in Bahia, Brazil, in: *Journal of Latin American Studies*, 29 (1997), 355-393.
47 Alessandro Stanziani, The Legal Statuts of Labour from the Seventeenth to the Nineteenth Century. Russia in a Comparative European Perspective, in: *International Review of Social History* 54 (2009), 359-389 (reprinted in this volume); idem, *Bondage. Labor and Rights in Eurasia from the Sixteenth to the Early Twentieth Century*, New York/Oxford 2014; idem (ed.), *Le Travail Contraint en Europe et en Asie, XVI–XXe siècles*, Paris 2010.
48 Alessandro Stanziani, The travelling panopticon: labor institutions and labor practices in Russia and Britain in the eighteenth and nineteenth century, in: *Comparative Studies in Society and History*, 51,4 (2009), 715–741, here: 732.

once slavery as an 'institution' became a public abomination, at least from the late eighteenth century on. In these contexts the clear divide between 'slavery' and 'freedom' turned into the source of all kinds of social and political anxieties and fostered various logics of continuity and discontinuity. On this topic, Brazilian historians have particularly stressed that during the nineteenth century no distinct division existed between slaves and 'freed' workers with regard to the utilization of extra-economic coercion. On the other hand, as their work shows, the ambivalence of the concept of 'freedom' indicated sharp social conflict on the ground, which was related to specific work arrangements. Among former slaves, 'freedom' was usually experienced as precarious, limited, even spurious, but it nevertheless constituted a relevant category and a crucial aspiration.[49]

One insight from this research is that even if there seems to be a long-term trend towards 'free wage labour', so-called free labour "cannot be seen as the only form of exploitation suitable for modern capitalism, but rather as one alternative among several".[50] Marcel van der Linden further suggests that rethinking the fuzzy boundaries between wage labour, self-employment and slavery helps to rethink the concept of the working class, itself a specific historical artefact that originated in nineteenth-century Europe. He refers to the observation that most workers not only belonged to households that combined several modes of labour, but that they could combine different modes of labour, both synchronically and diachronically. Thus, van der Linden argues, there has always been a large class of people within capitalism whose labour power was commodified in various ways. Its members are enormously varied: they include chattel slaves, sharecroppers, small artisans and wage earners.[51] Such an interpretation involves a substantial re-interpretation of the role of 'free wage labour' within capitalism and

---

49 See Henrique Espada Lima, Freedom, Precariousness, and the Law: Freed Persons contracting out their Labor in Nineteenth-Century Brazil, in: *International Review of Social History* 54,3 (2009), 391–416; Marcelo Badaró Mattos, Experiences in Common: Slavery and "Freedom" in the Process of Rio de Janeiro's Working Class Formation (1850-1910), in: *International Review of Social History*, 55,2 (2010), 193–213; Sidney Chaloub, The Precariousness of Freedom in a Slave Society (Brazil in the Nineteenth Century), in: *International Review of Social History*, 56,3 (2011), 405–439; idem, The Politics of Ambiguity. Conditional Manumission, Labor Contracts and Slave Emancipation in Brazil (1850s to 1888), in: *International Review of Social History*, 60,2 (2015), 161–191 (reprinted in this volume). These contributions also represent a new dialogue between historians of slavery and labour historians. For a thoughtful reflection on the unfree-free divide referring to the crucial contribution of Brazilian historians see Ravi Ahuja, A Freedom Still Enmeshed in Servitude. The Unruly 'Lascers' of the *SS City of Manila* or, a Micro-History of the 'Free Labour' Problem, in: idem, *Working Lives*, 97–133, esp. 97f.
50 Van der Linden, Labour History Beyond Borders, 368.
51 Ibid, 367. Also Van der Linden, *Workers of the World*, 32f.

makes a case for the fact that the relationship of capitalism and labour is neither homogenizing nor linear.⁵²

Finally, (racist) ideologies, stereotypes and claims of superiority shaped the history of work and have been taken up by historians in order to develop global perspectives on this aspect. In the colonial world in general, 'work' was assigned the task of overcoming the supposed 'backwardness' of the colonized people. 'Work' promised to open access to 'civilization', while colonial ideology claimed that it would take a long time to distil a sufficient amount of capitalist work ethics into Asians and especially Africans. The 'lazy native' soon became a classic stereotype of colonial literature.⁵³ This very persistent stereotype also demonstrates that European rule in the colonies was far from omnipotent. For instance, the characterization of African workers as 'lazy' implied that in the end colonizers had to accept the limits of colonial rule, that Africans were partially successful in their struggles over work – even under the harsh system of South African gold mining. Notwithstanding the severity of this context, Africans shaped the limits of their own exploitation, notably in generating pressure for systems of day labour or workers' guilds in cities or various forms of labour tenancy on farms, all of which allowed them to allocate family labour and shape work rhythms to a significant extent.⁵⁴ On the other hand, the way work was supposedly performed in Africa and other non-European regions was contrasted with the 'high quality' and 'standard' of 'national types of work'.⁵⁵

Nevertheless 'education for work' was a crucial element of colonial policies. Sebastian Conrad has argued that efforts to discipline the homeless in Germany in the late nineteenth and early twentieth centuries shaped the parallel project of 'civilizing' the Africans in the German colonies.⁵⁶ Moreover he claims that the 'colonial mission' had effects on debates and practices back in Germany. In the

---

52 The comeback of capitalism as a tool for historical analysis is demonstrated in Jürgen Kocka/Marcel van der Linden (eds.), *Capitalism. The Reemergence of a Historical Concept*, London 2016.
53 Syed H. Alatas, *The Myth of the Lazy Native*, London 1977. For a case study see Alamin Mazrui/Lupenga Mphande, Time and Labor in Colonial Africa: The Case of Kenya and Malawi, in: Joseph K. Adjaye (ed.), *Time in the Black Experience*, Westport/Conn. 1994, 97–119.
54 Frederick Cooper, Africa in a Capitalist World, in: Darlene Clark Hine/Jacqueline McLeod (eds.), *Crossing Boundaries. Comparative History of Black People in the Diaspora*, Bloomington 1999, 391–418, here: 401.
55 Sebastian Conrad, Circulation, "National Work" and Identity Debates About the Mobility of Work in Germany and Japan, 1890–1914, in: Wolf Lepenies (ed.), *Entangled Histories and Negotiated Universals. Centers and Peripheries in a Changing World*, Frankfurt 2003, 260–280.
56 Sebastian Conrad, "Eingeborenenpolitik" in Kolonie und Metropole. "Erziehung zur Arbeit" in Ostafrika und Ostwestfalen, in: idem/Jürgen Osterhammel (eds.), *Das Kaiserreich transnational. Deutschland in der Welt 1871–1914*, Göttingen 2004, 107–128; idem, *Globalisation and the Nation in Imperial Germany*, Cambridge 2010, Ch. 2.

end, however, there are very few clues that could justify the idea that there was a mutual linking-up of experiences, discourses and practices in 'East Africa and East Westphalia'. Without doubt, the parallel structure of educational projects in Germany and East Africa seems to fit like a glove. And the effects of the practices in the Reich upon practices in the East African colony are quite evident. However, it is far from clear whether the radicalization of the labour discourse in Germany has anything to do with colonial experiences and practices.

Challenges[57]

Conrad's attempts to link 'education for work' in the metropole and colony represent a major challenge to Global Labour History: While it is easy to show how labour regimes and working practices in the Americas, Africa and Asia have been shaped by North Atlantic influences, it is usually far more difficult to demonstrate how the realm of work in Europe has been influenced by its colonial experiences and practices. However, a number of studies now offer remarkable insights into the interconnections between different parts of the world, and look at people and at institutions, ideas and objects.[58] The search for entanglements entails risks though, for instance the tendency to assume an ever-increasing connection and compression of labour regimes and practices and thus reproducing the teleological perspective of the concept of globalization.[59] Along these lines, Franco Barchiesi casts doubt on the perception of 'the global' manifesting itself in Africa in the form of connections, but rather sees disconnection, segmentation and seg-

---

[57] A most interesting set of challenges and critical questions to Global Labour History is articulated in the feedback to van der Linden, Promise, published in: *International Labor and Working-Class History* 82 (2012). See, Franco Barchiesi, How Far from Africa's Shore? A Response to Marcel van der Linden's Map for Global Labor History, 77-84; Peter Winn, Global Labor History: The Future of the Field?, 85-91; Jürgen Kocka, Revising Labor History on a Global Scale: Some Comments to Marcel van der Linden, 92-98; Dorothy Sue Cobble, The Promise and Peril of the New Global Labor History, 99-107; Prasannan Parthasarathi, Global Labor History: A Dialogue with Marcel van der Linden, 108-113; and Marcel van der Linden's response: Global Labor History: Promising Challenges, in: *International Labor and Working-Class History* 84 (2013), 218–225. Some of the points made in these comments will be taken up in the following section.

[58] A crucial institution in this context is the International Labour Organization (ILO). See Jasmien Van Daele et al. (eds.), *ILO Histories: Essays on the International Labour Organization and Its Impact on the World During the Twentieth Century*, Berne 2011; Sandrine Kott/Joëlle Droux (eds.), *Globalizing Social Rights: The ILO and Beyond*, London 2012.

[59] For a powerful critique see Frederick Cooper, What is the Concept of Globalization Good For? An African historian's perspective, in: *African Affairs* 100, 399 (2001), 189–213.

regation. He specifically criticizes the idea of workers' 'teleconnections' in global commodity chains put forward by van der Linden. He argues instead, that "colonial and postcolonial Africa shows indeed that the globalization of capital did not only provide a minority of unionized workers with new opportunities to converse with the global working class. It has also, and more importantly, excluded and marginalized multitudes of producers, households, and communities."[60] Moreover, there is a certain general tendency within global history of 'doing history backwards' and to limit research to identifying the flows and nodal points of globalization.[61] In labour history, this trend finds its expression in the focus on seamen and other mobile sectors of the African and Asian labour force, which contributed to the emergence of global commodity and labour markets. While there is nothing wrong with this, it is crucial not to overlook other parts of the workforce – non-plantation rural labour, for instance – as the globalization of labour not only meant unbounded mobility, but spatial immobility as well, and we need to see the contradictions and unevenness of global processes of incorporation.

Marcel van der Linden has directed our attention to a central methodological problem of Global Labour History:[62] All core concepts of 'traditional' labour history are primarily based on experiences made in the North Atlantic region and are thus in need of critical reconsideration. The concept of 'labour' itself provides a good example of this problem. Several Western languages make a distinction between 'labour' and 'work'. In these cases, following Hannah Arendt, 'labour' often refers to toil and effort or to market-related activities, while 'work' refers to more creative processes. This binary meaning, however, does not exist in many other languages. In some languages there is no single word for abstractions like 'labour' and 'work', on the other hand we find changing meanings for local words such as the Swahili term *kazi* in Belgian Congo, which initially referred to slave and forced labour but transformed its meaning and designated wage labour.[63] To which extent are the concepts of 'labour' and 'work' trans-culturally usable? While it does not seem feasible for a useful historiographical dialogue to simply use local terms as we find them, the content of 'labour' and 'work' should be defined and contextualized much more precisely than is usually done. Where does 'labour' begin and 'work' end? Is it possible to draw a precise boundary between 'labour' and 'work', or is the boundary less obvious than is often assumed?

---

60 Barchiesi, How Far From Africa's Shore, 77.
61 Frederick Cooper, *Colonialism in Question. Theory, Knowledge, History*, Berkeley 2005, Ch.4.
62 Van der Linden, Labour History Beyond Borders, 365.
63 Julia Seibert, Kazi. Konzepte, Praktiken und Semantiken von Lohnarbeit im kolonialen Kongo, in: Leonhard/Steinmetz, *Semantiken*, 209–223.

The highly uneven existence of source material and availability of data for writing histories of labour around the world presents another challenge. A large IISH project entitled "Global Collaborative on the History of Labour Relations" shows both the possibilities and limits of large-scale data-based global labour history enterprises. The core of this project is a universal taxonomy of labour relations that aims to map different kinds of labour relations in various world regions between 1500 and 2000.[64] The taxonomy basically distinguishes between four types of labour: non-work, reciprocal labour, tributary labour, and commodified labour, either connected with the household, the community or the market. These types are further elaborated in nineteen different labour relations at the individual level, for instance, in the category of household: leading producers, kin producers, kin non-producers, servants and redistributive labourers. The project chose five-cross sections in time: 1500, 1650, 1800, 1900, and 2000, as well as 1950 for Africa. On the basis of the data collected by the participating specialists on specific regions and cross-sections, the 'collaboratory' attempted to analyse major shifts in labour relations by asking, for instance, when a specific type of labour relation gave way to another or how these transitions could be explained and connected in a global context. Without any doubt, this project offers a solid base from which to analyse shifts in labour relations over time within societies and allows for interregional and worldwide comparisons. One drawback seems to be the strong role of demographical data as a starting point for examining each geographical unit and cross-section, given the fact that for a continent like Africa, this data is very sketchy and unreliable until right into the twentieth century. Moreover, the taxonomy does not really allow for capturing overlaps and 'grey zones' in individual labour relations. The Africa-related publications that have emerged from this project so far provide interesting new insights but also refer to the limits of the database-driven approach to the history of African labour and its global connections, especially for the periods before 1900.[65]

The project set an example for collaboration between scholars from many parts of the world, including historians from what is now called the 'Global South'. Despite various and successful efforts, however, one cannot ignore the many ways in which structural inequalities shape the field of Global Labour History: For scholars in Asia or Africa, access to sources and literature is limited, funding for research and conferences rarely available. The important thing for the practice of Global Labour History is, according to Van der Linden, "to follow the

---

64 My presentation of the project follows Lucassen, New Directions, 68-70. For detailed information, see https://collab.iisg.nl/labourrelations.
65 See Karen Hofmeester et al., No Global Labor History without Africa: Reciprocal Comparison and Beyond, in: *History in Africa* 41 (2014), 249–276.

traces of interest to us wherever they may lead: across political and geographical frontiers, time frames, territories and disciplinary boundaries."[66] This journey presents a considerable demand not only to the intellectual and linguistic skills of the researcher, but also in terms of financing. Nevertheless, the scepticism about global history approaches is not only due to frustrations about the lack of resources. In many parts of the 'Global South', the persistent preoccupation with national history also represents an obstacle to global perspectives.[67] In essence, given the long history of Eurocentric knowledge production and academic hierarchies, there is a widespread sense of Global (Labour) History as just another hegemonic Western project.

The Chapters of the Volume

The articles reprinted in this reader have been published over the last decade or so and represent a selection from a very broad and lively field of historical research. This collection is meant to provide both an introduction and some insights into themes, debates and the methods of Global Labour History as they have been developed over the last few years. It is intended to be of use to students and scholars interested in familiarizing themselves with a burgeoning field of high academic *and* political relevance. This book has been divided into four sections, each comprising three articles. Section 1, "The Globalization of Labour History", is devoted to efforts to map the field and to discuss major historiographical developments. Marcel van der Linden's "The Promise and Challenges of Global Labour History" is a key text in this respect, and it succinctly describes the rise of Global Labour History, its major concerns as he sees them, its innovative aspects, and research topics to be pursued. Christian G. De Vito and Alex Lichtenstein's "Writing a Global Labour History of Convict Labour" contributes to the understanding of a specific theme within labour history – convict labour, from a global and long-term perspective – and takes up one of the central issues of Global Labour History, the unfree/free-divide. Phil Bonner, Jonathan Hyslop and Lucien van der Walt ("Rethinking Worlds of Labour. Southern African Labour History in International Context") discuss comparisons and the connection between the history of labour in South Africa and in other parts of the world. Using the example of what is arguably the most important labour historiography south of the Sahara, and which was long shaped by a rather parochial view of

---

66 Van der Linden, Promise, 62.
67 For Latin America, see Winn, Global Labour History.

the country's past, the authors sketch the possible benefits of 'globalizing' the perspectives on labour without losing sight of local developments.

Section II, "Varieties of Work", presents studies on different professions that have gained new attention in the context of an emerging Global Labour History, but also addresses the question of what is work and how to define it. Gopalan Balanchandran in his "Workers in the World: Indian Seafarers, c.1870s-1940s" offers a concise portrait of Indian seamen in the steamship era between the late nineteenth century and World War II and draws a picture of considerable mobility. Despite being relatively small in number, they appear to have travelled nearly everywhere in the world and could be labelled "India's earliest global workers". Alf Lüdtke's article "Soldiering and Working: Almost the Same? Reviewing Practices in Industry and the Military in Twentieth-Century Contexts" broadens dominant concepts of work. The author explores analogies and similarities between practices and experiences of work in modern industrial settings and practices and experiences in military organizations and modern wars. He also draws our attention to the frequently overlooked destructive implications of work. At the centre of Gerd Spittler's "Work – Transformation of Objects or Interaction between Subjects" are hunters and gatherers, herders and peasants, but also capitalist industrial work. He argues against a definition of work as purely instrumental and shows that the idea that animals, plants and even things possess their own sense of self-will (*Eigensinn*) is widespread in non-industrial, non-capitalist societies.

Section III, "Dynamics of Labour Relations", critically engages the boundaries of 'free' labour and the ambiguities contained in this concept but also addresses state interventions in labour regulations and historicizes informality. Sidney Chalhoub ("The Politics of Ambiguity. Conditional Manumission, Labour Contracts, and Slave Emancipation in Brazil") focuses on controversies regarding conditional manumission to explore the legal and social ambiguities between slavery and freedom that prevailed in nineteenth-century Brazilian society. "Regulated Informality. Legal Constructions of Labour Relations in Colonial India 1814-1926" by Prabhu Mohapatra investigates the genealogy of contemporary informal labour relations in India well into the nineteenth-century colonial period and traces the processes by which labour relations were constructed by colonial state action, especially through legislative intervention. The author argues that in the process of such construction, labour relations were deeply impressed by pervasive informality, and this shaped subsequent developments in the decades after independence. In his "The Legal Status of Labour from the Seventeenth to the Nineteenth Century. Russia in a Comparative European Perspective", Alessandro Stanziani emphasizes that until the end of the nineteenth century, the barrier between freedom and bondage was movable and negotiable. In most "Western" countries, he argues, labour was similar to service and wage conditions resembled those of domestic servants, with numerous constraints imposed on worker mobility. Thus the material and living conditions of 'free' workers and servants were not necessarily better than those of 'serfs'.

Section IV, "The End of Wage Labour?", takes up and critically engages a debate that emerged in the 1980s in many Western industrial countries about "the end of work society", the menacing disappearance of wage labour and the rise of informal labour not only in the 'Global South', but in Western countries as well. Michael Denning ("Wageless Life") provocatively reminds us that under capitalism, "the only thing worse than being exploited is not being exploited" and insists that 'proletarian' is not a synonym for 'wage labourer', but for dispossession, expropriation and radical dependence on the market. In her "The Problem with Work", Kathie Weeks focuses on the United States to discuss what she perceives as the widespread willingness to live for work and asks why work seems to be valued more than other pastimes and practices. She wonders about the lack of attention paid to the lived experiences and political textures of work within political theory, given the fact that work is crucial not only to those whose lives are centred around it, but also, in a society that expects people to work for wages, to those who are expelled or excluded from work and marginalized in relation to it. And finally, Rina Agarwala ("Reshaping the social contract. Emerging relations between the state and informal labour in India") takes up some of the arguments developed by Mohapatra in the previous section. She investigates the strategies of Indian informal workers to improve their livelihoods and relates them to the new forms of institutionalism that have developed in the current system of reduced state regulation of capital and blurred employer-employee relations. Argawala argues that experiences of informal workers in India suggest the continuing power of both states and workers in shaping the current phase of economic and political transition and thus challenges widespread views about the diminishing role of the state. This volume offers a comprehensive introduction to the new book series "Work in Global and Historical Perspective". Its articles map out the state-of-the-art of current research, and explore the latest debates in the scholarly landscape of labour history.

The Globalization of Labour History

Marcel van der Linden
The Promise and Challenges of Global Labor History[1]

> We, the workers of the fully industrialized, "civilized" countries of the West, can no longer "isolate" ourselves from the remainder of the world. Our movements are no longer (and our "theories" should not remain either) the comparatively independent expressions of certain *nationally* restricted processes. We are part and parcel of a veritable *one-world revolution*.
>
> Karl Korsch, letter to Irving B. Canter dated December 6, 1950

A long road

The idea that the histories of different regions in the world are interconnected is not particularly novel; it already existed several centuries ago. Thus, for example, when the German historian and playwright Friedrich Schiller was granted a chair at the University of Jena in 1789, he declared in his inaugural address that "the most remote regions of the world contribute to our luxury." After all, he continued, "The clothes we wear, the spices in our food, and the price for which we buy them, many of our strongest medicines, and also many new tools of our destruction – do they not presuppose a Columbus who discovered America, a Vasco da Gama who circumnavigated the tip of Africa"?[2] Nevertheless it took quite some time before professional historians began to consider these global connections seriously in their research. Colonial and "imperial" historians led the way. They were joined by economic historians. Labor historians became interested in intercontinental perspectives only more recently; until the 1970s, they typically locked themselves into the framework of individual nation-states. Even great innovators

---

[1] This article was first published under the same title in *International Labor and Working-Class History*, 82 (Fall 2012), pp. 57–76 doi:10.1017/S0147547912000270 © The International Labor and Working-Class History, Inc., published by Cambridge University Press, reproduced with permission. I am grateful to my colleagues Ulbe Bosma, Karin Hofmeester, Jan Lucassen, Christine Moll-Murata, and Elise van Nederveen Meerkerk for their comments on two earlier drafts, and to Jurriaan Bendien for translating this text from Dutch. For my earlier essays on this topic, with different angles, see especially Marcel van der Linden, "The 'Globalization' of Labor and Working Class History and Its Consequences," *ILWCH*, 65 (2004): 136–156; van der Linden, "Labor History: The Old, the New and the Global," *African Studies*, 66 (2007): 1–12; van der Linden, "Labour History Beyond Borders," in *Histories of Labour: National and International Perspectives*, ed. Joan Allen, Alan Campbell, and John McIlroy, *Histories of Labour: National and International Perspectives* (London, 2010), 353–383.
[2] Friedrich Schiller, "What Is, and to What End do We Study, Universal History," in *Poet of Freedom*, vol. II., trans. Caroline Stephan and Robert Trout (New York, 1988).

in the discipline, such as E. P. Thompson, thought mostly in terms of "national" working classes.

A significant turning point was reached in 1971. At a meeting of the American Historical Association, a study group was founded under the inspiring leadership of Bob Wheeler, which began publishing the *Newsletter, European Labor and Working Class History*. This event prefigured changes to come, in two ways: First, the *Newsletter* broke through the relative isolation of the various country specialists on both sides of the Atlantic; and second, the constraint of an exclusively "European" focus quite quickly lost its appeal. Within just a few years, the *Newsletter* also began to publish articles about the Mexican Revolution, modern and contemporary China, and so on. The alteration of the newsletter's title in 1976, from *European* to *International Labor and Working Class History*, reflected this trend.

Other developments in the same direction around that time were the founding in 1964 of the *Internationale Tagung der Historiker der Arbeiterbewegung* (ITH) in Austria – an annual Conference of labor historians from "socialist" and capitalist countries – and the founding in 1970 of the International Association of Labour History Institutions (IALHI), a collaborative organization for archives around the world but concentrated in the rich countries (which, unfortunately, remains the case).[3]

Substantively, the new trend first became visible in comparative studies of different countries. Comparative work had, of course, already appeared previously, but in the 1970s and especially in the 1980s, the number of such studies rose quickly. The countries investigated were usually relatively "large" ones, and primarily in the North Atlantic region. They included, above all, the United States and Britain (which had the added advantage that they could be compared, even if the researcher spoke only English), France, Germany, Italy, and Russia. The number of cases studied was almost always very small (two or three), because the research projects were normally carried out by individual researchers.[4] Later, from the late 1980s onward, some larger-scale projects followed, which were usually conceived at the International Institute of Social History in Amsterdam, and in which some twenty or more countries were often compared.[5]

---

3 Nowadays the ITH is called "International Conference of Labour and Social History." See www.ith.or.at (accessed October 15, 2012). The activities of the IALHI can be followed via www.ialhi.org (accessed October 15, 2012)

4 I have tried to give an overview in "A Bibliography of Comparative Labour History," in *Australian Labour and Regional Change. Essays in Honour of R.A. Gollan*, ed. Jim Hagan and Andrew Wells (Rushcutters Bay, NSW [Australia], 1998), 117–145.

5 In the first projects, the comparisons were still mainly contrasting, that is, highlighting similarities and differences between instances, without trying to *explain* these similarities and differ-

Separately from this trend, however, other developments also occurred. From the 1940s, labor and working-class histories began to appear in the Global South, partly encouraged by the independence struggles in African and Asian colonies, but also stimulated by the Cuban Revolution of 1953–1959.[6] Many works were institutional analyses, such as J. Norman Parmer's *Colonial Labor Policy and Administration* (1960) on the Malaysian rubber plantation industry, or Charles Gamba's *The Origins of Trade Unions in Malaya* (1962). But already early on attention was given to the perspective "from below," as illustrated by Jean Chesneaux's classic *Le mouvement ouvrier en Chine de 1919 à 1927* (1962), and Guillermo Lora's *Historia del movimiento obrero boliviana* (1967–1970). Other stimulating influences were the rise of Pan-Africanism; the discovery of border cultures and transnational identities in historical migration research; and of transnational cycles of protests and strikes.

When, from the early 1990s, scholarly interest in "world history" (and, a little later, "global history") also began to increase – probably in good part due to the collapse of "really existing socialism" in Eastern Europe and the Soviet Union – the need for a reorientation of labor and working-class history was felt more and more, including within the North Atlantic region. Against this background, my colleague Jan Lucassen and I published our *Prolegomena for a Global Labour History* in 1999, a short pamphlet in which the concept of Global Labor History (GLH) was introduced. The *Prolegomena* stressed the geographical, temporal, and thematic limitations of traditional labor history. It argued that a new approach was required, generating "a preference for studying developments traditionally overlooked by labor historians."

---

ences. In later studies, much more systematic attention was given to explanations. See, for important examples: Sam Davies, et al., (eds), *Dock Workers 1790–1970. International Explorations in Comparative Labour History*, 2 volumes (Aldershot, 2000); and Lex Heerma van Voss, eds., *The Ashgate Companion to the History of Textile Workers, 1650–2000* (Aldershot, 2010). Outside the IISH comparisons were organized as well, often for between six and twelve countries. See, for example, Dick Geary, ed., *Labour and Socialist Movements in Europe before 1914* (Oxford, 1989); Stefan Berger and David Broughton, eds., *The Force of Labour: The Western European Labour Movement and the Working Class in the Twentieth Century* (Oxford and Washington, 1995); Ulla Wikander et al., eds., *Protecting Women: Labor Legislation in Europe, the United States, and Australia, 1880–1920* (Urbana, IL, 1995); and Patrick Pasture and Johan Verberckmoes, eds., *Working-Class Internationalism and the Appeal of National Identity: Historical Debates and Current Perspectives (Oxford and New York, 1998).*

6 Already prior to the Second World War, a few important contributions to labor history in the Global South were published. Rajani Kanta Das, an employee of the International Labor Organization in Geneva, published three studies in one year: *Factory Labor in India* (Berlin, 1923); *Factory Legislation in India* (Berlin, 1923); and *Labor Movement in India* (Berlin, 1923). US historian Marjorie Ruth Clark wrote a pioneering work on *Organized Labor in Mexico* (New York, 1973 [originally 1934]).

More in particular, the *Prolegomena* stressed the need of transcontinental and diachronic comparisons, and suggested four partially overlapping areas of research: the rewriting of organizational histories (histories of trade unions, etc.) from a different perspective; the study of organizational forms neglected by research so far (mutual benefit societies, consumer cooperatives, etc.); the history of the working classes in the global south; and the history of preindustrial workers.

Now, thirteen years later, our *Prolegomena* has become obsolete in several respects. The demand for GLH has meanwhile increased strongly, as is proved also by the choice of topic for this *ILWCH jubileum* issue. At many conferences and in many publications, the concept is mentioned; it nowadays inspires a modest but increasing number of research projects worldwide. A few examples may illustrate the increasing interest:

- Already in 2005, the Association of Indian Labour Historians organized an international conference, "Towards Global Labour History: New Comparisons." A selection of the papers presented there was published in 2009.[7]
- In September 2006, the General Assembly of the ITH (International Conference of Labour and Social History) accepted a policy paper saying, "The ITH will focus on *Global Labour History*, the global history of all wage earners, slaves, sharecroppers, etc., including their organizations and associated social movements."[8]
- In June 2008, the University of Toronto (New College) organized an international Summer School on Global Labor History for graduate students.
- Also in 2008, the University of Witwatersrand, Johannesburg, organized a conference on "Labour Crossings: World, Work and History," which brought together labor historians from Brazil, Africa, and India.
- The electronic journal of the Brazilian labor history network *Revista Mundos do Trabalho* opened its first issue (2009) with the article "Labour History: The Old, the New and the Global," emphasizing the importance of the GLH perspective.[9]
- The Humboldt University in Berlin in 2009 opened its international research center, Work and Human Life Cycle in Global History, which annually brings together senior and junior fellows from different disciplines concerned with GLH.

---

7 Marcel van der Linden and Prabhu Mohapatra, eds., *Labour Matters: Towards Global Histories* (New Delhi, 2009).
8 See http://www.ith.or.at/ith_e/vorschlaege_ZuKO_e.htm (accessed October 15, 2012).
9 Marcel van der Linden, "História do Trabalho: o velho, o novo e o global," *Revista Mundos do Trabalho*, 1 (2009), 11–26. See http://www.periodicos.ufsc.br/index.php/mundosdotrabalho/issue/view/1130 (accessed October 15, 2012).

- The *Arbeitskreis Moderne Sozialgeschichte,* a half-yearly meeting of German-language professors of social history, organized discussions about GLH in 2010 and 2011.
- In early 2011, Lisbon's New University organized a big conference on "Strikes and Social Conflicts in the Twentieth Century," leading to the founding of a new association for the global historical study of social conflicts and a new electronic peer-reviewed journal, to be published at Campinas, Brazil.
- The Italian journal *Passato e Presente* recently published an enthusiastic survey article on GLH activities and their international resonance.[10] An Italian collection of essays on GLH came out this year.[11]
- The French journal *Le Mouvement Social* will in late 2012 publish an issue focusing on GLH.

These developments, of course, have not gone unnoticed in the United States, the country that proportionally still has more professional historians than all other countries. The US approach is often inter-American, though a further step toward global history is then not far off anymore. From 2002, the journal *Labor History* opened its pages for contributions to labor history from all world regions. The new journal *Labor: Studies in Working-Class History of the Americas,* which emerged out of a dispute around *Labor History* in 2004, featured the appointment of coeditors for Canada and Latin America. The circles around the journal *Labor* organized the international conference "Workers, the Nation-State, and Beyond" with the theme "Labor History across the Americas" (Chicago, September 2008). Much attention was given by participants to methodological and theoretical questions, but important extensions of the research field also occurred. Among other topics, there were contributions dealing with military labor, indigenous and caring labor; transnational labor recruitment and immigration control, and cross-border solidarity, for example, with fugitive slaves and among sailors.[12]

---

[10] Christian de Vito, "La proposta della *Global labour history* nell'era della 'globalizzazione'," *Passato e Presente,* no. 85 (January–April 2012), 177–188.

[11] Christian de Vito (ed.), *Global Labour History. La storia del lavoro al tempo della globalizzazione,* Verona, 2012.

[12] A number of papers are now available in Leon Fink, ed., *Workers Across the Americas: The Transnational Turn in Labor History* (New York, 2011).

What is global labor history?

The growing popularity of GLH has, until now, not been accompanied by a growing clarity about the concept itself. Jan Lucassen and myself originally neglected to provide a very clear and persuasive definition, and others working in this area of research did not – to my knowledge – do so either, though this omission was practically inevitable. After all, a poetess does not write an aesthetics before she begins to write poetry, and a dancer doesn't first sing a song before he begins his movement.[13] Now that the *practice* of GLH has really begun to develop, it seems wise to attempt a more exact definition of the object of study, as well as of the methods of the new approach.

I would emphasize one point straightaway: I consider GLH to be a distinctive field of research, just like art history or linguistics. Within that research area, different theories can be constructed and tested, whether inspired by Karl Marx, Max Weber, John Commons, or other thinkers. By implication, GLH itself is *not* a "theory" in its own right, and therefore it is *not* an alternative for Immanuel Wallerstein's world-systems theory, or any other interpretations of the capitalist world order. That being said, the question suggests itself of how we should define the dimensions and boundaries of this area of inquiry.

When is history "global"?

During the last thirty or forty years historians have had cause to relativize the boundaries of the nation-state. The nation-state is probably no more than two centuries old, but the concept has deeply anchored itself in our thinking. Just like most other historians, labor historians assumed for a long time that the nation-state was the obvious frame of reference within which developments had to be analyzed. Labor historians referred without hesitation to the "American," "Italian," or "Russian" workers' movement, as if such movements were neatly placed within separate geographical/political containers. Of course, there have always been problematic cases, such as multiethnic states (the Ottoman Empire, the Habsburg Empire, etc.) or movements of ethnic groups who did not possess their own state (Scots, Catalans, etc.). But these were supposedly the exceptions that proved the rule, examples of an uncompleted process of which the end result was more or less a foregone conclusion: Each nation has its own state.

---

[13] Arthur Schopenhauer, Die Welt als Wille und Vorstellung, Part II, Ch. 12 (Leipzig: Brockhaus, 1859).

Disquiet about this methodological nationalism expressed itself – especially from the 1970s onward – in comparative analyses that focused on the differences and common features among individual nation-states. These comparative studies nevertheless did not break with the nation-state paradigm because all the reconstructions revolved around the separate nation-states as independent and windowless "monads" (G.W. Leibniz). As methodological nationalism began to change its form, attempts were made to criticize this fixation implicitly. In the Global South, historians had already earlier reached the conclusion that it was impossible to write the labor history of a country as if it were a self-contained unit. How could the working-class history of, for example, Nigeria, Vietnam, or Indonesia be reconstructed without continually paying attention to the connections with their colonial motherlands Britain, France, and the Netherlands? Moreover, how could the history of wage earners in these countries be written without an eye for the history of other labor relations, like slavery (and the slave trade) or the exploitation of coolies? The Guyanese historian Walter Rodney, murdered for political reasons, was a pioneer in this area. The importance of his work can hardly be underestimated; his oeuvre discusses not only the influence of the slave trade on West Africa, but also the history of the Guyanese working people shaped by this trade. In this way, Rodney opened up a wholly new transcontinental perspective.[14] In the Global North, especially supporters of world-systems theories, provided pioneering studies among other things by drawing attention to intercontinental connections between different modes of labor exploitation.[15]

The more that the "monadology" was disputed, the more the terminological debate about alternatives intensified. Thus, for example, in France the concept of *histoire croisée* (crossed history) was invented, focusing on the reciprocal transfers between nations, civilizations, regions, etc., as well as emphasizing mutual influences and reception mechanisms.[16] In the English-speaking world, the concept of the *entangled history* has been introduced, which likewise gives attention to such interconnections. More frequently mentioned than these two terms, is the concept of *transnational history*. However, this concept takes the nation-state as the self-evident point of departure that needs to be transcended and is also often used for an international comparative historiography that does not pay atten-

---

14 Walter Rodney, *A History of the Upper Guinea Coast* (City, 1970); Rodney, *A History of the Guyanese Working People, 1881–1905* (Baltimore, 1981).
15 For more details, see chapter thirteen of my book *Workers of the World* (Leiden, 2008), 287–318.
16 Michael Werner and Bénédicte Zimmermann, eds., *De la comparaison à l'histoire croisée* (Paris, 2004); Michael Werner and Bénédicte Zimmermann, "Beyond Comparison: *Histoire Croisée* and the Challenge of Reflexivity," *History and Theory*, 45 (2006): 30–50.

tion to entanglements.[17] All of the three concepts are moreover usually (but not always) applied to the historiography of contiguous regions, even though very-long-distance connections can be involved. The concept of *world history* might offer a solution, except that much research published under this rubric (though certainly not all) is additive: At a certain point in time, *X* happened in Europe, *Y* in China, and *Z* in America. *Global history* overlaps significantly with world history but does not suffer from this limitation because the term refers to connections across the globe. Yet there is also a disadvantage of this concept: Global history creates the impression that only "big history" is included – the "great divergence" between China and Europe, for example, or the connection between world wars and hegemonies. Every term we might choose therefore has its drawbacks.

If we speak of global history, it is important to state clearly what we do and do not mean by it. In my view, global history is primarily concerned with *the description and explanation of the intensifying (or weakening) connections (interactions, influences, transfers) between different world regions, as well as of the economic, political, social, and cultural networks, institutions, and media that played a role in it*. This historiography is much more than the historiography of globalization alone unless we define globalization very broadly. Comparative studies, exploring the causes and consequences of combined and uneven differential developments, are an integral part of it.

Global history in this sense does not have to be large-scale only; it can include microhistory as well. It is quite feasible to write a global history of a small village, a work site, or a family. The important thing is that we should follow the traces of interest to us wherever they may lead: across political and geographic frontiers, time frames, territories, and disciplinary boundaries. Migration patterns, mass media, world markets and corporations, religious hierarchies, climate changes, wars, and so on can all be bridges to a wider world. Sometimes we will not travel far to discover the interconnections and explanations, and sometimes we will have to.

Obviously there have also been groups of people who lived in a relatively isolated way and were, at most, connected with others via sporadic long-distance trade. Though global history is not a "history of everything," these groups, too, belong to the field of inquiry, in as much as the interactions and transfers that did *not* eventuate are also of interest. To identify the big picture in small details (and vice versa, to discover microrealities in macroprocesses) – that is what it is all about! Global history is therefore in the first instance a question of mentality. Researchers should be bold in their inquiry and dare to venture outside their own familiar terrain.

---

17 That is how I did it myself in *Transnational Labour History. Explorations* (Aldershot, 2003).

What is the time frame?

If we want to write the history of labor on a world scale, we could take two sorts of approaches. One approach aspires to a "universal history of work," documenting the labor relations in different parts of the world as comprehensively as possible. Another approach aims for "a history of globalized work," that looks at labor relations and labor movements from the topical perspective of the "globalized" economy. Both approaches need not be mutually exclusive, however. Willem van Schendel proposed that the first approach could become "a dynamic and crucial field of inquiry," in which "the histories and identities of working people are compared and analyzed from different theoretical vantage points that attempt to see beyond the looking-glass of the North." The second approach ("histories of labor seen as studies of capitalism through its labor aspect") could be interpreted as "a special interest within this larger field, and it, too, could be approached from various theoretical angles."[18] I would endorse such a view, except that I favor prioritizing the second (more narrowly focused) approach in the meantime. My reasons are practical and political.

The practical reason is that both old and new labor historians have always centrally focused on labor in capitalist societies; it is obvious that GLH dovetails with that interest. The political reason is that the second approach directly contributes to understanding the world in which we live now – providing better insight into the tendencies that have brought us to where we are today.[19] The first-mentioned approach obviously does not lose any of its importance because of this priority. If GLH would in time extend its horizons beyond capitalist civilization, it would deepen our understanding of the specificity (or nonspecificity) of capitalist developments.[20]

---

[18] Willem van Schendel, "Stretching Labour Historiography," *International Review of Social History*, 51 (2006): 260–261.
[19] Bruce Mazlish correctly argues that "all history is contemporary history in the sense that the perspective brought to bear on past events is necessarily rooted in the present. In this light, global history may simply be more conscious of its perspective and interested in focusing it more directly on contemporary happenings, as well as on the past. Serious problems of selectivity or documentation then remain, as they do with any history." Mazlish, "Introduction to Global History," in Bruce Mazlish and Ralph Buultjens, eds., *Conceptualizing Global History* (Boulder, 1993), 3.
[20] I regard the Soviet Union, the Chinese People's Republic, and other "socialist" societies as elements of capitalist civilization, broadly speaking. They were, in my view, not "capitalist," but their rise or decline can only be understood in a world capitalist context. I provide a definition of capitalism in *Workers of the World* (Leiden, 2008), chapter sixteen. My interpretation of Soviet-type societies can be found in *Western Marxism and the Soviet Union* (Leiden, 2007).

What do we mean by "labor"?

Labor and working-class history were for a long time understood as "the history of wage earners" – workers who, as free individuals, can dispose of their labor power as their own commodity and who have no other commodity for sale.[21] Attention was focused especially on miners, industrial and transport workers, and, less frequently, on agricultural laborers. This narrow conceptualization is called in question by the "globalization" of the research terrain.

On the one hand, the experience of the *contemporary* Global South tells us that the distinctions between "classical" wage earners and some other subordinate groups are vague indeed. "Pure" wage workers have been a minority in the labor force of many countries in the Global South; there, a process of class formation often did not develop until the very end. Most of these wage earners do not freely dispose of their own labor power – for example, because these workers are tied down by debts – or they do not have any formal (legally recognized) contractual relationship with their employers. In addition, wage labor in the South is carried out by households and families whose survival very often remains partly dependent on subsistence labor as well, performed, especially but not exclusively by women, and on independent production of commodities for the market. The economic roles that different family members take on are often not fixed and permanent but instead signify a transient social relationship – one that can be replaced rather quickly by other sources of income. That is one reason why the dividing line between workers and so-called lumpenproletarians (people who survive by means of begging, crime, prostitution, and so on) is not always easy to draw.[22] Next to that, there are all kinds of forms of hidden wage labor, such as sharecropping, in which a peasant family supplies labor and the landowner supplies the land and means of production while the revenues are shared between them, according to some formula. Another form of "hidden" wage labor includes *self-employed workers*, who are formally employers without staff but in reality are often dependent on one specific client who is therefore their de facto employer.

On the other hand, *historical* studies reveal that in the past, the dividing line between chattel slaves, serfs, and other unfree subalterns taken together and

---

21 Marx, *Capital*, Vol. I (Harmondsworth, 1976), 272.
22 Referring to Africa, Vic Allen concluded some forty years ago that "[in] societies in which bare subsistence is the norm for a high proportion of all the working class, and where men, women, and children are compelled to seek alternative means of subsistence, as distinct from their traditional ones, the *lumpenproletariat* is barely distinguishable from much of the rest of the working class." V.L. Allen, "The Meaning of the Working Class in Africa," *Journal of Modern African Studies*, 10 (1972): 169–189, at 188.

"free" wage earners was rather vague at best. On the African east coast around 1900, for example, there lived quite a number of slaves who

> ... worked as self-employed artisans or skilled workers, some of whom had previously worked as day labourers but had learnt a more lucrative trade. They worked as sea captains, fishermen, hunters, sailors, boatmen, rope makers, halva makers, tailors, shoemakers, potters, mat makers, wood carvers, weavers, palm wine tappers, carpenters, boat builders, metalworkers, bricklayers, lime burners, stone masons and even as silversmiths. Others joined caravans as porters, petty traders, and itinerant artisans, some even as caravan leaders and guides. Finally, there were those who worked as professional mercenary soldiers. ... These self-employed slaves ... were respected for their knowledge and thus commanded exceedingly high prices in the market, but they were rarely for sale. With almost the same status as freed slaves, a number of them actually owned small garden plots, and occasionally even slaves.[23]

Brazilian historians especially have pointed to the fluid dividing line between "free" wage labor and chattel slavery, as in the case of the *ganhadores* (slaves for hire) who earned their own wage, part of which they had to hand over to their owners.[24] In South Asia other ambivalences occur, as in the case of indentured laborers (*coolies*) who were employed in South Asia itself, but also in the Caribbean, Malaya, Natal, Fiji, and elsewhere. Their situation is sometimes described as a "new form of slavery," but at other times as "nearly free" wage labor.[25] In Australia, after lengthy hesitations, labor historians have no difficulty anymore to describe the numerous convict laborers originally settling in the country as "working class" in the broad sense of the word, even though these workers performed forced labor.[26] And for Europe, the new research reveals that many so-called "free" workers were really *bonded* laborers, far into the nineteenth century. Master-and-servant laws, apprenticeship arrangements, and so forth, ensured that workers were tied to their employers and had significantly fewer

---

23 Jan-Georg Deutsch, *Emancipation without Abolition in German East Africa c.1884–1914* (Oxford, 2006), 71–72.
24 Groundbreaking was the article by Silvia Hunold Lara, "Escradivão, cidadania e história do trabalho no Brasil," *Projeto História*, 16 (1998): 25–38; See also the important case study by João José Reis, "'The Revolution of the *Ganhadores*': Urban Labour, Ethnicity and the African Strike of 1857 in Bahia, Brazil," *Journal of Latin American Studies*, 29 (1997): 355–393.
25 Hugh Tinker, *A New System of Slavery: The Export of India Labour Overseas, 1830–1920* (London, 1974).
26 An excellent overview is provided by David Andrew Roberts, "The 'Knotted Hands that Set Us High': Labour History and the Study of Convict Australia," *Labour History* [Sydney], 100 (2011): 33–50.

legal rights than the literature previously suggested. In this context, there has indeed been mention of "industrial serfdom."[27]

An additional difficulty is that the old conceptualizations have proved inadequate, because they exclude all occupational groups who supposedly "do not work." Such an interpretation is reached with criteria which are rarely explained, and which most often have a moral background. The term *lumpenproletariat*, for example, is usually applied to characterize people in very precarious circumstances who earn their keep with activities like rag-picking, prostitution, and begging. These activities are not considered to be "work," but that interpretation contains a moralistic bias. On closer inspection, ragmen, prostitutes, and beggars often turn out to be de facto wage workers, indentured laborers, or chattel slaves.[28]

Another controversy concerns people who execute repression and violence on behalf of the state, like policemen and soldiers. Labor historians have long ignored their history, even though – in most cases by far – they are workers. The Latin word *mercenarius* originally meant nothing more than someone who is paid for his work (in Latin, *merx* = commodity). The work of policemen is just as regimented and Taylorized as that of other wage earners.[29] It is therefore high time that we abandon moralistic judgements and include all these "dangerous classes" in their different meanings as a legitimate field of inquiry. That is quite feasible if we opt for a more neutral definition of work. For example, we might state that work is *the purposive production of useful objects or services*.[30] Two elements

---

[27] See, for example, Alan McKinlay, "From Industrial Serf to Wage-Labourer: The 1937 Apprentice Revolt in Britain," *International Review of Social History*, 31 (1986): 1–18. Comparative perspectives are offered in Robert J. Steinfeld, *The Invention of Free Labor: The Employment Relation in English and American Law and Culture, 1350–1870* (Chapel Hill, 1991); Douglas Hay and Paul Craven, eds., *Masters, Servants, and Magistrates in Britain and the Empire, 1562–1955* (Chapel Hill, 2004), and in Alessandro Stanziani, (ed., *Le travail contraint en Asie et en Europe: XVII–XXe siècles* (Paris, 2010).

[28] See, for example, J. Mark Ramseyer, "Indentured Prostitution in Imperial Japan: Credible Commitments in the Commercial Sex Industry," *Journal of Law, Economics, and Organization*, 7 (1991): 89–116; Alain Faure, "Sordid Class, Dangerous Class? Observations on Parisian Ragpickers and Their *Cites* During the Nineteenth Century," in Shahid Amin and Marcel van der Linden, eds., *'Peripheral' Labour? Studies in the History of Partial Proletarianization* (Cambridge, 1996), 157–176.

[29] Clive Emsley, "The Policeman as Worker: A Comparative Survey, c. 1800–1940," *International Review of Social History*, 45 (2000): 89–110.

[30] This definition is essentially the same as that of Charles and Chris Tilly: "Work includes any human effort adding use value to goods and services." Charles Tilly and Chris Tilly, *Work Under Capitalism* (Boulder, CO, 1998), 22. I prefer not to use the Marxian concept "use value" in this context since use values always exist in conjunction with exchange values (prices), and thus that definition is really only applicable to commodified labor.

are emphasized in such a definition: Work is both a *purposive* activity, and work creates objects or services that are *useful* to the people for whom the work is done. Usefulness is, of course, subjective: Some people may find extremely unuseful what others consider to be very useful. Warfare, for example, is – however else we may define it – also a kind of labor process, but this is not seen as a "useful activity" by many people.

These enlargements of the research terrain have far-reaching implications. To realize their broader approach, contacts between different subgroups of researchers should, I think, be significantly intensified. First, there should be more contact between labor historians in different regions. Second, a closer cooperation is desirable between the historians of wage labor and the historians of slavery, indenture, and peasantry. Initiatives in this direction are visible in parts of the Global South (India, Brazil, Southern Africa), but much more is feasible and desirable. Third, there is a significant overlap with economic, family, women's, and legal history, and area studies, which could be utilized better. And fourth, we should strive for more cooperation with social scientists (anthropologists, sociologists, political scientists, geographers, etc.). In the terrain of traditional labor history, such cooperation already occurs, but it could be intensified. Anthropologists, for example, can make an important contribution to our insight into the incorporation of noncapitalist societies in the capitalist world economy.

Bridging these gaps presents great challenges. Historians concerned with slavery, for example, form a separate, rather extensive community, with their own periodicals (such as the excellent *Slavery and Abolition*) that are normally not read by labor historians. But, inversely, the historians of slavery do not usually concern themselves with the history of wage labor, and only seldomly read *ILWCH* or the *International Review of Social History*. Initiatives aiming at cooperation between the historians of slave labor and wage labor originate mainly from Africa and Brazil; in recent times, they are finding cautious approval elsewhere as well.[31] To make GLH a success, much more of this kind of interaction will be necessary.

---

[31] Dick Geary, professor of history at the University of Nottingham (UK) has organized a so-called Leverhulme Research Interchange from 2002, with the topic "Labour in Slave and Non-Slave Societies: Brazil and Europe in the 18th and 19th Centuries." The aim was to establish a transcontinental dialogue between labor historians and historians of slavery. One resulting study was Douglas Cole Libby and Júnia Ferreira Furtado, eds., *Trabalho livre, trabalho escravo: Brasil e Europa, séculos XVII e XIX* (São Paulo, 2006).

What has already been done, and what could be done next?

It should be obvious that GLH is a huge field for research, which could be addressed with innumerable different research questions. It is likewise obvious that there can be no "objective" methodology for establishing the scientific priorities that all labor historians ought to have. In what follows, I can therefore share my own thoughts about the direction of research only with a proviso – I acknowledge in advance that other historians may find very different topics more urgent or significant to investigate. That need not cause any strife between us, I think; to the contrary, we might well complement each other's work.

Reconceptualizing the working class

The new global networks among researchers and the new discussions they enable suggest that we need to reconceptualize the working class – on the basis of inclusion rather than exclusion. This theoretical challenge has been taken up especially by Marxian historians. Marx himself regarded chattel slavery as an "anomaly opposite the bourgeois system itself," which was "possible at individual points within the bourgeois system of production," but "only because it does not exist at other points."[32] However, recently Marxian historians have mooted two possible reconceptualizations.

One proposal, advanced by Jairus Banaji and Rakesh Bhandari, is to do away with Marx's idea of "anomalies" and consider *all* forms of labor under capitalism (including unfree labor) as variations of "capital-positing" labor. This approach implies that the differences between chattel slaves, sharecroppers, and wage-earners are only a matter of degree, rather than being qualitative differences, since all of them work for capital and since all of them labor under economic and/or noneconomic compulsion:

> Finding the essence of wage-labour in capital-positing activity not only allows a change in the extension of the concept and thereby a challenge to the apologetic Eurocentric occlusion of slavery and colonialism in the writing of the history of capitalism, it also allows us to throw into relief the way in which wage-labour in whatever form is enslaved.[33]

---

32 Marx, *Grundrisse* (Harmondsworth, 1973), 464.
33 Rakesh Bhandari, "The Disguises of Wage-Labour: Juridical Illusions, Unfree Conditions and Novel Extensions," *Historical Materialism*, 16 (2008): 71–99, at 96. See also Rakesh Bhandari,

A slightly different proposal involves broadening the concept of the working class to include all *commodified* labor. From this perspective, the working class consists of all carriers of labor power whose labor power is sold or hired out to employers (who could be individuals, corporations, or institutions), whether under economic or noneconomic compulsion, regardless of whether these carriers of labor power are themselves selling or hiring out their labor power and also regardless of whether these carriers themselves own means of production.[34] This conceptual demarcation aims to indicate the common class-basis of all subaltern workers: he the *coerced* commodification of their labor power.

According to both approaches, what all members of this redefined working class have in common is their economic exploitation by employers and the commodification of their labor power. Therefore, they share a common class interest in transcending capitalism. Recent historical research has, for instance, revealed concrete cases of struggles conducted jointly by slaves and "free" wage earners.[35] At the same time, the short- and medium-term interests of particular segments in this "new broad-spectrum proletariat" can obviously diverge strongly.

Reconstructing the changing class composition

The analysis of the long-term development of the world working class in the broadest sense obviously presents an enormous challenge. As yet we lack any quantitative estimates for the evolution of the world working class in the broader sense. Even the size of the segment of wage earners *within* this extended working class can only be roughly estimated.[36] And, while there is – relatively speaking – a large amount of data available for the nineteenth and twentieth century, constructing comparative data sets for earlier periods is often very difficult.

"Slavery and Wage Labor in History," *Rethinking Marxism*, 19 (2007): 396–408; Jairus Banaji, *Theory as History: Essays on Modes of Production and Exploitation* (Leiden and Boston, 2010).
34 Marcel van der Linden, *Workers of the World*, chapter two. Those whose labor power is not commodified, while they possess no other means of livelihood than labor power (all jobless in the broad sense), are regarded as part of the subaltern working class, as well as family members of subaltern workers who perform subsistence labor, or who, because of age or state of health, cannot work.
35 For example, Peter Linebaugh and Marcus Rediker, *The Many-Headed Hydra*.
36 Preliminary attempts in Paul Bairoch and J.-M. Limbor, "Changes in the Industrial Distribution of the World Labour Force, by Region, 1880–1960," *International Labour Review*, 98 (1968): 311–336; Paul Bairoch, "Structure de la population active mondiale de 1700 à 1970," *Annales E.S.C.*, 26 (1971): 960–976; Deon Filmer, *Estimating the World at Work*, World Bank Policy Research Working Paper No. 1488 (Washington, DC: World Bank, 1995).

Much can nevertheless be discovered about the broad outlines of the process of class formation, as the activities of the "Global Collaboratory on the History of Labor Relations" have proven. Since 2007, this team of scholars from six continents works at a reconstruction of labor relations across the globe in five sample years: 1500, 1650, 1800, 1900, and 2000. The coordination of the project is provided by the International Institute of Social History, in Amsterdam. On the basis of pilot projects, the Collaboratory developed a taxonomy of eighteen varieties of labor relations, distinguishing different types of labor defined as "reciprocal," "tributary," and "commodified," plus the "nonworking." Although there are still many gaps in the data set, the provisional hypothesis suggests itself, that the range of *types* of labor (and combinations of labor relations) grew more complex until the early nineteenth century. A simplification in labor structures then followed, as "ordinary" wage labor became more prominent. In the next years, it will be possible to test this hypothesis further, with more elaborations and refinements of the data.[37] Building on these results, it should be possible to find explanations for the incidence of divergent modes of labor control in different regions and historical periods.[38]

Understanding differential class formation

In order to truly "dig deeper" as researchers, we require not only better data sets, but also problem-oriented case studies and international comparative research. In this regard, the new developments give cause for hope. The scholarly literature about diverse world regions is growing impetuously. The number of internationally comparative studies that do not restrict themselves to the rich countries has increased quickly in recent years. After attention had already been given to coal miners early on, large-scale studies have followed recently of longshoremen and textile workers, while similar projects for the history of shipbuilders, brickmakers, soldiers, and prostitutes are in the making.[39]

---

37 https://collab.iisg.nl/web/labourrelations. The project recalls an idea by Jan Lucassen. It is coordinated by Karin Hofmeester and Christine Moll-Murata and financed by the Netherlands Organization for Scientific Research (NWO) as well as the Gerda Henkel Foundation (Germany).
38 A pioneering attempt was made by Immanuel Wallerstein in his *Modern World System*, vols. I and II (New York, 1974 and 1980). For an appraisal with respect to the concerns of labor historians, see van der Linden, *Workers of the World,* chapter thirteen.
39 Gerald D. Feldman and Klaus Tenfelde, eds., *Workers, Owners and Politics in Coal Mining: An International Comparison of Industrial Relations* (New York, 1990); Sam Davies et al., eds., *Dock Workers*; Heerma van Voss et al., eds., *Ashgate Companion to Textile Workers*. The projects on shipbuilding (coordinator: Raquel Varela), brickmaking (coordinator: Jan Lucassen), soldiers

I think it is especially important to verify, informed by such studies, how the development of the working class in different continents was interconnected – and yet resulted in significant intraclass inequalities. Several different methodological approaches are possible here. One of them is the reconstruction of commodity chains. A commodity is normally the product of human labor, that is, the result of efforts by people who produce products with means of production that are subsequently sold or hired out by themselves or by others. But those means of production (raw materials, machines, energy, etc.) are themselves also the result of human labor. So a kind of "product chain" exists, which takes the form of "a tree-like sequence of production processes and exchanges by which a product for final consumption is produced. These linkages of raw materials, labor, the sustenance of labor, intermediate processing, final processing, transport, and final consumption materially connect most of the people within the contemporary world-system."[40] Thus, this concept identifies the reality that, even if the final consumer is blissfully unaware of it, each commodity has its own individual history, and if we trace out the histories of products, this can tell us a lot about global interconnections, or what I have elsewhere referred to as *teleconnections*.[41]

The literature about commodity chains has increased enormously since the 1990s, but a recent study nevertheless rightly concludes that "the framework has encountered major difficulties in incorporating into its analysis labour in particular, and class relations more generally."[42] Especially radical geographers have begun to change this situation. The analysis of commodity chains and global production networks can also help us to understand the material possibilities and limitations of solidarity between workers in different positions in the chains. After all, their short-term interests can diverge: The more "expensive" the workers at the beginning of the chain are, the more employers will try to exert downward pressure on the living standard of workers at the end of the chain.

A second way to analyze teleconnections relates to an old controversy: How much do workers in the advanced capitalist countries profit from the extra exploitation of workers in less developed and colonial regions? One answer was first formulated by Engels and Lenin, and subsequently elaborated in different

---

(coordinator: Erik-Jan Zürcher), and prostitution (coordinators: Lex Heerma van Voss and Magaly Rodriguez García) are initiatives of the International Institute of Social History in Amsterdam.
40 Christopher Chase-Dunn, *Global Formation: Structures of the World Economy* (Oxford and Cambridge, MA, 1989), 346.
41 Marcel van der Linden, *Workers of the World* (Leiden, 2008), 372–377.
42 Ben Selwyn, "Beyond Firm-Centrism: Re-integrating Labour and Capitalism into Global Commodity Chain Analysis," *Journal of Economic Geography*, 12 (2012), 205–226, at 205.

variants by Fritz Sternberg (1926) and Arghiri Emmanuel (1969).[43] It is a well-established fact that from the nineteenth century a growing disparity in wealth emerged between workers in developed and underdeveloped capitalism. And it is also quite certain that this trend restricted the possibilities for real international solidarity. But the big question remains of in what measure metropolitan "super-wages" have been a *direct consequence* of unequal exchange between rich and poor countries. To a significant extent, the salaries of strata of metropolitan workers may have been the result of their higher average productivity, skill level, and organizing ability – and of the endogenous economic growth which that made possible. This remains, I think, an important empirical issue in need of further critical scientific study.[44]

Understanding interconnections

Closely related to the study of international inequalities within the broad working class is the identification of *transfer mechanisms* between different parts of the world. Transfers emerge in various ways. One of them is migration, but even though much research has been done in this area, there often is a Eurocentric bias. It has become clear that the nineteenth-century trans-Atlantic migration circuit was in truth not larger than the contemporaneous migration circuits in south and northeast Asia.[45] A second *trait d'union* between world regions are the transport workers, in particular the seamen who so often formed multinational crews and sailed from one continent to another. It is not surprising that they have received a relatively large amount of scholarly attention in recent years.[46]

---

[43] Fritz Sternberg, *Der Imperialismus* (Berlin, 1926); Arghiri Emmanuel, *L'échange inégal. Essais sur les antagonismes dans les rapports économiques internationaux* (Paris, 1969).

[44] At least in part, one could agree with the "split labor market theory" of Edna Bonacich and others. See the clear overview in Edna Bonacich, "The Past, Present, and Future of Split Labor Market Theory," *Research in Race and Ethnic Relations*, 1 (1979): 17–64.

[45] The groundbreaking article on this topic is Adam McKeown, "Global Migration, 1846–1940," *Journal of World History*, 15 (2004): 155–189. A good overview of the earlier global migration history is provided in Dirk Hoerder, *Cultures in Contact: World Migrations in the Second Millennium* (Durham, NC, 2002). Since 2005 there is a "Global Migration History" project, which strives "to include the full migration experience of the non-Western world." See http://www.iisg.nl/research/gmhp.php (accessed October 15, 2012).

[46] Recent contributions include Gopalan Balachandran, "Circulation through Seafaring: Indian Seamen, 1890–1945," in Claude Markovits et al., eds., *Society and Circulation: Mobile People and Itinerant Cultures in South Asia, 1750–1950* (New Delhi, 2003), 89–130; Jan Lucassen, "A Multinational and its Labor Force: The Dutch East India Company, 1595–1795," *ILWCH*, 66 (2004): 12–39; Michael H. Fisher, "Working Across the Seas: Indian Maritime Labourers in India, Britain, and in

But other than people (migrants, sailors) who moved across the globe, there are also institutions, ideas, and objects that exerted influence across large distances. A clear example is the British state, which from 1807 tried to abolish the slave trade – a lengthy campaign that greatly influenced labor relations from the Americas and Africa to south and southeast Asia. In a certain sense, the International Labor Organization, founded in 1919, continued this campaign into the twentieth century by propagating a broad range of international labor standards – without, however, being able to enforce their implementation.[47] On the other side, it has become clear (1) that important labor-management techniques were invented outside the North Atlantic region (especially in the colonies) in the attempt to control *unfree* workers; (2) that some of these innovations date from long *before* the Industrial Revolution; and (3) that knowledge about such innovations traveled across all parts of the globe.[48] Such international connections are often hardly explored but promise to provide fascinating new insights.

Understanding class cultures

Cultural differences among workers in Europe can be great; this has been demonstrated beyond any doubt by labor historians. Richard Biernacki, for example, has shown, that from the sixteenth-century wage laborers in Germany and

---

Between, 1600–1857," and Ravi Ahuja, "Mobility and Containment: The Voyages of South Asian Seamen, c.1900–1960," both in Rana Behal and Marcel van der Linden, eds., *India's Labouring Poor: Historical Studies c. 1600–c.2000* (New Delhi, 2007), 21–45, and 111–141; Matthias van Rossum et al., "National and International Labour Markets for Sailors in European, Atlantic and Asian Waters, 1600–1850," *Research in Maritime History*, 43 (2010): 47–72; Leon Fink, *Sweatshops at Sea: Merchant Seamen in the World's First Globalized Industry, from 1812 to the Present* (Chapel Hill, NC, 2011). About the history of railway builders and workers there are many country studies. It would be interesting to use this literature as the basis for an integrated global reconstruction.

47 Jasmien Van Daele et al., eds., *ILO Histories: Essays on the International Labour Organization and Its Impact on the World During the Twentieth Century* (Berne, 2010); Isabelle Lespinet-Moret and Vincent Viet, eds., *L'Organisation internationale du travail. Origine, développement, avenir* (Rennes, 2011); Sandrine Kott and Joëlle Droux, eds., *Globalizing Social Rights: The ILO and Beyond* (London, 2012); Marcel van der Linden, ed., *Humanitarian Intervention and Changing Labor Relations. The Long-term Consequences of the Abolition of the Slave Trade* (Leiden and Boston, 2011).

48 Bill Cooke, "The Denial of Slavery in Management Studies," *Journal of Management Studies*, 40 (2003): 1895–1918; Elizabeth Esch and David Roediger, "One Symptom of Originality: Race and the Management of Labour in the History of the United States," *Historical Materialism*, 17 (2009): 3–43; Marcel van der Linden, "Re-constructing the Origins of Modern Labor Management," *Labor History*, 51 (2010): 509–522.

Britain developed different understandings of the conveyance of labor-power as a commodity, and that these diverging understandings "were reproduced among managers and workers through the execution of work rather than through the reception of a discourse."[49] By extension, we could hypothesize that the differences between working-class cultures on a world scale are even greater. But for now that remains pure speculation. To understand how working-class cultures emerge, adapt, and change, we obviously have to gain insight also into the socialization processes occurring in families, social networks, and in formal and informal education. Such an intercultural historiography of socialization processes is, however, still in an embryonic phase. Collaboration among ethnographers, historians, and social psychologists in this area would no doubt be fruitful.

Another issue concerns global awareness. Perhaps an example can clarify what I mean here. The mechanization of the British textile industry at the end of the eighteenth century for the most part destroyed manual weaving in Britain, while at the same time it increased the demand for cotton produced by North American slaves. When the trans-Atlantic trade stagnated during the American Civil War of 1861–1865, the resulting Lancashire "cotton famine" not only pauperized the British workers, but also caused a migration of workers to Australia and increased cotton production in, for example, Egypt and India. There, many farmers were robbed of their means of subsistence by commercialization, causing, among other things, more famines.[50] This causal chain – very briefly summarized – spanned some five countries: the United States, the United Kingdom, Egypt, British India, and Australia. Consequently, at least five collective memories also originated, the records of which remain largely disconnected from each other. Thus, the Australian memory of the immigration of the 1860s is quite unrelated to the Egyptian memory of agricultural change at roughly the same time, and unrelated to the American memory of civil war.

The question is raised: Under which conditions does consciousness of global connections emerge, and under which conditions does it remain absent? Why, for example, did transnational waves of enthusiasm emerge among workers and peasants after 1905 (the Japanese victory over Russia) and after 1917 (the October Revolution) that expressed themselves respectively in support to social movements in Indonesia, Iran, and Turkey – and in worldwide sympathy for Bolshe-

---

49 Richard Biernacki, *The Fabrication of Labor: Germany and Britain, 1640–1914* (Berkeley, 1995), 471.
50 I borrow this example from Rosa Luxemburg, "*Einführung in die Nationalökonomie*," in Luxemburg, *Gesammelte Werke*, vol. 5 (Berlin, 1985), 524–778, at 557–560. An English translation is available in section IV of Rosa Luxemburg, *What is Economics?* Translated by T. Edwards (New York, 1954); reprinted New York, 1968, 39–44.

vism? Has the global awareness of parts of the broad working class increased in the course of time? Are there important differences in this regard between peripheral and metropolitan parts of the world? And what do we make of events that are remembered in contrary ways by workers with different national, ethnic, and gender backgrounds?

One possible source for the study of workers' subjectivity, still hardly investigated, is the analysis of "global biographies," that is, the life histories of individuals who crossed large distances, sailed the oceans, or crossed political, cultural, and religious boundaries.[51] Such biographies exist for influential labor leaders and radical intellectuals but hardly for "ordinary" members of the broad working class. The important autobiography of Olaudah Equiano (c. 1745–1797) springs to mind, but it looks more like an exception that proves the rule.[52] Global labor historians have nevertheless started to become active on this terrain as well. Quite recently, for example, a scientific edition was published of the memoirs of Munshi Rahman Khan (1874–1972), an Indian coolie who migrated to Surinam at the age of twenty-four. For more than forty years, he kept notes of his experiences, which provide us with rich insights into the life and work of Indian indentured laborers in the Caribbean.[53]

Understanding self-organization and resistance

Forms of self-organization and resistance are increasingly being studied at the hand of international comparisons. Attention is being paid not just to spectacular forms of public protest such as strikes or mutinies, but also to inconspicuous activities such as the building of rotating savings and credit associations, mutual aid funds, and consumer cooperatives.[54] In this area (also known as *mutualism*)

---

[51] This description is taken from the introduction to Bernd Hausberger, ed., *Globale Lebensläufe. Menschen als Akteure im weltgeschichtlichen Geschehen* (Vienna, 2006).
[52] *The Interesting Narrative of the Life of Olaudah Equiano, or Gustavus Vassa, the African. Written by Himself* (New York, 1791).
[53] Kathinka Sinha-Kerkhoff et al., eds., *Autobiography of an Indian Indentured Labourer: Munshi Rahman Khan (1874–1972)* (New Delhi, 2005). Ravi Ahuja (University of Gottingen) is currently preparing a publication based on the memoirs of Amir Haider Khan (c. 1901–1989), a *lascar* (sailor) from British India.
[54] Sjaak van der Velden et al., eds., *Strikes Around the World, 1968–2005* (Amsterdam, 2007); Marcel van der Linden, ed., *Social Security Mutualism: The Comparative History of Mutual Benefit Societies* (Berne, 1996); Abram de Swaan and Marcel van der Linden, eds., *Mutualist Microfinance: Informal Savings Funds from the Global Periphery to the Core?* (Amsterdam, 2006). A conference about the global history of mutinies was staged at the IISH in June 2011 (coordinators: Marcus Rediker, Niklas Frykman, and Lex Heerma van Voss); a large-scale project about consum-

much remains to be done. Not only have mutualist organizations remained a "stepchild" of traditional labor history – probably because of their unheroic character – but forms of mutualism among unfree laborers have hardly been studied. There are, for example, indications that rotating savings funds existed amongst slaves, but little is known about it so far.

We know much more about the forms of overt protest, like the *marronage* of slaves in Africa and the Americas, strikes, and other forms of protest by "free" laborers. But here, too, a global approach can provide new insights. A traditional approach would suggest, for example, that strikes are a form of collective action associated especially with free wage laborers. But if we now examine the ways in which protest is expressed and pressure is exerted by the different groups of workers (including slaves, the self-employed, the *lumpenproletarians,* and the "free" wage laborers), these appear to overlap considerably. Slaves and coolies also went on strike, for example. At the same time, the inclusion of slaves and indentured laborers in the analysis demonstrates that the strike is a very important, but also a very specific, form of the collective refusal to work. So-called unfree workers have used many other forms of collective refusal that deserve to be integrated in our analysis – such as the downing of tools without any demands being made, or a collective exodus (e.g., the coolies at the tea plantations in Chargola Valley, Assam, in 1921).[55] Seen against this background, the strikes of so-called free wage earners constitute just *one* form of collective resistance against the exploitation of commodified labor. And we should also acknowledge that, conversely, *free* wage laborers have often used methods of struggle that are normally associated with *unfree* workers, such as lynching, rioting, arson, and bombing.

A global approach can also make a contribution to the historiography of wage laborers in the traditional sense. Despite some methodological weaknesses, the global strike data compiled from 1980 by the Research Working Group on World Labor of the Braudel Center (Binghamton) have provided a treasure trove of information about trends since the late nineteenth century, and particularly about the differences between the "core" and the "periphery" of the world system. The best-known study is, of course, Beverly Silver's *Forces of Labor,* published in 2003. Using the examples of the textile and car industries, Silver showed that the interrelationship between labor movements and capital has a certain logic. Depending on all kinds of factors (including product life cycles and interstate conflicts) and driven by recurrent workers' resistance, capital develops at least

---

er cooperatives is coordinated by the Swedish Arbetarrörelsens Arkiv och Bibliotek (Mary Hilson and Silke Neunsinger).
55 On the Chargola exodus, see Nitin Varma's forthcoming monograph.

four strategies in its attempt to maintain profitability: (1) the "spatial fix," that is, the geographical relocation to regions with cheaper and more docile workers; (2) the "technological/organizational fix," that is, the transformation of labor processes; (3) the "product fix," that is, the shift of capital to new industries and product lines; and (4) the "financial fix," that is, the shift of capital from production and trade to money lending and speculation. All these answers to labor protest "undermined established customs and livelihoods," but simultaneously "created and strengthened new working classes with strategic bargaining power in the expanding and profitable segments of the global economy."[56] Our broader concept of the working class allows us to add another variant, which we could call the "labor modes fix": Employers can, if they see their position threatened in one way or another, substitute one form of labor commodification for another, for example, by replacing "free" wage labor with debt bondage or self-employment.

The last issue I want to mention in this context concerns workers' political organizations. Labor, social democratic and communist parties are generally considered to be political representatives of the working class. Yet such parties emerged mainly in one specific historical period, namely between the 1880s and the 1930s. As Eric Hobsbawm explained thirty years ago,

> These parties, or their lineal successors, are still in being and often influential, but where they did not already exist, or the influence of socialists/communists was significant in labor movements before World War II, hardly any such parties have emerged out of the working classes since then, notably in the so-called "Third World."[57]

The most important exception to this rule was the founding of the Workers' Party in Brazil in 1980, which grew very large; for the rest, Hobsbawm's assessment appears to be right. What causal factors can explain this empirical observation? The new working classes in the Global South seem to articulate their discontent especially through radical religions. Is the growing influence of evangelical/charismatic and Islamic currents in poor countries an expression of class formation?

Spots on the horizon

Twenty-four centuries ago Plato, the Greek philosopher, suspected that the countries around the Mediterranean seaboard represented only a small part of a

---

56 Silver, *Forces of Labor*, 131–132.
57 Eric J. Hobsbawm, *Worlds of Labour: Further Studies in the History of Labour* (London, 1984), 60.

much larger world. Their inhabitants were, he wrote, "like ants and frogs about a marsh," quite unaware "that there are other inhabitants of many other like places."[58] In the same way, we as labor and working-class historians are now realizing that our discipline encompasses a much larger intellectual territory than we were previously taught. It will take quite some time yet before we can trace out all the far-flung corners of this "new world" on our mental maps. When we begin to succeed in this, we will also be able to renew our understanding of the original terrain of labor and working-class history in Europe and North America. Just as the history of the Global South can hardly be written without giving attention to the Global North, the history of the Global North cannot be understood without their linkages in the Global South. Much progress has already been made, but empirically and analytically we stand – for the most part – still only at the beginning.

---

[58] *Phaedo*, 109b. Trans. Benjamin Jowitt.

Christian G. De Vito / Alex Lichtenstein
Writing a Global History of Convict Labour[1]

Whatever their political perspective, historians of labour and work tend to associate the evolution of labour relations with the teleology of freedom. Various coercive labour practices – slavery, serfdom, indenture, vassalage – are regarded as giving way over time to free but commodified forms of labour, particularly with the expansion of capitalist modernity, free contract, and wage work. Yet, in nearly every society and in nearly every historical era, enforced work has in fact been deployed as a form of penal and/or administrative control of selected populations. Taking this perpetual nexus of labour and penality as its framework, this article examines the historically ubiquitous institution of convict labour from both a global and long-term perspective, and its place within a constellation of forms of unfree labour linked to the development of modernity. It does so in three main ways, corresponding to three mutually reinforcing sections of the bibliographic survey that follows.

In the first section, we frame convict labour within broader classifications of labour relations, in order to constitute penal work as a category of historical analysis, in much the same way as slavery, serfdom, wage labour, indentured labour, and so on have served as specific analytical categories and investigative tropes within labour historiography. Further, we point to the peculiar, socially constructed nature of the concept "convict", constituted as it is by legal regimes, state power, and private action that link unfreedom and punishment. Here we emphasize the need to address both the objective, structural factors that defined penal labour within a larger grid of relations of production *and* its subjective, experiential aspects by which prisoners defined their own consciousness. Finally,

---

[1] This article was first published under the same title in *International Review of Social History*, 58 (2013), pp. 285–325 doi 10.1017/S0020859012000818 © 2013 Internationaal Instituut voor Sociale Geschiedenis, published by Cambridge University Press. Draft versions of this article were discussed during the workshop on "Global Convict Labour" held at the International Institute of Social History, Amsterdam, 13–14 June 2012, at a staff meeting at the IISH, and with individual experts. We should like to thank the following scholars for the comments, critiques, and suggestions they provided: Carlos Aguirre, Clare Anderson, Touraj Atabaki, Rossana Barragan, Stefano Bellucci, Aad Blok, Ulbe Bosma, Marc Buggeln, Timothy Coates, Francesca Di Pasquale, Miko Flohr, Guy Geltner, Miriam J. Groen-Vallinga, Karin Hofmeester, Stacey Hynd, Padraic Kenney, Margo De Koster, Marcel van der Linden, Jan Lucassen, Hamish Maxwell-Stewart, Klaus Mühlhahn, Robert Perkinson, Jean-Lucien Sanchez, Willem van Schendel, and Lynne Viola. An edited volume presenting contributions on the topic has been published: C. G. De Vito, A. Lichtenstein (eds), *Global Convict Labour*, in: M. van der Linden (ed.), Studies in Global Social History, Vol. 19 (Leiden, 2015).

the question is raised of which conditions have proved most conducive to the emergence and transformation of convict labour over time, and the advantages of an approach that integrates economic, cultural, and political factors are underlined. In particular, we call attention to the role of penal labour in defining the nature of state power and in producing specific types of citizen and subject.

In the second section we provide a selective overview of some of the literature on convict labour in the form of an itinerary through time, space, and different regimes of punishment. By placing convict labour at the centre of our analysis, we aim to transcend the fragmentation of the existing historiography on the interconnections of labour, penality, and the denial of freedom. With this survey, the article points to the interconnections among different forms of punishment and the broader social, political, cultural, and economic context in which both penal labour and punishment more broadly have developed.

In the third and final section of the article we consider the possibility of a pre-capitalist *longue durée* of penal labour, extending our analysis prior to 1500, through a brief examination of transportation and imprisonment in ancient and medieval times. Moreover, we raise the question of how a genuinely *global* history of convict labour might be written, that is, a history that does not simply integrate existing knowledge and ongoing research on different parts of the world into pre-existing models of penal history, but that self-consciously looks for methodological approaches that avoid Eurocentric perspectives and point instead to transnational linkages as a constituent element in penal labour regimes.

Classifying convict labour

Convict labour can best be understood as a phenomenon located at the crossroads of two dynamic social processes: the commodification of labour and the enforced social definition of the "convict" as a person who has forfeited his or her right to freedom. Examination of the first process reminds us that convict labour has proved compatible with diverse modes of production and is perfectly compatible with modern social relations, such as the expansion of capitalism and the spread of wage labour. The second process calls attention to the importance of the state in shaping unfree labour relations, while also stressing subjective perceptions and representations of convict labour.

To frame convict labour within a broader history of labour relations, we might begin by considering the taxonomy constructed by the Global Collaboratory on the History of Labour Relations for a long-term project being conducted at the IISH "to establish a quantitative overview of labour relations worldwide for the period 1500–2000".[2] In this context, convicts appear as two sub-categories of "tributary labourers":[3] "forced labourers" and "tributary slaves". The former are defined as "those who have to work for the polity, and are remunerated mainly in kind", and include *corvée* labourers and conscripted soldiers as well as convicts. The "tributary slaves" are "those who are owned by and work for the polity indefinitely (deprived of the right to leave, to refuse to work, or to receive compensation for their labour)". The Global Collaboratory regards forced labourers in concentration camps as an example of these. The main advantage of this classification lies in the fact that it stresses the role of the state in the process of definition, selection, and exploitation of convict labour. However, this presents a serious limitation, since it almost exclusively underlines the otherness of convict labour in relation to the process of commodification of labour power.[4] In so doing, it seems

---

2 K. Hofmeester and C. Moll-Murata (eds), *The Joy and Pain of Work: Global Attitudes and Valuations, 1500–1650, International Review of Social History*, 56, Special Issue 19 (2011). This special issue is dedicated to the Global Collaboratory project. See in particular the introduction by K. Hofmeester and C. Moll-Murata (pp. 1–24). The taxonomy referred to in the text is published as Figure 1, p. 6; the definitions of labour relations are published in the Appendix, pp. 21–23. See also the website: https://collab.iisg.nl/web/labourrelations.

3 "Tributary labourers" in general are defined as those who "are obliged to work for the polity (often the state, though it could also be a feudal or religious authority). Their labour is not commodified and owned by the polity." The taxonomy also allows one to frame non-working convicts within the category "non-working" and then under the sub-category "cannot work or cannot be expected to work". In this case the impossibility to work does not relate to either age, disability, or the need to study, but to the legal impossibility of working *outside* penal or administrative control and the material impossibility of working *inside* penal or administrative institutions. This condition, for instance, is largely diffused among inmates in many contemporary Western prisons.

4 Another problem with this way of framing convict labour relates to the use of the concept of "slaves" for concentration camp prisoners. This association raises some fundamental issues that have been summarized by Marc Buggeln: (1) slavery is a system of labour in which the slave has a value for their private owner, while the concentration camp prisoner is the inmate of a state organization and is deprived of any (or a large part of his/her) value; (2) ex-concentration camp prisoners who defined themselves as slaves used the term in a non-economic, symbolic way; (3) much of the debate on the question "has rested on the absolute positioning of American slavery as the paradigmatic slave system for all times", while from a global and long-term perspective "slavery has proved to be an extremely multi-layered phenomenon that has shown itself capable of adapting to a wide variety of societal forms throughout history". In other words, even if one accepts that concentration camp prisoners were slaves, the question remains of what kind of slaves they were. For these reasons, Buggeln has pointed out that "the dangers implicit in this form of comparison [...] outweigh the benefits", and Rüdiger Hachtmann has stressed that "the term [slavery] is loaded with various connotations in historical research", and "cannot as a category really do justice to the specific forms of discrimination that the various groups of labourers compelled to unfree work deployments in German industry were subjected to during

to leave little space for the understanding of those connections convict labour has maintained with other forms of free and unfree labour, setting it largely outside of important considerations of political economy.

A potentially more dynamic means of including convict labourers as part of the global working classes is provided by Marcel van der Linden in his collection of essays, *Workers of the World*.[5] Van der Linden's work challenges the idea that only the labour power of free wage labourers is commodified, and thus opens up the possibility of considering various forms of both free and unfree labour *as part of* the process of commodification. By offering a far more supple definition of the "working class" than traditional Marxian accounts, one that is not dependent on the classic evolution of free wage labour and thus includes marginalized workers of all types, Van der Linden incorporates the experience of the majority of the population of the "Global South" into his account. In particular, he has distinguished four different types of possible labour commodification: "*autonomous* commodification, in which the carrier of labour power is also its possessor, and *heteronomous* commodification, in which the carrier of labour power is not its possessor; in both cases, the carrier's labour power can be offered by the carrier him- or herself or by another person". Most importantly for our purposes, Van der Linden identifies the "coerced commodification of labour power" as an important aspect of the making of a global working class. Indeed, using this model, convict labour can be considered as commodified labour insofar as the labour power of the convicts – who are carriers but not possessors of their labour power – is commodified by the authorities, under whose penal and/or administrative control they are held (at least initially).

The classification proposed by Van der Linden has a fundamental advantage in that it allows us to envisage convict labour in its connections with other forms of free and unfree labour rather than setting it off as an anomalous category. In so doing, it supplements the first classification proposed by the Collaboratory, joining in that project's effort to identify a global working class while recognizing the close ties between penality and the historical experience of labour and work in many contexts, including the commodification of labour. As we will argue in the following section, convict labour has been a part of fluid coercive networks

---

World War II". See M. Buggeln, "Were Concentration Camp Prisoners Slaves?: The Possibilities and Limits of Comparative History and Global Historical Perspectives", *International Review of Social History*, 53 (2008), pp. 101–129, 116 and 115. See also W. Sofsky, *The Order of Terror: The Concentration Camp* (Princeton, NJ, 1997); R. Hachtmann, "Fordism and Unfree Labour: Aspects of the Work Deployment of Concentration Camp Prisoners in German Industry between 1941 and 1944", *International Review of Social History*, 55 (2010), pp. 485–513, 488–489.

5 M. van der Linden, *Workers of the World* (Leiden, 2008). See especially ch. 2, and particularly pp. 18–20 and 34.

in the context of early modern and modern colonial empires as well as in more recent and even contemporary labour systems. Empirical research has repeatedly shown its multiple intertwining with other forms of unfree labour as well as with free labour. In fact, in many penal colonies convicts prepared the ground for indentured and free labour, indentured workers became convicts when caught after trying to escape or as a supplementary punishment, slaves and free workers condemned to death could be "liberated" upon transportation, and ex-convicts sometimes signed contracts of indenture or migrated on to new destinations.[6]

Nor is convict labour imbricated with other labour relations only on a structural level. Although a very complex topic for research, convicts' self-perception of their work also plays an important role here. This is the case, for example, with some ex-concentration camp prisoners who tried to make sense of their experience by evoking slavery. With reference to another context, Clare Anderson has shown that prisoners transported within the Indian Ocean sometimes did not perceive themselves as convicts at all and associated their experience with that of indenture, a status more common in their own families and communities. And a deep tradition of African-American cultural expression has made the convict labourer a central character in the longing for liberation in a society marked by racial repression.[7]

Such subjectivity plays an especially important role in the case of convict labour, given its very nature. Besides the commodification of labour, the process of defining the "convict" is the other social dynamic that shapes convict labour. While concepts such as wage labour or indentured work directly point to particular forms of labour relations rooted in contract,[8] the expression "convict labour"

---

6 C. Anderson, *Subaltern Lives: Biographies of Colonialism in the Indian Ocean, World, 1790–1920* (Cambridge, 2012). See also U. Bosma, "European Colonial Soldiers in the Nineteenth Century: Their Role in White Global Migration and Patterns of Colonial Settlement", *Journal of Global History*, 4 (2009), pp. 317–336. On p. 319 the author refers to the cases of Siberia and Australia and explicitly points to the fact that "[i]n the early phases of colonialism, soldiers and convicts were, if not the cheapest, certainly the most easily deployed source of labour in the extreme circumstances of a frontier". The two groups thus came to play a pivotal role as "primers of the pump for mass migration" and in preparing the ground for other forms of labour.
7 Anderson, *Subaltern Lives*. On subjectivity and the memory of imprisonment and forced labour, see also J.M. Gheith and K.R. Jolluck, *Gulag Voices: Oral Histories of Soviet Incarceration and Exile* (New York, 2011); on the African-American experience, see L. Gellert, *Negro Songs of Protest* (New York, 1936); B. Jackson, *Wake Up, Dead Man: Afro-American Work Songs from Texas Prisons* (Cambridge, MA, 1972); and H.B. Franklin, *Prison Literature in America: The Victim as Criminal and Artist* (New York, 1989).
8 However, an extended literature has discussed the need to overcome a rigid distinction between "free" and "unfree" labour and has even questioned the category of "free labour". See especially G. Prakash, "Colonialism, Capitalism and the Discourse of Freedom", in S. Amin and

points to an immanent labour relation into which individuals enter only *after* they have undergone a process of enforced social definition as convicts, a social definition that brands them as criminals, deviants, or non-citizens in need of isolation and correction. Therefore, although economic rationales have sometimes played a fundamental role in defining the geography and morphology of punishment and work, the impact of legal and administrative categories on these processes should never be underestimated. Moreover, since punishment (and sometimes other administrative forms of control) usually implies a definite amount of time, the experience of convict labour represents only a limited portion of the convict's life experience. Being a convict is often a temporary juridical or administrative status that eventually entails the reintegration of the prisoner into specific labour relations. It can be expected therefore that the convict's labour identity and ethics either remain connected to a previous occupation (or non-occupation) and location in the labour market and social order, or are projected after the end of punishment, as in the case of many transported convicts who subsequently settled in the new penal colonies.

Moreover, not only juridical and administrative factors, but also social, political, economic, and cultural processes are involved in the definition of "convict" (as well as in that of related concepts such as prisoner, internee, and inmate). As the sociology of punishment and the critical approaches to criminology have stressed, even in the highly formalized legal systems of contemporary democracies, political and media discourses on criminality, race, and security shape ideologies of punishment. The possibility of accessing the right of defence, the structure of penal codes and juridical administration, and the mentality of police, social, judicial, and penal actors all play a decisive role in the social construction of deviancy, crime, and convicts.[9] It seems safe to assume that this discretionality increases in the case of medieval and early modern contexts, where informal agencies and extrajudicial mechanisms played a fundamental role in punishment, and that it reaches its zenith in the case of administrative measures taken under "states of exception", especially in situations of war, colonization, and non-democratic regimes, that is, in most of the situations where convict labour has actually appeared in history. In democratic societies, such exceptionality

---

M. van der Linden (eds), *"Peripheral" Labour? Studies in the History of Partial Proletarianization* (Cambridge, 1997), pp. 9–25; T. Brass and M. van der Linden (eds), *Free and Unfree Labour: The Debate Continues* (Berne, 1997); R.P. Behal, "Changing Paradigm of South Asian Labour Historiography", in M. van der Linden and E. Himmelstoss (eds), *Labour History Beyond Borders: Concepts and Explorations* (Vienna, 2009), pp. 63–78; Van der Linden, *Workers of the World*.

9 See for instance P. Combessie, *Sociologie de la prison* (Paris, 2001); K. Carrington and R. Hogg, *Critical Criminology: Issues, Debates, Challenges* (Portland, OR, 2002).

may still be associated with the perpetuation of historical, racial, or ethnic domination, as seems to be the case for the current world leader in incarceration, the United States.[10]

For these reasons, while we might still want to build a taxonomy of labour relations that includes convict labour and allows quantitative comparative insights, in trying to make sense of convict labour any reification of the phenomenon should be avoided. One possible way to proceed is through a double move. On the one hand, we propose to define convict labour loosely as the work performed by individuals under penal and/or administrative control. This broad definition binds together different institutions across various periods and within all sorts of political regime. At the same time, it clearly differentiates convict labour from other historical situations where either forced labour or penal and/or administrative control were present, but did not come together. For instance, slavery or POW labour as such are clearly separated from convict labour; the work performed by slaves and POWs is considered convict labour here only insofar as it is enforced as the consequence of a supplementary penal or administrative measure (for example, as a punishment for a crime or a disciplinary infraction). Beyond this separation, however, areas of interpenetration between convict labour and other forms of forced labour become visible and can be addressed in empirical research.[11] Ultimately, because of its pragmatic rather than prescriptive approach, this definition points to the fact that the question "What is convict labour?" can be answered only with reference to specific historical contexts. On the other hand, with the goal of generalizing the findings of localized studies, the question "Why convict labour?" could be asked, or, to put it another way, empirical findings could be used to generalize about the historical conditions under which convict labour has been produced and exploited in the larger process of the commodification of labour.

Such a procedure entails understanding convict labour not in isolation but as part of an integrated labour market, that is, in dialectic with other (free and unfree) labour relations and their mutual combinations. And it requires an approach that brings together different strands of the literature that have stressed either economic explanations or social-political-cultural factors, such as racial or

---

10 M. Alexander, *The New Jim Crow: Mass Incarceration in the Age of Colorblindness* (New York, 2010).
11 Think, for instance, of the many cases, especially in non-Western European contexts, where labour was imposed on individuals through extra-judicial practice within households, communities, and guilds. Another case is that of the "free convicts" in the late 1950s and 1960s Chinese *laogai*, that is, individuals who had formally completed their sentences but were prevented from leaving the camps and forced to work in special brigades under the *jiu ye* system of "job placement".

colonial domination. As in the pioneering work of Georg Rusche and Otto Kirchheimer, the significance of economic approaches to punishment lies in pointing to the connection between economic cycles, incarceration, and convict labour.[12] Their approach prompts consideration of the place of convict labour in the labour market of particular economic sectors, the disciplining effect of convict labour on the free workforce, the productivity of convict labour, and so on. However, in order to avoid deterministic economic explanations, the importance of other factors also needs to be recognized. The function of convict labour, its characteristics, and its connection with other forms of labour relations have depended not just on rational economic motivations but also on social constructions that have influenced both the way the convicts have been imagined, selected, and differentiated, and the forms of punishment, the related institutions, and their localization. Discourses of ethnicity, race, class, and gender, in particular, have shaped notions of criminality as a whole and the lives of individuals under penal and administrative control. Precisely because coercive networks are highly differentiated and fluid, the coexistence of different forms of punishment has been possible and "rehabilitative" and "punitive" work have coexisted in differentiated parts of the convict population, in differentiated spaces, and at different times in the biography of a single individual.

Thinking about these non-economic aspects of convict labour brings us back to the widely influential question of "governmentality", a concept coined by Foucault in the late 1970s, and central to the subsequent deployment of Foucauldian accounts of the role of incarceration in constituting modern forms of state power. From this vantage point, historians might consider how different types of penal labour regime have served as an expression and projection of particular forms of bio-political sovereignty, one that can knit together conceptualizations of citizenship (or non-citizenship), work, and the legal (or extra-legal) power to punish at particular historical moments. Who is defined as "criminal" and why, how the state commands prisoners' capacity for productive labour and in what form,

---

[12] The key reference for this approach is still G. Rusche and O. Kirchheimer, *Punishment and Social Structure* (New York, 1939). The thesis had already been anticipated in G. Rusche, "Arbeitsmarkt und Strafvollzug. Gedanken zur Soziologie der Strafjustiz", *Zeitschrift für Sozialforschung* (1933), pp. 63–78. For more recent studies restating this materialist explanation, see D. Melossi and M. Pavarini, *Carcere e fabbrica: alle origini del sistema penitenziario (XVI–XIX secolo)* (Bologna, 1977), English translation: *The Prison and the Factory: Origins of the Penitentiary System* (London, 1981); I. Jankovich, "Labor Market and Imprisonment", *Crime and Social Justice*, 8 (1977), pp. 17–31; M. Killias and C. Grandjean, "Chômage et taux d'incarcération: l'exemple de la Suisse de 1890 à 1941", *Déviance et société*, 10 (1986), pp. 309–322; B. Laffargue and T. Godefroy, "La prison républicaine et son environment économique. Population en prison et marché du travail (1870–1914)", *Déviance et société*, 14 (1990) pp. 39–58.

and how such unfree labour is conceptualized as part of a larger social order all deserve further historical scrutiny.[13]

Nevertheless, in understanding how economic, political, social, and cultural factors have shaped the penal strategies of empires, states, and local authorities, the limits of governmentality also need to be investigated, as even Foucault himself came to acknowledge.[14] After all, even the most powerful authority has neither ever had an actual monopoly on social control and coercive discourses nor unlimited resources to implement them. Shifts from prisons to labour camps, for instance, have also stemmed from concrete problems such as systematic overcrowding, fiscal limitations, inadequate prison buildings, and the (perceived) lack of professional training of prisoners and guards. Similarly, the low productivity of convict labour, often exacerbated by prisoner resistance, has sometimes modified and even stopped plans for economic exploitation, transforming the everyday reality of many prisons and penal colonies into "a simple struggle for financial self-sufficiency".[15] Nor should governmentality be regarded as an ahistorical and impersonal force; in this respect, investigations of the agency of the historical actors need to be systematically extended.

Drawing on the classificatory model we sketch above, the following two sections address the available literature on convict labour. In the next section of this article we attempt to survey this literature. In doing so, we make no claim for completeness, not least because of limited space, the need for selection, and the disproportionate reference to scholarship in English. We aim rather to show the potentiality of the concept of convict labour for bringing together different strands of literature that have so far largely remained separated.[16] We therefore bind together knowledge and issues stemming from, among other areas of scholarship, the history of the penitentiary, the history of transportation, the history of the Nazi camps, Gulag studies, and the sociology and criminology of contemporary punishment. In the third and final section we attempt a synthesis of this literature as a model of global convict labour history, rather than from the perspective of each fragmented sub-discipline. We point to its main limitations and gaps and, in so doing, we seek to provide an agenda for future research in this field.

---

13 M. Foucault, "Governmentality", in G. Burchell, C. Gordon, and P. Miller (eds), *The Foucault Effect: Studies in Governmentality* (Chicago, IL, 1991), pp. 87–104. See especially Foucault's useful definition on p. 102.
14 Burchell, Gordon, and Miller, *The Foucault Effect*, p. 5.
15 Taylor C. Sherman, "Tensions of Colonial Punishment: Perspectives on Recent Developments in the Study of Coercive Networks in Asia, Africa and the Caribbean", *History Compass*, 7 (2009), pp. 659–677, 661.
16 For a similar approach, see P. Spierenburg, *The Prison Experience: Disciplinary Institutions and Their Inmates in Early Modern Europe* (New Brunswick, NJ [etc.], 1991), ch. 11, pp. 261–276.

A Global survey of convict labour

One of the earliest deployments of convict labour came in maritime transport and naval combat. Yet, contrary to a widespread popular image, no convict rowers were chained to the oars of the galleys during the Roman Empire – with the exception of Ptolemaic Egypt – and their use was also largely limited aboard early fourteenth-century Venetian and fifteenth-century Florentine galleys and in the navy of the Ottoman sultan Suleiman the Magnificent in the early sixteenth century.[17] While prisoners of war were sometimes used as galley slaves, the use of "free" (that is, conscripted or hired) rowers was largely preferred, not least because unlike prisoners they could be armed. It was the growing difficulty of sustaining galley costs that led private and state actors to turn to slaves and convicts during the sixteenth and seventeenth centuries. Only then did the *degredados,* together with slaves in Asia and Brazil, become essential on Portuguese galleys, and the *forzados,* consisting mainly of vagabonds, gypsies, and *moriscos,* come to make up the majority of workmen on Spanish galleys.

In the French case the use of convict labour on the galleys reached its climax in the second half of the seventeenth century.[18] Slaves – mainly North Africans (called *Turks),* but at times also schismatic Russians and Greeks, West Africans, and American Iroquois Indians – acted as the elite among the rowers. Lower in the rank stood the unskilled mass of the *forçats,* condemned to the galley *à perpetuité* or for a fixed period for crimes such as bigamy, theft, blasphemy, vagabond-

---

[17] On convict labour aboard galleys, see Paul Walden Bamford, "The Procurement of Oarsmen for French Galleys, 1660–1748", *American Historical Review,* 65 (1959), pp. 31–48; Lionel Casson, "Galley Slaves", *Transactions and Proceedings of the American Philological Association,* 97 (1966), pp. 35–44; M.E. Mallet, *The Florentine Galleys in the Fifteenth Century* (Oxford, 1967); I.A.A. Thompson, "A Map of Crime in Sixteenth-Century Spain", *Economic History Review,* 21 (1968), pp. 244–267; Henry Kamen, "Galley Service and Crime in Sixteenth- Century Spain", *Economic History Review,* 22 (1969), pp. 304–305; L. Casson, *Ships and Seamanship in the Ancient World* (Princeton, NJ, 1971); P.W. Bamford, *Fighting Ships and Prisons: The Mediterranean Galleys of France in the Age of Louis XIV* (London, 1974); L.T. Lehmann, *Galleys in the Netherlands* (Amsterdam, 1984); L. Casson, *The Ancient Mariners: Seafarers and Sea Fighters of the Mediterranean in Ancient Times* (Princeton, NJ, 1991); Colin Imber, "The Navy of Suleyman the Magnificent", *Archivum Ottomanicum,* 6 (1980), pp. 211–282; J.S. Morrison and R. Gardiner (eds), *The Age of the Galley: Mediterranean Oared Vessels Since Pre-Classical Times* (London, 1995); J.F. Guilmartin, *Galleons and Galleys* (London, 2002); L. Lo Basso, *Uomini da remo. Galee e galeotti del Mediterraneo in età moderna* (Milan, 2003); M. Capulli, *Le Navi della Serenissima – La 'Galea' di Lazise* (Venice, 2003); Anthony Gorman, "Regulation, Reform and Resistance in the Middle Eastern Prison", in F. Dikötter and I. Brown (eds), *Cultures of Confinement: A History of the Prison in Africa, Asia, and Latin America* (Ithaca, NY, 2007), pp. 95–146.
[18] See especially Bamford, "The Procurement".

age, and mendicancy, and for their belonging to the so-called *Religion pretendue reformée* after the revocation of the Edict of Nantes in 1685. In order to counter the shortage of manpower, in the mid-1680s the service was reorganized by the Secretary of State for the Navy, Jean-Baptiste Colbert, with 4,870 new *forçats* and 1,401 new slaves joining the forty galleys of the French fleet. By the early eighteenth century, however, galleys were phased out in favour of the technical superiority and the higher firepower of naval sailing ships. When the Corps des Galeres was officially abolished in 1748 "its few remaining vessels were essentially prison hulks for the accommodation of convicts who slept aboard, and usually worked ashore by day".[19] The hulks harboured in the London docks in the same period had the same function.

A similar trajectory of galley service can be observed in the Islamic empires. As Anthony Gorman has argued, in the sixteenth century penal or forced labour (*sukhri* or *tashkir*) was employed especially by the Ottomans "when the need for oarsmen saw service in the galleys *(kürek)* commonly prescribed as a punishment".[20] Three centuries later, however, sentence to the galleys had been transformed into work in agriculture and small-scale industry. Together with free labour, this "employment with chained feet" played a significant role in Muhammad Ali's programme of "modernization" in early nineteenth-century Egypt.

Thus, the sectoral deployment of penal labour often shifted according to shifts in political economy. Besides galley service and public works, penal servitude developed in the early modern period, especially in the form of transportation, to aid in populating and securing newly acquired imperial territory.[21] The rise

---

19 *Ibid.*, p. 47.
20 Gorman, "Regulation, Reform and Resistance in the Middle Eastern Prison", p. 118. Further information in the text is also taken from this essay.
21 On early modern transportation in the Portuguese and Spanish empires see Ruth Pike, "Penal Labor in Sixteenth-Century Spain: The Mines of Almadén", *Societas – A Review of Social History*, 3 (1973), pp. 193–206; idem, "Penal Servitude in the Spanish Empire: Presidio Labor in the Eighteenth Century", *Hispanic American Historical Review*, 58 (1978), pp. 21–40; idem, *Penal Servitude in Early Modern Spain* (Madison, WI, 1983); E. Troconis de Veracoechea, *Historia de las cárceles en Venezuela, 1600–1890* (Caracas, 1983); M.A. Lima Cruz, "Exiles and Renegades in Early Sixteenth Century Portuguese India", *Indian Economic and Social History Review*, 23 (1986), pp. 249–262; F. Pico, *El día menos pensado: historia de los presidiarios en Puerto Rico, 1793–1993* (Rió Piedras, 1994); Timothy Coates, "Crime and Punishment in the Fifteenth-Century Portuguese World: The Transition from Internal to Imperial Exile", in Donald Kagay and L.J. Andrew Villalon (eds), *The Final Argument: The Imprint of Violence on Society in Medieval and Early Modern Europe* (London, 1998), pp. 119–139; G. Haslip-Viera, *Crime and Punishment in Late Colonial Mexico City, 1692–1810* (Albuquerque, NM, 1999); M.L. Bush, *Servitude in Modern Times* (Cambridge, 2000); T. Coates, *Convicts and Orphans: Forced and State-Sponsored Colonizers in the Portuguese Empire, 1330–1733* (Stanford, CA, 2001); G. Pieroni and T. Coates, *De couto do pecado ecvila do*

of the Iberian empires typically involved a shift from *presidios* along the borders of Spain and Portugal to locations overseas. In the case of Portugal, havens and exile locales at home were phased out (with the exception of Castro Marim) and, according to Timothy Coates, at least 50,000 convicts and sinners were forced to relocate, largely overseas, in the early modern period.[22] Their destinations were mainly the new colonies in Goa, coastal West Africa (Azores, Madeira, Principe, São Tomé, and Cape Verde) and later, between 1740 and 1822, Pará, Maranhão, and Santa Catarina in Brazil. In the Spanish case, the mercury mines of Almadén and the maritime arsenal of Cartagena, La Carraca (Cadiz), and El Ferrol (Galicia) and the northern African *presidios* of Oran, Ceuta and Melilla, Peñón de Vélez, and Peñón de Alhucemas continued to host *presidiarios* involved in the heavy manual work of constructing, repairing, and maintaining roads, canals, fortifications, and other military facilities. To these, the Filipino *presidios* and then increasingly the Spanish American *presidios* were added.

Punishment, transportation, and penal labour all played instrumental roles in the capacity of the Iberian empires to expand their global frontiers, gain access to economic resources, and extend their political and military reach in this period.[23] Similarly, the Dutch convict transportation system played an integral role in linking distant imperial outposts. In this case, however, most traffic in forced labour was overseen by a private entity, the Dutch East India Company (VOC), which controlled the Indian Ocean flow of convicts between Batavia and the Cape of Good Hope in southern Africa. As Kerry Ward has shown, transported convict labour proved important to the "networks of empire" thrown across

---

sal: Castro Marim, 1330–1830 (Lisbon, 2002); Timothy Coates, "The Early Modern Portuguese Empire: A Commentary on Recent Studies", *Sixteenth Century Journal*, 37 (2006), pp. 83–90; idem, "European Forced Labor in the Early Modern Era", in David Eltis and Stanley L. Engerman (eds), *The Cambridge World History of Slavery* (Cambridge, 2011), III, pp. 631–649. On the penal servitude of Christians caught by North African pirates, see Ellen Friedman, "North African Piracy on the Coasts of Spain in the Seventeenth Century: A New Perspective on the Expulsion of the Moriscos", *International History Review*, 1 (1979), pp. 1–16. For a broader discussion of piracy and early modern empire, see Linda Colley, *Captives: Britain, Empire, and the World, 1600–1830* (London, 2002). The question of the way empires have been populated has been central in the "New Imperial Histories", although these studies have rarely addressed convict labour directly. For an introduction see F. Cooper and A.L. Stoler (eds), *Tensions of Empire: Colonial Cultures in a Bourgeois World* (Berkeley, CA [etc.], 1997); I. Gerasimov *et al.*, "In Search of a New Imperial History", *Ab Imperio*, 1 (2005), pp. 33–56; K. Wilson, "Old Imperialisms and New Imperial Histories: Rethinking the History of the Present", *Radical History Review*, 95 (2006), pp. 211–234; S. Howe (ed.), *The New Imperial Histories Reader* (London, 2008).
22 Coates, *Convicts and Orphans*; Pieroni and Coates, *Castro Marim*.
23 This argument complements that made by Robin Blackburn in *The Making of New World Slavery: From the Baroque to the Modern, 1492–1800* (London, 1998).

various territories by the VOC, which in doing so helped constitute "multiple and intersecting fields of partial sovereignty".[24]

Security and penal considerations played a significant role in the matching of prisoners and destinations. For instance, Ruth Pike has noted that in the Spanish Empire recidivist prisoners were less likely to be sent to north Africa, while deserters were shipped mainly to the New World.[25] However, the labour needs of the various *presidios* represented the general guiding principle for the choice of destination. Moreover, while penal servitude in metropolitan Spain was exclusively linked to the state's economic interests, in Spanish America, prisoners sentenced to hard labour by the colonial courts were also leased to private employers who used them in mines, manufactures, and mills, eventually to compensate for the severe shortage of labour due to the decline in the Indian population from the mid-sixteenth century. Particularly after Spain's losses to England during the Seven Years War (1756–1763), some hundreds of convicts – together with black slaves, their number progressively diminishing as that of convicts grew – were also involved in the fortification of Latin American ports such as Havana (Cuba) and San Juan (Puerto Rico). Havana served as the main hub for the New World *presidios*, and *presidiarios* came there from Mexico as well as from Spain. In Spain, following a system devised in the sixteenth century to supply convict rowers for the galleys, convicts awaited transportation to Spanish America in the central prisons of Toledo, Valladolid, and Seville and were shipped mainly through the port of Cadiz. Since they could be sent only on warships carrying troops, they often had to wait for years in the special *depósito* of La Carraca, subject to the informal practice, contrary to existing legislation, of exploiting the labour of convicts awaiting transportation.

In colonial settings, penal servitude was an integral part of a broader system of legal bondage that included slavery, serfdom, indentured service, and debt bondage, in which "unfree" labour played a fundamental role in the transition to "modernity".[26] Between 1607 and 1775, 54,500 convicts from England,

---

24 K. Ward, *Networks of Empire: Forced Migration in the Dutch East India Company* (Cambridge, 2008), p. 6.
25 See especially Pike, *Penal Servitude in Early Modern Spain*.
26 See Bush, *Servitude in Modern Times*; David Eltis (ed.), *Coerced and Free Migration: Global Perspectives* (Stanford, CA, 2002); E. Christopher, C. Pybus, and M. Rediker (eds), *Many Middle Passages: Forced Migration and the Making of the Modern World* (Berkeley, CA, 2007). The perspective of studying global migrations beyond the traditional focus on "free" migration is a central element of global migration history. See, for instance, D. Hoerder, *Cultures in Contact: World Migrations in the Second Millennium* (Durham, NC [etc.], 2002); J. Lucassen and L. Lucassen, "The Mobility Transition Revisited, 1500–1900: What the Case of Europe Can Offer to Global History", *Journal of Global Labour History*, 4 (2009), pp. 347–377; J. Lucassen, L. Lucassen, and P. Manning

Wales, Ireland, and Scotland crossed the Atlantic Ocean to reach the shores of the British colonies in North America.[27] Together with more than 310,000 African slaves, around 200,000 British, Dutch, German, and French indentured workers and around the same number of free European migrants they formed the "many-headed hydra" of a nascent Atlantic working class that Peter Linebaugh and Marcus Rediker have described in their volume of that title.[28] However, the independence of the American colonies deeply altered this trend. Already between 1776 and 1809, while 114,600 African slaves still reached North American shores, the number of free migrants along the same route rose to more than 250,000, while that of indentured servants and convicts dropped to 18,300 and 1,000 respectively. In the following decennium the transportation of convicts to North America virtually stopped, and the Australian continent became Britain's favoured penal destination.

In a new ideological climate that increasingly placed a premium on the ideal of "free labour", religious and scientific motivations and the economic interests of a part of the elite produced the rise of the penitentiary in the north-eastern American states during the nineteenth century.[29] In the debate between the sup-

---

(eds), *Migration History in World History: Multidisciplinary Approaches* (Leiden [etc.], 2010); J. Lucassen, "From Mobility Transition to Comparative Global Migration History", *Journal of Global History*, 6 (2011), pp. 299–307; U. Bosma, G. Kessler, and L. Lucassen (eds), *Migration and Membership Regimes in Global and Historical Perspective* (Leiden [etc.], forthcoming); D. Gabaccia and D. Hoerder (eds), *Connecting Seas and Connected Ocean Rims: Indian, Atlantic, and Pacific Oceans and China Seas Migrations from the 1830s to the 1930s* (Leiden [etc.], 2011). It should be noted, however, that up to this point these studies have paid only marginal attention to convict migration.

27 Aaron S. Fogleman, "From Slaves, Convicts, and Servants to Free Passengers: The Transformation of Immigration in the Era of the American Revolution", *Journal of American History*, 85 (1998), pp. 43–76. See also R.A. Ekirch, *Bound for America: The Transportation of British Convicts to the Colonies, 1718–1775* (Oxford, 1987); D. Jordan and M. Walsh, *White Cargo: The Forgotten History of Britain's White Slaves in America* (London, 2008).

28 P. Linebaugh and M. Rediker, *The Many-Headed Hydra: Sailors, Slaves, Commoners, and the Hidden History of the Revolutionary Atlantic* (Boston, MA, 2000).

29 G.A. Gildemeister, *Prison Labor and Convict Competition with Free Workers in Industrializing America, 1840–1890* (New York [etc.], 1987); A.J. Hirsch, *The Rise of the Penitentiary: Prisons and Punishment in Early America* (New Haven, CT, 1992); E.M. McGinn, *At Hard Labor: Inmate Labor at the Colorado State Penitentiary, 1871–1940* (New York, 1993); L. Goldsmith, *Penal Reform, Convict Labor, and Prison Culture in Massachusetts, 1800–1880* (Philadelphia, PA, 1994); M. Meranze, *Laboratories of Virtue: Punishment, Revolution, and Authority in Philadelphia, 1760–1835* (Chapel Hill, NC, 1996); M. Colvin, *Penitentiaries, Reformatories, and Chain Gangs: Social Theory and the History of Punishment in Nineteenth-Century America* (New York, 1997); R. McLennan, *The Crisis of Imprisonment: Protest, Politics, and the Making of the American Penal State, 1776–1941* (New York, 2008).

porters of the Pennsylvania model (continuous isolation and work confined to single-prisoner cells) and those of the Auburn and Sing Sing models (night-time isolation and congregate silent labour in a factory-like setting), the arrangement and exploitation of prisoners' work became absolutely central. By the 1850s all northern US state prisons had committed to the congregate system, which brought together the ideal of making the prisoner a "silent and insulated working machine"[30] and private capital's interests in the contract system, as opposed to the public account system dominating the Pennsylvania model. Moreover, workshop-based congregate labour proved a far more efficient deployment of penal labour, at least from capital's point of view, than the artisanal production required by the outmoded Pennsylvania system, which forced prisoners to work at handicrafts in isolation in their cells. In this emergent penal regime, the imperative of productive labour superseded the revolutionary era's ideals of punishment and penitence.

In various parts of the world, local elites eagerly demonstrated their commitment to "modernity" by replicating the debate on the Auburn and Philadelphia systems. Yet, the relationship between the American "model" and the new prisons created in subsequent decades cannot be conceived as one of mere transmission and reception.[31] In Europe, penal uses of convict labour continued to

---

[30] The sentence was used by Elam Lynds, first warden of Auburn; quoted in W.D. Lewis, *From Newgate to Dannemora: The Rise of the Penitentiary in New York, 1796–1848* (Ithaca, NY, 1965), p. 88.

[31] For a useful survey of the historiography on prisons that makes a similar argument, see Mary Gibson, "Global Perspectives on the Birth of the Prison", *American Historical Review,* 116 (2011), pp. 1040–1063. For a survey of the literature on colonial punishment, see Sherman, "Tensions of Colonial Punishment". The most important recent studies on the history of the prison are: D.D. Arnold, "The Colonial Prison: Power, Knowledge and Penology in Nineteenth-Century India", in *idem* and David Hardiman (eds), *Subaltern Studies VIII* (Delhi, 1994), pp. 148–187; N. Finzsch and R. Jütte (eds), *Institutions of Confinement: Hospitals, Asylums, and Prisons in Western Europe and North America, 1500–1950* (Cambridge, 1996); R.D. Salvatore and C. Aguirre (eds), *The Birth of the Penitentiary in Latin America: Essays on Criminology, Prison Reform, and Social Control, 1830–1940* (Austin, TX, 1996); N. Morris and D.J. Rothman (eds), *The Oxford History of the Prison: The Practice of Punishment in Western Society* (New York, 1998); F. Bernault (ed.), *Enfermement, prison et châtiments en Afrique du 19e siècle à nos jours* (Paris, 1999), revised English version: *A History of Prison and Confinement in Africa* (Portsmouth, NH, 2003); R.D. Salvatore, C. Aguirre, and G.M. Joseph (eds), *Crime and Punishment in Latin America: Law and Society since Late Colonial Times* (Durham, NC, 2001); P. Zinoman, *The Colonial Bastille: A History of Imprisonment in Vietnam, 1862–1940* (Berkeley, CA, 2001); Dikötter and Brown, *Cultures of Confinement*; M. Sen, *Prisons in Colonial Bengal, 1838–1919* (Calcutta, 2007); H. Johnston (ed.), *Punishment and Control in Historical Perspective* (Houndmills, 2008). Also relevant for this discussion: F. Snyder and D. Hay (eds), Labour, *Law and Crime: An Historical Perspective* (London [etc.], 1987); C. Anderson, *Legible Bodies: Race, Criminality and Colonialism in South Asia* (Oxford [etc.], 2004).

prevail over economic considerations.³² Meanwhile, in the economic periphery and plantation societies, the abolition of slavery in the first half of the nineteenth century, colonial forms of government, and local dynamics strongly contributed to make race a fundamental factor in shaping peculiar and articulated regimes of punishment. These responded to the need to fix ethnically defined populations to specific territories and labour markets, including in the southern states of the US. In this context, convict labour, together with corporal punishment and the criminalization of entire populations, played a central role, since it translated both the racist assumption that the black/indigenous population would not work except under some form of compulsion and the idea of the insufficiency of imprisonment alone as a means to discipline subalterns, now often defined as inherently criminal.³³

The most recent literature has given plenty of evidence of this process.³⁴ For instance, scholars have described the nineteenth-century road-gangs in India, the industrial workshops in the Cairo Prison, and the "agricultural penitentiaries" in

---

32 See especially John Conley, "Revising Conceptions about the Origin of Prisons: The Importance of Economic Considerations", *Social Science Quarterly*, 62 (1981), pp. 247-258; Spierenburg, *The Prison Experience*, pp. 122-125.

33 On the intertwining of corporal and carceral punishment, see, for instance, D. Paton, *No Bond but the Law: Punishment, Race, and Gender in Jamaican State Formation, 1780-1870* (Durham, NC, 2004). On the later impact of criminal anthropology on the redefinition of individuals and groups as inherently criminal, see M. Gibson, *Born to Crime: Cesare Lombroso and the Origins of Biological Criminology* (Westport, CT, 2002); P. Becker and R.F. Wetzell (eds), *Criminals and Their Scientists: The History of Criminology in International Perspective* (New York, 2006).

34 M.S. Hindus, *Prison and Plantation: Crime, Justice, and Authority in Massachusetts and South Carolina, 1767-1878* (Chapel Hill, NC, 1980); W. Worger, *South Africa's City of Diamonds: Mine Workers and Monopoly Capitalism in Kimberley, 1867-1895* (New Haven, CT, 1987); A. Lichtenstein, *Twice the Work of Free Labor: The Political Economy of Convict Labor in the New South* (New York, 1996); D.M. Oshinsky, *Worse Than Slavery: Parchman Farm and the Ordeal of Jim Crow Justice* (New York, 1996); M.J. Mancini, *One Dies, Get Another: Convict Leasing in the American South, 1866-1928* (Columbia, SC, 1996); Mary Ellen Curtin, *Black Prisoners and Their World: Alabama, 1865-1900* (Charlottesville, VA [etc.], 2000); Ricardo D. Salvatore, "Penitentiaries, Visions of Class, and Export Economies: Brazil and Argentina Compared", in idem and Aguirre, *Birth of the Penitentiary*, pp. 194-223; M.A. Myers, *Race, Labor, and Punishment in the New South* (Columbus, OH, 1998); Rudolph Peters, "Egypt and the Age of the Triumphant Prison: Legal Punishment in Nineteenth Century Egypt", *Annales Islamologiques*, 36 (2002), pp. 253-285; B. O'Laughlin, "Proletarianization, Agency and Changing Rural Livelihoods: Forced Labour and Resistance in Colonial Mozambique", *Journal of Southern African Studies*, 28 (2002), pp. 511-530; William H. Worger, "Convict Labour, Industrialists and the State in the US South and South Africa, 1870-1930", *Journal of Southern African Studies*, 30 (2004), pp. 63-86; M. Da Passano (ed.), *Le colonie penali nell'Europa dell'Ottocento* (Rome, 2004), pp. 89-128; S. Hynd, "Imperial Gallows: Capital Punishment, Violence and Colonial Rule in Britain's African Territories, c.1903-1968", D.Phil., University of Oxford, 2007; R. Perkinson, *Texas Tough: The Rise of America's Prison Empire* (New

French north Africa and Italian Tripolitania; and they have narrated the exploitation of convict labour in Cecil Rhodes's De Beers Mining Company in Kimberley, South Africa's first industrial city, and the *shibalo* system through which Mozambican men and women escaping contract labour were forced to work for local public works and private enterprises and in the mines in South Africa, Rhodesia, and the Congo up to the 1940s. But researchers have observed similar patterns for highly racially segregated non-colonial contexts, such as post-independence Brazil and the American South after the Civil War and the abolition of slavery.

In all these cases, convict labour proved instrumental in matching the economic interests of local and colonial entrepreneurs and authorities with a persistent racial hierarchy and mentality. This process cut across both the private and public use of prison labour, and could involve both "excarceration" beyond penitentiary walls and incarceration. Not surprisingly, then, in the American South the phasing out of the excarcerative convict lease in the late nineteenth century and the first decade of the twentieth century did not lead to a reformed system of "modern" incarceration, mimicking the northern states, but rather to the states' chain gangs. Convict labour was used then to build roads and other infrastructure or for state-controlled agricultural work, as in the infamous example of Parchman Farm in Mississippi, opened in 1904 and still notorious in the 1960s, when state authorities relied on the prison farm to break the will of the civil rights movement.

In the nineteenth century – allegedly "the age of the triumphant prison"[35] – and beyond, prison practice in most of the world therefore largely contradicted Michel Foucault's assumption of a sudden and definitive shift from corporal to disciplinary punishment, which in fact appears to be an artefact of a small corner of the emergent, modern, capitalist economies.[36] Moreover, even in these regions and states, the modern prison penitentiary coexisted with other forms of punishment. Convict labour, in the guise of both rehabilitation and punishment,

---

York, 2008); J. Seibert, *More Continuity Than Change? New Forms of Unfree Labor in the Belgian Congo, 1908–1930* (Leiden, 2011).

35 M. Perrot, "Délinquance et système pénitentiaire en France au XIXème siècle", *Annales ESC*, 30 (1975), p. 81. See also Peters, "Egypt and the Age of the Triumphant Prison".

36 M. Foucault, *Surveiller et punir. Naissance de la prison* (Paris, 1975), English translation: *Discipline and Punish: The Birth of the Prison* (New York, 1977). A similar thesis is put forward in D. Rothman, *The Discovery of the Asylum: Social Order and Disorder in the New Republic* (Boston, MA, 1973); M. Ignatieff, *A Just Measure of Pain: The Penitentiary in the Industrial Revolution, 1750–1850* (New York, 1978). The majority of the recent literature on the history of prisons (see previous note) is overtly critical of Foucault's thesis on this point. Earlier critiques can be found for instance in M. Perrot (ed.), *L'impossible prison. Recherches sur le système pénitentiaire aux XIXe siècle* (Paris, 1980).

remained a central feature of this more complex "coercive network".³⁷ Indeed, within colonial empires, the rise of the prison did not negate the continuation and expansion of transportation, and often flourished alongside it.³⁸ Both in Britain and in France, attempts to replace transportation to far-flung corners of the empire with metropolitan imprisonment and hard labour were repeatedly made, but failed because of the systematic opposition of political and economic lobbies.³⁹ In the nineteenth Century and part of the twentieth Century, therefore, an "extensive pan-imperial trade" in penal labour developed.⁴⁰

In the case of Britain, this traffic responded to the new Situation created by the independence of the American colonies, the abolition of slavery in the 1830s,

---

37 Sherman, "Tensions of Colonial Punishment", p. 669. For a broader discussion of the potentiality of this concept, see section two of the present article.
38 The most important studies on modern transportation in the British Empire include: R.I.M. Burnett, *Hard Labour, Hard Fare and a Hard Bed: New Zealand's Search for Its Own Penal Philosophy* (Wellington, 1995); C. Anderson, "Unfree Labour and its Discontents: Transportation from Mauritius to Australia, 1825–1845", *Australian Studies*, 13 (1998), pp. 116–133; C.F.E. Hollis Hallett, *Forty Years of Convict Labour: Bermuda, 1823–1863* (Bermuda, 1999); C. Anderson, *Convicts in the Indian Ocean: Transportation from South Asia to Mauritius, 1815–1853* (Basingstoke, 2000); C. Pybus and H. Maxwell-Stewart, *American Citizens, British Slaves: Yankee Political Prisoners in an Australian Penal Colony, 1839–1850* (Melbourne, 2000); S. Sen, *Disciplining Punishment: Colonialism and Convict Society in the Andaman Islands* (New Delhi, 2000); A. Brooke and D. Brandon, *Bound for Botany Bay: British Convict Voyages to Australia* (Kew, 2005); S. Nicholas (ed.), *Convict Workers: Reinterpreting Australia's Past* (Cambridge, 1989). For the French Empire see A. Zysberg, *Les galériens. Vies et destins de 60000 forçats sur les galères de France, 1680–1748* (Paris, 1987); A. Bullard, *Exile to Paradise: Savagery and Civilization in Paris and the South Pacific* (Stanford, CA, 2000); P. Redfield, *Space in the Tropics: From Convicts to Rockets in French Guiana* (Berkeley, CA, 2000); J. Vanmai, *Pilou Pilou* (Paris, 1998–2002), 3 vols; N. Castan and A. Zysberg, *Histoire des galères, bagnes et prisons en France de l'Ancien Régime* (Paris, 2002); J. Kergrist, *Les bagnards du canal de Nantes à Brest. La vie au camp de Glomel (1823–1832)* (Spézet, 2003); Jean-Lucien Sanchez, "Identifier, exclure, régénérer. La relégation des récidivistes en Guyane (1885–1938)", in Marco Cicchini and Michel Porret (eds), *Les sphères du pénal avec Michel Foucault* (Lausanne, 2007), pp. 139–153. For the Portuguese Empire see Coates, *Convicts and Orphans;* Timothy Coates, "The Imperial Prison of Luanda and 'Effective Occupation' of Angola", *Portuguese Literary and Cultural Studies*, 15/16 (2010), pp. 79–114.
39 S. Devereux, "The Making of the Penitentiary Act, 1775–1779", *Historical Journal*, 42 (1999), pp. 405–433. On the history of British prisons, see S. McConville, *A History of the English Prison Administration, 1750–1877* (London [etc.], 1981); M. DeLacy, *Prison Reform in Lancashire, 1700–1850* (Stanford, CA, 1986); C. Emsley, "The History of Crime and Crime Control Institutions, c.1770–c.1945", in M. Maguire, R. Morgan, and R. Reiner (eds), *The Oxford Handbook of Criminology* (Oxford, 1994), ch. 4. On the history of French prisons, see J.-G. Petit, *Ces peines obscures. La prison pénale en France, 1780–1875* (Paris, 1990); H. Gaillac, *Les maisons de correction 1830–1945* (Paris, 1991); M. Perrot, *Les ombres de l'histoire. Crime et châtiment au XIXe siècle* (Paris, 2001).
40 Anderson, Convicts in the Indian Ocean.

and later by the rise of nationalist movements in the Indian subcontinent, all of which shifted imperial flows of coerced labour and settlement. Between 1787 and 1868, with the North American colonies now closed off, British authorities shipped some 160,000 prisoners from Britain to New South Wales, Van Diemen's Land, and Western Australia. From the late eighteenth century to the mid-twentieth century, many thousands more convicts were sentenced to transportation from British India to penal settlements in the Malay Peninsula, Burma, Mauritius, and the Andaman Islands. Minor convict migrant streams also appear significant in some specific periods and in relation to particular events: for instance, a few thousand were transported from Ceylon to Mauritius and south-east Asia (1815–1868); 300 or 400 non-Anglo-Celtic convicts were transported from Canada, the Cape, and the West Indies to New South Wales and Van Diemen's Land; 100 convicts were sentenced to transportation in Mauritius and sent to the Australian settlements (1825–1845); from the 1830s to the 1860s several thousand Chinese and Malay convicts from Burma were transported to the Bengal and Madras presidencies and to Bombay. For all the differences in these experiences, the operation of the penal settlements depended heavily on convicts' productive capacities, and the governance of these settlements was organized around the transportation and labour that brought them into existence in the first place. To put it another way, an account of the imperial expansions of the nineteenth-century world remains incomplete without acknowledging the centrality of penal labour to this process, and penal transportation as a key aspect of imperial sovereignty.

In the case of the French Empire, the building of prison-manufactories – the *maisons centrales*, akin to the American penitentiaries observed by de Tocqueville and Beaumont in their 1831 visit to the US – in the period 1830–1835, where around 300,000 prisoners were held every year under terrible conditions, did not exclude the extensive use of alternative, excarcerative punitive practices. Following the abolition of slavery in the colonies (1848), the insurrections of 1848, and the expansion of its colonial empire, the French state (under imperial or republican governance in the metropole) resorted to transportation on a massive scale. A law passed on 30 May 1854 made Guyana the destination of both political and common-law *bagnards*; from 1861 New Caledonia was added as a place of transportation, for instance for those involved in the Commune, but in 1897 all deportees and *reléguées* – petty criminals who could be transported under a law of 1885 – were transported again to Guyana. Transportation within the French Empire therefore began later than in the British case, but continued well into the twentieth century, longer than its counterpart. With deportation eventually abolished by the Front Populaire in 1938 and the last *reléguées* returning to France in 1953, a total of nearly 100,000 men and women are believed to have been transported under French penal jurisdiction, 67,000 of them to Guyana (52,000 deportees and 15,000 *reléguées)* and the rest to New Caledonia (20,000 and 10,000 respectively).

Similar patterns can be observed for the Portuguese Empire. After the independence of Brazil in 1822 a fundamental reorganization took place within its system of transportation. Convicts from Portugal, Cape Verde, Portuguese Guinea, São Tomé, and Mozambique were sent instead to the *depósito* in Luanda, Angola, and convicts from Angola, Portuguese India, Macau, and Timor to an analogous institution on Mozambique Island off the south-east coast of Africa. Around 20,000 convicts were exiled there from 1880 to 1932, when the system ended in Portuguese colonial Africa.

Because of their close association with deportations and the massive transfer of populations, it is tempting to interpret twentieth-century labour camps as the modern incarnation of these imperial systems of colonial transportation and punishment. We will discuss this point further in the following section. More commonly, however, research on labour camps has focused on their links with the shift to total war and with totalitarian regimes.[41] Naturally, World War II has been the single largest focus of research in this area, and wartime Japanese, German, and Soviet camps have attracted most scholarly attention. Japa-

---

41 See the following notes for references in the text. Significant strands of the literature have dealt with the following other topics related to convict labour. (1) World War I, but mainly on POWs, such as in M. Spoerer, "The Mortality of Allied Prisoners of War and Belgian Civilian Deportees in German Custody during the First World War: A Reappraisal of the Effects of Forced Labour", *Population Studies*, 60 (2006), pp. 121–136; K. Tenfelde and H.-C. Seidel (eds), *Zwangsarbeit im Bergwerk* (Essen, 2005). (2) Other fascist regimes (especially Franco's Spain): R. Torres, *Los esclavos de Franco* (Madrid, 2000); R. Serrano and D. Serrano, *Toda España era una cárcel. Memoria de los presos del franquismo* (Madrid, 2001); I. Lafuente, *Esclavos por la patria* (Madrid, 2002); Julio Prada Rodriguez and Domingo Rodriguez Teijeiro, "El Trabajo os hará Libres: una Aproximación a la Explotación de la Mano de Obra Penal en el Ourense de Guerra y Posguerra", *Minius: Revista do Departamento de Historia, Arte e Xeografía*, 10 (2002), pp. 209–236; C. Molinero, M. Sala, and J. Sobreques (eds), *Una inmensa prisión. Los campos de concentración y las prisiones durante la guerra civil y el franquismo* (Barcelona, 2003); J.M. Gutiérrez Casalá, *Colonias penitenciarias militarizadas de Montijo. Represión franquista en la Comarca de Mérida* (Mérida, 2003); G. Acosta et al., *El canal de los presos (1940–1962). Trabajos forzados: de la represión política a la explotación económica* (Barcelona, 2004); S. Corvisieri, *La villeggiatura di Mussolini. Il confino da Bocchini a Berlusconi* (Milan, 2005); J. Rodrigo, *Cautivos. Campos de Concentración en la España franquista, 1936–1947* (Barcelona, 2005); C.S. Capogreco, *I campi del Duce. L'internamento civile nell'Italia fascista (1940–1943)* (Turin, 2006); J.M. Soarez Tavarez, *O campo de concentraçao do Taraffal (1936–1954). A origem e o quotidiano* (Lisbon, 2007); J. Ruiz, "'Work and Don't Lose Hope': Republican Forced Labour Camps during the Spanish Civil War", *Contemporary European History*, 18 (2009), pp. 419–441; Álvaro Falquina et al., "Arqueología de los destacamentos penales franquistas en el ferrocarril Madrid-Burgos: El caso de Bustarviejo", *Complutum*, 19 (2008), pp. 175–195.

nese occupants deported 1 million Korean men and women and at least 40,000 Chinese to Japan, while forcing millions more civilians to work in Korea, China, and other parts of south-east Asia.[42] A relatively well-studied case is that of nearly 60,000 Allied POWs who were employed in the construction of the Siam-Burma Railway, interned together with 240,000 other POWs in more than 200 camps in different parts of occupied south-east Asia.

The literature on the Nazi system of camps is virtually unlimited. For the purpose of this article it will suffice to stress that, especially from the 1990s, scholars have pointed to some issues important for the understanding of convict labour as a key aspect of the Nazi regime, beyond the usual focus on war and genocide. Among these are the following. First, while also expanding our knowledge on Jewish and political internees and prisoners, scholars have devoted more attention to other groups, such as POWs, Roma, gays, and common-law prisoners.[43] Secondly, historians of Nazism have addressed the complexity of the network of camps for POWs, civilian internees, and prisoners, together with its transformation as dictated by military, political, and economic strategies during the brief life of the Nazi regime. Thirdly, we have seen a renewed focus on the question of the alleged contradiction between ideological and economic motivations in the creation of camps, pointing to the defining role of the process of "continuous selection and replacement", based on the prisoner's ability to work, offset by both the nature of their work and by racial criteria.[44] Fourthly, there was the fate of the common-law

---

42 See, for instance, R. Roychowdhury, *Black Days in Andaman and Nicobar Islands* (New Delhi, 2004); T.R. Sareen, *Building the Siam-Burma Railway during World War II: A Documentary Study* (Delhi, 2005); M. Spoerer, "Zwangsarbeitsregimes im Vergleich. Deutschland und Japan im Ersten und Zweiten Weltkrieg", in Tenfelde and Seidel, *Zwangsarbeit*.

43 See especially K. Orth, *Das System der nationalsozialistischen Konzentrationslager. Eine politische Organisationsgeschichte* (Hamburg, 1999); idem, *Die Konzentrationslager-SS. Sozialstrukturelle Analysen und biographische Studien* (Göttingen, 2000); M. Spoerer, *Zwangsarbeit unter dem Hakenkreuz* (Stuttgart [etc.], 2001); idem and J. Fleischhacker, "Forced Laborers in Nazi Germany: Categories, Numbers, and Survivors", *Journal of Interdisciplinary History*, 33 (2002), pp. 169–204; M. Buggeln, "KZ-Häftlinge als letzte Arbeitskraftreserve der Bremer Rüstungswirtschaft", *Arbeiterbewegung und Sozialgeschichte*, 12 (2003), pp. 19–36; W. Benz and B. Distel (eds), *Geschichte der Konzentrationslager 1933–1945* (Berlin, 2004), 5 vols; M. Buggeln, *Arbeit und Gewalt. Das Außenlagersystem des KZ Neuengamme* (Göttingen, 2009); idem, "Building to Death: Prisoner Forced Labour in the German War Economy – The Neuengamme Subcamps, 1942–1945", *European History Quarterly*, 39 (2009), pp. 606–632; J. Caplan and N. Wachsmann (eds), *Concentration Camps in Nazi Germany: The New Histories* (London, 2010) – in this volume see especially J.C. Wagner, "Work and Extermination in the Concentration Camps", pp. 127–148.

44 A. Tooze, *Wages of Destruction: The Making and Breaking of the Nazi Economy* (London, 2006). For the previous debate, see U. Herbert, *Hitler's Foreign Workers: Enforced Foreign Labor in Germany under the Third Reich* (Cambridge, 1997); idem (ed.), *National Socialist Extermination*

prisoners forcibly put to work and the "annihilation through labour" programme.⁴⁵ Fifthly, mention should be made of the camps in the German African colonies as precedents and the fate of the colonial POWs.⁴⁶ Scholars have also turned their attention to the internment of ex-collaborationists after the end of the war.⁴⁷

Persistent interest in the history of totalitarianism, genocide, and the "Bloodlands" of east-central Europe has led as well to the significant expansion of research topics relating to the Soviet Gulags, especially as a system of labour "recruitment", mobilization, circulation, and exploitation (though many of these studies extend both prior to and after the war).⁴⁸ Here, too, scholars have

---

Policies: Contemporary German Perspectives and Controversies (New York, 2000); G. Aly and S. Heim, *Architects of Annihilation: Auschwitz and the Logic of Destruction* (Princeton, NJ, 2002).

45 See especially N. Wachsmann, "'Annihilation through Labor': The Killing of State Prisoners in the Third Reich", *Journal of Modern History*, 71 (1999), pp. 624–659; idem, *Hitler's Prisons: Legal Terror in Nazi Germany* (New Haven, CT [etc.], 2004). See also P. Pédron, *La prison sous Vichy* (Paris, 1993); G. von Frijtag, *Het recht van de sterkste. Duitse strafrechtspleging in bezet Nederland* (Amsterdam, 1999); A. Bancaud, *Une exception ordinaire. La magistrature en France, 1930–1950* (Paris, 2002); Tamara Altman, *"Les criminels de droit commun jugés par les conseils de guerre allemands durant la seconde guerre mondiale en Belgique: étude qualitative et quantitative sur base des Personalakten de la prison de Saint-Gilles"*, Ph.D., Université Libre de Bruxelles, 2004; C.G. De Vito, *Camosci e girachiavi. Storia del carcere in Italia, 1943–2007* (Rome, 2009); Dimitri Roden, "Van aanhouding tot strafuitvoering. De werking van het Duitse gerechtelijke apparaat in bezet België en Noord-Frankrijk, 1940–1944 ", *Cahiers d'histoire du temps présent – Bijdragen tot de eigentijdse geschiedenis*, 22 (2010), pp. 113-160. See also the ongoing project by Anna Tijsseling on "Gevangen onder Duitse besetting" (NIOD Institute for War, Holocaust and Genocide Studies, Amsterdam).

46 For instance, Helmut Bley, *South-West Africa under German Rule 1894–1914* (London, 1971); Jürgen Zimmerer, "Die Geburt des 'Ostlandes' aus dem Geiste des Kolonialismus. Die nationalsozialistische Eroberungs- und Beherrschungspolitik in (post-)kolonialer Perspektive", *Sozialgeschichte*, 19 (2004), pp. 10–43; idem, "Annihilation in Africa: The 'Race War' in German Southwest Africa (1904–1908) and its Significance for a Global History of Genocide", *Bulletin of the German Historical Institute (Washington)*, 37 (2005), pp. 51–58; Birthe Kundrus, "Kontinuitäten, Parallelen, Rezeptionen. Überlegungen zur 'Kolonialisierung' des Nationalsozialismus", *WerkstattGeschichte*, 15 (2006), pp. 45–62; S. Conrad, *German Colonialism: A Short History* (Cambridge, 2011). See also the papers presented at the workshop "Internment, Incarceration and Detention: Captivation Histories in Europe around the First and Second World War", Wassenaar, 3–4 November 2011, especially in the session on "Colonial Perspectives. An important workshop on this topic had previously been organized by Stacey Hynd and Taylor Sherman in 2008 at the History Faculty in Cambridge, entitled "Coercive Networks: Violence, Punishment and the Colonial Condition. The proceedings of the two workshops have not yet been published.

47 For example Helen Grevers, "Het leven in de interneringskampen en gevangenissen voor collaborateurs na de Tweede Wereldoorlog in België en Nederland" , *BVNG/ABHC*, 31 (2009), pp. 30–33.

48 Among the most recent studies are: G. Armanski, *Maschinen des Terrors: Das Lager (KZ und GULAG) in der Moderne* (Münster, 1993); E. Bacon, *The Gulag at War: Stalin's Forced Labour Sys-*

addressed the complexity of the Gulag system – 53 camps and 524 colonies in March 1941, on the eve of Soviet entry into the war – with some studies devoted to specific aspects, camps, and areas. The questions of the inmates' productivity and of the contribution of the camp system to the economy of the USSR have also been investigated, showing how some strategic sectors particularly benefited from convict labour, especially during the phase of industrialization in the 1930s and in the labour mobilization during World War II. An emphasis on the "rehabilitative" function of forced labour was also characteristic of the Stalinist camps, as part of the broader ideological aim of "building the socialist man". This holds true for other socialist countries as well.[49] For instance, administrative internment in Romania was mainly enforced for up to two years, but could be extended for five more years, according to the outcomes of the process of "re-education", where work played a central role. In this context, convict labour was used mainly for public works, as in the case of the Donau–Black Sea canal, started in 1949 and finally inaugurated by Nicolae Ceaușescu in 1984.

An important case of the exploitation of convicts in labour camps constructed by a self-proclaimed "socialist" regime in the name of "re-education" can be found in post-1949 China.[50] As the studies of Frank Dikötter and Klaus Mühlhahn

---

tem in the Light of the Archives (New York, 1994); P.H. Solomon, Jnr, *Soviet Criminal Justice under Stalin* (Cambridge, 1996); S. Wheatcroft, "The Scale and Nature of German and Soviet Repression and Mass Killings, 1930–1945", *Europe-Asia Studies*, 48 (1996), pp. 1319–1353; N. Bougai, *The Deportation of Peoples in the Soviet Union* (New York, 1996); J.R. Harris, "The Growth of the Gulag: Forced Labor in the Urals Region, 1929–31", *Russian Review*, 56 (1997), pp. 265–280; D.J. Nordlander, "Origins of a Gulag Capital: Magadan and Stalinist Control in the Early 1930s", *Slavic Review*, 57 (1998), pp. 791–812; Lynne Viola, "The Other Archipelago: Kulak Deportations to the North in 1930", *Slavic Review*, 60 (2001), pp. 730–755; Judith Pallot, "Forced Labour for Forestry: The Twentieth Century History of Colonization and Settlement in the North of Perm' Oblast", *Europe-Asia Studies*, 54 (2002), pp. 1055–1083; N. Adler, *The Gulag Survivor: Beyond the Soviet System* (New Brunswick, NJ, 2002); A. Applebaum, *Gulag: A History* (New York, 2003); P.R. Gregory and V. Lazarev (eds), *The Economics of Forced Labor: The Soviet Gulag* (Stanford, CA, 2003); L. Viola, *The Unknown Gulag: The Lost World of Stalin's Special Settlements* (Oxford, 2007); A. Barenberg, "Prisoners Without Borders: Zazonniki and the Transformation of Vorkuta after Stalin", *Jahrbücher für Geschichte Osteuropas*, 57 (2007), pp. 513–534; S.A. Barnes, *Death and Redemption: The Gulag and the Shaping of Soviet Society* (Princeton, NJ, 2011).
49 On the Soviet Gulag, see Barnes, *Death and Redemption*. On Romania, see I. Bălan, *Regimul concentrationar din Romania 1945–1964* (Bucharest, 2000). On North Korean labour camps: K. Chol-hwan, *The Aquariums of Pyongyang: Ten Years in a North Korean Gulag* (Oxford, 2001); K. Yong, *Long Road Home: Testimony of a North Korean Camps Survivor* (New York, 2009).
50 On Chinese prisons and camps: P.E. Griffin, *The Chinese Communist Treatment of Counter-revolutionaries, 1924–1949* (Princeton, NJ, 1976); J.-L. Domenach, *Chine: L'archipel oublié* (Paris, 1992); H.H. Wu, *Laogai: The Chinese Gulag* (Oxford, 1992); J.D. Seymour and R. Anderson, *New Ghosts, Old Ghosts: Prisons and Labor Reform Camps in China* (Amonk, NY, 1997); Frank Diköt-

have shown, pre-communist China largely followed the path of other countries. Penal servitude, gaols, and traditional forms of punishment prevailed in the late imperial period and later overlapped with the emerging penitentiary model during the republican period. For instance, the Beijing No. 1 Prison, modelled after London's Pentonville (modelled, in turn, on the Pennsylvania system in the US), opened in 1912, with its workshops (carpentry, weaving, typesetting, printing and bookbinding, tailoring, stonemasonry, and work with metal, leather, and bamboo) indicating a strong emphasis on reformation. During the Republican era, support for labour camps remained limited to the pro-Soviet milieu. It gained ground only as a pragmatic response to the specific conditions of civil war, and subsequently spread both in communist- and in nationalist-controlled territory during the 1930s and early 1940s.

With the proclamation of the People's Republic in 1949, however, two distinct forms of punishment – and therefore two distinct institutional systems – developed, both emphasizing the role of labour in re-education: the *laogai* (an abbreviation for *laodong gaizao*, i.e. "reform through labour"), aiming at the birth of a "new man" through the remoulding of every aspect of a prisoner's morals, ideas, and habits, but under a determinate sentence; and the *laojiao* (an abbreviation for *laodong jiaoyang suo,* i.e. "re-education through labour"), instituted in the mid-1950s, allowing the legal system to be bypassed and local governments to remove "undesirable elements" through indeterminate sentences.

Whether under militarized fascist regimes, socialist states at war or peace, or seemingly more benign forms of governance, labour camps thus mark the modern world and reprise persistent linkages of state efforts to restrict or define the limits of citizenship, mete out punishment, and enforce work that date back to earlier historical periods.[51] Indeed, far from being limited to authoritarian or totalitarian regimes, administrative detention – often coupled with forced labour – has also characterized the recent history of many Western democracies. This was especially the case in colonial contexts, and the experience in Kenya is par-

---

ter, "Crime and Punishment in Post-Liberation China: The Prisoners of a Beijing Gaol in the 1950s", *China Quarterly,* 149 (1997), pp. 147–159; idem, "Crime and Punishment in Early Republican China: Beijing's First Model Prison, 1912–1922", *Late Imperial China,* 21 (2000), pp. 140–162; idem, *Crime, Punishment, and the Prison in Modern China, 1895–1949* (New York, 2002); idem, "The Promise of Repentance: Prison Reform in Modern China", *British Journal of Criminology,* 42 (2002), pp. 240–249; F. Hualing, "Re-education Through Labour in Historical Perspective", *China Quarterly,* 184 (2005), pp. 811–830; K. Mühlhahn, *Criminal Justice in China: A History* (Cambridge, MA [etc.], 2009).

51 For an example from a democratic state, see Volker Janssen, "When the 'Jungle' Met the Forest: Public Work, Civil Defense, and Prison Camps in Postwar California", *Journal of American History,* 96 (2009), pp. 702–726.

ticularly telling, although not unique, in this respect.[52] As in other cases, conditions inside the detention camps created in Kenya in the 1910s and 1920s and in the prison camps opened in 1933 depended on the assumption that forced labour, together with corporal punishment, could actually serve as the only effective forms of penal discipline. However, the experience in Kenyan prisons and camps turned into an even more brutal experience by the end of 1954, at the zenith of the Mau Mau revolt, since police repression by far exceeded the capacity of the already overcrowded prisons, and the colonial government decided to establish a network of camps, collectively called the "Pipeline", characterized by violence, torture, and forced labour.

More recent experiences within Europe itself indicate the actuality of detention camps and point to the centrality of convict labour within them. Particularly significant are the networks of "re-education camps" for *asozialen* or *asocialen*, which functioned respectively in West Germany and the Netherlands from the late 1940s to the 1970s.[53] More linked to the penal system, networks of detention camps for (mainly) alcoholics existed in Scandinavian countries up until the 1970s, with forced labour viewed as a central feature in the process of their "treatment".[54] Moreover, it is tempting to see a historical continuity between these detention camps and some "therapeutic communities" created after the 1970s, for instance in Italy, conceived as an alternative to imprisonment for drug addicts convicted of minor crimes who are then forced to work without remuneration within factories inside the closed gates of the "community".[55] In a perverse inversion of colonial transportation, the present-day global landscape is also dominated by the exten-

---

[52] D. Branch, "Imprisonment and Colonialism in Kenya, c.1930–1952: Escaping the Carceral Archipelago", *International Journal of African Historical Studies*, 38 (2005), pp. 239–265; C. Elkins, *Imperial Reckoning: The Untold Story of Britain's Gulag in Kenya* (New York, 2005); D. Anderson, *Histories of the Hanged: The Dirty War in Kenya and the End of Empire* (New York [etc.], 2005).

[53] A. Dercksen and L. Verplanke, *Geschiedenis van de onmaatschappelijkheidsbestrijding in Nederland, 1914–1970* (Amsterdam, 1987); W. Ayass, *Das Arbeitshaus Breitenau. Bettler, Landstreicher, Prostituierte, Zuhälter und Fürsorgeempfänger in der Korrektions- und Landarmenanstalt Breitenau (1874–1949)* (Kassel, 1992); idem, "Die 'korrektionelle Nachhaft'. Zur Geschichte der strafrechtlichen Arbeitshausunterbringung in Deutschland", *Zeitschrift für Neuere Rechtsgeschichte*, 15 (1993), pp. 184–201; B. Maandag and T. van der Mee, *De 'asocialen'. Heropvoeding in Drentse kampen* (Rotterdam, 2005); Thomas Irmer, Barbara Reischl, and Kaspar Nürnberg, "Das Städtische Arbeits- und Bewahrungshaus Rummelsburg in Berlin-Lichtenberg", 2008, www.gedenkstaettenforum.de/nc/aktuelles/einzelansicht/news/das_staedtische_arbeits_und_bewahrungshaus_rummelsburg_in_berlin_lichtenberg/; last accessed on 6 May 2012.

[54] J. Edman and K. Stenius (eds), *On the Margins: Nordic Alcohol and Treatment 1885–2007* (Oslo, 2007).

[55] P. Giudicini and G. Pieretti, *San Patrignano tra Comunità e Società. Ricerca sui percorsi di vita di 711 ex-ospiti di San Patrignano* (Milan, 1994).

sive network of "detention centres" for undocumented immigrants created since the early 1990s.[56] Little research has been carried out on this topic, and what has is qualitatively insufficient. The apparent marginality of forced labour in those institutions, mainly used as temporary warehouses for people awaiting expulsion and deportation, therefore needs to be systematically examined, not least because the camps are rapidly differentiating and growing in number.

Expanding convict labour historiography

The survey in the previous section indicates the potentiality of a process-based approach to the history of convict labour and thus the need to overcome the present fragmentation of research into a number of sub-disciplines and geographic areas related to single regimes of punishment.[57] However, the survey also suggests the limitations of the available historiography on convict labour in at least two ways. On the one hand there exists a chronological limitation, especially as far as the pre-1500 period is concerned. On the other hand there is an undue focus in the historiography on a more or less explicit Eurocentric approach. Both of these limitations remain bound to the unwarranted teleology of penal reform and modernization that is assumed to move progressively towards stable forms of incarceration and rehabilitation, and away from brutality, unmitigated punishment, and naked coercion or enslavement. This view imagines the labour camps of totalitarian social orders as the negation of modernity. This section seeks to address these two issues, in order to put forward some suggestions for the development of a more global and long-term perspective on the history of convict labour, one less prone to reifying conceptions of punishment associated with "modernity".

---

56 See, for instance, P. Mares, *Borderline* (Sydney, 2001); Meaghan Amor and Janet Austin (eds), *From Nothing to Zero: Letters from Refugees in Australia's Detention Centres* (Melbourne, 2003); M. Dow, *American Gulag: Inside US Immigration Prisons* (Berkeley, CA, 2005); Jesuit Refugee Service Europe, *Detention in Europe: Administrative Detention of Asylum-Seekers and Irregular Migrants* (Brussels, 2005); M. Rovelli, *Lager italiani* (Rome, 2006); A. Kaur and I. Metcalfe (eds), *Mobility, Labour Migration and Border Controls in Asia* (London, 2006); Anton van Kalmthout, "Foreigners", in Miranda Boone and Martin Moerings (eds), *Dutch Prisons* (The Hague, 2007), pp. 101–126; C. Kobelinsky and C. Makaremi, *Enfermés dehors. Enquêtes sur le confinement des étrangers* (Paris, 2009); M. Ford, "Constructing Legality: The Management of Irregular Labour Migration in Thailand and Malaysia", in Van der Linden and Himmelstoss, *Labour History Beyond Borders*, pp. 177–200; A. Sciurba, *Campi di forza. Percorsi confinati di migranti in Europa* (Verona, 2009). For a global view, see http://www.globaldetentionproject.org/home.html; last accessed on 6 May 2012.
57 For a similar approach, see Spierenburg, *The Prison Experience*, ch. 11, pp. 261–276.

By extending our chronology back before 1500, two long-term trends can be observed. The first relates to the continuity or discontinuity of the experience of penal transportation.[58] The second refers to the "birth of the prison" as part of a broader shift in attitudes towards the socially marginal. Observing early modern and modern transportation, four conditions seem especially favourable for the development of penal transportation: first, centralized authority; secondly, control over large territories with an uneven distribution of resources; thirdly, a drive for (internal and/or external) colonization, often linked to military engagements; and, fourthly, fluidity between free and unfree labour. Notwithstanding the scarcity of sources and specific research, available studies on the Han Empire (206 BCE–220 CE) and on the (Western) Roman Empire (27 BCE–476 CE) reveal the consistency of these four characteristics with those ancient contexts as well.[59]

In the Roman Empire the *damnatio ad metalla* led to the transportation of convicts (*damnati*, or *damnati in metallum*) to the gold and silver mines of Numidia, the alabaster mines and the porphyry quarries of Egypt, the marble quarries on the island of Proconnesus (Marmara), and other sites in Cyprus, Sardinia, and

---

[58] Note also that Roman law remained the basis of early modern and modern imperial law on exile and penal transportation. See, for instance, Coates, *Convicts and Orphans*, pp. 22–23.
[59] On the Han Empire see C. Martin Wilbur, "Industrial Slavery in China during the Former Han Dynasty (206 BC–AD 25)", *Journal of Economic History*, 3 (1943), pp. 56–69; idem, *Slavery in China During the Former Han Dynasty, 206 BC–AD 25* (Chicago, IL, 1943). For long-term surveys, see also Philip F. Williams and Yenna Wu, *The Great Wall of Confinement: The Chinese Prison Camp through Contemporary Fiction and Reportage* (Berkeley, CA, 2004), p. 24; R.H. van Gulik, *Crime and Punishment in Ancient China: The T'ang-Yin-Pi-Shih* (Bangkok, 2007); Mühlhahn, *Criminal Justice in China*, pp. 14–57. For a later period see J. Waley-Cohen, *Exile in Mid-Qing China: Banishment to Xinjiang, 1758–1820* (New Haven, CT [etc.], 1991). On the Roman Empire see J.G. Davies, "Condemnation to the Mines: A Neglected Chapter in the History of the Persecutions", *University of Birmingham Historical Journal*, 6 (1958), pp. 99–107; P. Garnsey, *Social Status and Legal Privilege in the Roman Empire* (Oxford, 1970); Fergus Millar, "Condemnation to Hard Labour in the Roman Empire, from the Julio-Claudians to Constantine", *Papers of the British School at Rome*, 52 (1984), pp. 124–147; J. Clayton Fant, "The Roman Emperors in the Marble Business: Capitalists, Middlemen or Philanthropists?", in Norman Herz and Marc Waelkens (eds), *Classical Marble: Geochemistry, Technology, Trade* (Dordrecht, 1988), pp. 147–158; Mark Gustafson, "Condemnation to the Mines in the Later Roman Empire", *Harvard Theological Review*, 87 (1994), pp. 421–433; D. Lassandro, "I 'damnati in metalla' in alcune testimonianze antiche", in M. Sordi, *Coercizione e mobilità umana nel mondo antico* (Milan, 1995); J. Alexander, "Islam, Archaeology and Slavery in Africa", *World Archaeology*, 33 (2001), pp. 44–60 (on the possible continuation of the condemnation to hard labour in mining/quarrying). No specific information could be found on convict labour in the Assyrian Empire (1100–600 BCE). See for instance B.J. Parker, "Archaeological Manifestations of Empire: Assyria's Imprint on Southeastern Anatolia", *American Journal of Archaeology*, 107 (2003), pp. 525–557; M. Liverani, *Antico Oriente. Storia, società, economia* (Rome, 2009).

Palestine. In the Han Empire, convicts were transported to the government salt and iron monopolies, where they staged repeated revolts in the final part of the first century BCE. In both empires the employment of convict labour was linked with the trends in the demand and supply of slaves: in the case of the Roman Empire the rise of convict labour from the third century CE onward is probably due to the reduced influx of slaves, in turn possibly caused by the end of the wars of conquest; in the Han Empire of the second and first centuries BCE the "boundless supply of cheap corvee and convict labor"[60] appears to be a key explanation for the alleged absence of slaves in some economic sectors.

Moreover, the flexibility of labour relations has been especially stressed for the Roman Empire by ancient scholars who, moving away from its traditional characterization as a "slave society", have pointed to the existence of a considerable degree of inter-changeability between the work of freemen, slaves, and freed slaves within what has been defined as a "unified labour force".[61] Transported convicts could also be included in the latter. Central to this fluidity of labour relations was the "open" character of Roman slavery, marked by frequent manumissions, social mobility linked to positive incentives (salary, education, etc.), and the relatively high level of legal integration of ex-slaves into the citizenry. Similarly, the literature on the Han Empire refers to frequent general amnesties and special pardons for convicts of various classifications.

New research is certainly needed on this topic, together with greater cooperation between historians working on ancient and modern empires. However, it seems that a degree of continuity can be hypothesized between ancient, early modern, and nineteenth-century transportation. Furthermore, as suggested in the previous section, it is also tempting to propose that such continuity can be further traced between transportation and twentieth-century labour camps. Although the emphasis lies on the movement of inmates in the case of transportation, and on the locations of their final destinations in that of labour camps, transportation and camps can be seen as two different modes of a similar phenomenon of channelling and corralling the labour of subject or criminalized categories of the populace.[62] To begin with, the above four conditions apply to the

---

[60] Wilbur, "Industrial Slavery in China during the Former Han Dynasty", p. 66.
[61] Peter Temin, "The Labor Market of the Early Roman Empire", *Journal of Interdisciplinary History*, 34 (2004), pp. 513–538. See also P.A. Brunt, "Free Labor and Public Works at Rome", *Journal of Roman Studies*, 70 (1980), pp. 81–100. The key reference on ancient slavery is K. Bradley and P. Cartledge (eds), *The Cambridge World History of Slavery* (Cambridge, 2011), I.
[62] An earlier vein of scholarship, associated with criminologist Thorsten Sellin, posited just such continuity. See T. Sellin, *Slavery and the Penal System* (New York, 1976), and J.M. Moore, "Classic Text Revisited: *Slavery and the Penal System*", *Criminal Justice Matters*, 85 (2011), p. 40, for a recent retrospective appreciation of Sellin's work. One possible explanation for the different

twentieth-century camps too. Moreover, empirical evidence also points to this long-term continuity. For instance, agricultural penal colonies created outside Lisbon soon after the end of transportation to Portuguese Africa in 1932 were later used during the Salazar regime and, at least in the case of the Colónia Penal Agricola de "António Maceira" in Sintra, continue to function to this day.[63] Similarly, the long-term continuity between the Tsarist *katorga* and the Soviet Gulag can be understood in the context of Russian internal colonization of the eastern regions, especially once recent interpretations are taken into account that point to the deportation of millions of peasants to the "other archipelago" of the special settlements in the early 1930s.[64] This holds true as well for the network of Nazi concentration and labour camps.[65] In fact, deportation to Germany during World War II could be envisaged as an integrated system providing forced and convict

---

way of framing transportation and the labour camps lies in the fact that a separation exists between the historiography of transportation, prison, and labour camps in the twentieth century. Moreover, the demise of colonialism could have further accentuated this separation: Klaus Mühlhahn, on the contrary, has shown the global connections and transfers through which the concentration camps "moved" first from the European colonial domains to the European continent and later further throughout the world; "The Concentration Camp in Global Historical Perspective", *History Compass*, 8 (2010), pp. 543–561. A totalization of the twentieth-century experience of the camps has followed, especially as far as the Nazi concentration camps are concerned. The twentieth century has therefore been framed as "the century of the camps", and Agamben's theory of the state of exception and of the camps has avoided any reference to colonial policy and experience, although it extensively deals with institutions of Roman law and nineteenth- and twentieth-century European politics. See J. Kotek and P. Rigoulot, *Century of Concentration Camps: 100 Years of Radical Evil* (London, 2004); G. Agamben, *Homo Sacer: Sovereign Power and Bare Life* (Stanford, CA, 1998); idem, *State of Exception* (Chicago, IL, 2005). Some scholars, however, have seen the seeds of the Nazi camp system in German colonial policy in Southwest Africa in the suppression of the Herero Revolt; Bley, *South-West Africa under German Rule*; Conrad, *German Colonialism*; Mühlhahn, "The Concentration Camp in Global Historical Perspective", p. 546. When considering the long-term continuity between transportation and twentieth-century labour camps, an important issue is that of the role played by internment in both regimes.
63 *Coates, Convicts and Orphans.*
64 Viola, *The Unknown Gulag*, pp. 185–188. See also Abby M. Schrader, "Branding the Exile as 'Other': Corporal Punishment and the Construction of Boundaries in mid-Nineteenth-Century Russia", in D.L. Hoffmann and Y. Kotsonis (eds), *Russian Modernity* (London, 2000), pp. 19–40; Hellie Richard, "Migration in Early Modern Russia, I480s–1780s", in Eltis, *Coerced and Free Migration*; A.A. Gentes, *Exile to Siberia, 1590–1822: Corporeal Commodification and Administrative Systematization in Russia* (Houndmills, 2008); idem, *Exile, Murder and Madness in Siberia, 1823–61* (Houndmills, 2010). This was a point made by Sellin at the time.
65 See references in n. 42 above. For an extended explanation of this hypothesis, see C.G. De Vito, "Mussolini's Prisons, Final Act (1943–1945)", paper for the European Social Science History Conference, Glasgow, 11–14 April 2012.

labour from the Reich's annexed or controlled countries to specific sites in order to serve the needs of the Nazi war economy.

This long-term perspective on transportation also poses the question of the medieval experience of convict labour.[66] In fact, at least in the western European context, the Middle Ages witnessed the virtual disappearance of penal transportation. The four points mentioned above could suggest some explanations for this trend. With the reorientation of the Roman Empire towards the East, the European territory was essentially split into a series of political entities that were too many, too small, and too weak to conceive and organize the transportation of their small number of convicts. A "provincialization of politics" took place, since "local elites began to deal with the 'barbarian' powers rather than with the imperial government, which was by now too distant and decreasingly relevant".[67] Moreover, the shift from taxation to landowning as the basis of the state made the post-Roman kingdoms economically less strong and less complex. The structure of the feudal economy further accentuated the fragmentation of power and territory and could be reckoned to have impeded the fluidity between different labour relations by tying surplus labour to particular plots of land. Finally, Germanic influences made *weregild* a prevalent form of punishment, focusing on compensation and restitution rather than transportation and forced labour.

Characteristic of the new situation in medieval Europe was also the recourse to *exile* rather than to transportation, that is, to a form of punishment aimed at expelling someone *from* a certain territory rather than sending them *to* another territory for forced work. Such expulsion sought primarily to cleanse and protect the body politic, rather than to deploy "surplus" population in an effort to extend the effective reach of the imperial state (though certainly these two motives could easily join together, as they came to in Britain's North American colonies). Lack of funding and facilities for long-term imprisonment can also be held responsible for this shift. Not surprisingly then, "the reappearance of penal labor in western Europe at the end of the Middle Ages coincided with the emergence of the national state and an increase in its wealth and power".[68] The growing use of convict labour aboard the galleys in the same period confirms this, since it is

---

[66] For the considerations that follow in the text, see W. Chester Jordan, *From Servitude to Freedom: Manumission in the Sénonais in the Thirteenth Century* (Philadelphia, PA, 1986); P Brown, *The World of Late Antiquity, AD 150–750* (New York, 1989); C. Wickham, *Framing the Early Middle Ages: Europe and the Mediterranean, 400–800* (Oxford, 2004); idem, *The Inheritance of Rome: A History of Europe from 400 to 1000* (London, 2008).
[67] Wickham, *The Inheritance of Rome*, p. 108.
[68] Pike, *Penal Servitude in Early Modern Spain*, p. 4.

first to be observed in larger and more powerful political entities such as Venice and France.

The late Middle Ages have also been seen as the origin of another long-term transformation in punishment and convict labour, one that in this case actually ran counter to the impulse to exile social malefactors. Around the thirteen century, the emergence of a new mode of production in some European urban centres and the general change in mentality led to a new attitude towards the governing of social outcasts – from expulsion to containment.[69] In turn, this produced the creation of new "incarcerative" institutions – leper-houses, brothels, hospitals, almshouses, Jewish quarters – and a fundamental shift in the practice of imprisonment. Gaols – the large majority of whose population was made up of individuals imprisoned for debt – took on a more important role in city life and the urban imaginary and became internally more differentiated. This meant that carceral institutions departed from their traditional role as warehouses for individuals awaiting trial or punishment. On this basis Guy Geltner has argued for a medieval "birth of the prison", some five or six centuries before the chronology posed by Michel Foucault in *Discipline and Punish*.

To be sure, forced labour cannot be considered a major feature of these late medieval European prisons, but the shift in the attitude towards the socially excluded they suggested was a fundamental element in the emergence of other institutions explicitly designed to govern the urban poor and make them engage in productive or punitive labour. Examples of the latter are to be found especially

---

[69] G. Geltner, *The Medieval Prison: A Social History* (Princeton, NJ [etc.], 2008). Particularly in the 1970s and 1980s a broad debate developed among historians on the shift in attitude towards poverty and the emergence of new institutions between the late Middle Ages and the early modern period. Studies on the emergence of mental asylums also played a key role in this. Michel Foucault's *Histoire de la folie à l'âge classique* (Paris, 1961) in many ways anticipated this debate. See, for instance, J.-P Gutton, *La société et les pauvres. L'exemple de la Généralité de Lyon, 1534–1789* (Paris, 1971); O.H. Hufton, *The Poor of Eighteenth-Century France, 1750–1789* (Oxford, 1974); B. Geremek, *Les marginaux parisiens aux XIV et XVe siècles* (Paris, 1976); idem, *La potence ou la pitié. L'Europe et les pauvres du Moyen Age à nos jours* (Paris, 1978); M. Mollat, *Les pauvres au Moyen Age. Etude sociale* (Paris, 1978); J. Le Goff, "Les marginaux dans l'Occident mediéval", *Cahiers Jussieu*, 5 (1979), pp. 19–28; C. Lis and H. Soly, *Poverty and Capitalism in Pre-Industrial Europe* (Brighton, 1979); P Spierenburg, *The Emergence of Carceral Institutions: Prisons, Galleys and Lunatic Asylums, 1550–1900* (Rotterdam, 1984); S. Woof, *The Poor in Western Europe in the Eighteenth and Nineteenth Centuries* (London, 1986). While often linked to a Marxist perspective on the origins of capitalism, in some authors the long-term approach was inspired by Norbert Elias's classic *Über den Prozeß der Zivilisation. Soziogenetische und psychogenetische Untersuchungen* (Basel, 1939), 2 vols, English translation: *The Civilizing Process* (Oxford, 1969 and 1982). Other authors have also referred to Gerhard Oestreich, *Geist und Gestalt des frühmodernen Staates* (Berlin, 1969), English translation: *Neostoicism and the Early Modern State* (Cambridge, 1982).

in the prison workhouses – the Dutch *tuchthuizen*, the German *zuchthäuser*, and the English *bridewells* – that were created from the early seventeenth Century.[70] As shown by the path-breaking research by Pieter Spierenburg, long-term shifts in mentalities and in material conditions played a role in making work a central feature of these institutions. Most importantly, the study of the workhouses leads to the following issues: the productive or non-productive character of convict labour (and the problem of its competition with free labour); the rehabilitative or punitive function of work; the specialization of space in the institutions and the differentiation within the inmate population, often through the gendered-, age-, and socially constructed concept of the "able-bodied" labourer. These questions, and the prison workhouse model as such, proved to be central in the rise of the penitentiary during the nineteenth century.[71]

By examining the phenomenon of convict labour within a chronology going back before 1500, it is thus possible to address its role in the transition to modernity while at the same time avoiding a modernization-oriented approach that stresses a sudden transition accompanying the late eighteenth-century Industrial Revolution.[72] This approach entails a move away from teleological concepts such as "proto-industrialization" or "proletarianization" and frames convict labour as one form of labour relations involved in the process of commodification of labour. We have already explored this issue in the first section. What is important to add here is that, in order to proceed in this direction, a truly global perspective is needed, one that investigates the applicability of the scholarship on European medieval and early modern transportation, prisons, and workhouses described

---

[70] The key reference is Spierenburg, *The Prison Experience*. For a long-term approach to the history of the prison, see also X. Rousseaux, "Pour une histoire de la justice pénale en Belgique (13e–20e s.)", *Histoire de la Justice*, 8–9 (1995–1996), pp. 113–147; E.M. Peters, "Prison before the Prison: The Ancient and Medieval Worlds", in Morris and Rothman, *The Oxford History of the Prison*, pp. 3–43; X. Rousseaux, "Dalle città medievali agli stati nazionali: rassegna sulla storia della criminalità e della giustizia penale in Europa (1350–1850)", in L. Cajani (ed.), *Criminalità, giustizia penale e ordine pubblico nell'Europa moderna* (Milan, 1997); X. Rousseaux, "Historiographie du crime et de la justice criminelle dans l'espace francais (1990–2005). Partie I: du Moyen-Age à la fin de l'Ancien Régime", *Crime, Histoire et Sociétés*, 10 (2006), pp. 123–158; F. Bretschneider, *Gefangene Gesellschaft. Eine Geschichte der Einsperrung in Sachsen im 18. und 19. Jahrhundert* (Konstanz, 2008); A. Gestrich and R. Lutz (eds), *Inklusion/Exklusion. Studien zu Fremdheit und Armut von der Antike bis zur Gegenwart* (Frankfurt, 2008); G. Ammerer et al. (eds), *Orte der Verwahrung. Die innere Organisation von Gefängnissen, Hospitälern und Klöstern seit dem Spätmittelalter* (Leipzig, 2010); I. Heullant-Donat, J. Claustre, and E. Lusset (eds), *Enfermements. Le cloître et la prison (VIe–XVIIIe siècle)* (Paris, 2011).
[71] Colvin, *Penitentiaries, Reformatories, and Chain Gangs*.
[72] For a clear discussion of these two interpretations, see Spierenburg, *The Prison Experience*, pp. 1–11

above to non-European experiences. For instance, what kind of punitive Systems and convict labour were in use in the Abbassid, Mamluk, and Ottoman caliphates, in the Vijayanagara and Inca empires, and in the Aztec Triple Alliance?[73]

Together with the fragmentation of sub-disciplines corresponding to regimes of punishment and temporal limitations imposed by teleological assumptions of modernity and progress, the limited knowledge of non-Western areas is the other fundamental limitation of the available literature on convict labour. Moreover, not only does the historiography focus more on "the West" than on "the Rest", most of the research is marked by a Eurocentric mindset, one that takes the alleged progressive penal development of incarceration, rehabilitation, and social control associated with modernity as its template. This blind spot is in fact common to both the liberal humanitarian narrative and the critical anti-Enlightenment perspective, such as that provided by the Foucauldian approach to correctional history. Merely adding narratives of convict labour outside "the West" would then not be sufficient to move beyond this Eurocentric approach.[74] A non-Eurocentric understanding can emerge only when narratives, interpretations, and concepts are reconsidered from an integrated global perspective that no longer privileges the development of Western penal history, whether as a humane model or the poisoned taproot of total bio-power.

As with many other fields of research, colonial and post-colonial studies today represent the most innovative methodological sub-discipline within the historiography of convict labour. For although they too risk reproducing a form of Eurocentrism – the history of non-European countries considered only as far

---

[73] The following works deal with these contexts, but reveal the difficulty of finding specific information on convict labour: S. Falk Moore, *Power and Property in Inca Peru* (New York, 1958); H. Dieterich, "Some Theoretical and Methodological Observations about the Inca Empire and the Asiatic Mode of Production", *Latin American Perspectives*, 9:4 (1982), pp. 111–132; G.W. Conrad and A.A. Demarest, *Religion and Empire: The Dynamics of Aztec and Inca Expansionism* (New York, 1984); M.E. Smith and F.F. Berdan, "Archaeology of the Aztec Empire", *World Archaeology*, 23 (1992), pp. 353–367; I. Schneider, "Imprisonment in Pre-Classical and Classical Islamic Law", *Islamic Law and Society*, 2 (1995), pp. 157–173; C.M. Sinopoli and K.D. Morrison, "Dimensions of Imperial Control: The Vijayanagara Capital", *American Anthropologist*, 97 (1995), pp. 83–96. From a general point of view, the importance of expanding the perspective both to the pre-1500 period and to non-European experiences has been shown by J.L. Abu-Lughod, *Before European Hegemony: The World System AD 1250–1350* (New York [etc.], 1989).

[74] For a similar point about the limitations of a Eurocentric view of prison history, see Gibson, "Global Perspectives on the Birth of the Prison". In some of the 1980s' and 1990s' historiography on colonial prisons, for instance, the inapplicability of Foucault's *Surveiller et punir* scheme to the colonial systems of confinement had been observed, but it was framed in terms of the "pre-modernity" and the "backwardness" of the colonies rather than questioning Foucault's interpretation. On this see Sherman, "Tensions of Colonial Punishment".

as European colonization is involved – the post-colonial awareness of the need to radically rethink Eurocentric categories allows us to reconsider convict labour within a global framework. Not surprisingly then, it is in a recent survey article on the "tensions of colonial punishment" that Taylor C. Sherman has proposed the concept of a "coercive network" as a new framework to understand the mutual connections between different regimes of punishment and the links between punishment as a whole and the political, cultural, social, economic, and administrative context on a global, or at least imperial, scale.[75] Similarly, Clare Anderson, writing on the convict transportation networks in the Indian Ocean across several centuries, has pointed to the need to develop a "world history frame sensitive to the global and the local".[76]

As should be evident by now, this article accepts these suggestions and in turn argues that they should be extended to the study of convict labour beyond the colonial and post-colonial experience. Our view is that convict labour can provide a strategic perspective to connect research on the intersecting lines of penal history and labour history from a global perspective, much the same way transnational studies of slavery and emancipation have helped reconceptualize the study of labour in the eighteenth- and nineteenth-century Atlantic world. When studying convict labour, one should neither remain trapped within preconceived "national" borders nor imagine the "local" as a self-contained unit and the "global" as a monolithic entity. Rather, following the work of Doreen Massey, space could be visualized as "the product of interrelations", "the sphere of the possibility of the existence of multiplicity", and as something "always under construction".[77] It could then be possible to "follow the traces" of different persons, ideas, and phenomena through different localities and scales. For instance, historians of convict labour could study the exchanges of personnel, techniques, and technology, investigate global responses to specific events, trace the chains of production and consumption by convicts, compare the fate of different groups of prisoners, and follow the biographies of convicts, personnel, and other histor-

---

[75] *Ibid.*, p. 669.
[76] C. Anderson, "Convict Transportation in the Indian Ocean", paper for the "Global Convict Labour" conference, IISH, Amsterdam, 13–14 June 2012. The awareness of the need for a global and long-term perspective is also shown by the international conference on "Colonial Places, Convict Spaces: Penal Transportation in Global Context, c.1600–1940", Department of Economic & Social History, University of Leicester, 9–10 December 1999. The proceedings of the conference have never been published. Abstracts of the papers are available at http://iccs.arts.utas.edu.au/abstracts4.html; last accessed on 21 May 2012. See also Ward, *Networks of Empire*, for an example of what this approach might yield.
[77] D. Massey, *For Space* (London [etc.], 2005), p. 9.

ical actors.[78] This is particularly true given how dependent penal networks and the political economy of convict labour have been on the movement of bodies through geographic space, the reallocation of human productive power from territory to territory, or from one economic sector to another, when the "market" would not suffice. This is why attention to transportation or "excarceration", instead of incarceration alone, must be considered a central element in the history of convict labour.

Looking at convict labour beyond a rigid global/local dichotomy, the possibility also emerges to address fully human agency by a wide range of actors. In the past two decades scholars of penal history have paid significant attention to decision-making processes, interaction between various state and private authorities, and the plurality of consequences of attempts at reform. Efforts have also been made to locate the power to shape the policy of punishment and convict labour outside political and penal institutions, for example by the actions of convicts themselves, including resistance.[79] However, much work remains to be done in this field.

---

78 The expression "follow the traces" is in Marcel van der Linden, "Historia do trabalho: o Velho, o Novo e o Global", *Revista Mundos do trabalho*, 1 (2009), pp. 11–26. Other important methodological references are A. Lüdtke (ed.), *The History of Everyday Life: Reconstructing Historical Experiences and Ways of Life* (Princeton, NJ, 1995); J. Revel (ed.), *Jeux d'échelles. La micro-analyse à l'expérience* (Paris, 1996); M. Werner and B. Zimmermann, "Beyond Comparison: Histoire croisée and the Challenge of Reflexivity", *History and Theory*, 45 (2006), pp. 30–50; U. Freitag and A. von Oppen (eds), *Translocality: The Study of Globalising Processes from a Southern Perspective* (Leiden [etc.], 2010); Van der Linden, *Workers of the World*, pp. 372–378 (on the concept of "teleconnections"). For examples of a biographical or prosopographical approach to this social history, see C. Pybus, "The African Diaspora at the End of the World", in Dawne Curry, Eric Duke, and Marshanda Smith (eds), *Extending the Diaspora: New Histories of Black People* (Urbana, IL, 2009), pp. 157–177; I. Duffield, "From Slave Colonies to Penal Colonies: The West Indian Convict Transportees to Australia", *Slavery and Abolition*, 7 (1986), pp. 25–45, as well as several of the papers presented at the "Colonial Places, Convict Spaces: Penal Transportation in Global Context, c.1600–1940" conference. For a good recent example of the application of this method, see Anderson, *Subaltern Lives*.

79 McLennan, *Crisis of Imprisonment*; R.T. Chase, "'Slaves of the State' Revolt: Southern Prison Labor and a Prison-Made Civil Rights Movement, 1945–1980", in Robert Zieger (ed.), *Life and Labor in the New South* (Gainesville, FL, 2012); A. Lichtenstein, "Twice the Work of Free Labor? Labor, Punishment, and the Task System in Georgia's Convict Mines", in Gary Fink and Merl Reed (eds), *Race, Class, and Community in Southern Labor History* (Tuscaloosa, AL, 1994); Steven A. Barnes, *Death and Redemption: The Gulag and the Shaping of Soviet Society* (Princeton, NJ, 2011), ch. 6; idem, "'In a Manner Befitting Soviet Citizens': An Uprising in the Post-Stalin Gulag", *Slavic Review*, 64 (2005), pp. 823–850.

Only a handful of scattered studies, for instance, specifically deal with the key issue of the relationship between convict labour and the labour movement.[80] However, scholars have pointed to the importance of four aspects of this relationship: first, the "disciplining effect of convict labour" on free labour; secondly, the need to look at specific productive sectors when considering the issue of economic competition between convict and "free" labour; thirdly, the importance of labour organizations in limiting convict labour to state-owned sectors and, more often, to "domestic" labour inside penal establishments; and, fourthly, that the perceived "competition" of convict labour does not simply entail economic factors, but also relates to the negative image that convict labour could have shed on a particular class of people or on a certain location. In the latter case, opposition to convict labour could typically be expected from merchants and small entrepreneurs. On the other hand, at least in the recent history of the US, punishment has served as an engine of community economic redevelopment and job creation through "carceral Keynesianism" and in privatized corrections.[81]

Other visible gaps in the historiography regard the custodians and the impact of imprisonment and exile on convicts' families and friends.[82] More generally,

---

[80] K.A. Shapiro, *A New South Rebellion: The Battle against Convict Labor in the Tennessee Coalfields, 1871–1896* (Chapel Hill, NC [etc.], 1998); B. Greenberg, *Worker and Community: Response to Industrialization in a Nineteenth-century American City, Albany, New York, 1850–1884* (Albany, NY, 1984). See also "The Struggle against the Introduction of Convict and Reformatory Labour into Natal", *Archives Year Book for South African History* (1967), 2 vols; T. Mathiesen, *The Politics of Abolition* (London, 1974); Gildemeister, *Prison Labor and Convict Competition*; McLennan, *Crisis of Imprisonment*; K. Morgan, "Petitions against Convict Transportation, 1725–1735", *English Historical Review*, 104:410 (1989), pp. 110–113. See also the special issue of *Labor. Studies in Working-Class History of the Americas* (2011), including A. Lichtenstein, "A 'Labor History' of Mass Incarceration", *Labor: Studies in Working-Class History of the Americas*, 8:3 (2011), pp. 5–14.

[81] A. Lichtenstein and M. Kroll, "The Fortress Economy: The Economic Role of the US Prison System", in Elihu Rosenblatt (ed.), *Criminal Injustice: Confronting the Prison Crisis* (Boston, MA, 1996); Heather A. Thompson, "Why Mass Incarceration Matters: Rethinking Crisis, Decline and Transformation in Postwar American History", *Journal of American History*, 97 (2010), pp. 703–734; Mike Davis, *Ecology of Fear: Los Angeles and the Imagination of Disaster* (New York, 1999), p. 416; idem, "Hell Factories in the Field: A Prison-Industrial Complex", *The Nation*, 260:7 (20 February 1995).

[82] On prison guards see, for example, Ted Conover, *Newjack: Guarding Sing Sing* (New York, 2000); N. Morris, *Maconochie's Gentlemen: The Story of Norfolk Island and the Roots of Modern Prison Reform* (New York, 2003); F.V. Mochulsky, *Gulag Boss: A Soviet Memoir* (New York, 2011); J. Page, *The Toughest Beat: Politics, Punishment, and the Prison Officers' Union in California* (New York, 2011). On family and community, see, for example, Curtin, *Black Prisoners and their World*; W.Z. Goldman, *Inventing the Enemy: Denunciation and Terror in Stalin's Russia* (Cambridge, 2011); Gheith and Jolluck, *Gulag Voices*, chs 7–10; Heather A. Thompson, "Rethinking Working Class Struggle through the Lens of the Carceral State: Toward a Labor History of Inmates and Guards",

little is known about the social history and work life of the inmates before and after their internment, a lack of information that is probably due to a long-term prejudice about – and the historical invisibility of – the lumpenproletariat that has formed the vast majority of the convict population in many contexts.[83] Furthermore, although quantitatively consistent for some places and periods, the literature on the labour of female convicts – around 5–10 per cent of prisoners in most societies – appears poorly integrated in general overviews of convict labour.[84] Scant attention is paid to the gender dimension of penal labour as such,

---

Labor: Working Class Studies of the Americas, 8:3 (2011), pp. 15–45; C.A. Frierson and S.S. Vilensky, *Children of the Gulag* (New Haven, CT, 2010), chs 4–6. Attempts at a social history of penal life have been made, especially for penal colonies.

83 C. Aguirre, *The Criminals of Lima and Their Worlds: The Prison Experience, 1850–1935* (Durham, NC, 2005). On Marxism and lumpenproletariat see, for instance, H. Draper, "The Concept of the 'Lumpenproletariat' in Marx and Engels", *Economies et Sociétés*, 6 (1972), pp. 2285–2312; F. Bovenkerk, "The Rehabilitation of the Rabble: How and Why Marx and Engels Wrongly Depicted the Lumpenproletariat as a Reactionary Force", *Netherlands Journal of Sociology*, 20 (1984), pp. 13–41; P. Hayes, "*Utopia* and the Lumpenproletariat: Marx's Reasoning in *The Eighteenth Brumaire of Louis Bonaparte*", *Review of Politics*, 50 (1988), pp. 445–465.

84 Among the available studies: C. Lesselier, "Les femmes et la prison 1820–1939. Prison de femmes et reproduction de la société patriarcale", in J.-G. Petit, *La prison, le bagne et l'histoire* (Paris [etc.], 1984); O. Krakovitch, *Les femmes bagnardes* (Paris, 1990); E. Campelli et al., *Donne in carcere. Ricerca sulla detenzione femminile in Italia* (Milan, 1992); J. Damousi, "'Depravity and Disorder': The Sexuality of Convict Women", *Labour History*, 68 (1995), pp. 30–45; D. Oxley, *Convict Maids: The Forced Migration of Women to Australia* (Cambridge, 1996); M.S. Zarate, "Vicious Women, Virtuous Women: The Female Delinquent and the Santiago de Chile Correctional House, 1860–1900", in Salvatore and Aguirre, *The Birth of the Penitentiary*, pp. 78–100; K. Daniels, *Convict Women* (Sydney, 1998); E. Conlin Casella, "'Doing Trade': A Sexual Economy of Nineteenth-Century Australian Female Convict Prisons", *World Archaeology*, 32 (2000), pp. 209–221; A. Pillay, "Prisoners Are Women Too: A Case Study of Women Prisoners at Westville Prison", *Alternation*, 7 (2000), pp. 156–169; M. Gibson, "Le carceri femminili nell'Italia liberale", *Storica*, 16 (2000), pp. 135–154; D.J. Guy, "Girls in Prison: The Role of the Buenos Aires Casa Correccional de Mujeres as an Institution for Child Rescue, 1890–1940", in Salvatore, Aguirre, and Joseph, *Crime and Punishment in Latin America*, pp. 369–390; S. Sen, "The Female Jails of Colonial India", *Indian Economic and Social History Review*, 39 (2002), pp. 417–438; L. Mara Dodge, *"Whores and Thieves of the Worst Kind": A Study of Women, Crime, and Prisons, 1835–2000* (DeKalb, IL, 2002); K. Ruggiero, "'Houses of Deposit' and the Exclusion of Women in Turn-of-the-Century Argentina", in C. Strange and A. Bashford (eds), *Isolation: Places and Practices of Exclusion* (New York, 2003), pp. 111–124; S. Trombetta, *Punizione e carità. Carceri femminili nell'Italia dell'Ottocento* (Bologna, 2004); S. Leukel, *Strafanstalt und Geschlecht. Geschichte des Frauenstrafvollzugs im 19. Jahrhundert (Baden und Preußen)* (Leipzig 2010); G. Geltner, "No-Woman's Land? On Female Crime and Incarceration, Past, Present, and Future", *Justice Policy Journal*, 7:2 (2010), n.p., www.cjcj.org/files/No_Woman.pdf; last accessed 11 December 2012; Talitha LeFlouria, "'The Hand that Rocks the Cradle Cuts Cordwood': Exploring Black Women's Lives and Labor in Georgia's Convict Camps, 1865–1917", *Labor: Studies in Working-Class History of the Americas*, 8:3 (2011),

as well as to the importance of age and generations. Particularly noticeable is the lack of specific studies on juvenile convict labour.[85]

As far as the convicts' agency is concerned, the picture remains highly uneven. Much historiography has focused on political convicts subjected to penal servitude and in prisons, where work has often played a highly particular role in regimes of punishment.[86] On non-political prisoners, important studies have been published on those transported across the Indian Ocean,[87] and on the individual and collective resistance of internees in the Nazi lagers and in the Stalinist

---

pp. 47–63; J. Pallot and L. Piacentini, *Gender, Geography, and Punishment: The Experience of Women in Carceral Russia* (Oxford, 2012).

[85] For some studies on juvenile convict labour, see, for example, M.-S. Dupont-Bouchat, *De la prison à l'école. Les pénitenciers pour enfants en Belgique au XIXe siècle (1840–1914)* (Kortrijk, 1996); idem and E. Pierre (eds), *Enfance et justice au XIXe siècle. Essais d'histoire comparée de la protection de l'enfance 1820–1914* (Paris, 2001); Castan and Zysberg, *Histoire de galères*; M. De Koster, "Jongeren en criminaliteit: Een lange geschiedenis van de Middeleeuwen tot heden", *Tijdschrift voor Criminologie*, 52 (2010), pp. 308-317; Frierson and Vilensky, *Children of the Gulag*, pp. 6–63. For the French case, see also the special issue of the *Revue d'histoire de l'enfance irrégulière*, 7 (2005).

[86] A preliminary question is of course that of defining "political prisoner". On this, the ongoing research by Padraic Kenney is especially relevant. For some references on political prisoners' resistance see U. Kumar Singh, *Political Prisoners in India* (New Delhi, 1998); Peter Zinoman, "Colonial Prisons and Anti-Colonial Resistance in French Indochina: The Thai Nguyen Rebellion, 1917", *Modern Asia Studies*, 34 (2000), pp. 57-98; L. McKeown, *Out of Time: Irish Republican Prisoners, Long Kesh 1972–2000* (Belfast, 2001); F.L. Buntman, *Robben Island and Prisoner Resistance to Apartheid* (New York, 2003); P. Gready, *Writing as Resistance: Life Stories of Imprisonment, Exile, and Homecoming from Apartheid South Africa* (Oxford, 2003); D. Arnold, "The Self and the Cell: Indian Prison Narratives as Life Histories", in idem and S. Blackburn (eds), *Telling Lives in India: Biography, Autobiography, and Life History* (New Delhi, 2004), pp. 29–53; P.F. Williams and Yenna Wu (eds), *Remolding and Resistance Among Writers of the Chinese Prison Camp* (New York, 2006); F. Rule, *Un allegro muy largo: de la vida social y cultural en las cárceles de la dictadura militar argentina, 1976–1983* (Buenos Aires, 2006); M.R. Prette (ed.), *Il carcere speciale* (Dogliani, 2006); C. Anderson, *The Indian Uprising of 1857–8: Prisons, Prisoners and Rebellion* (London, 2007).

[87] See, for instance, L. Frost and H. Maxwell-Stewart, *Chain Letters: Narrating Convict Lives* (Melbourne, 2001); Clare Anderson, "The Bel Ombre Rebellion: Indian Convicts in Mauritius, 1815–53", in G. Campbell (ed.), *Abolition and its Aftermath in Indian Ocean Africa and Asia* (London, 2005), pp. 46–59; Clare Anderson, "'The Ferringees are Flying – the Ship is Ours!': The Convict Middle Passage in Colonial South and Southeast Asia, 1790–1860", *Indian Economic and Social History Review*, 42 (2005), pp. 143–186; idem, "Sepoys, Servants and Settlers: Convict Transportation in the Indian Ocean, 1787–1945", in Dikötter and Brown, *Cultures of Confinement*, pp. 185–220; A.A. Yang, "Indian Convict Workers in Southeast Asia in the Late Eighteenth and Early Nineteenth Centuries", *Journal of World History*, 14 (2003), pp. 179–208.

Gulags (also in relation to forced labour),[88] but little is known about detention camps in other historical and geographical contexts. Similarly, much work has been done in recent decades on prisoner resistance to the convict lease and the chain gang in the US South in the second half of the nineteenth century, but no systematic study is available on resistance to forced labour in gaols, prisons, and penitentiaries.[89] Research on the latter could certainly benefit from an interdisciplinary approach that brings together historical findings and the long tradition of sociological, criminological, and ethnographical studies on life within "total institutions".[90] And comparative research could reveal the role played by work and labour relations in common law prisoners' rights movements, like those that erupted in the US and in western Europe during the 1960s and 1970s.[91]

The lack of attention paid to agency also appears as the major weakness of the vast sociological and political literature on the process of mass incarceration in the US and elsewhere since the 1990s.[92] Here, abstract and supposedly non-mod-

---

[88] See, for instance, Caplan and Wachsmann, *Concentration Camps in Nazi Germany*; Barnes, "'In a Manner Befitting Soviet Citizens'".

[89] See, for instance, Curtin, *Black Prisoners and Their World*. See also C. van Onselen, "Crime and Total Institutions in the Making of Modern South Africa: The Life of Nongoloza Mathebula, 1867–1948", *History Workshop*, 19 (1985), pp. 62–81; McLennan, *Crisis of Imprisonment*; Chase, "'Slaves of the State' Revolt".

[90] N.S. Hayner and E. Ash, "The Prisoner Community as a Social Group", *American Sociological Review*, 4 (1939), pp. 362–363; D. Clemmer, *The Prison Community* (Boston, MA, 1940); M.G. Caldwell, "Group Dynamics in the Prison Community", *Journal of Criminal Law, Criminology and Police Science*, 46 (1956), pp. 648–657; G.M. Sykes, *The Society of Captives: A Study of a Maximum Security Prison* (Princeton, NJ, 1958); E. Goffman, *Asylums: Essays on the Social Situation of Mental Patients and Other Inmates* (New York, 1961); T. Mathiesen, *The Defences of the Weak: A Sociological Study of a Norwegian Correctional Institution* (London, 1965); J.B. Jacobs, *Stateville: The Penitentiary in Mass Society* (Chicago, IL [etc.], 1977); Falk Bretschneider, Martin Scheutz, and Alfred Stefan Weiß (eds), *Personal und Insassen von 'Totalen Institutionen" – zwischen Konfrontation und Verflechtung* (Leipzig, 2011).

[91] Mathiesen, *The Politics of Abolition*; *Rebelión en las cárceles* (Madrid, 1978); R. Adams, *Prison Riots in Britain and the USA* (Houndmills, 1994); Philippe Artières, Laurent Quéro, and Michelle Zancarini-Fournel, *Le Groupe d'information sur les prisons. Archives d'une lutte, 1970–1972* (Paris, 2003); César L. Rubio, "La revuelta de los comunes. El movimiento de presos sociales durante la Transición", in *Por la memoria anticapitalista. Reflexiones sobre la autonomía* (Madrid, 2008); H. Smits, *Strafrechthervormers en hemelbestormers. Opkomst en teloorgang van de Coornhert-Liga* (Amsterdam, 2008); C.G. De Vito and S. Vaiani, "Ci siamo presi la libertà di lottare. Movimenti dei detenuti in Europa Occidentale", *Zapruder*, 16 (2008), pp. 8–22; Thompson, "Rethinking Working Class Struggle"; Perkinson, *Texas Tough*; Chase, "'Slaves of the State' Revolt". For a recent example of work on the prisoners' rights movement and Black power, see D.F. Tibbs, *From Black Power to Prison Power: The Making of Jones v North Carolina Prisoners' Labor Union* (New York, 2011).

[92] For some contributions to this debate see L. Wacquant, *Les prisons de la misère* (Paris, 1999); A. De Giorgi, *Zero tolleranza. Strategie e pratiche della società di controllo* (Rome, 2000); N.

ifiable forces such as "globalization", "neoliberalism", and (in the US) the "prison-industrial complex" are described as imposing control on the "post-industrial proletariat", "multitudes", and "poor" through incarceration. Although these descriptions have played an important role in creating awareness of the political relevance of this ongoing process, they fail to provide a broader framework to locate it historically. Moreover, because they do not always effectively identify specific agents that either promote or resist the shift in penal policy, these accounts can produce a sense of inevitability and thus impotence. Finally, this literature typically refers exclusively to Western penal systems – and most often to the US – but generalizes its conclusions to the whole world.

The same limitations characterize the way convict labour itself is approached in this strand of literature. Most frequently absent from the picture, it is otherwise depicted as an undifferentiated form of "modern slavery" in a way that suggests a regression to earlier stages of civilization. However, when contemporary convict labour is looked at through a global and comparative perspective the same intertwining of economic, social, political, and cultural factors appears that has operated in previous historical contexts.[93] Moreover, as in the past, convict labour in the contemporary world is not limited to penal institutions. Labour camps, in particular, continue to play an important role, as the Chinese *laojiao* and *laogai* dramatically show.

Yet today, even while incarceration expands as a form of punishment, penal labour itself often appears redundant. The complex interaction of different factors on different scales thus points to another possibility: the forces that have led to the emergence of convict labour in certain historical contexts could actually be reversed. An analysis is thus possible of the objective and subjective factors that have led away from the exploitation of penal labour in relation to certain catego-

---

Christie, *Crime Control as Industry: Towards Gulags, Western Style* (New York, 2000); D. Garland (ed.), *Mass Imprisonment: Social Causes and Consequences* (London [etc.], 2001); R. Matthews and P. Francis (eds), *Prisons 2000: An International Perspective on the Current State and Future of Imprisonment* (Houndmills, 2001); D. van Zyl Smit and F. Dünkel (eds), *Imprisonment Today and Tomorrow: International Perspectives on Prisoners' Rights and Prison Conditions* (The Hague, 2001); P. Artières and P. Lascoumes (eds), *Gouverner, enfermer. La prison, un modèle indépassable?* (Paris, 2004); L. Re, *Carcere e globalizzazione. Il boom penitenziario negli Stati Uniti e in Europa* (Rome, 2006); Thompson, "Why Mass Incarceration Matters"; Mary Louise Frampton, Ian Haney Lopez, and Jonathan Simon (eds), *After the War on Crime: Race, Democracy, and a New Reconstruction* (New York, 2008); Ruth Wilson Gilmore, *Golden Gulag: Prisons, Surplus, Crisis, and Opposition in Globalizing California* (Berkeley, CA, 2007).

93 Dirk van Zyl Smit and Frieder Dünkel (eds), *Prison Labour: Salvation or Slavery?* (London, 1999); E. Shea, *Le travail pénitentiaire: un défi européen. Etude comparée: France, Angleterre, Allemagne* (Paris, 2006); J. Sarkin, "Global Prison Crisis: How Does Africa Rate?", *South African Labour Bulletin*, 32:5 (2008), pp. 25–27.

ries of or even all prisoners in a given time and space. Under what conditions does punishment *not* produce rehabilitative or retributive convict labour? Why is there *no* convict labour? By answering these questions, dramatic human experiences may emerge, such as exile, repatriation, extreme isolation (as in US "supermax" prisons), extermination, and genocide or attempted genocide, not to mention the more mundane tasks of simply managing "surplus" populations in a post-industrial political economy.[94] But this approach might also reveal new patterns of agency, resistance, alternatives, and, perhaps, abolition.

---

94 See, for instance, J. Walston, "History and Memory of the Italian Concentration Camps", *Historical Journal*, 40 (1997), pp. 169–183; M. Frucht Levy, "The Ustasa Genocide against Serbs: 1941–1945", in M. Neerland Soleim (ed.), *Prisoners of War and Forced Labour: Histories of War and Occupation* (Cambridge, 2010), pp. 89–104.

Philip Bonner, Jonathan Hyslop and Lucien van der Walt
Rethinking Worlds of Labour
Southern African Labour History in International Context[1]

South African historians and social scientists have often bemoaned 'South African exceptionalism': in other words a tendency to see the country's historical trajectory as absolutely unique. Yet they have also been strangely reluctant to place their findings in a more global context. The articles which comprise this edition were papers given at a University of the Witwatersrand (Wits) History Workshop and Sociology of Work Unit international conference entitled 'Rethinking Worlds of Labour: southern African labour history in international context' held from 28 to 31 July 2006.

The conference provided an opportunity to move away from South African exceptionalism in practice, by considering *comparisons* and *connections* between the history of labour in South Africa and in other parts of the world. The title also reflected the conviction of the conference organisers that such a shift away from parochialism would contribute to a 'rethinking' of some of the fundamental assumptions of labour history in southern Africa, and contributes to a revivification of the field. Furthermore, we meant 'worlds' in a dual sense – signalling not just the physical spaces through which people move, but also social worlds, and our special interest in the subjective ways in which the world is understood by workers.

Globalisation and labour history

There has, during the first decade of the twenty-first century, been a clear rise in historians' interest in working at a more international level (Hopkins 2002; Bayly 2004). This is certainly rooted in the sense that globalisation – however that is understood – is making an enormous impact on our daily lives. This causes a reappraisal of many certainties, economic, social and political, and gives rise to a historical curiosity about the antecedents of globalisation.

---

[1] This article was first published under the same title in *African Studies*, 66, 2–3, August–December 2007, pp. 137–168 DOI: 10.1080/00020180701482628 © 2007 Taylor & Francis Group Ltd on behalf of the University of Witwatersrand.

Indeed, it may be argued that historians have a particularly valuable contribution to make to globalisation debates. Very often we are told that features of 'globalisation' are absolutely new, or unique to the present. But social scientists sometimes do this without any very careful attention to the past, which they are considering. Closer enquiry may in fact show that some features of globalisation have clear precedents. In this perspective we are only now re-emerging into something like the globalised world of before 1914.

John Gray (1998) has pointed out that it is not helpful to conflate, as commonly happens, the international turn toward free market policies in the 1980s with 'globalisation' understood as the history of intensifying transnational connections as a whole. Globalisation has proceeded at many levels – political, social, and cultural – besides the economic. It has a long history, and is likely to survive the demise of recently influential economic ideologies. Indeed Bayly (2004) has convincingly advanced the notion of 'archaic globalisation', linking empires and societies previous to modern capitalism. In her path-breaking study of the world of the twelfth to the fourteenth centuries, Janet Abu Lughod (1989) likewise made a powerful case for the existence of a China-centred world economy before the rise of European colonisation. Indeed, many historians of the late nineteenth and early twentieth century would argue that there was in that era a 'first globalisation', followed by a strengthening of nation-based structures after the First World War. So it would seem that claims about what is, and is not, original about current globalisation would benefit from a much stronger baseline of historical comparison.

In this context, labour history is a field with particular claims for attention informed by a more global outlook. The glory days of the discipline internationally were in the 1960s to the early 1980s, and in that era there is no doubt that the interest in labour's past was driven by the extraordinary waves of industrial militancy in the United Kingdom, France, Italy, Poland, Brazil, Argentina, India and many other countries during those years. Yet it is equally the case that subsequent developments caused a salutary re-examination of some of the notions that informed labour history. The defeats suffered by labour movements, the decline of the size of the industrial workforce in many major economies, the emergence of new forms of global flows of capital, and new patterns of production and consumption, all put question marks over any triumphalism about the cause of labour. Critics, many of them informed by post-structuralist theory, with some justification raised questions over labour historians' neglect of the analysis of discourse and language (Steadman Jones 1983), its failure to engage adequately with feminist theory (Scott 1988), and its teleological politics (Joyce 1994).

Yet though there was much that was valid in these critiques, and although the world of the 1990s was inhospitable for labour history, the subject of the working classes and their histories remains an inescapable one for any serious study of the modern world. There are also strong signs of a practical and theoretical revival of labour history that speaks to questions thrown up by globalisation. What has been striking over the last few years has been a revival of labour history, particularly within the semi-industrial countries. At the same time, labour history has become increasingly attuned to the global dimensions of working-class formation. As Marcel van der Linden notes in his contribution to this collection, labour history is today not only more globalised in its practice, but it is also more global in its outlook.

One of the major limitations of classical labour history was that it was largely confined within the boundaries of national histories. The greatest of all the works of labour history in its golden era was after all, EP Thompson's (1991) book on *The Making of the English Working Class*. The Scots, Welsh and Irish only got walk-on parts in Thompson's great drama, while peoples further a field were almost entirely ignored, notwithstanding the larger British imperial context. In general, labour historians have followed this approach, writing about the German, Australian, South African, Brazilian, Nigerian etc. working classes.

Now, obviously the formation of nation-states was one of the major features of the nineteenth, and more especially the twentieth centuries, and working classes have often orientated politically towards such 'national' frameworks. However, nationally based labour studies face several related problems. Taking the nation-state as the self-evident unit of analysis tends to naturalise what must be seen as a fairly novel (and for much of the modern period, unusual) state form, and the related assumption that labour must develop a *national* character. *Relativizing* and *historicizing* the nation-state can reveal much about the history of labour, help avoid teleological assumptions about the historical trajectory of labour movements, and undermine the sense of national uniqueness that produces a sense of 'exceptionalism'. Nationally based labour histories have also tended to homogenise local variations *within* nation-states, inadvertently playing down regional specificity. Moreover, they have tended to ignore the point that many of the most important processes within the world of labour occurred *across* national boundaries. International flows of migrant workers, capital, political agitators, publications, cultures and public spheres are crucial to the histories of working classes in the modern world.

Much can be gained by escaping from such confines. For all Thompson's great achievement, consider how much fuller is the picture of the late eighteenth century English working class that is presented in Peter Linebaugh and Marcus Rediker's *The Many-Headed Hydra* (2000). Their argument for the existence of an 'Atlantic working class' of sailors, labourers, slaves, freedmen and renegades linking Britain, West Africa, the Caribbean and North America has crucially expanded labour historians' understanding of the seventeenth and eighteenth century world. It has drawn attention to the importance of understanding connections between continents and across different labouring groups, and the need to rediscover and rethink popular imaginations.

The theoretical groundwork for such approaches was laid by important interrogations of the nation-state in the 1980s. By showing that the nation-state was a relatively recent phenomenon (Gellner 1983) – based on 'imagined communities' constituted through print capitalism and other instrumentalities (Anderson 1991) and legitimised through 'invented traditions' and the ideological work of military service and schooling (Hobsbawm 1990) – social scientists and historians radically destabilised and denaturalised the nation state. In turn, these interventions made it much more possible for scholars to recognise the somewhat fictive character of the claims of the state, more generally, and the possibility that states could fail to make good these claims. For labour studies, this pointed to examining the relationship between changing state form and working-class movements, and questioning the view that empires and other types of state forms could be regarded as simply the prehistory of the nation-state.

In a way, it was odd that labour historians had become so hypnotised by the nationstate, given that Marxism was so crucial to the intellectual formation of the discipline. Marxism was, in intent at least, an internationalist project, and Marx and Engel's paean to the destructive and constructive powers of capitalism celebrated how commodities battered down 'Chinese Walls', denied that the proletariat had a 'fatherland', and, of course, famously proclaimed: 'Workers of All Countries – Unite!' The emergence of a historiography organised in largely national terms can be partly explained by the pragmatic reality of world politics, and by Lenin's systematic re-orientation of Marxism towards strategic alliances with nationalist movements in the 'colonial and semi-colonial world'. Aside from the revision of Marx's arguments this entailed (Warren 1982), and the difficulty of reconciling class analysis with class alliances that must continually arise, the practical success of Lenin's approach had the effect of making the 'national' a central category within Marxist thought and politics.[2]

Nevertheless, there are notable works by Marxist historians that transcend approaches rooted in methodological nationalism. Perhaps most outstanding is Eric Hobsbawm's (1977a, 1977b, 1987) great trilogy on the world of the 'long' nineteenth century. Hobsbawm's extraordinary portrait of the rise of a globally connected world is exemplary in the way in which it goes beyond national history.

---

2 Indeed, many contemporary Marxists seem to regard 'progressive' or 'anti-imperialist' nationalist movements as intrinsically radical, an approach that can sometimes be used to support some of the most reprehensible regimes, like that of Robert Mugabe.

Its sensitivity to the cultural level of analysis, and its deep engagement with Latin American and Asian experiences in many ways anticipated the work of contemporary transnational historians. (It must be said though that sub-Saharan Africa remained something of a blind spot for the great historian.)

Thinking globally

It is our view that labour history can benefit greatly from the application of a more transnational approach. What would be different about the approach that we are suggesting? Perhaps it would be best to clear the ground by saying first of all what we do *not* envisage.

Firstly, we do not want to adopt the slogan of 'World History' (Pomper, Elphick and Vann 1998), which since at least the 1960s has been a fairly mainstream branch of historiography (setting aside somewhat eccentric predecessors like Oswald Spengler (1926, 1928) and Arnold Toynbee (1960)). This trend did, as we do, seek to overcome parochialism, and it did produce some remarkable works of scholarship such as William H. McNeill's outstanding books on the global history of epidemic disease (1977) and of warfare (1983). However, even the most outstanding practitioners of World History, including McNeill, have tended to approach their task through the lens of analysis of Civilizations, which are usually defined through some form of cultural attributes.

The difficulty here is that, even in the hands of an able historian like McNeill, these world cultures seem to be monolithic, static, mutually exclusive and essentialised. It is striking that even in the work of an historian as great and innovative as Fernand Braudel (1982), the master's commitment to a notion of culturally intact civilization drove him eventually toward a distinctively protective posture towards French identity. The *reductio ad absurdum* of this approach is found in Samuel Huntington's (1996) belief in an inevitable 'Clash of Civilizations'. Moreover, when practised by less erudite and skilled historians than Braudel or McNeill, the project of a comprehensive history of the world can become overambitious, even farcical. Few historians can write with much plausibility about developments over a single century, let alone all human history. So, moving history outside national frameworks does not mean that one should make a hubristic attempt at comprehensiveness.

Secondly, we are specifically not advocating what has been the most influential framework for global history in recent decades: the World Systems Theory (WST) of Immanuel Wallerstein (1974). Wallerstein postulated that the expansion of Europe at the turn of the sixteenth century saw the creation of a single capitalist world system, one of a series of 'world systems': the modern world system was understood as a system of states, with a 'core' in the West, a 'periphery' subjected to the 'core' by imperialism, and a 'semi-periphery' of intermediate states that acted as 'agents' of the 'core' while striving for 'core' status. Economic 'surpluses' are 'drained' to the 'core', enriching it at the expense of the other regions, which become 'underdeveloped'. States can with difficulty change their position within the world system, but the system persists.

The objections to such a schema are so obvious that it is hard to understand the power that it has exercised over the minds of scholars. Its evident attraction is its very simplicity, as a universal explanation; the same simplicity is its weakness, too, for it posits a closed social analysis, conceived within a functionalist approach, and tends to operate through the static logic of systems theory. It is difficult to see any room for resistance, for the role of ideas, or for ruptures in the structure (Adas 1998), while the meaning of the core idea, 'underdevelopment', is vague, shifting and very often tautological (Warren 1980). By displacing class exploitation *within* countries by international exploitation *between* countries, the framework displaces class, and perhaps more importantly, the role of class struggles, from its analysis. The idea of nations remains relatively taken for granted and unexamined, and mapped onto the different regions.

Many WST practitioners purport to be Marxist, yet the model of the world system is rooted not in a Marxist analysis of production, but rather in flows of trade (Brenner 1977; Laclau 1982), with the argument for 'exploitation' between countries rooted, in the final analysis, in the liberal theory of 'exploitation' as monopoly pricing (Leys 1996). WST may be right, but it cannot be both right *and* Marxist, and the result is a radical theoretical incoherence. WST can only argue with great difficulty that the Spanish and Portuguese adventurers, who initiated the modern world economy, were in any meaningful sense modern capitalists. With its vision of single systemic logic, WST is ill-equipped to analyse non-Western empires, and unable to explain the rise of newly industrialised countries in late nineteenth, and again in the late twentieth century, world.

Comparative studies of different countries have, on the other hand, a long and honourable tradition in the social sciences. By seeking to place two cases alongside one another, not only are we immediately led to question our assumptions and to look at what is similar and different in distinct historical contexts, but also our conceptual and empirical horizons are rapidly expanded.

South African historians have, for example, almost universally accepted that 'super-exploited' large-scale cyclical labour migrancy was a definitive feature of South African capitalism, and attributed this situation in large part to segregation and apartheid. However, as Philip Bonner (2004) has shown in a study of Indian and South African urbanisation, there are remarkable similarities in patterns of labour migrancy in the two countries, despite the general absence of any significant state interventions in the colonial Indian labour market.

This is one of several themes that Sumit Sakar's article in this collection develops through a comparative discussion. Sakar notes, for example, that the interventions of the South African state in the fields of labour markets and social policy were far more extensive and ambitious than those undertaken in the British Raj: there was, for example, simply no equivalent in colonial India to South African-style township construction, social segregation and labour coercion. He cautions, consequently, against the tendency of some post-colonial theory to homogenise the colonial experience, and to downplay the importance of pre-colonial legacies. In India, unlike southern Africa, pre-colonial social stratification was extensive, and it was this that allowed the recruitment of a large labour force without direct interventions like land restrictions. Peter Alexander's contribution to this collection, which compares collieries in South Africa and India, makes the key point that female miners were almost unknown in South Africa as compared to India, and adds that daily pay for Indian miners was half of African miners'. This suggests that the 'concept of "cheap labour" ... involves a comparison with white South African labour, is parochial, and ... should now be discarded' (Alexander 2006:7).

Comparative approaches, in other words, help create the basis for a re-examination of some of the conventional wisdom in the field. Perhaps some of the resistance of South African social scientists and historians to comparative work is based, though, on the important misunderstanding that comparing two situations entails making the case that they are somehow the same. This is absolutely not the case, for many of the most important comparative analyses are those that study *different* historical paths. A notable example is Barrington Moore's (1987) *Social Origins of Dictatorship and Democracy*, which explains the different routes that agrarian societies took to modernity, and their long-term political and social consequences. Similarly, Perry Anderson's (1974) *Lineages of the Absolutist State* sought to explain the very different socioeconomic trajectories of eastern and western Europe.

What constitutes a valid comparison? Some time ago, Mahmood Mamdani (1998) led a rather moralistic campaign about the need to place studies of South Africa in an African context. Whether one makes African or non-African comparisons should depend on the usefulness of the comparison to what one is studying, and the way it can illuminate particular issues. Thus, Jeremy Seekings' comparison of the South African welfare system with those of Latin America, which appears in this collection, works exceptionally well because there is a sufficient degree of similarity and difference in the cases to make them illuminating.

Allison Drew's comparison of the agrarian engagement of Algerian and South African communists in this edition works so well because of the intellectual framing she gives it, rather than simply because the two cases examined are drawn from Africa. Similarly, Gay Seidman's (1994) comparison of the South African and Brazilian labour movements was productive given the comparable economic and social contexts. It would be difficult to compare the modern South African labour movement with that of a country without major industries. On the other hand, it is clear that in many areas – for example popular culture, traditional authority and political democratisation – comparisons between South Africa and other African countries are extremely illuminating. There is, in short, no moral obligation on researchers to accept certain forms of comparison, and refuse others.

One way in which the growing scepticism about national histories can be extremely helpful is in developing international comparisons that take regional variation into account, rather than compare countries as a whole. Thus Peter Alexander's comparison of collieries has a keen sense of the social specificity of the region in which his Indian case is located, and of the distinctions between the Transvaal and Natal coal industries in South Africa. Similarly, while comparisons been South African and the United States as a whole can become rather unwieldy, a focused comparison of processes in particular regions can be very helpful: the career of segregation in the *southern* US and South Africa have, for instance, been usefully compared by Greenberg (1980), Cell (1982) and others.

Transnational labour history

We can now turn to transnational labour history. Let us offer a modest definition: transnational labour history does not assume that the nation-state is the necessary framework for historical analysis. It is interested in perspectives that move beyond the level of the 'nation' to look at flows of people, commodities, ideas and organisations across national boundaries. It also considers the possibility that regions or cities within nation-states may have closer links with regions or cities lodged in other nation-states than with their own hinterlands. It does not seek to be comprehensive: rather it simply does not accept that its field of enquiry should stop at the 'national' border, or that a 'national' unit is a self-evident, or necessarily a particularly useful unit of analysis. It argues for approaches that examine connections across countries, continents and cultures, for comparative studies, for transnational perspectives, and for rethinking the conceptual vocabulary of labour and working-class history.

To say this is clearly not to pose a transnational perspective as the theoretical panacea for all historiographical problems. Nor does it suggest that the 'national' is not a useful level of analysis, or deny that the nation-state and nationalism have been central forces in the modern period, or will remain powerful forces in any conceivable medium-term future. At the very least, a transnational view asks the scholar to hesitate before starting the analysis with the assumption that the nation-state is the relevant unit of analysis. And even the study of nationalism itself can benefit from this, for one of the features of current historiography is its revelation of the way in which nationalisms form *across* national boundaries. For example, in his extraordinary book, *Americana*, James Dunkerley (2000) brilliantly illuminates the emergence of US and Latin American political identities in the mid-nineteenth century by treating both the North and South American continents as a single political arena, and by relating them in turn to political and cultural developments in Ireland, and elsewhere in Europe.

What methodological benefits might this sort of perspective bring to labour history? Firstly, it refocuses attention on the phenomenon of global migration. Of course, the world of the nineteenth and twentieth centuries has been continually re-shaped by mass migrations, of which working-class people were a central component. Now, a perspective that emphasises national labour histories can lead to the idea that migration simply involves a flow of workers from country A to country B, where they assimilate and form a component of the 'national' working class. The reality, however, is more complex, as migrants often cling tenaciously to political identities from their place of origin, and infuse these into movements in the host country. Not only, for example, did radicals in the late nineteenth and early twentieth century US draw in large numbers of immigrants, but they also communicated with them through a polyglot press. Thus, the first anarchist daily newspaper in the world seems to have been the *Chicagoer Arbeiter-Zeitung*, a German-language paper published in Chicago in the 1880s, which was then called the second largest German city in the world (Bekken 1995).

Moreover, migration is often oscillating or lateral, rather than simply a move from country A to country B. Migrants dream of returning to their home country and often do so, and others move between several countries in the course of their migration. Thus, for example, at the beginning of the Witwatersrand mining industry, not only did many Cornish miners return to their families in Cornwall after several years on the Rand, but there was also a constant flow of Cornish miners between South Australia, West Australia, southern Africa, and western America: more adventurous Cornishmen could be found down mines from Malaya to Bolivia. Migration is a process, without a necessary 'national' end point.

One phenomenon that is now starting to receive more adequate attention, partly as a result of a more transnational outlook, is nineteenth and twentieth century Chinese and Indian indentured labour. The institution of this system in the backwash of the British Empire's abolition of slavery had significant effects on South Africa and in many other regions of the world. Whether one agrees with Hugh Tinker's (1974) famous contention that this was *A New System of Slavery*, or whether one accepts the more optimistic view that indenture played a significant role in enabling labourers to accumulate capital and begin breaking out of a semifeudal village life (Northrup 1995), it clearly entailed vast mortality, suffering and social disruption. It is not generally recognised that the number of 'coolies' shipped around the world was comparable to the numbers transported in the African slave trade. Indenture deserves a much more central place in labour history, and including indenture starts to raise significant questions about how 'labour' and the 'working class' are defined, and to what extent 'free' labour is characteristic of industrial modernity.

Secondly, a transnational perspective leads to a reassessment of labour's political movements. The present authors have sought to make a contribution to this project in their other work. Lucien van der Walt (1999, 2004), for example, has shown that the early twentieth century South African labour movement's ideologies and actions cannot be understood without due attention to the global impact of anarchist and syndicalist ideologies and movements, often brought to South Africa by migrants and spread through an international press. This has been almost entirely ignored by South African labour historians. By placing South African developments in a global context, and examining the importance of transnational connections and influences, Jonathan Hyslop (1999), too, has mounted a case that the trade unions of British immigrants in the same era are best understood as part of an 'imperial working class' which straddled the British Empire.

This reassessment is especially necessary in relation to the history of Communism. Writers sympathetic to communist parties have emphasised the rootedness of their ideologies and activities in national struggles and conditions (for example, Isserman 1982), while their critics have stressed the heavy hand of Moscow through the Communist International (Comintern), the Cominform and funding (for example Klehr, Haynes and Firsov 1995). Both approaches are narrow and one-sided: the weight of evidence of tight connections between communist parties and the Soviet Union is overwhelming, and communist ideology stressed the importance of these links; on the other hand, the parties only became significant where they were able to make genuine connections with national and local social grievances, cultural traditions and political struggles. It is useful, then, to understand Communism from a transnational perspective that recognises its parties were simultaneously shaped by both their relation to the Soviet

Union and their national contexts. The work of Geoff Eley (2002) is distinguished amongst historians of the left for striking this sort of equilibrium on this issue.

Thirdly, transnational labour history opens up exciting and illuminating possibilities in micro-history and biographical research. A transnational perspective poses key methodological issues, and it is striking that some of the greatest insights into global processes can be gleaned from a study of individual lives. In particular, following an individual travelling labour activist as he or she moves around the world illuminates complex global networks and flows of ideas. Karen Hunt's article in this edition provides an excellent example of what can be accomplished here. By looking at Dora Montefiore, a British socialist and feminist who travelled the world of the imperial working class, Hunt shows how ideas and movements can be (re)shaped by experiences in different, yet interconnected, contexts. A key work is Benedict Anderson's (2005) study of the anarchist-influenced Filipino revolutionary intellectuals of the late nineteenth century. Anderson brilliantly shows the extraordinary personal linkages in the 1890s between the left in Europe, the rebellion against the Spanish in Cuba, and the wars of the Philippine rebels against both Spanish colonists and American liberators. (He also notes how the Anglo-Boer War, a key moment in South Africa, became a key symbol of anti-imperialist resistance worldwide at the time.)

Fourthly, following from the previous point, a transnational approach highlights the point that not nation-states, but empires, have been the typical state form over the past centuries (Stoler and Cooper 1997). Until the First World War, the empires of the British, French and Dutch (and their feebler Austro-Hungarian, Portuguese, Russian and Ottoman rivals) bestrode the world, and it was only after the Second World War that formal empires (like the Soviet Union) became rarities, rather than the norm. For much of the nineteenth and twentieth centuries, labour must be understood in imperial, not national, contexts. Passports were rarely used before the First World War (Torpey 2000), one indication of the relative unimportance of national types of state: indeed, it was considerably easier for workers to move around the world before 1914 than it is today. It is thoroughly anachronistic for labour historians to project current national structures back in time.

Fifthly, oceanic history must be an important component of contemporary history beyond national boundaries. Braudel's (1972–3) great work on the Mediterranean is an important starting point, showing how maritime space can provide the arena for a dense social and economic overlapping of political entities. This insight has already been applied to the Atlantic Ocean with considerable effect (Linebaugh and Rediker 2000), and is now being mobilised in the labour history of the Indian Ocean (for example, Metcalf 2007). In turn, the more serious interest in oceanic contexts has been associated with a lively historiography that seeks to understand the world of the ship as a world of work (Dening 1992; Ewald 2000). The ship has been an important site of social life, and especially labour action, in the making of our world, as well as an important carrier of ideas and movements.

Sixthly, and perhaps paradoxically, a transnational perspective leads us back to a focus on the city. The metropolis is often more connected to metropolises in other countries than to its own hinterland. As Ferguson (2006) memorably puts it, in Africa capital (and labour!) does not so much 'flow' as 'hop'. This means, at one level, that due attention needs to be paid to variation within countries; at another, it means taking cities seriously as cosmopolitan sites, as nodes in transnational networks, and as sites of state power and class formation. It is worth asking whether we are not perhaps coming to inhabit, in some regions at least, a world of weak states and strong cities, rather like late-medieval Europe.

Merely concentrating masses of people into shared workplaces and neighbourhoods in large cities does not, however, necessarily imply class unity. Cosmopolitan contexts can as easily accentuate differences as limit their significance: it is striking, for example, that it was in South Africa, and not India, that the expatriate Mohandas Gandhi came to see himself as first, and foremost, an Indian (Markovits 2004:81). In understanding these dynamics, it is important to consider the complicated role of cosmopolitan centres as forcing houses of ideas, as nodes in networks, and as sites of both competition and cooperation in the popular classes.

Finally, a transnational perspective has an important role to play in the very necessary task of rescuing labour history from what has undoubtedly been a very strong tendency to economistic forms of analysis. Although EP Thompson was extremely sensitive to the impact of literature and religion on the working class, and although Herbert Gutman (1976) made a powerful case for the centrality of culture to labour history, their successors have not always taken these points sufficiently on board. While the Wits History Workshop has had a strong commitment to issues of popular culture, we have not been sufficiently sensitive to issues like literacy, and its social and political impact. And some labour studies have been balefully economistic, treating workers as lacking any interest in such issues as ethnic identity, religion, sexuality, chiefly politics, sports, language or reading.

The work of Karl Polanyi (1991) is enjoying something of a vogue in labour studies, in part because of his rejection of liberal economics. Yet Polanyi's larger point is that society is never purely structured by economic relations: interactions need to be understood in radically social terms, and not reduced to the 'economy' or 'politics'. With the 'great acceleration of communications and transport in the nineteenth century' (Bayly 2004) and the contemporary 'compression of time and space' (Harvey 1991), it is important to recognise that the flow of ideas cannot conceivably be understood in terms of the cultural production of a single country, or simply as the result of an autonomous and pure 'national' process.

To understand the social worlds of labour in a given place, we need to study popular culture, but to situate this within a cultural arena formed by ideas flowing across international boundaries, in relation to the manner in which different medias circulate them, and, again, in relation to the ways in which people reinterpret them in specific contexts. In the contemporary situation we as historians need to start thinking more systematically about the way in which the Internet is changing worlds of labour. The sociologist of religion Olivier Roy (2006) has, for instance, recently argued that the Internet is the key site where new militant Islamist ideologies are formed. And religious formations are of course eminently global with their claims to universal community, in the reach and technological sophistication of their propaganda: sometimes harnessed to nationalism, religious aspirations can also subvert the nation-state project with claims to a global community and project.

South African labour, or labour in South(ern) Africa?

A transnational perspective can make an important contribution to the labour history of southern Africa, where scholarship on labour history is unevenly developed in the region, concentrated in South Africa, and generally been placed within the framework of the nation-state. Labour history in South Africa has derived from two main traditions: activist and scholarly work. Activist writing on labour, largely produced outside of academia, goes back to the 1920s. The earliest work came from white labour (Gitsham and Trembath 1926; Walker and Weinbren 1961), followed by writings by Communist Party of South Africa (CPSA) members in the 1940s (Andrews 1941; Cope c. 1943; Harrison n.d.; Roux [1944] 1993), Trotskyist analyses in the 1950s (notably Majeke 1952; Mnguni 1952; Tabata 1950; for a partial overview, see Nasson 1990), and a wave of works by writers associated with the CPSA's successor, the South African Communist Party (SACP) from the 1950s onwards (for example, Bunting 1975; Forman [1959] 1992; Lerumo 1971; Simons and Simons 1969 [1983]; for a partial overview, see Drew 1997).[3]

---

3 The work of Baruch Hirson, exiled South African Trotskyist, on the history of labour and the left, can also be usefully placed within the activist tradition: for a partial compilation, see Hirson and Hirson (2005) and also see Hirson (1989).

Leaving aside a few liberal analyses of labour that had some historical content (Horrell 1969), the scholarly tradition of labour history emerged in the 1970s in British and South African universities, and was influenced by Marxism and class analysis. This 'revisionist' literature challenged older liberal approaches that emphasised the negative effects of apartheid and segregation on South African capitalism: in its starkest formulations, the revisionists portrayed the racial order as nothing but a function of capitalist imperatives, with capitalism supposedly unable to function without apartheid (Johnstone 1970; Legassick 1974; Wolpe 1972). The impact of structuralist approaches in the 1970s was also evident in the use of Nicos Poulantzas' analysis of state policy as shaped by 'fractions' of capital (Davies, Kaplan, Morris and O'Meara 1976), the use of WST (Bundy 1979; Legassick 1977), and also a tendency to read labour history off labour processes (Lewis 1984).

In large part as a response to the structuralists' failure to examine popular agency and consciousness (Bonner 1994), and in contrast to the 'old labour history' focus of much of the activist literature, the late 1970s saw the blossoming of a local social history in the Thompsonian mode, which stressed experience and culture (the key works would include Bonner, Hofmeyr and James 1989; Bonner, Delius and Posel 1993; Bozzoli 1979, 1983, 1987; Bozzoli and Delius 1990; Beinart, Delius and Trapido 1986; Marks and Rathbone 1982; Marks and Trapido 1987; Van Onselen 1982a, 1982b; for overviews, see Bonner 1994; Bozzoli and Delius 1990; Saunders 1988). The Wits History Workshop, formed in 1977 and focused on the Witwatersrand, was the main organised expression of this shift, but only one of several social history initiatives at the time. The new labour history developed as part of this social history project. In contrast to the functionalism and reductionism of the structuralists, the social historians stressed contingency, contradictions, ruptures and the reconstruction of 'history from below'.

What both the activist and revisionist traditions, structuralists and social historians alike, shared was a tendency to write the history of labour in South Africa as a specifically 'South African' labour history. Of course, both traditions were well aware of the importance of international processes and connections in shaping a 'South African' society, and routinely made implicit or explicit comparisons between South Africa and other countries, generally with the emphasis on the 'exceptional' character of South Africa. Attention to the global was inevitable, given that the industrial revolution on the Witwatersrand in the late nineteenth century was spurred on the one hand by foreign direct investment in the 'first globalisation' lasting roughly from the 1880s to the 1920s; on the other, it developed in tandem with the expansion of British and Portuguese imperial power in the region.

It was also recognised, to some degree that the working class that emerged in South Africa was a multinational and multiracial one, drawn from across southern Africa, the British Empire and beyond. South African capitalism was embedded in a regional political economy, and in regional, as well as transcontinental, labour markets. In addition, there were several fruitful applications of revisionist perspectives elsewhere in southern Africa, most notably Mozambique (for example, Harries 1994; Penvenne 1984, 1995) and Zimbabwe (formerly Southern Rhodesia, notably Palmer and Parsons 1977; Phimister 1988; Phimister and Van Onselen 1979; Ranger 1970; Van Onselen 1976).

Nonetheless, activist and revisionist scholars tended to take South Africa as the unit of analysis, and to examine labour history as *South African* labour history. Cross-border connections were examined largely from the perspective of their contribution to South African history; the regional labour markets were examined largely in terms of their importance to South African labour employers. The white unionists noted international influences on the emergence of union traditions, but treated this as a passing phase before the mature period of a specifically 'South African movement' acting on a South African stage (Gitsham and Trembath 1926:11). The CPSA writers agreed, while many Trotskyists adopted an overtly nationalist narrative, with '300 years' of oppression (Mnguni 1952) leading to the 'awakening of a people' (Tabata 1950).

SACP writers likewise framed matters in a national framework, adding a large dash of teleology: the two 'streams' of class and national movements 'merged', apparently inevitably, in the 1950s when the CPSA/SACP allied with the nationalist African National Congress (ANC) (Bunting 1975; Forman [1959] 1992; Simons and Simons [1969] 1983). CPSA and SACP writers were, of course, well aware that the rise of Communism was closely linked to the rise of the Soviet Union, and shaped by that state. However, they stressed the 'national' character of the party and its rootedness in the struggles of 'our people'. There were substantial overlaps between SACP and nationalist ANC historiography (for a sophisticated example, see Meli 1988; for an overview, see Lodge 1990). For the SACP writers, not only was the CPSA's 1928 adoption of the Native Republic thesis – stressing the immediate task as a struggle against feudalism and imperialism, for the creation of a non-racial bourgeois society, rather than socialism – *not* imposed by Moscow, but was supposedly actually largely 'initiated' by CPSA members (Simons and Simons [1969] 1983:405; Bunting 1993). This is a typical example of the trend of pro-communist writers to stress the national character of parties.

The same limitations were clear in the revisionist historiography. The social historians were accused by the structuralists of failing to move beyond culturalist and local studies to examine the larger political economy (Morris 1987; Murray 1989). However, with a few exceptions (notably Legassick 1977) the structuralists took the larger political economy as a 'national' and South African formation. To the extent that there was an attempt by the structuralists to discuss southern Africa as a unit, the emphasis was on South Africa's dominant role. WST ideas of 'unequal exchange' played some role in these approaches, with the corollary that the region was analysed in terms of competing states, rather than viewed from the vantage point of empire, or examined as a unit with dynamics that were not simply the sum of (national) parts.

The structuralist charge that the social historians eschewed theory was not very well founded. The Wits History Workshop project, at least, was explicitly concerned with examining the significance of popular struggles for the system of 'racial capitalism', and of using local cases to inform larger models (see, for instance, Bonner, Delius and Posel 1993; Bozzoli 1979, 1983, 1987; Marks and Trapido 1987).

Nonetheless, the generalisations developed by the social historians were themselves typically posed at the level of South Africa, rather than, for example, southern Africa. If, however, the popular classes sprawled across the borders of South Africa, and if their experiences, ideas and struggles were not confined by borders, then it is not clear why generalisations from social history should have been made largely at the 'national' level. Given that the popular classes in South Africa were not necessarily South African, and that South Africa was part of a regional political economy and enmeshed within a web of major transnational linkages, it is striking that a general 'history from below' of the region was not developed. While South Africa was compared to other countries or regions within countries, as noted above, it is striking that there were almost no comparative analyses of labour *within* southern Africa (for an exception, see Phimister 1977), or a social history synthesis that grappled with the fact of a *southern* African, rather South African, working class.

This was the state of play by the mid-1990s, when labour history in South Africa went into a sharp decline. Besides the international factors that affected labour history worldwide at this time, there were also local factors that came into play: the end of apartheid removed much of the oppositional political energy that fed into revisionist writing, and the lack of direction coincided with a series of critical onslaughts on revisionist approaches for failing to seriously engage with race and its meanings (Posel, Hyslop and Nieftagodien 2001), for forcing social history into a teleological history of anti-apartheid resistance (Minkley and Rassool 1998), and for remaining a largely white intellectual project (Bonner 1994; Bozzoli and Delius 1990; Worger 1991).

Finally, the post-apartheid state's project of creating a new, official, national (and nationalist) history limited the space for revisionist history. On the one hand many of the themes of revisionist history have been incorporated into this new history; on the other, the record of 'history from below' has often been forced into a monolithic narrative of a single struggle (*'the* struggle'), supposedly led throughout by the ANC (for examples of this genre, see Magubane 2004, 2006). As Martin Legassick documented in an important paper at the 2006 conference, which will be published elsewhere, this has involved heavy-handed official control of work by independent scholars that has been commissioned for the new history.

Southern Africa, Latin America and North Africa

The fortunes of labour history have changed in recent years, with a growing output of work dealing with both the pre-industrial and industrial periods in South Africa, as well as in the larger region. Some of this work has challenged the CPSA and SACP versions of the history of the left through the recovery of alternative left traditions and an examination of the social history of local Communism (Drew 2002; Hirson and Hirson 2005; Hirson with Williams 1995; Van der Walt 1999, 2004). Comparative analysis, which played a role in the older labour history (in addition to earlier citations, see Cooper 1991; Trapido 1971) has been revitalised, with more attention to other parts of the British Empire, Africa and Latin America (see Alexander and Halpern 2000, 2004; Bonner 2004; Greenstein 1998; Mamdani 1996; Marx 1998). Labour and social history have revived in other parts of southern Africa, often in response to the resurgence of labour movements in the 1990s, notably for Zambia (formerly Northern Rhodesia, Larmer 2007) and Zimbabwe (see, *inter alia,* Raftopolous and Phimister 1997; Raftopolous and Yoshikuni 1999). If the increasing isolation of South Africa from the 1940s played an important role in the somewhat parochial outlooks, it may be that the current globalisation has played a role in the widening horizons of current labour history. The implications of applying a transnational perspective to labour history in South Africa and southern Africa are considerable, and in the remaining section we will indicate several areas where such a perspective may be fruitfully applied. One area is that of labour markets, which we touched on above. The racial wage gap on South African mines is well known, and it has also been noted that as early as the 1890s wages for skilled miners in what became South Africa were generally double (and sometimes five times higher) than the wages of comparable categories in mining areas elsewhere (Katz 1994:67, 75–7).

This process has often been explained in largely South African terms, as a response to the high cost of living, the bargaining power and aspirations of the whites, and employer strategies. However, a transnational perspective suggests this is too simplistic: unlike other white dominions in the British Empire, the South African state not only did not subsidise European immigration, but actively frustrated it, and white immigration was close to a net loss by the 1920s (Bradlow 1990:178–186, 192–193). The result was that employers in South Africa had to compete with other regions through unusually high wages.

The peculiarities of South African immigration policy are, at one level, to be explained by reference to Afrikaner-English divisions amongst whites, and the anti-immigration policies of Afrikaner nationalists. At another level, however, the imperial context must be taken as central, for the South African state, alone in colonial southern Africa, had dominion status.[4] This allowed state managers to defy imperial immigration policy, and to move towards important-substitution-industrialisation (ISI) policies in the 1920s. This was thirty years before most other African countries, but closely paralleled the policy shifts in contemporary Latin America as some commentators (Cooper 1991; De Noon 1983; Seidman 1994) have noted. If, as Mamdani claimed, there were substantial parallels between British imperial systems of indirect rule and South African apartheid (Mamdani 1996), then, it would be a grave mistake to treat South Africa as simply a typical African colony; at the same time, the specificities of South Africa are nonetheless closely linked to its particular insertion within the imperial system.

The existence of a large white working class, including many 'poor whites', is also sometimes regarded as an important element of South African exceptionalism. Again, a transnational perspective raises questions about this assumption. There were substantial white working classes in Angola, Mozambique, Zambia and Zimbabwe; in Mozambique, whites were heavily concentrated in unskilled work (Capela 1981); and in Southern Rhodesia, a 'poor white problem' concerned officials in the 1920s (Morrel 1992).

Migration, regional struggles and the movement of ideas

As van der Walt's article in this collection shows, moreover, these white working classes were interconnected through migration (the opening up of mines to the north of South Africa was crucial), and that there was a spread of repertoires of

---

4 Only Southern Rhodesia, with the achievement of self-government in 1923, came close to the South African experience, and was able to make early protectionist economic policies by the 1930s (Phimister 1988; also see Bond, Miller and Ruiters 2001). Protectionist policies were adopted in Mozambique in the 1910s, but largely as a result of initiatives by Portugal itself (see Capela 1981; Penvenne 1995).

struggle and organisational models throughout the region: the segregationist South African Labour Party, launched in 1910, was, for example, only the forerunner of a series of such parties in the region that were influenced by White Labourism. This was, in turn, profoundly influenced by the White Australia policy and the segregationist policies of the Australian Labor Party, ideas that were transmitted into South Africa by immigrants (Hyslop 1999). The 1922 Rand Revolt, so ably discussed in Jeremy Krikler's recent study (2005), was, van der Walt suggests, not only part of the international labour militancy of the late 1910s and early 1920s, but also the peak of a *regional* wave of black and white workers' struggles across southern Africa that has not been previously recognised.

The growth of Chinese indentured labour on the mines in South Africa in the early twentieth century is another important dimension of these regional and international struggles over labour supplies and wage levels. Brought in by the British from 1903 to 1907, the 60,000 indentured workers were to break the post-Anglo-Boer War shortage of African labour that amounted to an informal strike. The 'Chinese question' was absolutely central to the rise of White Labourism in southern Africa in the twentieth century, which was influenced by Australia's ban on Chinese and Polynesian labour in 1900.

Interestingly, as Kally Forrest's contribution to this collection notes, an Australian connection plays an important role in the contemporary labour movement in South Africa. Her article, which draws attention to another fascinating example of the traffic of ideas and actors across borders, examines how the (predominantly African) National Union of Metalworkers of South Africa (Numsa) sought to reposition itself on the eve of the demise of apartheid in the 1990s. Frustrated with ongoing adversarial conflicts with employers, Numsa leaders sought to promote worker control of production, skills development and advancement through tripartite forums as a road to socialism. The main model that informed this approach was provided by Australian labour; Australian union personnel were drafted in to reposition the unions, in a fascinating parallel to the Australian connection of a century before.

Now, if the white working class in southern Africa had a large immigrant component, was influenced by ideas from abroad, and existed as a regional force, at what point can we start to speak of a *South African* white working class? The 1920s would seem to mark an important moment in the 'nationalisation' of white labour: not only did a national level class compromise get forged after 1922, but immigration fell sharply, white labour became increasingly stabilised in families, and the state began to move towards systematic social policy and mass education (on these developments, see Lange 2003:12, 79, 153–157). Internationally, it is also worth noting, the 1920s arguably marked the onset of a period in which working-class people and movements were increasingly nationalised elsewhere, through factors like mass schooling, national class compromises, and the increasingly closed 'national' economies that were characteristic of the period into the 1970s.

Seekings' article is interesting in this regard, as it begins to examine the relationship between class struggles and social policy. Comparisons with Latin America are notably rare in South African studies, but as Seekings shows, can be most illuminating. Argentina had a fairly similar economic structure to South Africa, and a similar path to industrialisation. However, South Africa's welfare system is rather unusual amongst semi-industrial countries, including those of Latin America, for it centres on tax-financed non-contributory grants, rather than social insurance schemes.

The potential for this divergence arose, in large part, from the character of the South African state created in 1910: it was a far more effective and bureaucratic state apparatus than its Argentinean counterpart, and able to raise public revenue more effectively. This, we might add, was the result of the imperial state engineering after 1902. However, Seekings stresses, it was the different character of labour struggles, the political landscape and the structure of the ruling group that was critical to the divergence between the two cases.

South African policy-makers, in addition, evinced a concern for managing 'poor whites' and maintaining racial order that was absent in Argentina. While the majority of the poor in Argentina were regarded as white, this was not seen as necessitating special interventions, and was not understood as a 'poor white' problem. To this we might add the point that Latin America indicates that large-scale white immigration need not translate into the development of a labour aristocracy: in late nineteenth and early twentieth centuries in Brazil, for instance, white immigrants undercut *black* wages (Andrews 1988), quite the reverse of the South African scenario.

We know, in short, surprisingly little about how state policy reshaped white working-class cultures, identities, and imaginaries in Africa in the twentieth century, and probably even less about the situation for other layers of workers. In large part this is because the assumption that labour in South Africa equals *South African* labour has prevented the question of the 'nationalisation' of labour being posed at all. When people speak of the South African labour movement as a self-evident category, they do not always recognise that the first truly countrywide union federations in South Africa only emerged by the early 1950s, with the South African Trades and Labour Council and the South African Congress of Trade Unions.[5]

---

5 While the South African Industrial Federation was formed in 1914, the Cape Federation of Labour remained outside the fold of this federation and its successors for nearly forty years. Neither

Related to this, it is also worthy emphasising that very little is known about the role of working-class reading cultures and publics in the period of the first globalisation, or in the period of de-globalisation that followed. Print media may, Sakar suggests, have played a relatively limited role in working-class movements in South Africa, as compared to India, with its early development of a mass popular press. The rise (and fall) of the working-class press in South Africa (and southern Africa) is, however, an issue that has only recently begun to be explored (Visser 2004), and there are enormous gaps in our understanding. The Indian case suggests important contrasts, which could be fruitfully explored.

Comparisons between southern Africa and Latin America seem, then, a fruitful avenue for further research, and North Africa also seems eminently suitable for such comparisons. Algeria, a settler colony with the second largest white population in Africa, has only rarely been compared to South Africa. Drew's paper is quite ground-breaking in examining the different trajectories of Algerian and South African Communism. Drew steers a path that avoids the simple dichotomy of domination by, or autonomy from, Moscow, and stresses the importance of the timing of the implementation of sectarian New Line policies in the late 1920s in each country, the different ways in which the policies were understood and implemented, and the way in which the local context conditioned the ability of communists to organise in the rural areas. Such comparisons could be extended to other periods of left and labour history: like South Africa (van der Walt, 1999; 2004), African countries like Egypt had significant anarchist and syndicalist influences before the 1920s (see Gorman 2005; Khuri-Makdisi 2003).

Drew's paper highlights the importance of examining the interaction between global and local factors in the shaping of political traditions, and underlines the importance of a more transnational understanding of traditions like Communism. We noted above, for example, that SACP writers have stressed the autonomy and initiative of the party with regard to the Native Republic thesis, which was adopted along with the New Line. Clearly, this approach is too simplistic: the Native Republic thesis was the South African variant of the two-stage policy implemented by the Comintern throughout what was called the 'colonial and semi-colonial world', and it is exceedingly unlikely that the Comintern's global policies were decisively shaped by the views of a section of the small CPSA. On the other hand, the Native Republic thesis was amenable to many interpretations: in the 1940s, for instance, party journals like *Vryheid-Freedom* debated whether the policy really entailed two stages at all, or, if so, whether Afrikaner national-

---

the Federation of Non-European Trade Unions, formed in 1927, nor later bodies like the Council of Non-European Trade Unions were countrywide ('national') federations.

ism was a possible ally for the first stage, or whether the CPSA should lead both stages.

Local context clearly played an important role, and it is perhaps not accidental that the Native Republic was reformulated as Colonialism of a Special Type (CST) in the 1950s. While the Native Republic thesis stressed the struggle against British imperialism, CST described 'black South Africa' as the 'internal colony' of 'white South Africa', which effectively removed the British Empire from the agenda. The two-stage approach was maintained, in other words, but the antiimperialist element of the policy was transposed from the empire to South Africa. This shift took place in the 1950s, at the height of de-globalisation, the collapse of the empire, with a white republic on the horizon, the Comintern dissolved and the white working class (and perhaps the African working class as well?) increasingly nationalised.

It is by placing the question of empire centre-stage, as part of a larger transnational focus that we are alerted to such shifts, shifts that are often hidden by a more narrowly 'national' focus on South Africa. This allows us to rethink the way in which the social and ideological worlds of labour evolve and change, but never entirely as an endogenous 'national' process.

The migration of white labour northwards from South Africa was paralleled by the migration of coloured workers from South Africa into Namibia (formerly South West Africa), Swaziland and Zimbabwe, as well as by the migration of African workers across the region. The movement of Africans across the region, with roots going back to the pre-industrial period, has been examined by various authors (for example, Harries 1994; Katzenellenbogen 1982; Van Onselen 1976; Vellut 1983; Yudelman and Jeeves 1986).

Nonetheless, this work has often been structured by the image of 'South Africa's labour empire' (Crush, Jeeves and Yudelman 1991). This has the merit of highlighting South Africa's predominance in the migrant labour system, but carries the danger of suggesting a narrow focus on South Africa, and of seeing migrant labour as a specifically South African device, part of a 'distinctive cheap labour system' (Alexander and Halpern 2004:10).

A more transnational perspective suggests important qualifications to such approaches, and the need to examine the eminently transnational process of African migrancy on a larger scale than the vantage point provided by a particular state. Structuralist accounts have portrayed the African migrant labour system as engineered from above, and as characterised by systematic labour control and coercion. However, a striking feature of the regional political economy was precisely the disjuncture between labour markets and states, and the absence of any single organisation that could control regional labour flows. The different colonial states competed with one another for labour, as did employers in different sectors, and in different regions within countries.

It was partly in response to this situation that corporations established supranational labour recruitment bodies, notably the South African-based Native Recruitment Corporation (NRC) and Witwatersrand Native Labour Association (WNLA). These, too, however, did not have a truly regional control. The NRC and WNLA were quickly emulated by rival capitalists across the region, who formed competing bodies on the South African model: the Rhodesian Native Labour Board (RNLB) was consciously modelled on the NRC and WNLA (Van Onselen 1979:93), and the same seems true of the South West African Native Labour Association (SWANLA) (Moorson 1978).

If mining in Kimberley was the template for labour controls on the Witwatersrand, then the Witwatersrand was in turn the template for labour controls throughout southern Africa. By examining the regional labour system from the vantage point of South Africa, and by viewing 'racial capitalism' as a monolithic top-down process, scholars have sometimes ignored the rather disorganised character of African labour recruitment that a regional perspective reveals, as well as the fact that 'racial capitalism' was less distinctively South African than characteristic of *southern* Africa as a whole.

Now, precisely because there was no general regional mechanism to direct flows of African labour, African workers were able to navigate competing claims on their labour power in search of the best jobs across the region. Charles van Onselen (1976, 1979) memorably examined this process in Zimbabwe, and far more needs to be known about it in other contexts, as well as the way it played out at a regional level at different times. A narrow focus on South Africa as a distinctively low wage capitalist economy ignores the point that, in the regional context, the Witwatersrand mines provided, on the contrary, the best paid jobs (Van Onselen 1979), and, in addition, fails to recognise that racial wage gaps on the mines were highest, not in South Africa, but Zambia (see Meebelo 1986).

The regional dimensions of the labour market and migrant labour system are not fully understood, and far more needs to be known about the role and significance of migration *outside* of official channels like the NRC, WNLA, RNLB and SWANLA, as well as migration outside of mining, like rural-to-rural circular migration. The labour history of agriculture is not well developed in southern Africa, particularly outside of South Africa, and Wazha Morapedi's contribution to this collection is to be welcomed. Morapedi examines farm labour in Botswana (formerly Bechuanaland) on predominantly white-owned commercial farms, and develops a comparison with farm labour in South Africa. His analysis examines the significance of different labour markets within the country, of competition with South African mines, the use of migrant labour, the role of ethnicity in the labour process, interaction of 'the worst sort of white South African farm exploitation' with 'indigenous Botswana ethnic discrimination'.

Cross-border migration, by its very nature, is not easily studied on a country-by-country basis, while close attention to varying wage zones *within* as well as *between* countries cautions against assuming that the different colonies were internally homogenous in terms of levels of economic development or state capacity. The boundaries of the colonial states were not only often quite arbitrary, but the borders were often very porous and commonly ignored, evaded or transgressed by Africans.

We have repeatedly used the term 'transnational', which still suggests the centrality of the 'national', but the extreme variations within different countries in southern Africa must also be noted. Given the fractured legal systems involved in indirect rule and apartheid (Mamdani 1996), and uneven economic development within countries, it may be worth thinking of the significance of internal labour migration across *internal* 'borders' within countries: the experience of migration from the Eastern Cape reserves to Johannesburg could, arguably, be as significant as that of migration from Gaza in Mozambique.

It was noted earlier that white labour migration into South Africa was important to the transmission of union traditions, White Labourism, anarchism and syndicalism; it could be added that immigrants were also central to the communist parties of South Africa in the 1920s and 1930s (Drew 2002) and Southern Rhodesia in the 1940s (Lessing 1995). Southern Africa's integration into regional and international labour markets enabled a constant circulation of ideas and linkages into ideas circulating in labour and left circles worldwide in the period of the first globalisation. At the same time, the regional labour market was fractured and racialised, and different ethnic groups laid claim to particular occupations, which partly accounts for what van der Walt describes as the tendency of ideas, organisational models and repertoires of struggles to flow along ethnic and racial conduits (although radical and internationalist left traditions could burst out of these channels).

Colonisation and capitalism in Africa created new transnational connections, and international diasporas and networks of various types. George Gona's article in this collection explores examples of both in colonial East Africa, and draws the lessons of an older history of regional unionism for current labour movement strategies. He shows that the labour movement in the region assumed a regional character from the 1920s to the 1950s, and that migrants and travelling organisers played an important role in linking workers' movements in the different colonies. The East African Trade Union Congress (EATUC) formed in Kenya in 1949 organised a wide variety of occupations, and, strikingly, set out to organise labour in Uganda and Tanzania (formerly Tanganyika) as well. The ethos of this union tradition was anti-colonialist but internationalist, and Indian workers – a significant component of the East African labour force – played a prominent role, most notably the self-declared communist Makhan Singh.

African migrant labour and migrant networks also played a critical role in the spread of subversive and transformative ideas over a vast area. Religion provides one example. In 1903, for example, a labour migrant from Malawi (formerly Nyasaland) called Elliot Kamwana was introduced to Jehovah Witness (Watch Tower) doctrines while working in Cape Town. From 1906 Kamwana preached an apocalyptic Watch Tower doctrine in Malawi, recruiting thousands. Kamwana was later exiled, but Watch Tower spread, largely through migrant networks, into the mining compounds of Zimbabwe, and subsequently into Zambia and the Republic of the Congo (formerly the Belgian Congo) (McCracken 2000; Phimister 1988; Ranger 1970; Raftopoulous and Phimister 1997).

It is difficult to believe that Watch Tower did not get entangled with that other important labour current in southern Africa, and in which Malawian networks also played a central role: the Industrial and Commercial Workers' Union of Africa, or ICU. Van der Walt notes that the ICU, itself influenced by currents brought from abroad like Garveyism and syndicalism, was in many ways a transnational movement operating across southern Africa, paralleling in some ways the EATUC in East Africa. Certainly, shifts and cross fertilisation between religious and trade union dispositions have been common ever since throughout southern Africa, with the role of a church background, for instance, in the development of skills in oratory and organising an issue that merits closer examination.

The overlap between religious traditions and labour organising is an area that remains largely unexplored, and an examination of the spread across borders of popular religious traditions, amongst workers of all races, provides an excellent way in which to explore the transnational formations and connections of working classes. The social history of unions and parties, more generally, is not well developed in southern Africa, topics where 'old labour history', focused on organisations, policies and leaders, has tended to predominate. The interaction between labour and left currents in South Africa and elsewhere was complicated and interactive, and the balance of influence of transnational, 'national' and other factors varied over time. Not only was the official imperial ideology of empire (which is often not taken seriously enough) appropriated and reworked by subject peoples (Ranger 1983), but so, too, were international labour and left traditions.

Conclusion

This introduction has argued for a labour history that takes regional and transnational processes seriously, and for situating South Africa in southern Africa, and southern Africa in the larger world. In eschewing what Van der Linden calls 'methodological nationalism', and thinking about a *southern* African, rather than a South African, working class (Bond, Miller and Ruiters 2001), and in noting that working classes and working-class movements are not forged in autonomous 'national' contexts, we emphasised connections and comparisons. While our discussion has raised questions about 'cheap labour', migrancy and their relationship to social imaginations, we have left the question of the conceptual vocabulary of labour studies open. This article is a contribution to opening transnational labour history, not its conclusion.

References

Abu Lughod, J. 1989. Before European Hegemony: The World System A.D. 1250–1350. New York: Oxford University Press.
Adas, M. 1998. "Bringing Ideas and Agency Back In: Representation and the Comparative Approach to World History", in Pomper *et al.*
Alexander, P. 2006. 'Harold and History'. Keynote address delivered at the Harold Wolpe Memorial Trust's Tenth Anniversary Colloquium, 'Engaging Silences and Unresolved Issues in the Political Economy of South Africa', 21–23 September, Cape Town, South Africa.
Alexander. P. and Halpern, R. (eds). 2000. *Racialising Class, Classifying Race: Labour and Difference in Britain, the USA, and Africa*. New York: St. Martin's Press, in association with St. Antony's College, Oxford.
Alexander, P. and Halpern, R. (eds). 2004. 'Introduction: Comparing Race and Labour in South Africa and the United States'. Journal of Southern African Studies 30(1).
Anderson, Benedict. 1991. Imagined Communities: Reflections on the Origin and Spread of Nationalism. London: Verso.
Anderson, Benedict. 2005. Under Three Flags: Anarchism and the Anti-Colonial Imagination. London: Verso.
Anderson, P. 1974. Lineages of the Absolutist State. London: NLB.
Andrews, G.R. 1988. 'Black and White Workers: São Paulo, Brazil, 1888–1928'. *Hispanic American Historical Review* 68(3).
Andrews, W.H. 1941. Class Struggles in South Africa: Two Lectures Given on South African Trade Unionism by W.H. Andrews before the People's College, Cape Town, on October 7th and 14th, 1940, with foreword by E.S. Sachs, General Secretary, Garment Workers Union. Cape Town: Stewart Printing.
Bayly, C.A. 2004. The Birth of the Modern World 1780–1914. Oxford: Blackwell.
Bekken, J. 1995. 'The First Daily Anarchist Newspaper: The *Chicagoer ArbeiterZeitung*'. *Anarchist Studies* 3.

Bond, P., Miller, D. and Ruiters, G. 2001. 'The Production, Reproduction and Politics of the Southern African Working Class: Regional Class Struggle During Sustained Economic Crisis', in L. Panitch (ed), *Socialist Register 2001*. London: Merlin Press.

Bonner, P. 1994. 'New Nation, New History: The History Workshop in South Africa, 1977–1994'. *The Journal of American History* 18(3).

Bonner, P. 2004. 'Migration, Urbanisation and Urban Social Movements in Twentieth Century India and South Africa'. *Studies in History* 20(2).

Bonner, P., Delius, P. and Posel, D. (eds). 1993. *Apartheid's Genesis, 1935–1962*. Johannesburg: Ravan, Witwatersrand University Press.

Bonner, P., Hofmeyer, I. and James, D. (eds). 1989. *Holding their Ground: Class, Locality and Culture in 19th and 20th Century South Africa*. Johannesburg: Witwatersrand University Press.

Bozzoli, B. (ed). 1979. Labour, Townships and Protest: Studies in the Social History of the Witwatersrand. Johannesburg: Ravan.

Bozzoli, B. (ed). 1983. Town and Countryside in the Transvaal: Capitalist Penetration and Popular *Response*. Johannesburg: Ravan.

Bozzoli, B. (ed). 1987. Class, Community, and Conflict: South African Perspectives. Johannesburg: Ravan.

Bozzoli, B. and Delius, P. 1990. 'Radical History and South African Society'. *Radical History Review* 46/47.

Bradlow, E. 1990. 'Empire Settlement and South African Immigration Policy, 1910–1948', in S. Constantine (ed), *Emigrants and Empire: British Settlement in the Dominions between the Wars*. Manchester, New York: Manchester University Press.

Brenner, R. 1977. 'The Origins of Capitalist Development: A Critique of Neo-Smithian Marxism'. *New Left Review* 104.

Braudel, F. 1972–1973. The Mediterranean and the Mediterranean World in the Age of Philip II. London: Collins (2 volumes).

Braudel, F. 1982. Civilization and Capitalism: 15th–18th Century. London: Collins (3 volumes).

Bundy, C. 1979. The Rise and Fall of the South African Peasantry. London: Heinemann.

Bunting, B. 1975. Moses Kotane: South African Revolutionary. London: Inkululeko.

Bunting, B. [1944] 1993. 'Introduction', in Roux.

Capela, J. 1981. O Movimento Operário em Lourenço Marques, 1898–1927. Porto: Edic es Afrontamento.

Cell, J.W. 1982. The Highest Stage of White Supremacy: The Origins of Segregation and the American South. Cambridge: Cambridge University Press.

Cooper, D. 1991. 'Locating South Africa in the Third World: Comparative Perspectives on Patterns of Industrialisation and Political Trade Unionism in South America'. *Social Dynamics* 17(2).

Cope, R.K. c. 1943. Comrade Bill: The Life and Times of W.H. Andrews, Workers' Leader. Cape Town: Stewart Printing.

Crush, J.S., Jeeves, A. and Yudelman, D. 1991. South Africa's Labour Empire: A History of Black Migrancy to the Gold Mines. Cape Town: David Philip.

De Noon, D. 1983. Settler Capitalism: The Dynamics of Dependent Development in the Southern Hemisphere. New York: Oxford University Press.

Davies, R., Kaplan, D., Morris, M. and O'Meara, D. 1976. 'Class Struggle and the Periodisation of the State in South Africa'. *Review of African Political Economy* 3(7).

Beinart, W., Delius, P. and Trapido, S. (eds). 1986. Putting a Plough to the Ground: Accumulation and Dispossession in Rural South Africa, 1850–1930. Johannesburg: Ravan.
Dening, G. 1992. Mr Bligh's Bad Language: Passion, Power and Theatre on H.M. Armed Vessel Bounty. Cambridge: Cambridge University Press.
Drew, A. 1997. 'Writing South African Communist History'. *Science and Society* 61(1).
Drew, A. 2002. Discordant Comrades: Identities and Loyalties on the South African Left. Pretoria: University of South Africa Press.
Dunkerley, J. 2000. Americana: The Americas in the World, Around 1850 (Or 'Seeing the Elephant' as the Theme for an Imaginary Western). London: Verso.
Eley, G. 2002. Forging Democracy: The History of the Left in Europe, 1850–2000. New York: Oxford University Press.
Ewald, J.J. 2000. 'Crossers of the Sea: Slaves, Freedmen and Other Migrants in the Indian Ocean c.1750–1914'. *American Historical Review* 105(1).
Ferguson, J. 2006. Global Shadows: Africa in the Neoliberal World Order. Durham: Duke.
Forman, L. [1959] 1992. 'Chapters in the History of the March for Freedom', in S. Forman and A. Odendaal (eds), *Lionel Forman: A Trumpet from the Rooftops*. London: Zed Books.
Gellner, E. 1983. *Nations and Nationalism*. Oxford: Blackwell.
Gitsham, E. and Trembath, J.F. 1926. *A First Account of Labour Organisation in South Africa*. Durban: EP and Commercial Printing Co.
Gorman, A. 2005. 'Anarchists in Education: The Free Popular University in Egypt (1901)'. *Middle Eastern Studies* 41(3).
Gray, J. 1998. False Dawn: The Delusions of Global Capitalism. London: Granta.
Greenberg, S.B. 1980. Race and State in Capitalist Development: South Africa in Comparative Perspective. Johannesburg: Ravan.
Greenstein, R. (ed). 1998. *Comparative Perspectives on South Africa*. London, Macmillan.
Gutkind, C.W.P., Cohen, R. and Copans, J. (eds). *African Labor History*. Beverly Hills: Sage.
Gutman, H. 1976. Work, Culture and Society in Industrializing America: Essays in American Working Class and Social History. Oxford: Blackwell.
Harries, P. 1994. Work, Culture and Identity: Migrant Labourers in Mozambique and South Africa c. 1860–1910. Johannesburg: Witwatersrand University Press.
Harrison, W.H. n.d. *Memoirs of a Socialist in South Africa 1903–47*. Cape Town: Stewart Printing.
Harvey, D. 1991. The Condition of Postmodernity: An Enquiry into the Origins of Cultural Change. Oxford: Blackwell.
Hirson, B. 1989. Yours for the Union: Class and Community Struggles in South Africa, 1930–1947. London: Zed Books.
Hirson, B. and Hirson, Y. 2005. *History of the Left in South Africa: Writings of Baruch Hirson*. New York: International Library of African Studies, I.B. Tauris.
Hirson, B., with Williams, G.A. 1995. *The Delegate for Africa: David Ivon Jones, 1883–1924*. London: Core Publications.
Hobsbawm, E.J. 1977a. *The Age of Revolution: 1789–1848*. London: Sphere.
Hobsbawm, E.J. 1977b. The Age of Capital: 1848–1875. London: Sphere.
Hobsbawm, E.J. 1987. *The Age of Empire: 1875–1914*. London: Wedenfeld and Nicholson.

Hobsbawm, E.J. 1990. Nations and Nationalism since 1780: Programme, Myth, Reality. Cambridge: Cambridge University Press.
Hopkins A.G. (ed). 2002. *Globalization in World History*. London: Pimlico.

Horrell, M. 1969. *South Africa's Workers*. Johannesburg: South African Institute of Race Relations.
Huntington, S.P. 1996. The Clash of Civilizations and the Remaking of World Order. New York: Simon and Schuster.
Hyslop, J. 1999. 'The Imperial Working Class Makes Itself "White": White Labourism in Britain, Australia and South Africa before the First World War'. *Journal of Historical Sociology* 14.
Isserman, M. 1982. Which Side Were You On? The American Communist Party during the Second World War. Middletown: Wesleyan University Press.
Johnstone, F.A. 1970. 'White Prosperity and White Supremacy in South Africa Today'. *African Affairs* 69.
Joyce, P. 1994. Democratic Subjects: The Self and the Social in Nineteenth Century England. Cambridge: Cambridge University Press.
Katz, E. 1994. The White Death: Silicosis on the Witwatersrand Gold Mines, 1886–1910. Johannesburg: Witwatersrand University Press.
Katzenellenbogen, S.E. 1982. South Africa and Southern Mozambique: Labour, Railways and Trade in the Making of a Relationship. Manchester, New York: Manchester University Press.
Khuri-Makdisi, I. 2003. 'Levantine Trajectories: The Formulation and Dissemination of Radical Ideas in and between Beirut, Cairo and Alexandria, 1860–1914'. PhD thesis, Harvard.
Klehr, H., Haynes, J.E. and Firsov, F.I. 1995. *The Secret World of American Communism*. New Haven: Yale University Press.
Krikler, J. 2005, Rand Revolt: The 1922 Insurrection and Racial Killings in South Africa. Cape Town: Jonathan Ball.
Laclau, E. 1982. Politics and Ideology in Marxist Theory. London: Verso.
Lange, L. 2003. White, Poor and Angry: White Working Class Families in Johannesburg. Aldershot, Hampshire and Burlington, VT: Ashgate.
Larmer, M. 2007. Mineworkers in Zambia: Labour and Political Change in Post-Colonial Africa. Palgrave Macmillan.
Legassick, M. 1974. "South Africa: Capital Accumulation and Violence". *Economy and Society* 3.
Legassick, M. 1977. 'Gold, Agriculture and Secondary Industry in South Africa, 1885–1970', in Palmer and Parsons (eds).
Lerumo, A. 1971. Fifty Fighting Years: The Communist Party of South Africa 1921–71. London: Inkululeko.
Lessing, D. 1995. Under my Skin: Volume One of my Autobiography, to 1949. London: Harper Collins.
Lewis, J. 1984. Industrialisation and Trade Union Organisation in South Africa, 192455: The Rise and Fall of the South African Trades and Labour Council. Cambridge: Cambridge University Press.
Leys, C. 1996. The Rise and Fall of Development Theory. London: J. Currey.
Linebaugh. P. and Rediker, M. 2000. The Many-Headed Hydra: Sailors, Slaves, Commoners, and the Hidden History of the Revolutionary Atlantic. Boston: Beacon Press.
Lodge, T. 1990. 'Charters from the Past? The African National Congress and its Historiographical Traditions'. *Radical History Review* 46/47.
Magubane, B. (ed). 2004, 2006. *The Road to Democracy in South Africa*. Cape Town: Zebra Press, for the South African Democracy Education Trust (2 volumes).
Majeke, N. 1952. *The Role of the Missionaries in Conquest*. Johannesburg: Society of Young Africa.

Mamdani, M. 1996. Citizen and Subject: Contemporary Africa and the Legacy of Late Colonialism. Kampala: Fountain.
Mamdani, M. 1998. 'Is African Studies to be Turned into a New Home for Bantu Education at UCT?' http://www.hartford-hwp.com/archives/30/136.html
Markovits, C. 2004. The unGandhian Gandhi: The Life and Afterlife of the Mahatma. London: Anthem Press.
Marx, A. 1998. Making Race and Nation: A Comparison of the United States, South Africa, and Brazil. Cambridge: Cambridge University Press.
Marks, S. and Rathbone, R. (eds). 1982. Industrialisation and Social Change in South Africa: African Class Formation, Culture and Consciousness, 1870–1930. Harlow: Longman.
Marks, S. and Trapido, S. (eds). 1987. The Politics of Race, Class and Nationalism in Twentieth Century South Africa. London: Longman.
McCracken, J. 2000. *Politics and Christianity in Malawi, 1875–1940: The Impact of the Livingstonia Mission in the Northern Province.* Blantyre: Christian Literature Association in Malawi.
McNeill, W.H. 1977. *Plagues and Peoples.* London: Blackwell.
McNeil, W.H. 1983. The Pursuit of Power: Technology, Armed Force and Society since A.D. 1000. Oxford: Blackwell.
Meebelo, H.S. 1986. African Proletarians and Colonial Capitalism: The Origins, Growth and Struggles of the Zambian Labour Movement to 1964. Lusaka: Kenneth Kaunda Foundation.
Meli, F. 1988. *South Africa Belongs to Us: A History of the ANC.* Zimbabwe: Zimbabwe Publishing House.
Metcalf, T.R. 2007. Imperial Connections: India in the Indian Ocean Arena 1860–1920. Berkeley: University of California Press.
Minkley, G. and Rassool, C. 1998. 'Orality, Memory and Social History in South Africa', in S. Nuttall and C. Coetzee (eds), *Negotiating the Past: The Making of Memory in South Africa.* Cape Town: Oxford University Press.
Mnguni (Jaffe, H.) 1952. Three Hundred Years: A History of South Africa. Cumberwood: APdUSA.
Moore, B. Jr. 1987. Social Origins of Dictatorship and Democracy: Lord and Peasant in the Modern World. Harmondsworth: Penguin.
Moorson, R.J.B. 1978. 'Migrant Labourers and Formation of SWANLA, 1900–1926'. *South African Labour Bulletin* 4(1/2).
Morrel, R. (ed). 1992. White but Poor: Essays on the History of Poor Whites in Southern Africa 1880–1940. Pretoria: University of South Africa.
Morris, M. 1987. 'Social History and the Transition to Capitalism in the South African Countryside'. *Africa Perspective* (new series) 1(5/6).
Murray, M.J. 1989. 'Origins of Agrarian Capitalism in South Africa: A Critique of the "Social History" Perspective'. *Journal of Southern African Studies* 15(4).
Nasson, B. 1990. 'The Unity Movement: Its Legacy in Historical Consciousness'. *Radical History Review* 46/47.
Northrup, D. 1995. *Indentured Labour in the Age of Imperialism 1834–1922.* Cambridge: Cambridge University Press.
Palmer, R. and Parsons, N. (eds). 1977. *The Roots of Rural Poverty in Central and Southern Africa.* London: Heinemann.
Penvenne, J.M. 1984. 'Labour Struggles at the Port of Lourenço Marques, 1900–1933'. Review: Journal of the Fernand Braudel Centre for the Study of Economies, Historical Systems and Civilizations 8(2).

Penvenne, J.M. 1995. African Workers and Colonial Racism: Mozambican Strategies and Struggles *in Lourenço-Marques, 1877–1962*. Johannesburg: Witwatersrand University Press.

Phimister, I. 1977. 'White Miners in Historical Perspective: Southern Rhodesia, 1890–1953'. *Journal of Southern African Studies* 3(2).

Phimister, I. 1988. An Economic and Social History of Zimbabwe, 1890–1948: Capital Accumulation and Class Struggle. London: Longman.

Phimister, I. and Van Onselen, C. (eds). 1979. *Studies in the History of African Mine Labour in Colonial Zimbabwe*. Gwelo: Mambo Press.

Polanyi, K. 1991. The Great Transformation: Political and Economic Origins of our Time. Boston: Beacon.

Pomper, P., Elphick, R. and Vann, R.T. (eds). 1998. *World History: Ideologies, Structures and Identities*. Oxford: Blackwell.

Posel, D., Hyslop, J. and Nieftagodien, N. 2001. 'Debating "Race" in South African Scholarship'. *Transformation* 47.

Raftopoulous, B. and Phimister, I. (eds). 1997. *Keep on Knocking: A History of the Labour Movement in Zimbabwe, 1900–97*. Harare: Baobab Books, for the Zimbabwe Congress of Trade Unions and the Friedrich Ebert Stiftung.

Raftopolous, B. and Yoshikuni, T. (eds). 1999. *Sites of Struggle: Essays in Zimbabwe's Urban History*. Harare: Weaver Press.

Ranger, T.O. 1970. The African Voice in Southern Rhodesia, 1898–1930. London, Ibadan.

Ranger, T.O. 1983. 'The Invention of Tradition in Colonial Africa', in E.J. Hobsbawm and T.O. Ranger (eds), *The Invention of Tradition*. Cambridge: Cambridge University Press.

Roux, E. [1944] 1993. *S.P. Bunting: A Political Biography*. Bellville: Mayibuye Books, University of the Western Cape.

Roy, O. 2006. *Globalised Islam: The Search for a New Umma*. New York: Columbia University Press.

Saunders, C. 1988. The Making of the South African Past: Major Historians on Race and Class. Cape Town, Johannesburg: David Philips.

Scott, J.W. 1988. *Gender and the Politics of History*. New York: Columbia University Press.

Seidman, G. 1994. Manufacturing Militancy: Worker's Movements in Brazil and South Africa, 1970–1985. Berkeley: University of California Press.

Simons, J. and Simons, R. [1969] 1983. *Class and Colour in South Africa, 1850–1950*. London: International Defence and Aid Fund.

Spengler, O. 1926, 1928. *The Decline of the West*. New York: Alfred A. Knopf (2 volumes).

Stedman-Jones, G. 1983. Languages of Class: Studies in English Working Class History 1832–1892. Cambridge: Cambridge University Press.

Stoler, A.L. and Cooper, F. (eds). 1997. *Tensions of Empire: Colonial Cultures in a Bourgeois World*. Berkeley: University of California Press.

Tabata, I.B. 1950. *The Awakening of a People*. London: Spokesman Books (revised edition).

Thompson, E.P. 1991. The Making of the English Working Class. London: Penguin.

Tinker, Hugh. 1974. *A New System of Slavery*. Oxford: Oxford University Press.

Torpey, J. 2000. The Invention of the Passport: Surveillance, Citizenship and the State. Cambridge: Cambridge University Press.

Toynbee, A. 1960. *A Study of History: Abridgement of Volume I–X in One Volume*. Edited by D.C. Somervell. Oxford University Press.

Trapido, S. 1971. 'South Africa in a Comparative Study of Industrialisation'. *The Journal of Development Studies* 7(3).
Van Onselen, C. 1976. Chibaro: African Mine Labour in Southern Rhodesia. Johannesburg: Ravan.
Van der Walt, L. 1999. '"The Industrial Union is the Embryo of the Socialist Commonwealth": The International Socialist League and Revolutionary Syndicalism in South Africa, 1915–1920'. *Comparative Studies of South Asia, Africa and the Middle East* 19(1).
Van der Walt, L. 2004. 'Bakunin's Heirs in South Africa: Race and Revolutionary Syndicalism from the IWW to the International Socialist League, 1910–21'. *Politikon* 31(1).
Van der Walt, L. 1979. 'Black Workers in Central African Historiography: A Critical Essay on the Historiography and Sociology of Rhodesia', in Phimister and Van Onselen (eds).
Van der Walt, L. 1982a. Studies in the Social and Economic History of the Witwatersrand, 1886–1914, Volume One, New Babylon. Johannesburg: Ravan.
Van der Walt, L. 1982b. Studies in the Social and Economic History of the Witwatersrand, 1886–1914, Volume Two, New Nineveh. Johannesburg: Ravan.
Vellut, J. 1983. 'Mining in the Belgian Congo', in D. Birmingham and P.M. Martin (eds), *History of Central Africa, Volume Two*. London, New York: Longman.
Visser, W. 2004. '"To Fight the Battles of the Workers": The Emergence of Pro-Strike Publications in Early Twentieth-Century South Africa'. *International Review of Social History* 49(3).
Wallerstein, I. 1974. The Modern World System: Capitalist Agriculture and the Origins of the European World-Economy in the Sixteenth Century. New York: Academic Press.
Warren, B. 1980. Imperialism: Pioneer of Capitalism. London: Verso.
Walker, I.L. and Weinbren, B. 1961. 2,000 Casualties: A History of the Trade Unions and the Labour Movement in the History of South Africa. Johannesburg: South African Trade Union Council.
Wolpe, H. 1972. 'Capitalism and Cheap Labour-Power in South Africa'. *Economy and Society* 1(4).
Worger, W. 1991. 'White Radical History in South Africa'. *South African Historical Journal* 24.
Yudelman, D. and Jeeves, A. 1986. 'New Labour Frontiers for Old: Black Migrants to the South African Gold Mines, 1920–85'. *Journal of Southern African Studies* 13(1).

Varieties of Work

G. Balachandran
Workers in the World

Indian Seafarers, c. 1870s–1940s[1]

If the employment of foreign-domiciled seafarers in international shipping is any indication, the global off-shoring of employment is almost as old (or new) as the modern world economy. With its vessels preponderant in world shipping, this phenomenon was particularly marked in British shipping. After 1850, when Britain repealed navigation laws restricting their employment, there was a steady rise in the proportion of foreign nationals working on British ships to over 20 % by 1891 and nearly one-third by 1904.[2] Crews of British ships now comprised every conceivable nationality: American, Swede, Norwegian, Russian, Danish, Dutch, Belgian, French, German, Austrian, Italian, Greek, Spaniard, Turk, Portuguese, Indian, Maldivian, Malay, Sinhala, Chinese, Arab, Somali, Maltese and Cypriot, Kru men from West Africa, and men from the Caribbean islands. Britannia may have ruled the waves. But the workers of the world rode them for her.

From the 1870s a growing number of Indian seafarers went to work on foreign vessels, the large majority (over two-thirds) on British ships. In 1886 there were reportedly 16,600 'lascars' on British vessels.[3] By 1891 there were 24,000 Indian seafarers on British ships (10 % of the workforce), and by 1914 52,000 (20 %).[4] The slump in world trade and British shipping drove numbers down. Yet in 1937 44,000 sub-continental seafarers made up a third of Britain's maritime workforce. During the war this number rose to over 60,000 (about 40 %).[5]

These figures exclude Indian seafarers who were ashore between engagements, and crews of other foreign-owned vessels such as those of the German Hansa line. Before 1914 the Hansa line was Bombay's second largest maritime

---

[1] This article was first published in French under the title "Les marins indiens et leurs univers, 1870–1949 in *La Découverte* 2012/4, pp. 65–84 © 2012 Éditions La Découverte, www.editionsladecouverte.fr
[2] Conrad Dixon, 'Lascars: The Forgotten Seamen', in Rosemary Ommer and Gerald Panting (eds), *The Working Men Who Got Wet*, St Johns', Newfoundland, 1980, p. 281; Ronald Hope, *A New History of British Shipping*, London, 1990, pp. 383, 392.
[3] UK National Archives (hereafter PRO), MT 9/506, note 16 Feb. 1894.
[4] Dixon, 'Lascars', p. 281; Hope, *New History*, pp. 383, 392; V.C. Burton, 'Counting Seafarers: The Published Records of the Registry of Merchant Seamen', *Mariner's Mirror* (71: 3, 1985) p. 318.
[5] *Daily Herald*, 24 May 1939; British Library, Oriental and India Office Collections (OIOC), L/E/R/300, 'Lascar seafarers', undated wartime memorandum; OIOC, Hope, *New History*, pp. 383, 392.

employer after the Peninsular & Oriental Steam Navigation Company (or P&O). The Austrian Lloyds were another large employer, as were American cargo liners and American and Scandinavian tramps in the Asian trade. During World War II Australian and Dutch vessels also employed hundreds of Indian seamen.

In all there were said to be some 235,000 Indian seafarers at its major ports. However this figure excluded crews of the innumerable small, sailing and steam-powered vessels that bustled around the dozens of smaller ports along the Indian coast and the waters abutting them, carrying people and cargoes to ports in the Indian Ocean region, China, West Africa, or even to Pacific islands such as Fiji.[6] Besides Indian merchants, these vessels were owned by Arab and other Asian merchants based in the ports of the Indian Ocean littoral; so that there was, in addition to the maritime labour market catering to large, Western-owned steam, and later oil-fired ships, another continent-wide market catering to indigenous and indigenously-owned seagoing craft and vessels.

Indian seafarers who sailed the Western world's merchant shipping fleets were mostly engaged in Bombay or Calcutta. Arriving here from their mainly village homes, they ended one journey in preparation for the next. Down, round, and up India's peninsular coast from Calcutta, or directly into the Arabian Sea from Bombay, up the Red Sea through the Suez Canal into the Mediterranean, they headed east and north towards Brindisi and Trieste, or bore west and north to Marseilles whence, after depositing the wealthier passengers and express mails for transfer to the faster 'boat train', they rounded Gibraltar to navigate the rough seas of the Bay of Biscay en route to northerly European ports. From there, or directly across the Atlantic from Gibraltar, they sailed further west to ports along the US east coast, sometimes then heading south to Brazil and the River Plate, or after its opening, westwards through the Panama Canal to ports on the US west coast.

Less frequented routes took them directly southwards from Bombay and Calcutta towards the African coast, rounding the Cape into western Africa or towards South America. They might sail rather more regularly to Colombo and Singapore; then further south to Australia or Fiji; or north from Singapore towards Hong Kong and Shanghai and further north to Japan. From the 1920s Indian crews also spent the summer working in the emerging North European pleasure cruise industry and on British tramps to Russia.

---

6 A.C. Staples, 'Indian Maritime Transport in 1840', *Indian Economic and Social History Review* (6: 1, 1970) pp. 61–90; Douglas McLean, 'Maritime Trucking: India's Coastal Sailing Shipping on the Eve of the Great War', South Asia Research Unit, Curtin University of Technology, Bentley (W.A), undated.

Indian seafarers manned decks on the world's ships, and crewed engine rooms, saloons, cabins, and galleys. They inhabited a world deeply marked by race which determined what they would do, how much they would be paid, and how they could be treated. Virtually until World War II barring the odd Parsi doctor, officers on European ships were almost all white. Sometimes on deck, Indian crews were supplemented by a few Europeans, mainly carpenters (who could also be Chinese), sail-makers, and able-bodied seamen (or ABs). The racial divide ran deeper than rank, yet nowhere was it more complete than the engine room where the engineers were all European, as were those recognized to possess any skill, such as boiler-makers. Indian crews did the hot and heavy work of heaving coal and stoking the fires.

On deck Indian crews dropped and heaved anchor, kept watch, steered the vessel, sounded lead, tended to the ropes, and scrubbed, washed, and painted decks to produce the emblems of apparent order that frenzied officers found reassuring. Below decks in the sweltering heat of the engine room, where temperatures especially in the Red Sea could exceed 60°C, the frenzy was driven by the ceaseless need to keep the steam up by heaving vast quantities of coal into giant boilers with unending appetites for the fuel; while other men prepared, moved, and sized the fuel, and cleaned and greased engines, valves, pipes, and boilers. In the cabins, saloons, and galleys above, crews cooked, baked, served, and cleaned, and carried out the innumerable routines of shipboard life.

In times of peace Indian seafarers helped keep British shipping competitive especially in the eastern trades.[7] Shipping, in turn, was a vital strategic and symbolic resource for Britain's expansive yet rapidly integrating trading empire.

Take for example the P&O, the largest employer of Indian crews during our period. The P&O received generous mail subsidies from imperial and colonial governments. It moreover held effective monopoly of the Bombay end of the signature trade of the 19th century British Empire, viz. opium exports to China; and commanded the rock solid custom of imperial and colonial public officials. P&O steamers have rightly been called the 'flagships of imperialism'.[8] Assembled reassuringly each morning on deck for drills in their *faux*-oriental costumes, lined up in 'picturesque costumes' for *tableaux vivants* to relieve the 'monotony of the

---

[7] On margins in Asian shipping see Chih-lung Liu, 'British Shipping in the Orient, 1933–39: Reasons for its failure to compete', *International Journal of Maritime History* (20: 1, June 2008) pp. 153–172.

[8] Freda Harcourt, 'The P&O Company: Flagships of Imperialism', in Sarah Palmer and Glyndwr Williams, eds, *Charted and Uncharted Waters: Proceedings of a Conference on the Study of British Maritime History* (London: National Maritime Museum and Queen Mary College, 1981), epigraph, p. 6; and p. 21.

Red Sea', or assembled to play the pipe for visiting dignitaries, Indian crews on P&O boats served also as exotic trophies of imperial conquest.[9] Equally they were set-piece accessories in the formulaic instruction of wide-eyed, yet swaggering apprentice colonialists for whom sea passage offered a stage to rehearse their pomp, bearing, and manner in anticipation of the life awaiting them in India.[10] As Britain's grip over India began to loosen, summer cruise vessels carrying native crews offered nostalgic imperial hands and others, the vicarious thrill of the empire as an enclosed theme park in the familiar waters of the North Sea. At other times, as during the world wars when they died in the thousands and suffered imprisonment by the hundreds to keep its merchant fleet sailing, Indian seafarers made a difference for Britain between life and death, survival and starvation, victory and defeat.

The footprints of Indian seafarers may be found on every continent. Despite being relatively small in number, they appear to have been nearly everywhere in the steamship era, i.e. the late-19th century through World War II: attending political meetings in Britain, working in Detroit car factories and California farms, and featuring in Hollywood films. Some ended up destitute, in hospitals, workhouses, and jails. Others opened shops, restaurants, cafés, and lodging houses overseas. Some never returned to India, striking relationships and roots, marrying and raising families abroad. In their travels and sojourns Indian seafarers encountered employers and public officials, missionaries and trade unions, local communities, and other travellers and sojourners like themselves in distant lands. In short they were India's earliest global workers and among the earliest such workers anywhere in the world, pioneers and precursors of India's overseas presence today, and forbears as it were of the Indian or south Asian 'diaspora'. Prising open doors of insular societies long before 'multiculturalism' became fashionable, they were also the earliest mass carriers of south Asian cuisines and cultures to Europe.

Their employment on European vessels implicated Indian seafarers in conflicts between ship-owners and seafarers in other countries, notably Britain where seafarers' unions derided them as cheap coolies who had stolen jobs rightfully belonging to white seafarers.

Marginalized and isolated, seafarers from the sub-continent were also silent, selectively mobilized, and dispensable accoutrements of political ambition and public visibility for struggling Indian politicians and middle class figures in Britain: filling up auditoria seats and crowding political meetings where too, as

---

9 National Maritime Museum, Greenwich (NMM), P&O 16/8, reports from passenger voyage diaries; also see 21/1 and 89/6.
10 Rajeshwar Dayal, *A Life of our Times* (Hyderabad: Orient Longman, 1998), p. 32.

on P&O vessels and later in Hollywood films such as *Calcutta*, they were useful for 'creating atmosphere'; acting as carriers (only sporadically as objects or emissaries) of radical, subversive propaganda; and as the collective cover and mask for radical Indian activists eluding agents of the imperial state as they made their ways across the world to Weimar Germany or the Soviet Union. Indian seamen became objects of visible concern (and overt repression) when they struck work in 1939–1940 shortly after World War II began, and again in 1942 when the imperial state was at pains to retain their loyalties during the Quit India movement.[11]

The majority of Indian seafarers came from the regions that became Pakistan in 1947 and viewed the prospect of Partition with trepidation. When it came Partition disrupted their itineraries of work and movement and conscripted them into rival nationalist projects.[12]

Footprints on water

Yet until recently Indian seafarers have languished as a historically invisible underclass.

For a start, the colonial state did everything possible to render their everyday presence invisible. It regulated nearly every detail of the engagement of Indian seafarers on oceanic shipping to minimize the danger of political and cultural contact, and channel potential conflicts through routine bureaucratic agency. Besides aggressive paternalism, this agency was premised on the belief which in turn it helped realize, that Indian seafarers were undependable peasants who turned to the sea for temporary employment. Hence the paradox that despite the regulated nature of their employment, the maritime labour market was often indistinguishable from casual labour markets at Indian ports.

Nationalist accounts of India's past maritime prowess also disdained to acknowledge Indian maritime workers as heirs to this tradition. Echoing the *swadeshi* spirit of the day Radha Kumud Mookerji's 1912 account of Indian shipping, for example, dutifully extolled India's past as a great trading and ship-building nation.[13] But the book was silent on the people who sailed the vessels, or

---

11 OIOC, L/PJ/12/46, intelligence reports, 13 Sept., 30 Sept., 9 Oct. 1922, and 28 Feb. 1923; 12/47, report, 16 Jan. 1923; PRO, HO 344/32, A.P. Godfrey's letter to Waldron Smithers, 16 Dec. 1924; Maharashtra State Archives (MSA), Special Branch, 543(4)A, notes, 8 and 9 Oct. 1923.
12 G. Balachandran, *Globalizing Labour? Indian Seafarers and World Shipping, c. 1870–1945* (Delhi and Oxford: Oxford University Press, 2012), Epilogue.
13 *Indian Shipping: A History of the Sea-Borne Trade and Maritime Activity of the Indians from the Earliest Times* (London: Longmans Green, 1912).

even their navigational skills and practices. On the other hand a 1902 British mercantile marine committee defending the employment of Indian crews on British ships underlined the traditional importance of maritime employment for India's coastal communities. Only, unlike the nationalists who in seeking to cleanse Indian maritime entrepreneurship of any taint of labour or marginality stressed commerce and ship-building, the British committee, being loathe to acknowledge the capacity of the colonized for entrepreneurship and keen to affirm emerging spatial patterns of accumulation and specialization, emphasized India's role as a supplier of wage-labour for British-owned ships.[14]

In appearing not to display unqualified allegiance to either nation in the subcontinent after its 1947 Partition, Indian seafarers also came somewhat to resemble Partition's women, physically claimed by both states yet trusted by neither to uphold the new political and moral certitudes required to normalize their separate existence. Yet unlike Partition's women whose stories are now being told, seafarers from the subcontinent do not figure in the histories of the two nations or of the processes of their modern creation.

Until rather recently, Indian seafarers have also suffered relative neglect in historical studies of labour and the working class. One explanation could be that, neither peasants nor proletarians, and palpably committed neither to ship nor harbour, sea nor land, port nor hinterland, Asia nor Europe, town nor village, urban nor rural, industry nor agriculture, 'modern' nor 'traditional', they appear as distant stragglers after the neat categories that still frame our social imaginations. Freely relativizing and interrogating boundaries by crossing them repeatedly, Indian seafarers have also eluded the attention of scholars whose purported object has been to critique and move beyond such markers.

Fluid meanings, cosmopolitan spaces

'Lascar' carried many meanings varying with context and usage. The term is believed to have been first used in the maritime context by the Portuguese and Dutch to describe seafarers from India and the Indian Ocean region. It endured thereafter in Indian and British maritime laws. British laws had special clauses for 'lascars' down to 1963. Informally the term remained in use until more recently to describe seafarers from the subcontinent.

---

[14] G. Balachandran, 'Sovereignty, Subjectivities, Narrations: Nations and Other Stories from the Sea', *International Journal of Maritime History* (vol. 21: 2, December 2009), pp. 5–7.

According to Hobson-Jobson, 'lascar' originated from the Persian *lashkar*, meaning 'an army' or 'a camp', similar to the Arabic *al'askar*. Lascar was apparently a corruption introduced into European maritime usage by the Portuguese, in the form of *lasquarin, lascari*, etc., and taken over by the Dutch (*lascarein*) and the British. Even in its maritime usage, 'lascar' may have had military origins. Portuguese vessels defending forts and other possessions along the coast carried a large number of fighting men from Abyssinia, the Omani coast, as well as Malabar. The term's maritime associations and meanings may have arisen from the Portuguese, and later the Dutch and English, training 'gun-lascars' to man the artillery on trading vessels. In the 18th century, as vessels became more specialized, 'lascar' also began to denote a sailor rather than merely an indigenous soldier on a trading vessel.

Despite figuring in British and Indian merchant shipping laws and procedures from the early 19th century, the maritime meaning of 'lascar' remained malleable till after World War I. The overwhelming majority of Indian seafarers employed on deep-sea British vessels contracted under 'lascar agreements' or 'lascar articles' which, unlike the single voyage agreements more typical for European and American seafarers, represented in its main variant a contract of extended duration (of one to two years) covering several voyages criss-crossing the world.

Until the 20th century, 'lascar' continued to be used in British India to describe porters and 'unskilled' workers employed in the army, railways, and public works departments. Hence the term lent itself easily to generic or conflated meanings. For instance a colonial official appearing as an 'expert witness' at a wreck inquiry into the loss of the steamship *Roumania* could assert without fear of contradiction that he had 'considerable experience of these lascars in India ... up on the hills', and found them 'absolutely useless in cold weather ....'[15]

In this last usage the lascar was a 'common coolie'. 'Coolie' is a familiar 19th century figure in accounts of indentured labour migration to plantation colonies from India, China, and other parts of Asia. The ships outfitted to carry them were also called 'coolie ships'. Thanks to colonial prejudice, business strategies, and the dispositions of language, the Indian worker was for long represented as a 'coolie'. The coolie was as much a figure in the jute mills of Calcutta and the cotton mills of Bombay and Kanpur as he was on board a merchant vessel. From deploying 'lascar' as a generic term for all types of 'unskilled' workers, the de-skilling of maritime work, and the institution of steeper, racialized work hierarchies on steam ships, it was a small step to constructing the maritime 'lascar' also in the image of a 'coolie'. Indeed, 'lascar' quickly became a marker of coolie

---

[15] PRO, BT, MT9/469B M 4354/1894, note, 8 March 1893.

status, with even British trade unionists routinely describing Indian seamen as 'coolie labour', or using the terms 'lascar' and 'coolie' interchangeably.[16]

'Lascar' had however a very specific meaning on board a steam ship. Each department of a steam vessel was in charge of a serang, or in the case of the saloon a chief steward or butler, assisted by one or more deputies, called tindals. The deck serang was akin to a boatswain, and was often the highest ranking Indian on a foreign-owned vessel. Apart from the three departments, Indian quartermasters or helmsmen (whom the British insisted on describing as *sukhanis* or *seacunnies*) were hired separately from the other crew and occupied a strategic position on board a vessel.

Ordinary Indian crews in the engine-room could be *aagwalas*, *paniwalas*, *cassabs*, etc, and those in the saloon stewards, bakers, cooks, pantry-keepers, saloon-boy, cabin-boy, officers' boy, etc. On board the ship itself, 'lascar' referred exclusively to an ordinary *deck* hand. It excluded even the deck serang and deck tindals, let alone crews of other departments.

However in official, employer, and popular usage ashore in Britain, all Indian seafarers irrespective of the nature of their work they did on a vessel, were lumped together as *lascars*.

Between the 16th and early-20th centuries 'lascar', 'Indian', 'native', and 'Asiatic' were also interchangeable terms for seafarers of non-European origin from the vast Indian Ocean region sailing (or earlier fighting) on European vessels. Identities were consequently fluid: as British merchant vessels began to engage more Asian and African crews from the 1850s, 'lascar' was used to describe seafarers from the Indian subcontinent as well as Chinese, Malay, Sinhalese, Arab, and East African seafarers. Some sources even referred to Turkish seafarers as 'lascars'. Though by the 1920s 'lascars' came only to index seafarers from the subcontinent, their genealogies and stories nevertheless shed light on the complex, cosmopolitan working environments in mid-19th century shipping, particularly in the Asian and Indian Ocean trade. No less resilient for being complex, the cosmopolitanism remained resistant to metropolitan efforts to cleanse or discipline it through at least the early 20th century.[17]

Take for instance the *Indus*, which sailed from Bombay to a Thames port in 1881. Though mainly from Surat, the deck crew included men from Bombay,

---

[16] On the political and discursive construction of the 'coolie' and Indian seafarers' efforts to claim their identity workers, see G. Balachandran, 'Making Coolies, (Un)making Workers: "Globalizing" Labour in the Late-19th and Early-20th Centuries', *Journal of Historical Sociology* (vol. 24: 3, September 2011).

[17] See here G. Balachandran, 'Subaltern Cosmopolitanism, Racial Governance and Multiculturalism: Britain, c. 1900–45', *Social History* (vol. 39: 4, December 2014).

Gogha, Mangalore and Tellicherry. The serang of its 36-strong engine room crew was from Bombay. His tindal came from Punjab. The rest of the crew included a contingent of Zanzibaris, a handful of men from Bombay, and a few from Surat, Sylhet, Kutch, Karachi, Muscat, Bahrain, Aden, and Mozambique.[18]

Not only crews. Life experiences of individual seafarers on board and ashore might also be quite diverse. The *Ellora* docked in London in 1881 after a voyage from Calcutta with a serang from Madras. The two tindals belonged to Calcutta and Jeddah. The other members of the 23-member crew included half a dozen from Jeddah, four each from Calcutta and Muscat, two each from Madras and Aden, as well as men from Zanzibar, Hyderabad, Ghazipur, and Cannanore. One of the men from Madras on this ship was Ram Samy, said to be 45 years of age in 1881, who is recorded in the local parish's baptism register as living since 1861 at Horseferry Road in West London, with his wife Julia Ormond and two children Sam and Mary.[19]

Two examples from the other end of the world suffice to underline the point. The *Coromandel* of Liverpool that arrived at Sydney at the end of a voyage from London in 1854 had a serang from Penang. Two of his three tindals came from Calcutta, the third from Bombay. The rest of the crew comprised seven men from Calcutta, five men from Jeddah, four each from Madras and Visakhapatnam, and one member each from Aden, Penang, Manila, and Patna.[20] The deck crew of the *Sun Foo* of London, also on a voyage from London to Sydney in 1873 was led by a serang from Calcutta. His two tindals were Goriah and Poortes, who along with one Balajee, belonged to Visakhapatnam on the Coromondal coast. Alongside them lived and worked two men each from Calcutta and Hainan (China), and three men each from Jeddah and Manila. The engine room crew of *Sun Foo* had a serang from Jeddah and a tindal from Muscat, and was made up of five men from Zanzibar, three from Aden/Port Said, two each from Muscat and Dalmatia (on the Adriatic coast), and one each from Calcutta and Cape Verde. The crew's Chinese cook was from Hainan.[21]

---

[18] Crews of the *Indus* and *Ellora* below were enumerated in the 1881 UK census. See http://www.censusuk.co.uk/1881new.htm (last seen 23 October 2012).
[19] Westminster City Council Library and Archives, Black Presence exhibition, online at http://www.westminster.gov.uk/archives/blackpresence/22.cfm (last seen 23 October 2012).
[20] State Records Authority of New South Wales SRNSW: Shipping Master's Office; Passengers Arriving 1855–1922; SRNSW, NRS 13278, [X91] Reel 400 at http://mariners.records.nsw.gov.au/1854/10/5410.htm (last seen 23 October 2012).
[21] SRNSW, Shipping Master's Office; CGS 13278, Passengers Arriving 1855–1922; X129–130, SR Reel 429, 1873 at http://mariners.records.nsw.gov.au/1873/12/055sun.htm (last seen 23 October 2012).

Crews reflected the diversity of the maritime labour milieu at the main hiring ports, viz. Calcutta and Bombay. Under the impetus of speedier voyages and heavier sea-borne traffic, Calcutta and Bombay had transformed by the 1860s into cosmopolitan sites for the working poor from many parts of the world including thousands of European seafarers looking for work. Fearful of European destitution and crime eroding British racial authority in India, the colonial government intervened to racialize destitution by hiring policemen and jail officials from the ranks of unemployed British seafarers. It also took steps to stop ships discharging European seafarers at Indian ports and forcibly shipping home those already present.[22]

In the absence of an Anglo-US treaty to apprehend deserters, Bombay and Calcutta became a haven for American seafarers.[23] Calcutta was home to hundreds of Chinese seafarers many of whom ended up in the city's general labouring population. Some early P&O engine-room crews comprised slaves captured by British vessels and landed in Bombay where sizeable communities of East African and Arab seafarers endured until the 1920s.[24]

The fluidity, though not yet the cosmopolitanism, began partly to harden from the early 20th century. The growth of seafarers' unions crystallized British working class opposition to foreign seafarers. The opposition was partly racial: 'we may tolerate Germans, Scandinavians, and Dutch', a Salford union official declared, but not 'Greeks, Italians, Spaniards, Arabs, etc'.[25] Debate over the merits of engaging 'lascars' grew muted after a 1902 parliamentary committee endorsed their employment. However, it prompted prolonged legal and political wrangling over who could be classified as 'lascars and other native seafarers', and as 'natives of India'. This continued till the 1920s.[26]

---

22 Harald Fischer-Tiné, 'Flotsam and Jetsam of the Empire?', in Ashwini Tambe and Harald Fischer-Tiné, eds, *The Limits of British Colonial Control in South Asia* (Abingdon: Routledge, 2008).
23 West Bengal State Archives (WBSA), Bengal judicial proceedings, 13 Jan. 1859, No. 65, Police commissioner's letter, 30 Dec. 1858.
24 National Archives of India (NAI), CI-SR/MS, Nov. 1880, 2022A, acting shipping master's letter, 27 Oct. 1879.
25 PRO, MT 9/698/165/1902, f. 1118, union's letter to the Board of Trade, 18 Jan. 1902; also see Parthasarathi Gupta, *Imperialism and the British Labour Movement, 1914–1964* (New Delhi: Sage Publications, 2002), p. 52.
26 Balachandran, *Globalizing Labour*, pp. 30–34.

'All give way to the Asiatic'?

Several factors explain the rapid growth in employment of Indian crews on British ships. First, as already noted, was the nature of the industry itself: after the navigation laws were repealed British ship-owners lost no time in exploiting the mobility of their fixed capital.

Technological changes no doubt played a role. The ascendancy of steam transformed seafaring, with some ship-board work split into separate departments requiring skills quite removed from the world of sail and closer to those on land. Engine rooms of steam vessels resembled industrial boiler rooms more than anything on sailing vessels, and work in the saloon department that in the emerging hotel industry. Technological changes, the rapid expansion of shipping, speedier and thanks to canals, shorter, voyages, and access to new labour markets also contributed to stratifying skills and de-skilling maritime employment. Together these factors also plausibly increased the impetus for the shift from sail to steam.

'Deskilling' was discursive and political more than technological let alone occupational. Many of the new sub-continental engine-room crews came from Punjab, Mirpur, and other parts of the north-west. Catching their first glimpse of the deep sea probably from their foc'stle portholes, their first days at sea tended often to be traumatic.[27] Yet over time these crews gained notable mastery in the engine room, including the ability to undertake engineering repairs. But employers did not regard such skills seriously, it appears partly because they were themselves confounded by the great variety of ships' engine designs and did not believe self-taught engine-room crews possessed any portable skills.[28] Steam ships still demanded traditional seamanship skills on deck. Yet in general, 'de-skilling', the enforced invisibility of some skills, and an environment marked by steep and racial skill hierarchies made steam vessels with Indian crews a highly stratified work environment.

With low and irregular wages, frequent absences from home, and arbitrary discharges at foreign ports, seafaring became increasingly an unattractive occupation in late-19th century Britain. Tight-fisted ship-owners went to further lengths to achieve small wage economies, for instance by paying off British crews

---

[27] As a result a new fireman's first days at sea were nothing short of traumatic: Gabor Korvin, ed., *Memoirs of Khawajah Muhammad Bux, Australian Businessman* (translated from Urdu by Syed Haider Hassan), Rawalpindi, 2006, pp. 19–20.

[28] For some idea of negotiations about skill in different engine-room environments, see Hassan N. Gardezi, ed., *Chains to Lose: Life and Struggles of a Revolutionary – Memoirs of Dada Amir Haider Khan* (New Delhi: Patriot Publishers, 1989), especially ch. 3.

at Indian ports with depreciating rupees in the 1880s and replacing them with cheaper local crews.[29]

Wages rose in line with labour productivity in most parts of the industrializing West and Japan before World War I. But in Britain seafarers' real wages declined according to one estimate by 5 % between 1890 and 1905 at a time when Britain's per capita real national product rose by eight per cent.[30] Low relative wages were a further blow at the occupational status of seafaring in Britain.

Owners and officers also claimed British seafarers were unruly and violent. 'British seafarers drink, fight, quarrel and are insubordinate', a former P&O commander intoned. His company had ceased employing British crews because they 'were turbulent and half ... were constantly in jail ....'[31]

Complaints of this nature coincided with the growth of unions. British ship-owners were notoriously against trade unions, and set up the Shipping Federation expressly to break strikes. In the authoritarian environment of a merchant ship it was easy to damn any sign of shop floor activity as insubordination. Consequently the morale of British seamen declined as rapidly as their alleged reputation.[32] Nor did contemporary observers miss the connection between growing unionism in Britain and the employment of colonial and foreign seafarers.[33]

Some blamed the behaviour of British crews on the effects of tropical heat. As late as the 1970s the National Union of Seamen (NUS) accepted 'heat problems in [the] accommodation' as a valid reason to employ Asian seafarers.[34] Stereotypes about the vulnerability of European crews to heat complemented prejudices about the vulnerability of Indian crews to cold. The latter served to justify geographical restrictions on their employment until World War II.[35]

Officers' fears of unruly British crews grew worse east and south of the Suez Canal.

These fears deserve also to be viewed in the light of officers' insecurities over the changes sweeping through merchant shipping at this time. The growth of shipping and steam propulsion created new opportunities for engineers, many

---

[29] Balachandran, *Globalizing Labour*, p. 38.
[30] C.H. Dixon, 'Seafarers and the Law: An Examination of Legislation on the British Merchant seamen's Lot, 1580–1918', unpublished Ph.D. thesis, University College, London, 1981, pp. 233–234.
[31] NAI, FC, SC, March 1901, 135–42A, enclosures to A.M.'s note, 8 Oct. 1900.
[32] Luke Trainor, 'The Historians and Maritime Labour, c. 1850–1930', *Research in Maritime History* (no. 9, December 1995), pp. 277–294.
[33] NAI, SC, 1275–80B–July 1890, Bombay shipping master's report.
[34] Modern Records Centre, Warwick (MRC), MSS 175A/126, NMB, WP10 memorandum, 'UK Ships Manning Agreements: Non-domiciled Ratings', undated.
[35] Balachandran, *Globalizing Labour*, pp. 126–135.

from struggling middle-class families with no tradition or experience of the sea. Even on deck younger officers may have felt challenged to face down older sailors who had spent much of their lives on sailing vessels.

There were unsettling professional changes as well. Shipping companies with heavy new investments in steam sought crewing economies at the expense of officers and engineers who were felt to be 'much too expensive for the changed maritime environment'.[36] The 1894 British merchant shipping act threatened further changes, notably by stipulating more formal norms for promotions and punishments which included suspending certificates for professional and personal offences. The telegraph made masters more directly accountable to ship-owners, enhanced the role of shipping agents relative to the master and his mates, and spurred early attempts to centralize the management of tramp shipping. The telegraph also enabled shorter halts at ports and more complex tramp itineraries which in turn meant longer absences from home.[37] For masters, diminished responsibility for the business side of shipping entailed lower commissions on cargoes and profits, and diminished authority.[38]

The apparent amenability of Indian crews hence represented a welcome affirmation of masters' and officers' status and authority. As a former P&O master boasted, Indian seafarers were 'contented with their lot ..., amenable to ordinary discipline', and generally inclined to 'do their work as they should'. They 'harmonize[d] more freely than Europeans ... and shift[ed] around to help each other' when one of them fell out from illness or exhaustion. Indian seafarers did not regulate their work by the clock and were willing to work long hours. Therefore, employing Indian crews ensured officers kept watch instead of taking their coats 'off ... and bustl[ing] about like a bo'sn's mate ....' Indian seafarers were consequently 'more completely the servants of the ship-owner ... than any other group of men'.[39] European crews could not 'compete with, endure and thrive in the same healthy manner' as Indian crews. 'All give way to the Asiatic ....'.[40]

However officers felt, ultimately crewing decisions were dictated by ship-owners for whom employing Indian seafarers meant major cost advantages. There

---

36 J. Forbes Munro, *Maritime Enterprise and Empire: Sir William Mackinnon and his Business Network, 1823–93* (Suffolk: The Boydell Press, 2003), p. 125.
37 Byron Lew and Bruce Cater, 'The Telegraph, Coordination of Tramp Shipping, and Growth in World Trade, 1870–1910', *European Review of Economic History* (10: 1, 2006), pp. 147–173.
38 Munro, *Maritime Enterprise*, p. 125.
39 W.H. Hood, *The Blight of Insubordination: The Lascar Question and Rights and Wrongs of the British Shipmaster. Including the Mercantile Marine Committee Report* (London: Spottiswoode and Co., 1903), pp. 42–50; also L.G. W. White, *Ships, Coolies, and Rice* (London: Sampson Low & Co., 1936), pp. 62–63.
40 Hood, *Blight of Insubordination*, pp. 7–13.

were three major components to crew cost: wages, accommodation on board, and provisioning. Indian crews were cheaper than other crews in all three respects. Employing them also led indirectly to other economies.

Direct wage comparisons are difficult because Indian crew ranks and wages were more stratified than among European crews. This said, on a rough average Indian seafarers were paid a fifth to a quarter of a British seaman's wage. They were also paid less than Chinese, Malay, or other Asian seafarers.

Nor did wages increase much before World War II. The monthly wage of a serang on a British vessel was about Rs 35 in 1884, while that of a tindal varied between Rs 25 and 28. Wages of lascars and firemen averaged about Rs 18 on a well run ship. While by 1925 a serang's wages had risen to nearly Rs 60 per month, wages of tindals, cassabs, donkeymen, oilmen, greasers, and lascars ranged between Rs. 26 to 30, and those of ordinary lascars and firemen between Rs 18 to 24.[41] In contrast, British seafarers' monthly wages doubled from £ 4/10 in 1914 to £ 9 in 1939.

Not much is known about Chinese and Malay wages which seem to have varied with port and time of engagement. Malay deck crews commanded a premium in Calcutta in the winter thanks to seasonal restrictions on employing Indian crews in North Atlantic waters. Chinese seafarers in Hong Kong and Shanghai were paid less than their compatriots in Singapore. In Singapore in 1939 a Chinese sailor received about two and half times an Indian sailor's wage, and a Malay sailor about twice. But Chinese seafarers in Hong Kong and Shanghai were paid only fractionally more than Indian seafarers, while those engaged in Calcutta were paid slightly less than Malay seafarers.[42]

These wage differences did not translate into proportional cost differentials because of manning levels. Believing safety to lie in numbers when they were affordable, ship-owners hired three to four Indian seafarers for jobs for which they would only have hired two British seafarers even if that meant, as unions justifiably complained, going to sea in undermanned vessels. Yet given the wage differentials, even replacing a barely sufficient British crew with a much more adequate Indian crew meant a substantial reduction in the wage bill. By inhibiting exertion and preventing improvements to efficiency, low wages may have led to over-manning. Employers' insistence, when Indian crews became eligible for overtime compensation in the late-1930s, that this should take the form of time

---

[41] OIOC, L/R/5/300, 'Lascar seafarers', p. 5; Royal Commission on Labour in India (hereafter RCL), vol. V, part 1, *Written Evidence*, 'Memorandum of the Indian Seamen's Union', section XII, pp. 249–250.
[42] NAI, CD, MMII, 11MII (2)/31, May 1936, 1–41A.

off, rather than monetary payments, suggests they were aware of the over-manning but were unable or unwilling to do anything about it.

Overall wage cost differentials between Chinese, Malay, and Indian crews were much smaller. Hence crewing decisions across these choices depended on voyage schedules and crew logistics. In the 1920s and 1930s the MV *Oakbank* engaged Indian, Chinese, and Malay crews at Calcutta.[43] Its Chinese, Malay, and Indian deck crews comprised 15, 18, and 20 men respectively. The monthly wage cost of a Malay crew came to Rs 940. The Indian crew cost the least (Rs 732) and the Chinese crew cost slightly more (Rs 740). The vessel engaged Indian or Chinese crews in the saloon and engine room. With seven members each in the engine room and saloon, the Chinese crews cost Rs 400 and Rs 370 respectively. The 12-member Indian engine room crew cost Rs 360 and the seven-strong saloon crew, Rs 330.

Larger crews could have meant setting aside more space for accommodation. But Indian shipping laws ensured ship-owners would not find this a burden.

In 1860 Indian crews had bunks measuring four 'superficial feet' (or 24 cubic feet) and British crews, bunks of nine 'superficial feet' or 54 cubic feet to each. In 1876 these bunk sizes were increased to six superficial feet (36 cubic feet) and 10 superficial feet (60 cubic feet) respectively. By 1894 British crew bunk-sizes had increased to 12 square feet (72 cubic feet), and by 2006 to 15 square feet (or 120 cubic feet now with deck heights rising to eight feet).

Since the 19th century, Indian merchant shipping regulations specified diets for Indian seafarers. Until 1906 ship-owners employing British crews were under no similar obligation. Yet the diets of Indian seafarers were inferior to the diets to which British seafarers were accustomed, as well as cheaper. Indian seafarers also cost significantly less to provision than Arab or Chinese seafarers.

Once statutory scales were introduced the quantity, quality, and variety of British seafarers' diets improved rapidly. Indian seafarers' diets contained little or no variety. Attempts to introduce variety were as stoutly resisted as new conceptions of selves and social relationships. As an ignorant official remarked disdainfully about Bombay seafarers' demands for including coffee, a substance they brought on board and already consumed at their own expense, in their official diets, 'This has probably been demanded because it is included in the European scale. Coffee does not form part of the lascars' ordinary diet and there appears to be no good reason for its inclusion.'[44]

Longer agreements covering multiple voyages also meant lower employer outlays on shipping office, brokerage, and fees for crew engagement and dis-

---

43 NAI, CD, MMII, 11MII (2)/31, May 1936, 1–41A.
44 NAI, CD, MMII, Nov. 1931, 1–23 A, J.A. Woodhead's minute, 27 June 1930.

charge, besides greater flexibility to plan ships' voyages and itineraries. Indian seafarers also worked longer hours – 72 to 84 hour weeks were not unknown – and even after regulated working hours were introduced in the 1930s overtime work by Indian crews was compensated by time off rather than additional wages.

Indian seafarers could not obtain discharges outside the subcontinent. The overt intention was to protect them from being stranded and left destitute at foreign ports. Yet given prevalent wage differentials few ship-owners cavilled at a restriction that enhanced their control over Indian crews. They also opposed timid attempts to relax this restriction, yet in 1931 wrested the right to discharge Indian seafarers at foreign ports.[45]

Indian seamen were less prone to desert than seamen of other nationalities.[46] Consequently they formed a smaller and less visible presence even at British ports, than their Arab and Chinese counterparts. They were also not feared as vehicles of oriental subversion of western values, morals, and womanhood in the same way as Chinese seafarers with their presumed proclivity for trafficking in opium and operating 'dens of oriental vice'. These differences are reflected in popular fiction where the 'lascar' was a less ubiquitous and more ambivalent figure (for example in Arthur Conan Doyle) than Chinese seamen. The latter were more frequently vilified, most notoriously in the novels of the pseudonymous Sax Rohmer but also at the hands of otherwise sympathetic observers such as Stan Hugill, for criminal vices, and as sources of 'Oriental contagion' and corruption particularly of women – Canton Kitty being a popular name for a white woman with a Chinese companion, or worse for someone who had 'opium-smoked herself into a strange likeness of a Chinaman'.[47] Therefore, despite enduring union opposition, Indian seamen were on the whole a less controversial presence in the British merchant marine than Arab or Chinese seamen.

British Trade Unions and Indian seafarers

Almost immediately after they came into existence in the 1880s, British seafarers' unions began campaigning against Asian crews. This opposition varied in

---

45 See NAI, CD, MMII, 11 MII(9)/31, Nov. 1933, 1–19A.
46 Balachandran, *Globalizing Labour?*, pp. 177–184.
47 Stan Hugill, *Sailortown* (London: Routledge and K. Paul, 1967), pp. 123–124; Joseph Salter, *The East in the West or Work among the Asiatics and Africans in London* (London: Partridge and Co., c. 1896), chs 3–4; on sexualized fears of moral contagion, see Barry Milligan, *Pleasures and Pains: Opium and the Orient in 19th Century British Culture* (Charlottesville: University of Virginia Press, 1995), ch. 5.

scope and intensity, peaking round the turn of the century and in the 1930s when the Labour party also came out in explicit support of a British-only employment policy, yet with the exception of the two world wars remained unremitting until the 1970s. By the 1900s and more perceptibly from the 1920s, this opposition spread to port officials, missionaries, the local police, as well as the Home Office. In 1911 ship-owners agreed to make additional contributions to the British seamen's pension fund in proportion to the number of Indian crews they employed. Meant to protect the benefits of fund's current members, this agreement proved a durable safeguard from the employers' point of view. Needless to add, Indian seafarers were not admitted to the fund. In the 1970s the NUS took this to a logical conclusion when it began charging owners a 'union levy' for hiring Indian crews.[48]

British unions' efforts to check the employment of Indian seafarers took many forms. In the 1890s the National Sailors' and Firemen's Union (NSFU) demanded equal bunk spaces for Indian and British crews. However the NSFU's most prominent leader J. Havelock Wilson thought nothing of demanding larger spaces for 'cheap "Coolie" firemen' in the same breath as protesting their 'preferential employment'. Nor did he attempt to hide his true intent, viz. reduce or eliminate Indian crews on British ships.[49]

Health officials at British ports also complained about crowded spaces and insanitary conditions. But they encountered resistance from shipping companies led by the P&O to whom larger crew spaces were a particular threat. Seafarers from the subcontinent made up an overwhelming proportion of P&O crews. Its existing vessels were specially outfitted to carry them, and new space regulations would have meant expensive modifications to. The P&O consequently mobilized along a wide front, swapping cultural claims about Asian 'living and sleeping habits', the flavour of 'ghee and condiments', and the odours of 'Indian marine cooking' and political claims about the sovereignty of colonial Indian law; and orchestrating petitions on behalf of Indian seamen protesting being made victims of the 'benevolent intentions' and 'fatal philanthropy' of individuals intent on sacrificing their livelihoods for comfortable lodgings on board.[50] A 'native lascar' was only half as capable as a European seaman, one of these petitions read, and no employer could afford to treat them on par. Besides 'the vessels we sail are like palaces, and our quarters there are far and away superior to what we can

---

48 Hope, *New History*, p. 455; on the 'levy', see MRC, MSS 175A/Box 125, in particular 'Non-European Manning', memorandum, 18 Sept. 1974.
49 PRO, MT 23/92, letter, 9 Dec. 1895.
50 NAI, LD, Oct. 1895, prog. 265, app. 79, J. Playfair's speech.

ever hope to obtain ourselves on land.'[51] The high point of the P&O's intervention came in 1900 when Alexander Mackay (later Baron Inchcape) arrived in Calcutta where in the course of a single meeting he converted key colonial officials to his company's view.[52]

The NSFU demanded equal pay and working conditions for crews of all nationalities. This was empty rhetoric. In reality the union's opposition to Indian seafarers on grounds of presumed ability repudiated any notion of equality. Its routine tactic of deriding Indian seamen as 'lascars' or 'coolies' was calculated to deny them admission to the mystical fraternity of the sea and the modern working class, and reflected/reinforced this inequality. In practice too, by the 1930s the NUS, deeply implicated since 1919 in a corporatist alliance with British ship-owners, had grown intent on sustaining and reproducing this inequality. For instance it rejected the 1936 ILO working hours' convention and negotiated a longer working week for Indian crews in opposition to the wishes of the latter's unions which, in contrast to the NUS, had actively championed and voted for the 1936 convention.[53]

The NSFU (and later the NUS) claimed Indian seafarers put British lives at risk. Such claims struck a chord especially following accidents at sea. Another tactic was to protest the use of Indian crews on ships carrying British women and children.[54]

It was frequently claimed that Indian seafarers were incapable of working in the cold and were useless in a storm. Partisan and polarized, 'expert opinion' only helped relay and reproduce such prejudices because of which Indian crews worked and lived under the close, unflinching scrutiny of officers and passengers which, oddly enough, intensified rather than diminished during times of danger or emergency.[55]

The charge that Indian deck crews were useless in the cold spoke directly to racial prejudices. Fear and fatalism were other familiar tropes in accounts relaying vivid images of Indian seafarers huddled against the cold and cowering in fear

---

[51] NAI, LD, Oct. 1895, proceeding 262A, app. 78 and 267A, app. 81; on the P&O role in this campaign, see OIOC, L/E/7/696, A. Challis to Board of Trade, 13 Jan. 1911.

[52] NAI, LD, Jan. 1893, nos. 51–153, J.E. O'Conor's note, 12 Jan. 1901. In 1900 the British courts ruled that British ships had to follow British law in British waters. This left the P&O and other companies free to allocate crew spaces as per Indian law south of the Suez and on Indian Ocean voyages: see NAI, FC-SC, 231–44A.

[53] For more details, see Balachandran, *Globalizing Labour*, ch. 7.

[54] PRO, MT9/469B M 4354/1894, note, 8 March 1893; OIOC, L/E/9/970, parliamentary replies, 17 Oct. 1940.

[55] For example, see London Metropolitan Archives (LMA), PS/TH/W/01/014, record of the inquiry into the sinking of the *Oceana*, 1912.

when their ship ran into trouble. As a reporter for the *Hull Daily Mail* described his voyage from Bombay to Aden on a 'dirty monsoon night' when the ship's wheel chains broke in the small hours of the morning,

> half a dozen 'coolies' were called in to assist in the repairs, the vessel was making bad weather of it, and in the pitch darkness not a lascar was to be found on the deck .... They were on the deck, oh, yes! Two were hiding inside ventilators, one at the fore part of the engine-room skylight, and the others under the main barrels of the winch like half-drowned rats! They were essentially lacking in 'two o'clock morning courage', which is the great trait of the British sailor's character.[56]

Or in Prime Minister Lloyd George's words spoken in the middle of a war in which nearly 4000 Indian seafarers paid with their lives, 'lascars' lacked the 'grit of the white men'.[57]

Rhetorical claims for the 'true British seaman' were, as Isaac Land notes, composed of 'two mutually reinforcing parts', viz., 'a racial identity inflected by gender, and a masculinity that was ... an expression of inborn ethnic traits.' General discourses about race and adaptability to extreme climatic conditions also echoed with hidden resonances of class and claims to rule.[58]

Public and parliamentary concern over the effects of employing foreign merchant seamen on Britain's wartime naval reserve led to an inquiry in 1902.[59] Insisting they were indispensable to British shipping, shipowners said Indian seafarers made such capable all-weather crews that many masters would never hire European crews when Indian crews were available. Despite Havelock Wilson's overt hostility the 1902 committee endorsed the employment of 'lascars' who were as a rule 'temperate', and made 'amenable and contented crews'. Besides they were British subjects with a justified claim to employment on British ships which had also displaced 'native trading vessels' along the Indian coast.[60]

The committee's report helped blunt opposition to Indian seafarers for the next two decades. Union anger was thereafter directed mainly at Chinese and Arab seafarers until the 1920s.

---

56 16 Jan. 1902.
57 PRO, MT 9/1087 M. 5189/17, speech to trade unionists, 31 Jan. 1917.
58 Isaac Land, 'Customs Of The Sea: Flogging, Empire, and the "True British Seaman", 1770 to 1870', *Interventions* (3: 2, 2001) p. 172.
59 British Parliamentary Papers (BPP), vol. 62, 1903, Cd. 1608.
60 BPP, vol. 62, 1903, Cd. 1607, paras. 14–16.

'Muscles of Empire'

It is commonplace that the British Empire was glued together by railways, the navy, and the telegraph. As Ian Kerr notes in the context of the railways, colonial labour was an invisible ingredient in this glue.[61] Though the employment of colonial workers in its merchant fleet evoked protests in Britain, it is debatable whether the supply of native (i.e. white British) labour would have kept pace with the rapid growth of Britain's merchant navy at a time when the Royal Navy too, was expanding rapidly. As a NUS memorandum acknowledged in 1977, Indian crews proved indispensable to British shipping only partly on account of low relative wages in the industry. Even had wages been higher, it was a 'matter for speculation' whether enough British seafarers would have come forward, or whether 'reliance on high cost British labour would have proved an impediment to ... [the] growth [of the British merchant navy].'[62]

The 1902 committee cited Britain's monopoly of Indian shipping to justify the employment of Indian seafarers on British ships. The committee could not have been expected to recognize that this monopoly was also sustained by subsidies from Indian revenues. But by the 1930s Indian nationalists protesting wage and employment discrimination against sub-continental seafarers on British vessels argued that without the subsidized access it commanded to India, China, Africa, and the Arab coast, employment in British shipping would shrink to 30,000 low-paid ratings.[63]

The imperial state had a direct interest in employing cheap colonial maritime labour. In 1870 the P&O received a mail subsidy of £ 450,000 for India and China. By 1900 imperial shipping subsidies totalled nearly £ 2 million, of which a third came from colonial budgets.[64] Widely considered extravagant, this subsidy amounted to 17 pence (or 17d) per pound of mail for India, compared to 11 d for the US, and 14 d for South Africa and Australia. According to Freda Harcourt, mail subsidies exceeded a third of the P&O's total receipts in the 1870s and averaged a fifth over 1840–1914.[65] Contemporaries believed these subsidies, which also exceeded the company's dividends, enabled P&O's anti-competitive practices.

---

[61] Ian Kerr, *Building the Railways of the Raj, 1850–1900* (Delhi: Oxford University Press, 1995).
[62] MRC, MSS 175A, Box 127, 'Legislature and the Lascars', January 1977.
[63] NAI, CD, MMII, Nov. 1935, 24 MM-II/35, 1C, Mehta to Lansbury, 1 April 1935; Nehru Memorial Museum and Library (NMML), Master Papers, MA 25/1, David Erulkar's letter, 2 Feb. 1934.
[64] Daniel Headrick, *Tools of Empire: Technological Transfer in the Age of Imperialism, 1850–1940* (Oxford: Oxford University Press, 1988), pp. 36–37.
[65] Freda Harcourt, 'British Oceanic Mail Contracts in the Age of Steam, 1838–1914', *Journal of Transport History* (9: 1, 1988), p. 6.

It is moot how much larger the subsidy would have been had the P&O not had access to cheap Indian crews.

Mail subsidies are a good example of the mutually beneficially nexus between state and the principal shipping companies in the British Empire, and between imperial power and commercial profit. Sometimes this nexus verged on cronyism or corruption. Thus for example in 1925 the India Office persistently ignored the P&O breaking rules to employ Indian crews for its summer North sea cruises whose passengers included its own very senior officials![66] Often imperial interest and private profit had to be reconciled at the public expense. To the extent cheap Indian crews reduced the burden of such reconciliation on government revenues, they were an imperial asset deserving of protection.

Indian maritime workers became an indispensable asset when the empire went to war. In the world wars, besides merchant vessels, Indian seamen crewed troopships, hospital ships, supply ships, and other admiralty charters. About 3500 Indian seafarers were killed in World War I, about 5000 in World War II. 1200 Indian seamen were taken prisoner in each war. At the end of World War II British ship-owners declared that 'the Indian seaman ... [had] a record in Peace and War second to none'.[67] This was partly self-interested bombast.[68] Yet more than ever during the two world wars, Indian seafarers became, in Frank Broeze's apt description, 'muscles of the empire'.[69]

---

66 OIOC, L/E/9/956, especially Kershaw's note, 27 July 1925.
67 PRO, MT/4266, F. 101812, 'Report of sub-committee', 11 Oct. 1945, p. 5.
68 For the context, see Balachandran, *Globalizing Labour?*, ch. 7.
69 Frank Broeze, 'The Muscles of Empire: Indian Seamen and the Raj, 1919–1939', *Indian Economic and Social History Review* (18: 1, 1981) pp. 43–67.

Alf Lüdtke
Soldiering and Working: Almost the Same?
Reviewing Practices in Industry and the Military in Twentieth-Century Contexts[1]

A colonial moment

> The infantry fired steadily and stolidly, without hurry or excitement, for the enemy were far away and the officers careful. Besides, the soldiers were interested in the work and took great pains. But presently the mere physical act became tedious. The tiny figures seen over the slide of the back-sight seemed a little larger but also fewer at each successive volley. The rifles grew hot – so hot that they had to be changed for those of the reserve companies. The Maxim guns exhausted all the water in their jackets, and several had to be refreshed from the water-bottles of the Cameron Highlanders before they could go on with their deadly work. The empty cartridge-cases, tinkling to the ground, formed small but growing heaps beside each man. And all the time out on the plain on the other side bullets were shearing through flesh, smashing and splintering bones; blood spouted from terrible wounds; valiant men were struggling on through a hell of whistling metal, exploding shells, and spurting dust – suffering, despairing, dying.[2]

A young gentleman and trained cavalry officer drafted this report several weeks after having witnessed this action of British troops in Sudan in 1898. The author was Winston S. Churchill, who participated in one of these colonial wars. In his account, Churchill once again makes visible to the wider public what had never vanished from colonial and imperial politics: the physical annihilation of those who did not bend to the various 'civilizing missions' of the agents of the West.
The soldiers Churchill observed at their 'work' were professionally trained 'six-year-old British soldiers'.[3] In his view, they fundamentally differed from those 'boys' or 'conscripts' who would follow 'their officers in blind ignorance' and

---
1 This article was first published under the same title in Jürgen Kocka (ed.), Work in a Modern Society. The German Historical Experience in Comparative Perspective. New York, London: Berghahn 2010, pp. 109–130 © 2010 Berghahn Books. Reproduced by permission of Berghahn Books Inc.
2 Winston Churchill, *The River War: An Historical Account of the Reconquest of the Soudan*, [vol. 3 of *The Collected Works of Sir Winston Churchill*] (1974; 1st edn, London: Longmans, Green and Co, 1899), pp. 247–248.
3 Frederick Woods (ed.), *Winston S. Churchill: War Correspondent, 1895–1900* (London: Leo Cooper, 1992), pp. 150–151; dispatch of 11 September 1898, two days after the battle of Omdurman and the cavalry charge that Churchill referred to.

march 'in a row to their death' as they staffed the armies on the European continent. With these British troops, however, 'every man was an intelligent human being who thought for himself, acted for himself, took pride in himself and knew his own mind'. Thus, 'spontaneity, not mere passive obedience, was the characteristic of their charge'. These soldiers had undergone intensive training on the exercise grounds at home, and most of them had served at various locations in the empire. Churchill therefore saw himself as a witness to the actions of a well-trained body of seasoned experts whose conduct emphasized keeping cool. In this way, the men would stay in control of themselves and of their tools and could continue to cooperate with both comrades and superiors.

Repetitious action

The regularity of repetitious action was a central feature of industrial division of labour since its beginning in the eighteenth century. The advancement of industrial work processes had been both fervently acclaimed and bitterly contested. Still, whatever position contemporaries took, they agreed that industrial work would dramatically change the role of 'living', or human, labour. In this sense, Karl Marx articulated a commonly held opinion: industry would turn man into the 'mere appendix' of machinery.[4]

The image of machinery resonated with expectations of a well-ordered and steady flow of production. However, more recent case studies of industrial work provide a different view. They reveal fundamentally ambivalent and partly contradictory situations at the very heart of production. Workers permanently faced uncertainty, risk or danger when, for instance, handling open fire at a furnace or operating a small boat in an off-shore fishing operation. Moreover, environmental constraints, such as heat and stench, demanded adaptation of disciplinary regulations and the intricacies of time- and piece-rates. Yet such conditions never seem to constitute what Erving Goffman has called a 'total institution'. These studies also show how workers cope with and appropriate the specific settings of work and, thus, make them their own. Yet workers' efforts to carve out niches for themselves and re-adjust the 'system' do not resonate with heroic attitudes. On the contrary, it is the striving for survival and 'making do' that informs workers' behaviour.[5]

---

4 Karl Marx, *Das Kapital*, 3 vols (1965; 1st edn Berlin: Dietz, 1865), vol.1, pp. 445, 674.
5 Michael Burawoy, *Manufacturing Consent: Changes in the Labor Process under Monopoly Capitalism* (Chicago: Chicago University Press, 1979); Horst Kern and Michael Schumann, *Das Ende der Arbeitsteilung: Rationalisierung in der industriellen Produktion* (4th edn, Munich: Beck, 1990).

For decades academic studies revolved only on selection of workers and their adaptation to industry. Cases in point are the studies on individual companies designed and supervised by Alfred and Max Weber prior to 1914 (Marie Bernays et al., sponsored by the *Verein für Socialpolitik*). In the mid- and late 1920s the range of research broadened.[6] Concomitantly, German industrial managers began to focus on how women and men actively shape the process of production: they handle tools and materials in their own ways, sometimes in a stubbornly self-willed, or *eigensinnig*, fashion. Such growing awareness of workers' appropriation of work triggered policies of rationalization that were critical of and deviant from Taylorism. In fact, in the 1920s, industrial rationalization movements in Germany relied explicitly on the specific dexterity and skill of the workers, whether trained or untrained. Their hands and heads had to be stimulated and 'put to work' at tools or conveyor belts (few as they were). Only then would an 'optimum [of working and producing] ... be possible'.

Of course, one can dispose of such management-driven analyses just as one can abandon the romanticizing attitudes favoured by many labour historians. Micro-historical explorations of workers' everyday practices show that these people were not 'automatons'. Here, they appear as individual actors, employing their sensual perceptivity, stamina and dexterity. Only occasionally did they join forces – or fight – with workmates.

Room for manoeuvre versus the threat of death

In the battles in Sudan, the British employed Maxim guns (machine guns), shrapnel ammunition and magazine rifles: the three 'weapons of civilization' (as they appeared in Churchill's account).[7] But it was not just such guns or shells that enhanced the firepower of European troops tremendously. The industrialization of warfare since the American Civil War and, in particular, during the First World War has often been described.[8] Rather than going into the details of this process,

---

6 See Alf Lüdtke, '"Deutsche Qualitätsarbeit", "Spielereien" am Arbeitsplatz und "Fliehen" aus der Fabrik: Industrielle Arbeitsprozesse und Arbeiterverhalten in den 1920er Jahren', in Friedhelm Boll (ed.), *Arbeiterkulturen zwischen Alltag und Politik* (Vienna: Europa Verlag, 1986), pp. 155–197, esp. p. 155–167, 173–177; Mary Nolan, *Visions of Modernity: American Business and the Modernization of Germany* (Oxford: Oxford University Press, 1994).
7 Churchill in Woods, *War Correspondent*, p. 133; dispatch 8 September 1898.
8 Bruno Thoß and Hans-Erich Volkmann (eds), *Erster Weltkrieg – Zweiter Weltkrieg: ein Vergleich* (Paderborn: Schöningh, 2002); Gerhard Hirschfeld (ed.), *Enzyklopädie Erster Weltkrieg* (Paderborn: Schöningh, 2003).

I want to emphasize here the parallels to industrial production outlined above. Complex apparatuses remained dependent on human performance, ranging from dexterously handling systems of transportation and communication to ever new generations of machines of destruction. Foot soldiers operated guns, flame throwers and tanks; sailors ran battleships and submarines; aviators made airships and airplanes 'work'.

In this context, it is imperative to inspect the logic of command and obedience, which is routinely misunderstood, from the inside. Churchill distinguished between the individual capacities of British professional soldiers, who were recruited as volunteers, from continental armies, which were based on the draft. Both manuals and recollections from the German armies, however, reveal a line similar to the British one. Not only officers, but basically every military person ought to be able to 'act according to the general purpose [of a specific action or of that very war in general], even if orders are lacking'. Textbooks for military training already emphasized this point prior to 1914. This quote, however, stems from the widely popularized version of the regulation for the infantry of the *Wehrmacht* in its 1940 version, the *Reibert*.[9]

Against this background, I want to pursue a twofold thesis. First, room for manoeuvre at the respective point of production was crucial to both industrial work and soldiering. Demands for skilfully moving and using one's body were similar, if not largely identical, in both areas. Only with these demands fulfilled would specific varieties of behaviour combine efficiency with effectiveness. Second, the areas of action and, even more, the specific performances of workers and soldiers still remained fundamentally different. This sense of difference was grounded in, or at least resonated with, the experience and expectation of being killed or – what often was worse in soldiers' recollections – being wounded.

Even more poignant was another sort of soldiers' experience: to encounter the power to kill as something that was not only terrorizing, but also appealing. The extent to which such emotionally heightened responses reflected the dangers and isolation in combat or, instead, distanced participants from these factors must be left open to speculation. The spectrum of soldiers' feelings obviously ranged from disgust and shame to pride, if not pleasure, time and again seemingly combining all of them. But regardless of whether soldiers felt it disturbing or appealing (or both), killing helped transform the meaning of 'doing a good job' into the excitement of an ultimate transgression.

---

9 Wilhelm Reibert, *Der Dienstunterricht im Heere: Ausgabe der Schützenkompanie* (12th edn, Berlin: E.S. Mittler, 1940), p. 237. See also my article, '"Fehlgreifen in der Wahl der Mittel". Optionen im Alltag militärischen Handelns', *Mittelweg 36* (2003): 61–73, esp. 64–65.

The army as a 'steel mill'?

In 1941 Curzio Malaparte reported for several months on the German invasion into the U.S.S.R. This author had a rather erratic career, moving from staunchly supporting Mussolini and his *Fascisti* in 1922 to a more critical stance, which caused his writing to be temporarily banned in 1929. After some years, however, he had reaffirmed his cooperation with the powers that be. Malaparte's ambition to appear as an autonomous person also reverberated in his reports for the Italian daily *Corriere Della Sera*. Instead of following German war correspondents, who denounced the soldiers of the Red Army as unfit or cowards, Malaparte recognized a similar 'workers' morale' among combatants on either side. He perceived 'two armies at the core formed from specialized workers and "industrialized" peasants'. It would therefore be 'the first time in the history of warfare that two armies fight against each other and the military morale is intricately connected with workers' morale, thus blending military discipline with a technical discipline of work since both armies are manned and run by skilled workers'.[10]

Malaparte took an even closer look: he scrutinized the corpses of Soviet soldiers killed in action. He spotted, for instance, two dead Russians and took notice of their 'stout' bodies and 'long arms'. He saw 'their bright eyes ... wide open'; to him these were 'specialists, two *Stachanov* workers'. And he went on:

> These are new breeds, totally "new" and just delivered; look at their mouths and strong lips. Peasants? Workers? These are specialists, working people. Some of those thousands and thousands who work the communal farms – or some of those thousands and thousands who run the factories of the Soviet Union ... All [of these people] are the same, produced in a series. Each of them is like the others are. This is a hard race. These are corpses of workers killed at their workplace.[11]

But Malaparte had started this sequence with an observation that alluded to technology and industrialized work processes. Observing the German troops advancing, he detected:

> not just an army but a huge moving workshop, a colossal steel mill on wheels. It looked as if a thousand chimneys, a thousand cranes, a thousand iron bridges, a thousand steel fortresses, thousands and thousands of ball bearings, of gearings, hundreds of furnaces and steel mills of Westphalia – as if the whole *Ruhrgebiet* was marching on the planes of Bessarabia. As if the huge *Krupp-Werke* ... had started to attack the hills around Zaicani ...

---

10 Curzio Malaparte, *Die Wolga entspringt in Europa* (Köln: Kiepenheuer and Witsch, 1989), p. 44; earlier edns, (Paris, 1948), (Rome 1952); transl. from the German here and in the subsequent quotations by A.L.
11 Malaparte, *Wolga*, p. 45.

I saw not an army but a colossal steel mill with a huge workforce of specialized workers who pursued their tasks according to precise schemes, at first glance hiding the intensity of their work.[12]

Malaparte continued by noting that this 'steel mill on wheels' appeared to move across the fields without inflicting any harm on the villages around it. Only the towns would be attacked. He also observed soldiers whose tank had killed a hog. Some peasants rushed to save the remnants of the animal: still, so the report went on, the German soldiers guaranteed cash compensation to the proprietor. In Malaparte's account, this almost peaceful exchange seemed to spring directly from the reign of modern machinery and industrial work over people's minds and morale. It is particularly this passage that raises serious doubts, though, as internal army reports, letters from the front and recollections of survivors describe a substantially different conduct by victorious troops.[13] They mention destroyed villages and towns in abundance, as well as rather distanced, if not hostile actions of German troops who did not refrain from heavy looting and violence against civilians, without any compensation.

In Malaparte's view, the imagery of the 'steel mill' represented the gist of what armies and soldiers stood for and practised. Such an overarching trope of modernity applied to either side: in Malaparte's account, the troops of Nazi Germany and the armies of the Soviet Union did not differ in this respect, but pursued the same rationale. But what sort of network of meanings did the iconic image of the steel mill invoke? First, the immediate reference is to the mill's gigantic dimensions. Usually a steel mill stretches for several kilometres. Similarly, many of its components and sub-sections are huge and, in any case, larger than man.

Second, a steel mill stands for the professional handling of a large-scale transformation of substances, while controlling any possible dangers for people's lives and bodies. The glow of the furnaces stems from heating up iron and other substances to their respective melting points. This process and its result, fluid steel, not only contain, but display destructive energy ready to consume living people. The effort to securely handle this danger alludes to the third layer of resonances: although the steel mill is a huge complex and employs hundreds, if not

---

12 Malaparte, *Wolga*, p. 32.
13 See Martin Humburg, *Das Gesicht des Krieges: Feldpostbriefe von Wehrmachtssoldaten aus der Sowjetunion 1941–1944* (Opladen: Westdeutscher Verlag, 1998); Hannes Heer (ed.), *"Stets zu erschießen sind Frauen, die in der Roten Armee dienen": Geständnisse deutscher Kriegsgefangener über ihren Einsatz an der Ostfront*, (2nd edn, Hamburg: Hamburger Edition, 1996); Klaus Latzel, *Deutsche Soldaten nationalsozialistischer Krieg?: Kriegserlebnis – Kriegserfahrung; 1939–1945*, (2nd edn, Paderborn: Schöningh, 2000); Peter Jahn and Ulrike Schmiegelt (eds), *Foto-Feldpost: geknipste Kriegserlebnisse 1939–1945* (Berlin: Elefantenpress, 2000).

thousands, of people, its workers are individuals who complete multiple tasks with tools. They are supposed to employ their minds and hands accordingly. At the same time, they form specific work teams that not only connect and assign different tasks, but also provide support. Thus, the image of the steel mill invokes the concrete practice at the point of production: to keep a complex operation going day and night. Especially while running the furnace, 'necessary cooperation' must be performed in its various, but minute, details. People have to sustain the very ability to cooperate with workmates and colleagues. People's dexterity and individual stamina, but also their courage, remain reliable only if everyone keeps a delicate balance between leaving colleagues their own space and interfering when necessary.[14]

Fourth, the imagery of the dexterous and, at the same time, strong hands and bodies of the operators invokes the experiences and pride of those who tamed the dangers of the system. These are the men who make it possible to exploit this production process. A more concrete inspection shows that during their shift, work teams of about twenty people commonly take steps that range from filling the furnace to handling its products until the steel cools off. During the subsequent steps of production, work teams of a similar size move and roll the slabs and bars. Of course, they fulfil specific tasks, but most of the men are capable of taking over when a colleague from their team is missing or tiring, or commits an error.

This process revolves not only around the furnace. The fifth aspect of this imagery is the interconnectedness that exists beyond the furnace. Molten steel is but the first link in a chain of manufacturing processes, from rolling bars to finishing products ranging from solid tracks to construction bars, armour plates and paper-thin metal foils. In addition, a sixth element comes into play: at least at the furnace, the work is also a process in another sense. For financial and technical reasons it never stops, but runs uninterruptedly day and night, seven days a week. Thus, it is just a small step from – a seventh aspect – connecting the concrete impressions and sensations of those directly involved in production to the actual end. Above all, it evokes the mythical notions of the origin of industry and industrialization: open fire in all its aspects, from lighting the environment to melting and fusing raw materials, transforming them, for instance, from ore and coal to iron and steel. What emerges is the steel mill as both site and symbol of

---

[14] Heinrich Popitz, *Technik und Industriearbeit: Soziologische Untersuchungen in der Hüttenindustrie*, (3rd edn, 1976; 1st edn, Tübingen: Mohr Siebeck, 1957), passim; cf., for other industrial branches and tasks, Alf Lüdtke, 'Deutsche Qualitätsarbeit' in Boll, *Arbeiterkulturen*, pp. 155–197; Lüdtke, 'Polymorphous Synchrony' in *International Review of Social History*, Supplement (1993): 39–84.

creation. Thus, the steel mill represents man's control of fire for producing usable items: in general, for man's production of human progress.

In contrast to the self-explanatory potential of the steel mill, Malaparte in his journalistic-cum-literary account neither alluded to nor directly addressed what soldiers encounter or, at least, never can neglect: the danger of being wounded, if not killed, but also the likeliness of using their weapon and, possibly, harming if not killing other people or 'the enemy'. Malaparte's presentation of the imagery of the steel mill served as a perfect device to metaphorically transpose the killing fields of destruction onto a totally different plane. In such a light, the grinding mill of warfare would glow only as an icon of productivity and creative power.

Small teams

Operating in teams of about twenty people can be seen as a characteristic of both military action and manufacturing. This assumption does not ignore the presence of regulations and constraints upon the respective military and industrial fields. Regardless of the concrete forms and their transformation, in either field teams and individuals were tied to chains of command and connected with networks of cooperation and communication.[15]

Different authors have aimed at rewriting the history of industrialization by tracing two profoundly different, but parallel configurations of industrial production. They show that 'mass production' (with its temporary craze for Taylorism and Fordism) was paralleled, if not outdistanced, by branches based on and stimulating 'flexible specialization'.[16] However, this distinction does not affect the micro-level observation that small teams played a crucial role in production, as studies on metallurgical works and steel mills confirm. These studies show that 'mass production' has re-evaluated the pivotal role of individual 'production

---

[15] Small teams (of about twenty or fewer people) are mostly located in the branches of metal processing and machine construction. However, the pivots of the putting-out system and cottage industry in textiles had also been small teams and family units. Here, however, mechanization in factory production allowed for a rapid intensification of the division of labour. Oftentimes, this meant the separation of single women (and men) at their specific workplaces, but also an effort to degrade the knowledge of their craft. Still, recent interpretations underline that even in textiles, one cannot observe 'a trend towards any single structure', see Maxine Berg, *The Age of Manufactures, 1700–1820* (London: Fontana Press, 1985), p. 228; Berg, *The Age of Manufactures* (2nd edn, London: Routledge, 1994), pp. 257–279.

[16] Charles Sabel and Jonathan Zeitlin, 'Historical Alternatives to Mass Production: Politics, Markets and Technology in 19th Century Industrialization', in *Past and Present* 108 (Aug. 1985): 133–176.

workers' and small teams.[17] Charles Sabel and Jonathan Zeitlin have argued that dominant notions as, for instance, Taylorism or Fordism (or for this matter: the steel mill) grossly misrepresent both multifaceted historical processes and actual practices of historical actors. In their emphasis on 'one best way', they misrepresent the practices of working people.

A similar investigation of the paths of change in the military since the late eighteenth century would show a comparable width and range of trajectories for the armies of the European and North American powers. For instance, in the Second World War combustion engines powered airplanes and tanks, but also trucks and motorcycles in *Wehrmacht* units. Still, the majority of German soldiers moved and fought on foot or literally relied on horsepower for transport of baggage, food and ammunition.[18] Even artillery or engineering units of the *Wehrmacht* primarily employed horses for transporting and moving canons, guns and other gear, whether bulky or not. Tending to the horses and driving them was a multifaceted job for one group of soldiers. Others drove and repaired trucks, tanks or motorcycles. Tanks had been the symbolic spearheads of the ground forces' military successes between 1939 and late 1941.[19] But it was the newsreels that gave tanks and airplanes (and motorcycles) their ubiquitous presence in people's minds.

Thus, gas, diesel or electric engines, as well as advanced technology in communications, were part of military planning and practice and, hence, of soldiers' tasks. But the actual number of these soldiers remained limited; on the German side, it even shrank considerably in the course of the war. Regardless of the total number of soldiers involved, many German soldiers tended to six or eight horses each. In this capacity, they operated largely on their own, although they were still part of, for instance, the artillery battery that they had been assigned to.[20] In similar ways, the operators of cars, trucks, switchboards or wireless telegraphs were often on their own and had some leeway in fulfilling their tasks. Repair shops, bakeries and many of those rearguard small or medium-sized units that

---

[17] Kern Schumann, *Das Ende der Arbeitsteilung?*
[18] Militärgeschichtliches Forschungsamt, *Das Deutsche Reich und der Zweite Weltkrieg*, vol. 4: *Der Angriff auf die Sowjetunion* (Stuttgart: Deutsche Verlagsanstalt, 1983), pp. 1138f. and vol. 5, part 2: *Organisation und Mobilisierung des deutschen Machtbereichs* (Munich: Deutsche Verlagsanstalt, 1999), pp. 636f., 648ff.
[19] Cf. Karl-Heinz Frieser, *The Blitzkrieg Legend: The 1940 Campaign in the West* (Annapolis: Naval Institute Press, 2005; 1st edn, Munich: Oldenbourg, 1995); Evan Mawdsley, *Thunder in the East: The Nazi-Soviet War 1941–1945* (London: Hodder Arnold, 2005).
[20] See the case discussed in detail by Magnus Koch, '"... wenn der Tod mit seinen furchtbaren Arten seine Ernte holt". Deutungen physischer Gewalt am Beispiel des Wehrmachtsgefreiten Hermann Rombach', in *Historische Anthropologie* 12 (2004): 179–198.

provided calories and ammunition to keep the army going, worked differently. Here, teamwork prevailed to a much larger extent, so the situation was similar to the style of performance in civilian workshops, but also in combat units.

Emotional and cultural dynamics

Debates about industry and wage work conventionally assume that those involved direct their behaviours and activities according to rational calculations of their (dis)advantages. Only gradually did observers and those actively working in industry develop a sense for the multifaceted emotional and cultural dynamics that drove people to work or not to work.

Studies of artisan production have pioneered this opening-up by exploring multiple arenas of work. These investigations scrupulously traced the handling of tools and materials. However, their emphasis was on the many folds and trajectories that resonated between working people's strivings for survival and their performances of and at work. This view has revealed in concrete terms (and images) how 'eating, drinking, housing, marrying, bequeathing or inheriting property or rights to property [was part of] work itself'.[21] In his analysis of journeymen's behaviour in eighteenth-century Paris, Michael Sonenscher shows that these reproductive practices 'made up a part of the environment of nonmonetary manoeuvre and symbolic negotiation in which masters and journeymen encountered and dealt with one another'. Thus, if researchers ignore this context, they miss, for instance, what 'wage' meant and implied, not to mention the very buying power of cash, as it was not visible in specific amounts demanded, paid or received.

In a similar vein, Robert Darnton has focused on the cultural dimensions of artisan work. In his seminal study of 'the great cat massacre', he analyses an account rendered by a former participant in a demonstrative action of Parisian journeymen against their master and his wife in the 1730s.[22] The historian carefully traces the symbolic and material claims for status and control as acted out by the different inhabitants of the *patrons* household-cum-workshop. Thus, Darnton reconstructs a field of forces that were produced and employed in the everyday lives

---

[21] Michael Sonenscher, 'Work and Wages in Paris in the Eighteenth Century', in Maxine Berg, Pat Hudson and Michael Sonenscher (eds), *Manufacturer in Town and Country Before the Factory* (Cambridge: Cambridge University Press, 1983), pp. 147–172, esp. p. 171; in more traditional parlance: of the inter-relations between production and reproduction, ibid.

[22] Robert Darnton, 'Workers Revolt: The Great Cat Massacre of the Rue Saint-Séverin', in Darnton (ed.), *The Great Cat Massacre and Other Episodes in French Cultural History* (London: Vintage, 1984), pp. 75–104, 270–272.

of people who, in a very limited physical space, strove for survival and recognition. The journeymen and particularly the apprentices felt themselves treated unjustly: not only did the patron give them orders, but his 'middleman', his wife, did as well. Still more offensive to them was the contempt embodied in the meagre, if not distasteful, food dished out to them. Such daily meals were part of their wage while, at the same time, the cats of the *patronesse* were treated exquisitely. Darnton then emphasizes the potential for revolt in a carnival-like ritual: in a nightly raid several journeymen and apprentices killed those very cats that were fondly cherished and fed by the patron's wife. By taking this action, the workers protested and 'turned things upside down'. Thus, the journeymen stated their claims in violent terms; however, they did not transgress or physically attack the bodies or other properties of the two people whom they wanted to hurt and humiliate.

Historic-ethnographical studies[23] focus on both the simultaneities and the resonances of worker's signs, gestures and material actions. They explore interrelations between people's activities for producing survival and their relating themselves to (or distancing themselves from) others whom they considers as equal to, 'above' or 'below' themselves. A case in point is Gerald Sider's research on the Newfoundland cod fishery, which investigates work and the social interactions that revolved around it both in the present and the past.

Sider traces the behaviour of the men who for generations had formed the boat crews and brought in the catch. He also closely observed the women who processed the catch on the shore, thus 'making' the fish. Sider emphasizes the seasonal occurrence of interactions and experiences: not during, but after the fishing season, people 'acted out' and showed what had occupied them during recent months. They vented the pleasures and anger they had harboured for weeks or months 'inside'. Even in a crew that would 'ideally, consist of patrikinsmen' the members encountered tensions. In turn, kinfolk tended to 'avoid each other completely' after the summer season was over. However, they came back together in mid-winter when they, for instance, 'jointly beg[a]n to rebuild their equipment'.[24]

---

[23] See Gerald Sider, 'Christmas Mumming and the New Year in Outport Newfoundland', in *Past and Present* 71 (1976): 102–125, esp. 108f. As to industry, cf. Burawoy, *Manufacturing Consent*; Tamara Hareven, *Family Time and Industrial Time: The Relationship between the Family and Work in a New England Industrial Community* (Cambridge: University Press of America, 1982). In their efforts of finding and deciphering traces, historians have renewed scrutiny *modo ethnographico*, see Joan Scott, *The Glassworkers of Carmaux* (Cambridge, Mass.: Harvard University Press, 1974); Patrick Joyce, *Work, Society and Politics: The Culture of the Factory in Later Victorian England* (Brighton: Harvester, 1980); Franz-J. Brüggemeier, *Leben vor Ort: Ruhrbergleute und Ruhrbergbau 1889–1919* (Munich: Beck, 1983); Dorothee Wierling, *Mädchen für alles: Arbeitsalltag und Lebensgeschichte städtischer Dienstmädchen um die Jahrhundertwende* (Berlin: Dietz, 1987).
[24] Sider, 'Christmas Mumming', p. 108f.

A specific form of flexibility seemed present in almost all relationships and (self-) presentations. This intensity was re-informed by ritual activities that revolved around Christmas: carnival-like 'mumming' and a short-lived but boisterous 'turning the world upside down'. This mixture of playfulness and calculated action re-established the possibility of returning to the normalcy of the everyday. Such normalcy involved well-ordered, but not strictly hierarchical cooperation and burden sharing, which remained rigidly gendered.[25]

Similarities between the fisher-folk and military crews are striking. In both instances, the communities not only worked together, but lived together day and night. The permanent presence of workmates and comrades in the barracks, at camp or 'in action', as well as the immediacy of superiors, creates similar situations in each case. There is an analogy in the simultaneous presence of tensions and easy going cooperation. Rituals and the multitude of performative actions in a military setting are, therefore, of similar importance to those described in the studies undertaken by Gerald Sider.

Killing: a narrative void?

Ernst Jünger's accounts of the First World War, written during the 1920s, especially his *Storm of Steel*,[26] have too often been misread as just another loop of the never-ending spiral of officers' attempts at heroic self-presentation. Still, even the hindsight and officer's point of view that are both obviously employed by the author should not blind the reader to the other aspects of the text. Jünger rendered life 'at the front' in superb nuances: especially moments of combat with their intense mixture of fear and joy. Both fear and joy appear in his writings as intricately connected: the recognition of imminent danger with the feeling of utter fulfilment and 'being real' for the first time.[27]

Feelings of insecurity and anxiety are often mentioned – if in abbreviated form – in diaries, letters and accounts written in hindsight; and those looking

---

[25] Husbands and sons, brothers and fathers (also nephews and uncles) operated the boats. While at port, the female half of the families and households devoted, in turn, their time and energy to the task of processing the catch and 'making' fish, Sider, 'Christmas Mumming', p. 109.
[26] Ernst Jünger, *Storm of Steel* (first published 1920, *In Stahlgewittern* (London 1928); see Bernd Weisbrod, 'Military Violence and Male Fundamentalism: Ernst Jünger's Contribution to the Conservative Revolution', *History Workshop Journal* 49 (2000): 69–94.
[27] See Eric J. Leed, *No Mans Land: Combat and Identity in World War I* (Cambridge: Cambridge University Press, 1979), pp. 150–162; also Paul Fussel, *The Great War and Modern Memory* (Oxford: Oxford University Press, 1975).

back on the Second World War are not very different from those describing the First World War. As different as these respective texts may be, perceptions and sensual reactions triggered by the authors' own killing or wounding of people are mostly passed over in silence. It does not matter whether this happens 'face to face' or the other appears only as a barely visible 'dot' in the distance. However, recollections time and again refer to the either/or alternative: 'either he or I' will survive. To invoke an existential urge for survival does more than recall moments of the past; it also sheds some light on moral or cultural codes that might restrict killing actions. At the same time, the emotional intensity of these recollections – so striking with Jünger – becomes even more apparent if the wording in other texts is restrained or clumsy (as in many oral recollections).[28]

Michael Geyer reminded historians some years ago that military and even war history has almost totally neglected 'killing'.[29] A similar point can be made about the neglect of feelings. Analyses ignore the fact that joyful feelings of success and fulfilment were seemingly intertwined with fear and anxiety in war. Perhaps it was this overlap, if not simultaneity, that ran contrary to the various 'normalities' people had encountered in their peacetime settings (of course, also in the military).[30] These dimensions of 'real war' that 'never get in the books'[31] remain preserved in silences or evocative abbreviations: if they are not funnelled to less visible arenas such as the public house or *Stammtisch*, or afternoon tea. On both levels, though, it is not detailed descriptions of specific activities, but short phrases that dominate: the other is *erledigt* ('finished off'), *niedergemacht* or *liquidiert*.[32]

Stories and practices of 'comradeship'

Autobiographical and literary accounts of both the First and the Second World War revolve heavily around stories of *Kameradschaft* ('fellowship' or 'comrade-

---

28 Hans Joachim Schröder, *Die gestohlenen Jahre. Erzählgeschichten und Geschichtserzählung im Interview: Der Zweite Weltkrieg aus der Sicht ehemaliger Mannschaftssoldaten* (Tübingen: Niemeyer, 1992).
29 Michael Geyer, 'Von einer Kriegsgeschichte, die vom Töten spricht', in Thomas Lindenberger and Alf Lüdtke (eds), *Physische Gewalt* (Frankfurt am Main: Suhrkamp, 1995), pp. 136–161.
30 On this very level an otherwise most insightful study on the 'military culture' and its 'habitual practices' in Imperial Germany falls short: Isabel Hull, *Absolute Destruction: Military Culture and the Practices of War in Imperial Germany* (Ithaca/London: Cornell University Press, 2005), p. 92, 98ff.
31 Joanna Bourke, *An Intimate History of Killing: Face-to-face Killing in Twentieth-Century Wars* (London: Basic Books, 1998), pp. 267ff.
32 Schröder, *Die gestohlenen Jahre*, p. 565.

ship'). This pertains to all combatants, regardless of the side on which they found themselves. Thus, it is not surprising that sociologists Samuel Marshall and Samuel Stouffer confirmed the pivotal importance of small group relationships for the U.S. military.[33] Thomas Kühne has explored this kind of relationship in regard to the German armies as well, relating it to other forms of trust. He argues that soldiers employ a specific 'faceless' trust, as generated in and reproduced by the small groups they are operating and, in fact, living in. Technically speaking, one is looking into sub-unit relationships: squads (sections) or, at the utmost, platoons; that is, about thirty people.[34]

In this view, reciprocal relationships among comrades were fundamental for coping with physical and mental hardship, especially at the Eastern Front. The relationship of trust also allowed them to outwit the military hierarchy and its harsh disciplinary impositions. It was trust that would muffle the waves of aggressiveness in exchanges not only between superiors and their underlings, but also among rank-and-file soldiers. From this perspective, traditional ideas, as well as those emphasizing the dominance of Nazi ideology in general and Nazi antisemitism in particular (as stressed by Omer Bartov), seem overstated.[35] To be sure, efforts by military leaders and, especially, the newly introduced NS-*Führungsoffiziere* to fanaticize the troops were not completely meaningless. But evidence such as letters home from the front, diaries, and death announcements in newspapers indicate that people in many ways blended racism with notions of the 'fatherland under siege' that, again, created all sorts of resonances with experiences of companionship among the military work team.

The specific traits that Kühne describes as crucial for military companionship correspond closely to characteristics of industrial work teams. A certain familiarity with the code of conduct, the knowledge of how to treat peers and how to deal with superiors, materials and various constraints and demands (time schedules, wage schemes) was as common on the shop floor as in (or behind) the combat zones. What is missing in Kühne's account, at least partly, applies equally to the small group relationships in industry and the military: the darker side of socia-

---

33 Samuel L.A. Marshall, *Men Against Fire: The Problem of Battle Command in Future War* (New York: University of Oklahoma Press, 1947); Samuel Stouffer, *The American Soldier: Combat and Its Aftermath* (Princeton: Princeton University Press, 1949), pp. 130–137.
34 Thomas Kühne, 'Vertrauen und Kameradschaft. Soziales Kapital im "Endkampf" der Wehrmacht', in Ute Frevert (ed.), *Vertrauen* (Göttingen: Vandenhoeck and Ruprecht, 2003), pp. 245–278, esp. pp. 256–257, 263–264; see also his comprehensive account *Kameradschaft: die Soldaten des nationalsozialistischen Krieges und das 20. Jahrhundert* (Göttingen: Vandenhoeck and Ruprecht, 2006).
35 Omer Bartov, *The Eastern Front 1941–1945: German Troops and the Barbarisation of Warfare* (Basingstoke: Macmillan, 1985).

bility, namely, social control and social pressure.³⁶ It is the analysis of such relationships and, particularly, pressures on possible dissenters that has become the main line in Christopher Browning's analyses of the dynamics within the companies of Police Battalion 101. He explores how 'ordinary men' turned into killers in the context of the Holocaust in occupied Poland in 1942 and 1943.

Individual trajectories I

Individual trajectories are pivotal for this perspective. However, the issue is not to map 'typical', or 'normal' life courses. What matters are the specific details: they allow us to explore the range of potentialities. Dominik Richert was a soldier in the Prussian army from the beginning of the war until the summer of 1918, when he deserted. Born in 1893 in an Alsatian village, the young man was earning his living as a farm labourer when he was drafted in October 1913. Having done his basic training with a *Badische* Infantry regiment, he served first at the Western front. Eventually, his unit was redeployed to the East, only to be later transferred back to the Western front. Only several months after his desertion, he wrote a lengthy text, which survived by chance and was found and edited only a few years ago.³⁷

Richert narrates in detail combat situations from the viewpoint of the rank and file. He dwells on the everyday agonizing about one's own and, even more importantly, the enemy's whereabouts 'on the map': or, as it increasingly seemed, the 'troglodytes' in the trenches and underground.³⁸ He does not exclude eyewitness accounts of people dying; regardless of whether these were close comrades or enemy soldiers. This is never detached from the living conditions and the experiences of unequal treatment of officers and soldiers. He comments bitterly on officers who show no respect for soldiers and treat them brutally while enjoying enormous liberty (and, not to be forgotten, culinary delicacies). Richert also

---

36 See Lüdtke, '"Deutsche Qualitätsarbeit"' in Boll, *Arbeiterkulturen*, pp. 155–197; for military units see Christopher Browning, *Ordinary Men: Reserve Police Battalion 101 and the Final Solution in Poland* (New York: Harper Perennial, 1992). Cf. a recollection relating a specific kind of fear with one's desire for recognition: 'It was the fear of not performing as expected, making the wrong decision at a critical time, and letting my crew down.' This particular recollection stems from the memory of an American bomber pilot, James M. Davis; Davis, *In Hostile Skies: An American B-24 Pilot in WW II*, ed. by David L. Snead (Denton: Texas A and M University Press, 2006), p. 92.
37 Dominik Richert, *Beste Gelegenheit zum Sterben: Meine Erlebnisse im Kriege 1914–1918*, ed. by Angelika Tramitz and Bernd Ulrich (Munich: Knesebeck, 1989).
38 Cf. Leed, *No Mens Land*, quoting Henri Barbusse, p. 139.

depicts leisure time and, as one of its highlights, a sports festival of his regiment. In many ways the author reconstructs the cosmos of a soldier who suffers from his constant engagement with the cause – if not primarily from his performance 'on the job'.[39]

In early 1918 Richert, who had been promoted to non-commissioned office (NCO), became the leader of a machine-gun squad. The stories he recalls give a concrete picture of his aptness as a military leader, if not his eagerness to be a 'good' soldier. He operated the machine gun and guided his squad, gaining as much room to manoeuvre as possible and thereby effectively keeping the enemy down and his men alive. The German High Command had introduced these specific teams as segments of newly formed assault units in 1915. Close inspection renders similar, if not identical, features of the everyday practices of soldiers and NCOs on the one hand, and workers and industrial masters on the other. In both settings, the actors strove to perform 'German quality work': crucial was the individual handling of tools and materials, as well as of social relationships with both superiors and workmates. Sensitivity for both the material and social features of the task was central; similarly important was the ability to actively shape the handling of the situation.

Let us compare these findings with analyses of industrial work processes. Room to manoeuvre was vital on the shop floor: in the 1910s, as in the 1920s, 1930s and 1940s. The individual operator of a tool had to make decisions about specific performances when manipulating both tools and materials. This included, of course, management of time and energy. It also comprised – and this was no less important – the care for social relationships with comrades and workmates. The latter two were necessary for a job performance ensuring both work safety and a calculable wage.

Therefore, such 'cooperation of necessity' not only framed, but also stimulated individual behaviour. Richert, as NCO, encountered room for manoeuvre especially in his position as leader of a machine gun squad. In these small assault units, the twenty-five to thirty men directly cooperated with or integrated various specialists operating, for example, light cannons (*Infanteriegeschütz*), flame throwers or light mortars. Both training and actual combat demands focused on independent action of these small units and, in the end, of every individual. Finally, the NCOs were no longer those who had 'to push' soldiers from behind; in

---

[39] The rift between officers and ordinary soldiers was not experienced by Richert alone. Investigations of the German military after the war emphasized this particular trait as decisive for the final collapse in 1918. See more generally Wilhelm Deist, 'Verdeckter Militärstreik im Kriegsjahr 1918?', in Wolfram Wette (ed.), *Der Krieg des kleinen Mannes. Eine Militärgeschichte von unten* (Munich/Zurich: Piper, 1992), pp. 146–167.

the new scheme they had to lead from the front, interchangeable with subaltern officers. Thus, the mission-oriented tactics of the German (in particular of the Prussian) army in these new tactics directly affected the 'masses' of NCOs and even rank and file.

The same was true for the industrial work unit. Constant and rigid body drill was, however, special to the military. The aim was to instil a sense of immediate readiness for action into every soldier, so that they would overcome fear and keep cool in actual or imminent combat. It was particular to the German effort to emphasize the importance of coherence in order to ensure the cooperation of units and teams. NCOs and commanding officers were never removed during stints in a reserved position, contrary to British and French practices. In addition, drill never determined mission tactics. In fact, the latter was increasingly highlighted on the German side in war games, not only on the level of the general staff, but also in regular units down to company and even squad level. This regular practice furthered a climate of questioning routines and of experimenting throughout the army, including subaltern officers and NCOs. War gaming became an ever increasing feature of soldiering.[40]

Individual trajectories II

Children of Richert's age group, born after 1910, filled not only the rank and file, but also the posts of NCOs and subaltern officers in the *Wehrmacht*. One of them was Walter Janka. In the late 1920s this skilled metalworker had become an active Communist who was incarcerated for two years by the Nazis in 1933. Upon his release, he fled into exile and joined the Republican forces fighting the Franco rebels in Spain in 1936.

Janka survived and reached a high-ranking position in the publishing industry in East Germany in the mid-1950s. However, he was ousted from both his job and his position with the ruling Socialist Unity Party in 1957, having been sentenced to jail on account of accusations of treacherous anti-party conspiracy. He started to write an autobiography including episodes of soldiering in the Spanish Civil War. Among others, he recalled an incident where he had served as company commander in a Spanish division (not in the 'International Brigades'). His men had hidden machine guns in the ditches beside the road awaiting busloads of Franco's soldiers:

---

[40] Bruce I. Gudmundsson, *Storm Troop Tactics: Innovation in the German army, 1914–1918* (New York/London: Praeger Press, 1989), pp. 50–53, 173–177.

> Upon first sight of these buses ... I gave a signal ... Within minutes the road became hell: windows burst, oil and gas spread across the road. Most vehicles caught fire. Anyone who had not been gunned down in the buses was killed by the hand grenades of the second company, and those who hoped to escape were killed by gun fire. After twenty minutes there was nothing but fuming wracks, stench and death. We did not take prisoners. We did not have time to spare for prisoners ... The obvious success on the roads heightened the spirits. In fact, this was the second success on this very day.[41]

Calculated and concentrated application of mechanized (and partly automatized) firepower was at the centre of the work processes of these soldiers. They coordinated all their energies and body movements in order to use their tools as swiftly and efficiently as possible to survive themselves and wound or kill the 'others'. Janka, however, at least in hindsight, almost in the same instant started to reflect: 'Killing people is not work. But maybe a soldier sees it that way and most of the soldiers are workers. What they do is just work.' In his account, Janka lets his soldiers speak: they took their action as 'work'. In concrete terms, they had gunned down the enemy soldiers. Their commander recalled this action as both gruesome and tedious, nothing to be fond of. In fact, in hindsight it appeared as hard work, toilsome but also bloody. At least for Janka, the important difference between soldiers' actions and enjoyable activities was, obviously, bloodshed.

Still, what can one make of this remark? The author notifies readers of his unease: is it appropriate, can it be right to render a killing action as work? Janka in the late 1950s was a dissident of the Socialist Unity Party in East Germany. In his account, Janka invoked both the antifascist cause of the Spanish Republic and the socialist and Communist labour movements of Weimar Germany. Central to both was an imagery that presented work as the primordial activity of man. Thus, not only the toil, but also the satisfaction of 'living labour' drove the progress of humankind to produce used values or usable products. Production and productivity had, therefore, broadly framed societal and political vistas as well as the pragmatics of workers' politics on the shop floor. In other words, work drew its aura from its interconnectedness with production. In combat, Janka recalled, worker-soldiers produced destruction. More specifically, with all of their energy, they worked towards killing others.

---

41 Walter Janka, *Spuren eines Lebens* (Reinbek: Rowohlt, 1992), pp. 109–110; the author could only publish his text, however, after the implosion of the GDR.

From wage-working to soldiering in the Second World War

In the Second World War large numbers of both draftees and volunteers of the *Wehrmacht* were wage workers. In their civilian life, they had worked in blue-collar or white-collar jobs, and many had grown up in working class neighbourhoods and milieus. In another context, I have made use of the letters that some soldiers from such backgrounds sent home to their workmates at their respective hometown companies: in this case, Leipzig-based companies.[42] Regardless of whether these letters were mailed in 1940 from France or two or three years later from the Eastern Front, until the spring of 1945 the writers emphasized how much soldiering resembled working in an industrial plant or, for that matter, in a hospital or an administrative office. They stressed tediousness, routine if not boredom, physical toil and exhaustion, and also division of labour and lack of supervision. Comrades are present, too, in these letters, as is 'necessary cooperation' (although 'trust' is less present).[43] A rare find is, however, the letter of a *Luftwaffe* NCO from June 1943. He describes a flight in a plane that had a few days previously circled over Warsaw, immediately after the Jewish ghetto had been destroyed. After referring to this destruction, the NCO finishes with this remark: 'Our troops did a pretty good job *[gute Arbeit]* when destroying the Jewish quarter of that city.'[44]

Such a destruction of this part of the city must have included the killing of inhabitants or other people seeking shelter: soldier's activities that the writer summarily described as 'work'. The lack of more nuanced words is a telling reference to a void. Of course, this void, when submitted to analysis, seems to be totally filled if one considers feelings and their driving power among historical actors themselves. It is that simultaneity of coolness and fulfilment, of terror and fury, and of numbness and activity that is found in documents and traces of small and large battle settings and fighting and killing actions.

---

[42] See Alf Lüdtke, 'Arbeit, Arbeitserfahrungen und Arbeiterpolitik', in Lüdtke, *Eigen-Sinn. Arbeiter, Arbeitserfahrungen und Politik vom Kaiserreich bis in den Faschismus* (Hamburg: Ergebnisse Verlag, 1993), pp. 351–440, 406–409.
[43] Cf. letters of a medical doctor and officer, born 1907, from the Eastern Front: Ingo Stander (ed.), '*Ihr daheim und wir hier draußen. Ein Briefwechsel zwischen Ostfront und Heimat, Juni 1941–März 1943* (Cologne: Böhlau, 2006).
[44] Cf. Lüdtke, 'Arbeit, Arbeitserfahrungen und Arbeiterpolitik', p. 408.

Carrying on, 1943 to 1945

Two different but related questions emerge. First, what made these *Wehrmacht* soldiers fight on until the very last instance and even beyond? Second, what caused the ongoing, if not intensified, brutality? This was especially present among many who engaged in what had begun as anti-partisan warfare, at the Eastern Front but increasingly also in the southeast and south.

If one considers, again, the comradeship and cooperation of small-scale military units, the pictures largely overlap with scenarios of industrial work. Accordingly, numerous accounts confirm that the shock reported from first encounters with the killing fields did not last. Soldiers coped through self-willed stubbornness *(Eigen-Sinn)*. In fact, the title of the last feature film Nazi propagandists finished and released in 1945 contained the line: 'Life goes on' *[Das Leben geht weiter]*.[45] Here, a blend of nonchalance and self-will emerges. It was a sense of cool determination that fuelled people's strivings for every possible relationship, just as it fuelled any material means of survival.

Such images reflected the flexible endurance apparently widespread among seasoned soldiers. However, newly drafted soldiers and volunteering youngsters encountered both the stubborn clinging to old-style rigidity of the military institution *(Kommiss)* and the 'out-of-bounds' of the imminent battle zone. To explore these overlaps, but also their limits, let us embark on the recollections from a semi-military unit of German *Flakhelfer* in the second half of the Second World War.

Like many other young males who were aged sixteen or seventeen, Rolf Schörken and his peers were drafted in 1943 or 1944 for the anti-aircraft batteries *(Flak)* at the home front. Most of them attended high school and all belonged to the 'Hitler Youth', or *Hy*. Training to become gunners, these *Flakhelfer* were concentrated in separate barracks to attend class by day and operate anti-aircraft guns by night. One of the outstanding facets Schörken recalls is what the military hierarchy that the *Hy* had so eagerly adopted meant in their everyday lives: namely that 'someone permanently demanded something from you'.[46] In turn, Schörken and his companions tenaciously strove to preserve as much as possible of their own ways of life. In particular, all of them aimed at keeping a low profile and avoiding situations where superiors 'could reach you'. Their expectation that nobody could 'stem the tide' and defeat the Allied powers generated

---

[45] Werner Blumenberg, *Das Leben geht weiter. Der letzte Film des Dritten Reiches* (Berlin: Rowohlt, 1993).
[46] Rolf Schörken, *Luftwaffenhelfer und Drittes Reich: Die Entstehung eines politischen Bewusstseins* (Stuttgart: Klett-Cotta, 1984), p. 141.

less relief than gloomy visions of the future. In turn, intensified activity became a means to overcome such visions, if only for a few hours at a time. For these young men, the heightened intensity of action, especially of firing their guns, became a sought-after way out.[47] In the intervals between alarms, these gunners cherished every trace of mutual recognition and respect from family or friends.

On another level, however, individuals at least occasionally voiced their desire, not for identification between working and soldiering, but for their strict separation. Heinrich Böll, a rank-and-file soldier with the infantry, described a 'split' he saw in himself in his letters from the front. In one way, he saw himself as the grudgingly obedient soldier, whereas the other Böll was a 'fanatic individualist'.[48] The 'soldier Böll' would keep his military efforts to a minimum in order to survive threats from enemies and superiors (and, for that matter, from his companions). The 'other Böll' appeared perhaps more often in the dreams and fantasies of the writer. This was the independent spirit who did not care in the least about orders of hierarchy, including superiors. However, the 'other Böll' might not have been content within this bracket of 'fanatic individualism'. Would he not be tempted to seize the opportunity for (re-)producing the simultaneity of coolness and fulfilment, of terror and fury? Perhaps there were too many occasions in which to yield to this temptation, one that not only allowed for, but stimulated brutality in soldiers' actions.[49]

---

[47] Cf. also the biographical reconstruction of a soldier from a rural background, who was born in 1924 and eagerly expected the draft in 1942, aiming to join the navy or the *panzers:* Bernhard Haupert and Franz Josef Schäfer, *Jugend zwischen Kreuz und Hakenkreuz* (Frankfurt am Main: Suhrkamp, 1991), pp. 191–209, 135–237. See the remark of a communications officer, born in 1917, in a letter from occupied France to his girlfriend in June of 1940: he wanted to volunteer for the paratroopers and noted that, 'if there is war I cannot survive it in the rear'. In 1943 he courageously stood against the persecution of the family of Sophie Scholl: Sophie Scholl and Fritz Hartnagel, *Damit wir uns nicht verlieren. Briefwechsel 1937–1943*, ed. by Thomas Hartnagel, (Frankfurt am Main: Fischer, 2005), p. 180.

[48] Heinrich Böll, *Briefe aus dem Krieg*, ed. by. Jochen Schubert, vols. 1 and 2 (Cologne: Kiepenheuer & Witsch, 2001), p. 343. This remark from Summer 1940 finds no direct resonance in his writings of the years at the front that followed. For instance, in several notes of November 1943 he distinguishes strictly between the horrors and terrors of war and their concreteness in 'the East' on the one hand and on the feeling of undeserved luck of surviving and enjoying, yet again, the little pleasures of relief after 'another' round of combat on the other, see pp. 948–961.

[49] See Benjamin Ziemann, 'Die Eskalation des Tötens in zwei Weltkriegen', in Richard van Dülmen (ed.), *Erfindung des Menschen: Schöpfungsträume und Körperbilder 1500–2000* (Vienna: Böhlau, 1998), pp. 411–429, 424–428; Hamburger Institut für Sozialforschung, *Verbrechen der Wehrmacht: Dimensionen des Vernichtungskrieges 1941–1944* (Hamburg: Hamburger Edition, 2001); especially insightful, and relating brutality primarily to rearguard troops and less to frontline units, is Christoph Rass, *'Menschenmaterial: Deutsche Soldaten an der Ostfront. Innenansichten einer Infanteriedivision, 1939–1945* (Paderborn: Schöningh, 2003).

This other or second person may, then, resonate with a peculiar facet of soldiering: the overwhelming, instantaneous pleasure of actively being involved, which contrasts with working: whether it be in industrial, agrarian, or domestic settings. That pleasure might even cut into the field of obedience: working towards a good cause and engaging oneself according to a given blueprint could allow for grand feelings of and for oneself.[50] In order to further understand the interrelationship between rule and self-activity in this setting, one would have to consider Ernst Jünger's tract of 1932 on the worker-soldier, *Der Arbeiter*.

Normal work: and/or the fury of the killing fields

Ernst Jünger envisioned the worker as a *Gestalt* representing a new era. This idealized (and, hence, stereotyped) industrial worker diverged in principle from the image of an alienated 'appendix of machinery' common among Marxists in particular and intellectuals more generally. The worker Jünger portrayed appeared as 'driven by a will to power' and would blend working with warfare. Hence, Jünger referred to the First World War as a 'comprehensive working process' and to military action as 'battle work' entailing 'work of attack' as well as 'work of the lost post'.[51]

However, the 'heroic realism' Jünger pleaded for did not withstand the actual 'storm of steel' that became imminent in the wars of the late 1930s and 1940s. Walter Janka's sceptical account quoted above poses the question: could one really regard any effective action, killing dozens of enemy fighters, as work? For many German soldiers of the Second World War, whether draftees or volunteers, dexterous performance and effective pursuit of their respective tasks made this 'work'. To many of them, the practices of soldiering that allowed for the active input and cooperation of the rank and file resembled 'German quality work'. In the more distanced view of the observer, similarities between such military teams and fishing crews like those analysed by Gerald Sider emerge. Both involve the harsh conditions of getting by, to the imminent dangers of injury and death, to the formation of intricate relationships. These teams or crews connected one or two dozen males. Most of them had unequal skills and performance levels but, for the time being, they joined forces and acted to survive, at any cost.

---

50 See the praise of the automaton in eighteenth-century theories of individualization: Barbara Stollberg-Rilinger, *Der Staat als Maschine: Zur politischen Metaphorik des absoluten Fürstenstaats* (Berlin: Duncker and Humblot, 1986).
51 Ernst Jünger, *Der Arbeiter: Herrschaft und Gestalt* (Stuttgart: Klett Cotta, 1982; 1st edn, 1932), p. 66; the three subsequent quotations pp. 153, 82, 113.

Ben Shepherd has recently traced the varieties and intensities of the brutality German troops (and their indigenous helpers) committed in one segment of the Eastern Front. But he also came across occupiers who meandered between ruthlessness and restraint in treating non-combatants (and 'partisans').[52] This account can easily be read as a perfect case in point for the 'split personality' alluded to by Böll.[53] However, the image of the 'split personality' may obscure ongoing relationships or permanent resonances between the two antagonistic poles. The potential simultaneity of both Böll, the fanatic individualist, and Böll, the cooperating soldier, may have emotionally charged the individual before, during and after combat. It could therefore also appeal to the 'fanatic individualist' and, thus, lure him into – possibly collective – military action. In this vein, the 'split', as it were, between the 'fanatic individualist' Heinrich Böll, who withdrew or opposed, and the 'other' Böll, who cooperated and 'did his job', was oftentimes blurred. One can sense an undercurrent that differed from the joy of workers: to re-produce an 'order of things'. This was a longing for fulfilment born out of the fears of uncertainties and ruptures, but also the pleasures, of entering – and of exiting – the killing fields alive.[54]

Allusions to 'work' allowed soldiers to normalize their actions and behaviour. At the same time, however, the intensity of terror and fury on the killing fields enticed these soldiers to move beyond the very normality they longed for, but also despised. It was this attraction of terror and fury that unsettled the claims soldiers (and bystanders) made that their actions were 'nothing but work'.

---

52 Ben Shepherd, 'The Continuum of Brutality: Wehrmacht Security Divisions in Central Russia, 1942', in *German History* 21 (2003): 49–81; for a similar line, see Theo Schulte, *The German Army and Nazi Policies in Occupied Russia* (New York: Berg, 1989).
53 Böll in one of his letters admiringly describes what appeared to him to be a scene of radiant beauty: his lieutenant approaching the unit on horseback from afar. Obviously, the impression this image made on the private Böll also affected the 'other' Böll, the 'individualist'; see Böll, *Briefe aus dem Krieg*, vol. 1, p. 343–344, letter of 22 May 1942 ('From the West').
54 See also the notes of a U.S. combatant in Vietnam who in his literary account refers to soldiers' fear of the 'blush of dishonour' and, thus, fighting and also killing. He concomitantly depicts scenes where 'war wasn't all terror and violence. Sometimes things could get almost sweet', Tim O'Brien, *The Things They Carried* (New York: Broadway, 1998; 1st edn 1990), pp. 21, 31.

Gerd Spittler
Work – Transformation of Objects or Interaction Between Subjects?[*][1]

One of the essential features of every definition of work is utility, the purpose external to the work (Spittler 2001). But how is this purpose achieved? Work can be basically conceived of in two different ways:
- as transformation of an object
- as interaction with a subject.

The first paradigm – I call it the technical paradigm – implies the transformation of a passive object. The process is controllable and can be planned. When one has the appropriate knowledge, skill, and power, one can form an object according to one's ideas. The means for this are tools or machines. The second paradigm, which I call the interactive paradigm, assumes an object that is not fully controllable. An element of unpredictability is involved. One devotes great attention to the object. One interprets the messages that this object emits and reacts to them. The object possesses a subject character.

The first paradigm is constitutive of the modern position. We "work over" a piece of wood in order to make a spoon. We work on a piece of raw stone and produce a club or a blade. We transform the soil in order to make it agriculturally useful. Production means for us making a product through the transformation of material, of things. This is most obvious in our ideas on transforming dead materials. But we produce not only clubs, spoons and cars, but also wheat, grapes, milk, and pork by "working on" plants and animals. Treating animals as things is not without controversy, but it has been accepted within the technical paradigm at least ever since Descartes.

Habermas assumes the existence of this technical paradigm. In both of his essays "Arbeit und Interaktion" (Work and Interaction) (1968) and "Technik und Wissenschaft als Ideologie" (Technique and Knowledge as Ideology) (1968) he makes a distinction – based on an Interpretation of Hegel and Marx – between two types of action, "work" and "interaction". Work is "instrumental action" and follows technical rules. Interaction is "communicative" action and follows its own norms. Both types of action have to be kept strictly separated. Work is absolutely essential, but as Habermas observes – critically of Marx – interaction

---

[*] This article was first published under the same title in Brigitta Benzing/Bernd Herrmann (Hgg.), Exploitation and Overexploitation in Societies Past and Present. IUAES-Intercongress 2001 Goettingen. Münster 2003, pp. 327–338.

cannot derive from work. Conversely, and here Habermas directs himself against Herbert Marcuse, work cannot be organized as an interaction. If we want to be technically successful, we cannot communicate with nature; we have to work on it. Work belongs to the area of technique and economy. The task of the cultural sciences is to examine interaction. Habermas consistently held this approach and worked it out in his "Theorie des kommunikativen Handelns" (Theory of Communicative Action) (1981).

Can work and interaction really be so clearly divided? Is interaction free of instrumentality? The foremost question in my discussion is: Is work indeed purely instrumental? Is it only a matter of working on objects or is it not also a matter of interaction between subjects? The idea that not only humans possess their own sense of self-will / selfdetermination (Eigensinn, Eigenwillen), but also animals, plants, and even things, which we regard as dead material, is widespread in non-industrial, non-capitalist societies. The objects, or rather subjects, not only have their own peculiar characteristics (Eigenarten), which one must know and take into account, but have also a self-will, which is not fully controllable. This self-will can be so strong that these subjects are as powerful as humans or even may dominate them. Work becomes a game, a fight, a service, a care, an exchange.

I shall treat these questions first in relation to hunters and gatherers (I), then herders (II) and peasants (III), and finally in relation to capitalist industrial work (IV).

Work among hunters and gatherers

I am not starting with ethnographic examples, but rather with Ortega y Gasset's "Prólogo a un Tratado de Montería" (1944; english "About the Hunt") because the specific nature of hunting is better analyzed here than in most anthropological studies. Regardless of whether hunting is for subsistence as in the case with the Paleolithic hunters or for purposes of sport as among the aristocracy, wild game has a chance to escape. The hunted animal is an autonomous actor, a subject. Its behavior is not exactly calculated. In hunting there is no guarantee of success. That might be a cause of frustration. But, this is precisely what makes it attractive. Thus, hunting is a happy experience and so differs from arduous work. Happiness does not mean simply pleasure, for the effort involved in hunting is the same whether for sport or for work. But one freely undertakes this effort and with full freedom and for the sake of joy, "while work is an effort which one undertakes with a view to its result". Here Ortega y Gasset contradicts his comments about the Paleolithic hunters, who did not hunt for purposes of sport but to secure their subsistence. Thus, hunting can be just as much work, but it is a work of a specific sort, which cannot be interpreted as domination of an object, but rather as an interaction between subjects.

Ortega analyzed this better than social anthropologists taking the approach of "Cultural Materialism" and "Ecological Anthropology" where the idea of instrumental work dominates. What is hunted and gathered is explained by the "theory of optimal search for food" (Harris 1987). Hunters and gatherers optimize their returns in that they optimize the relation between work effort and return on calories obtained from different animals and plants. This theory has its merits but it can offer only a limited explanation. Hunting is a notoriously insecure activity. Hunters differ greatly in their knowledge, skill, and luck. Among the !Kung San studied by Lee (1979) the men spend more time hunting than the women gathering, but the returns are less. More than half of the food (when calculated in calories) comes from the women. However, meat is valued over plant food. While gathering has a constant return, the individual differences in hunting are enormous. That begins with the fact that not all men go hunting. During a study of a period of one month, 7 out of 11 men from one camp went hunting. Only every fourth day was successful and the individual differences again were great. The good hunters went hunting every second day and were disproportionally successful. One hunter, who went hunting only for four days, did not bag one wild animal.

Descola (1986) in a study on the Achuar in Ecuador found that the hunting returns are small because the hunters often return home without success. While 80 minutes of planting a garden can attain 2500 calories, the same amount of time in hunting brings only 600 calories. In respect to protein supply, fishing is the most productive. From a purely utilitarian point of view one could do completely without hunting; the protein requirements can be met with less work effort by planting gardens and catching fish. But here one sees the limitation of input-output calculations and the principle of minimal expenditure of effort. Hunting is fun. The men are out 8 to 10 hours hunting. This activity is not, however, seen as work. When one goes hunting, one speaks of "going to the forest" or "going for a walk".

The interactive character of hunting is evidenced not only in the hunter's behavior. The hunters are conscious of the interaction (Ingold 1994). While we tend to exclude technical aspects as instrumental from social relations, Ingold thinks that this is an unjustified imposition of our culture on the culture of hunters. For them tools are not instruments for ruling nature, but rather are mediums for creating a social relationship. Arrows serve the interaction between humans and animals. When it does not reach its goal, then it is because the animal is not ready to enter into a relation. Ingold asserts a contrast between hunting and herding cultures. In contrast to herders, who dominate their animals and will break their self-will, hunters leave the animals to their own will.

Even when we do not accept the interpretation of the hunters for ourselves, everyone can understand that hunting is more like an uncertain interaction than a successful instrumental activity. For that reason it is argued not only by Ortega y Gasset that hunting is not to be designated as work. Eduard Hahn equates the "Origin of Economic Work" ("Entstehung der wirtschaftlichen Arbeit", 1908) with the steady activities of the gatherers and the preparation of food by women. Men have fun with insecure hunting, but it is not work. This definitional typecasting of work associates it above all with toil, a position which often corresponds to emic ideas. But if we want to do comparative research, and if we stick to the analytical definition formulated at the start of this paper, then hunting within a subsistence economy is a matter of work.

Not only hunters, but also gatherers (men and women) interact with nature. The interaction is often seen as a gift or exchange relationship. Australian hunters and gatherers speak with the land on which they hunt and gather. Through their sweat and their talk they put the land in a favorable mood. The land is then ready to put at their disposal wild game and fruits (Povinelli 1993). It is reported that the Mbuti, African hunters and gatherers, see themselves as children of the forest. They like to go to the forest in order to be together with their counterparts and nature and to gather at this time the fruits. They sing together with the spirits of the forest and the latter give them their food (Bird-David 1992).

The work of herders

That animals not only have their own distinctiveness (Eigenarten), but also their own self-will (Eigenwillen, Eigensinn) would be conceded by most of us. The question is whether this self-will is respected. Ingold disputed this in regard to herders (in contrast to hunters). My own studies on herders' work among the Tuareg (Spittler 1998) show other results. According to the Kel Ewey Tuareg, humans and animals, even things, have a well developed self-will. This self-will may turn into resistance as soon as others try to influence it. Consequently there are limits to feasibility and upbringing.

Not only humans have their own sense of self and self-will, animals do too. One tries partly to overcome this opposition, but one also respects it to a certain degree. Animals are no machines that can be ruled by the proper technique. They are rather living beings with their own will. According to one idea that was formerly widespread, but today is in retreat, the goats give, for example, less milk when the cheese produced from the milk is sold instead of being consumed in the household. Tugey, to refuse, is a word frequently used which emphasizes the sense of self and self-will of humans, animals, and things. Tugey puts a limit on the upbringing of humans and the domination of animals and things. The daughter who refuses to go to the goat sheds in the grazing area, the son, who refuses to work in the garden, the goats which refuse to come at the call of their women herders – these all encompass types of refusal that are familiar to us. It becomes more difficult when we hear that the goats refuse to give milk or indeed that the dates refuse to be sold, or a language refuses to cooperate. When my progress in learning the Tuareg language lagged behind my hopes, then I was often comforted by the Tuareg with the words: "The Tuareg language refuses", i.e. the reason was seen to be less my incapacity than the will of the language.

The idea of tugey limits the work principle in several aspects. The limits of what is feasible and what can be educated are narrowly drawn. This is not only because one sees opposition at work; that could be overcome in many cases. Important is that the refusal is often respected, even when it could be technically overcome. The woman herder could force the dog to go to the pastures with her, but she respects its refusal, without asking whether the dog is "justified" in refusing.

This respect is often shown in the handling of camels or goats. Goats are especially self-willed. Even we have, or have had, this view, for the Word "capricious" comes from capra, goat. Goats have different characters, which are evidenced in the names which the Tuareg give them. There is inter alia the gazelle, which is shy towards the herder and behaves likes a gazelle; the quarrelsome, which is always fighting with the other goats; the strayer, who distances itself from the herd; the indifferent, which does not hear the calls of the goat herder; the coy, which has to be tempted with nice words to come to the water trough. These goats make the work of the herdswomen difficult. For example, the goats designated as gazelles do not allow themselves to be milked at all or several women herders have first to capture them. The milking, which normally can be done in a few minutes, lasts half an hour and requires the cooperation of several women.

Capricious goats exist everywhere. But we would sort them out by selling or slaughtering them so that the work becomes easier and these characteristics are not further reproduced in successive generations. Such considerations are not foreign to the herdswomen. But as a rule they dismiss these thoughts and say that one has to respect the goats' self-will just as of humans. They accept the extra work. But one can also imagine that this makes the work more fun. If the women were to see the goats as pure instruments for achieving their aims, then the lonely work in the wilderness would be intolerable. To watch a quarrelsome goat is fun. To capture a shy goat is a game that relieves the monotonous milking work.

Respect for the distinctive personality and self-will of animals can be developed into a specific service ethic. A conception of work as a service is common among nomads. Much more so than farmers or stationary cattle holders, nomads adapt their entire way of living to the needs of the animals in that they are as mobile as the animals. Kurt Beck has described this in detail in relation to the nomads in Kordofan (Beck 1994, 1996). The herders are to put their life at the service of the herd. That does not mean that they must always work, but they must always be ready for the herd.

Work among peasants

It is a widespread conception among peasants that work is care. Work alone cannot create a vegetable product but can only help in its growth. In the final analysis, the affluence of nature must be traced back to the will of God.

Anthropologists, like other people, often romanticize the work of peasants in pointing out its harmony with nature or its peaceful interaction with nature. But we should not forget that agricultural work always starts with the destruction of nature. Before sowing and planting can be done, the existing vegetation has to be destroyed. Clearing the field consists of cutting and burning down trees. To prepare fallow land for sowing means uprooting shrubs and grass. The destruction continues even after the sowing. Hoeing to make space for useful plants destroys the weeds. The soil is torn up with the hoe. Interaction with nature does not imply only peaceful exchange or care, but very often a battle. This fight may be dangerous. Tools like axes and hoes resemble weapons, with which the peasant can injure not only other people but himself as well.

In the following, I shall describe an extreme case of fighting found among the Bemba in Zambia. The basis of my description is Audrey Richards well known book "Land, Labour and Diet in Northern Rhodesia" (1939). Richards describes in great detail the agricultural work process, which is organized in a different way than in neighbouring societies. The martial tradition of the Bemba accounts for the difference. Whereas in many societies peaceful agriculture constitutes the opposite of war, the Bemba organize their most important agricultural work like war. This system has become known under its indigenous name citemene.

Clearing among the Bemba does not consist in destroying the trees completely, but in cutting the branches. To this end, the young men have to climb to the top of the trees. This work is seen as play, as pleasurable and exciting. But it is also very dangerous. Every year several young men fall to their death in this way. Richards gives a vivid description of the climbing: "At the top of the tree the work becomes more and more dangerous. A man may be left standing on a fork at the summit with one of the vertical stems as yet uncut. He has to clasp it with one hand to steady himself, while with the other he slashes at the trunk he is clinging to. He swings his axe till he hears the warning crack and feels the branch sway. Then he slides his body quick as a flash down the mutilated stump of the tree, yelling in triumph as he hears the bough fall". The Bemba particularly pride themselves on this citemene System. "Look at that man! He is an absolute monkey" is a high compliment to pay to a cultivator.

Audrey Richards was once asked whether Englishmen practised the citemene system in their own country. She gave a long and detailed description of the merits of English agriculture, but as she spoke she heard one of the young men behind her observe to his friend with a sort of derision: "Hm! Afraid to climb, I suppose."

Capitalist industrial work

Up to this point I have spoken about hunters and gatherers, peasants, and herders. They all have something to do with "nature", with plants and animals. At least when it comes to animals, most of us I suspect would be ready to accept their subject character. In regard to plants it is more difficult. But what about the craftsman who works with "raw materials", with dead wood, with stone and metals? Is there here an interaction between subjects or is there only a working of objects? Social anthropology has long realized that things are not just dead objects for their owners. The argument in Marcel Mauss' famous "Essai sur le don" (Mauss 1925) rests on the premise that "archaic societies" conceive of things having souls. Mauss studied what consequences this has for the gift, but he did not deal with the consequences for work.

The most important test for the question of interaction is not the handling of tools by a craftsman, but rather capitalist industrial work. This is the prototype of instrumental activity; it is the model for Marx's, Weber's, and Habermas' conceptions of work. As the technical or economic paradigms are dominating in research nearly all studies assume this framework. There are, however, some noteworthy exceptions: sociologists and social anthropologists, using the method of participant observation, arrived at other views and were at least on the track of an interactive work.

"Manufacturing Consent. Changes in the Labor Process under Monopoly Capitalism" is the title of a book by Michael Burawoy (1979). The subject of the book is an old topic: How can it be explained that humans are ready to perform incessant and strenuous work? Burawoy's study is based on his own experiences. For a year he was a worker in a machine manufacturing factory. Burawoy found that supervision, salary attractions, and punishments could not sufficiently explain the achievements of the workers. It was not force or salary attractions which guaranteed a successful production, but rather the game. "Game" has nothing to do with "playing" in contrast to work. Rather it is an essential part of the work process. The playful-antagonistic character with which this work is done and conflicts settled with management and other workers gives a meaning to the work which would otherwise be absent under Tayloristic conditions. It simply drives away boredom. Time passes more quickly when "making out". One becomes less tired. The game makes the basic deprivations that work brings with it tolerable or renders it satisfactory.

Burawoy studied especially the game of "making out". In piecework one can either earn the basic salary without any further efforts, or one can play the game of salary raises by increasing output (making out). In the latter variation all turns on this game: one's own actions, contacts and talks with work colleagues, and supervisors. It is a game insofar as it promises a profit, has elements of insecurity, which arouses ambition, and stimulates competition and cooperation with other workers. It is less the higher salary as such than the forces aroused through the game which results in higher performance. Contrary to the assumption made by Marx and others that under capitalistic conditions the game or playful character of work is lost, and equally contrary to the assumption made by Ortega y Gasset, which postulates an absolute contrariness between hunting and work, play is an element of work even under the extreme conditions of capitalist factory work.

Nearly all of the studies on this, however, focus on the interaction between humans. Humans' self-determination ("Eigensinn") and games between them are examined. Working with objects is less discussed. Burawoy mentions playing with machines, but they are more an instrument in the game between coworkers than a partner or opponent. As a rule it is supposed that objects are worked on and transformed and that through work they are completely controlled. In reality this is not the case. Dealing with things is not the equivalent of dominating things. One of the few studies focusing on the interaction with machines is Julian E. Orr's "Talking about Machines. An Ethnography of a Modern Job" (1996). It examines the triangular relation between service technicians, customers, and copy machines. Orr worked many years as a service technician before he undertook his anthropological research.

Part of the technical service and repair work corresponds to the technical paradigm: "Technical service work is commonly perceived to be the fixing by rote procedure of uniform machines, and routine repair is indeed common." This applies, however, only to a part of the work. Orr continues after the above sentence: "However, individual machines are quite idiosyncratic, new failure modes appear continuously, and rote procedure cannot address unknown problems... Work in such circumstances is resistant to rationalization, since the expertise vital to such contingent and extemporaneous practice cannot easily be codified."

Machines are not objects, but rather subjects, in this case partner and opponent. "War Stories" are told about the machines. These deal not only with heroic success, but also often with defeats in handling the machines. Even the heroic stories assume that the machines are difficult and incalculable. "These tales of the heroism required to service early machines seem balanced between celebrations of the perversity of the machines and celebrations of the technicians coping. It is not clear whether the technicians more admire the coping or the perversity." Each machine is an individual, even when many are of the same type. They are named individually by their users. A technician can differentiate between each machine in his herd. The machines are (like a livestock herd) in principle domesticated, but only in principle. When describing the negative characteristics of machines, one uses moral and value judgments. Machines can be "filthy", "perverse", "crotchety", "odd". These characteristics are seen not only as negative. "The machines are both perverse and fascinating. Earlier models featured both fires and explosions, and the technicians speak with a fond pride of the labor involved in recovering from such disasters. Catastrophes resulting from oversight are described with the same pride as part of the process of becoming a real technician... Indeed, how could they resent the machines, for such a machine is a worthy opponent, partner, other."

Orr compares the way technicians deal with the machine with the description by Levi-Strauss (1962) of the bricoleur, who works with what is momentarily available. This corresponds, however, only partially to the self-image of the technician. In practice the technician interacts with the machine as though it is an individual. Their stories are character descriptions and moral value judgments. On the other hand they have a technical world view insofar as they warn to harness the chaos especially with orderly and systematic behavior, based on knowledge and skill.

Conclusion

Empirically we can establish that the interactive conception of work is widespread. This can be most easily seen in respect to hunters and gatherers, peasants and herders, first because of the living nature of the work objects and secondly because of the historical dimension. These forms of work dominate in a pre-modem world. Clearly, though, even in capitalist industrial work one finds a strong interactive element.

How can one explain, from the point of view of the technical paradigm, the wide extent of work with subjects?

Where interaction is indisputable (for example, in hunting), work proves to be inefficient. The hunters return often to the camp with nothing useful. The effort is high, the failure rate equally high. The average work productivity is thus low. As a consequence, the evolution is towards more efficient economic forms like agriculture and livestock raising.

Where the interaction rests on non-scientific world views, that is, they contradict our ideas, it is a matter of a magical world view and of superstition, which equally leads to inefficiency. This is also supplanted by an evolution in favor of a more efficient economic form. The demystifying of the world (Weber: "Entzauberung der Welt") leads to increasing rationality. Today the remains of such magical views merely show that the Enlightenment has not yet succeeded.

What the social anthropologists describe as an emic world view is often only a metaphor (e.g. wringing with nature), which does not correspond to reality.

There are several objections to these arguments:

Let us start with the latter argument (the interaction metaphor): This argument is indeed to be taken seriously. The protagonists of a culturalistic perspective in social anthropology limit themselves often to a semantic approach in studying work. It is simply supposed this is relevant for action. In my opinion that is anything but obvious. Work goes beyond talking, it has to be done.

To my mind, the neglect of the action level and the limitation to the discourse level miss the object.

The technical paradigm assumes either the universality of its principles or an evolutionary perspective. The first assumption can be easily refuted. Work has never functioned alone according to the model of the technical paradigm. Rather it has always contained interactive elements. This is frequently overlooked, because of the dominance of the technical paradigm in the description and analysis of work. The evolutionary perspective too, which postulates an increasingly technical control of the world, cannot be sustained. Even when one is not a follower of the radical thesis of Latour ("We were never modern," 1995), then it is valid to say of the world of work today that interaction and communication, which evade a simple mechanistic perspective, are increasing, not decreasing. Here the technical paradigm is a poor adviser. This is possibly the case not only for the interaction among humans, but also with machines, e.g. computers.

The technical paradigm overlooks not only the subject in the object, but also in the actor, who works. It assumes a rational actor, in effect a machine (Rabinbach 1990), without thematizing the anthropological or cultural context of the actor. Work as interaction in any case is more fun than a successful domination of the object which excludes every surprise. Hunting is the best example of this. This is also valid for agricultural work, raising livestock, and industry as I have described above. Having fun at work is a value in itself. It also often increases work productivity as has been known since Fourier. Burawoy (1979) shows this persuasively for capitalist industrial work. Work can be not only a matter of fun, but also a fight. There are victories and defeats in interacting with other subjects. This is so not only for hunters, but also for herders, peasants, and industrial workers.

Persons (actors) and their actions have to be defined substantially in terms of culture. This applies as well to technical and interactive action. Anyone prepared to take risks will conduct work in a risky way (example: the Bemba). Whoever because of religious ideas finds that living in the wilderness is incompatible with human dignity will organize herding work differently from one who feels at home in the wilderness (Beck 1994; 1996; Spittler 1998). When modern persons define themselves as flexible individuals, then they will organize their work in a new way (Boltanski and Chiapello 1999). When the actor finds that the aim of work lies not only in practical utility, but also in playfulness and aesthetics, then he will perform the work in another way. The concepts of an actor mentioned here do not necessarily imply an interactive perspective; they do promote it.

(Translation by Chris Jones-Pauly)

References

Beck, Kurt. 1994. Die kulturelle Dimension der Arbeit in den nordkordofanischen Hirtengesellschaften, in: M.S. Laubscher und B. Turner (eds.). Völkerkundetagung 1991, vol. I, pp.157–176. München: anacon.
Beck, Kurt. 1996. Islam, Arbeitsethik, Lebensführung, in: Kurt Beck und Gerd Spittler (eds.) Arbeit in Afrika, pp. 161–178. Hamburg: Lit.
Bird-David, Nurit. 1992, Beyond "The Original Affluent Society". A Culturalist Reformulation in·Current Anthropology, 33: 25–47.
Boltanski, Luc und Eve Chiapello. 1999. Le nouvel esprit du capitalisme. Paris: Gallimard.
Burawoy, Michael. 1979. Manufacturing Consent. Changes in the Labor Process under Monopoly Capitalism. Chicago: Univ. of Chicago Press.
Descola, Philippe. 1986. La nature domestique. Symbolisme et praxis dans l'écologie des Achouar. Paris: Ed. de la Maison des Sciences de l'Homme.
Habermas, Jürgen. 1968. Arbeit und Interaktion, in: Technik und Wissenschaft als Ideologie, pp. 9–47 Frankfurt: Suhrkamp.
Habermas, Jürgen. 1968. Technik und Wissenschaft als Ideologie. Frankfurt: Suhrkamp.

Habermas, Jürgen. 1981. Theorie des kommunikativen Handelns. Frankfurt: Suhrkamp.
Hahn, Eduard. 1908. Die Entstehung der wirtschaftlichen Arbeit. Heidelberg: Winter.
Harris, Marvin. 1987. Cultural Anthropology. New York: Harpers & Row.
Ingold, Tim. 1994. Tool-use, Sociality and Intelligence, in: Gibson, Kathleen und Tim Ingold (eds.), Tools, Language, and Cognition in Human Evolution, pp. 429–445. Cambridge: Cambridge University Press.
Latour, Bruno. 1995. Wir sind nie modern gewesen. Versuch einer symmetrischen Anthropologie. Berlin: Akademie.
Lee, Richard B. 1979. The !Kung San. Men, Women, and Work in a Foraging Society. Cambridge: Cambridge University Press.
Lévi-Strauss, Claude. 1962. La pensée sauvage. Paris.
Lüdtke, Alf. 1992. Practising Eigensinn: Workers Beyond Domination and Resistance, in: Focaal No. 19: 16–35.
Mauss, Marcel. 1925. Essai sur le don. Paris.
Orr, Julian E. 1996. Talking about Machines. An Ethnography of a Modern Job. Ithaca: Cornell University Press.
Ortega y Gasset, José. 1944. Prólogo a un Tratado de Montería. Madrid.
Povinelli, Elizabeth A. 1993. Labor's Lot. The Power, History, and Culture of Aboriginal Action. Chicago: University of Chicago Press.
Rabinbach, Anson. 1990. The Human Motor. Energy, Fatigue, and the Origins of Modernity. New York: Basic Books.
Richards, Audrey I. 1939. Land. Labour, and Diet in Northern Rhodesia. London: International African Institute.
Spittler, Gerd. 1998. Hirtenarbeit. Die Welt der Kamelhirten und Ziegenhirtinnen von Timia. Köln: Köppe.
Spittler, Gerd. 2001. Work: Anthropological Aspects, in: International Encyclopedia of the Social and Behavioral Sciences, pp. 16565–1656. Amsterdam: Pergamon.

Dynamics of Labour Relations

Sidney Chalhoub
The Politics of Ambiguity

Conditional Manumission, Labor Contracts, and Slave Emancipation in Brazil (1850s–1888)*

Introduction

The historical process that made liberalism, old and new, the guiding ideology of Western societies brought with it the invention of new forms of unfree labor. Liberalism and free labor, ancien regime and serfdom and/or slavery are no longer unproblematic pairs of historical intelligibility. The first half of the nineteenth century did not see the weakening of slavery in the Americas at all, but just the partial relocation of it. The institution of slavery gradually disappeared in the British and French Caribbean while it became stronger in Brazil, Cuba, and the US South.[1] In the second half of the nineteenth century, as the nightmare of an international order based on slavery was finally defeated in the American Civil War,[2] there emerged extremely aggressive racist ideologies that justified Western imperial expansion and the persistence of forced labor in Africa and elsewhere. Actually, it boggles the mind to think that for so long it seemed possible to conceive of the nineteenth century as a time of transition from slavery to freedom, from bondage to contractual and/or free labor. In fact, contract labor, however diverse in its forms, was often thought of as a form of coerced labor, with workers

---

* This article was first published under the same title in *International Review of Social History*, Vol. 60 (2015), pp. 161–191 doi:10.1017/S0020859015000176 © 2015 Internationaal Instituut voor Sociale Geschiedenis, published by Cambridge University Press, reproduced with permission. It is a sequel to Sidney Chalhoub, "The Precariousness of Freedom in a Slave Society (Brazil in the Nineteenth Century)", *International Review of Social History*, 56 (2011), pp. 405–439. A first draft was written while I was a fellow at IGK Work and Human Lifecycle in Global History, Humboldt Universität, Berlin, January–July 2013. Research in Brazil was funded by the Conselho Nacional de Pesquisa (CNPq) and the Fundação de Amparo à Pesquisa do Estado de São Paulo (FAPESP). My thanks to Michael Hall and Robert Slenes for their critical comments and corrections of my English.
1 For a comparative overview of this process see, for instance, Dale W. Tomich, *Through the Prism of Slavery: Labor, Capital, and World Economy* (Lanham, MD, 2004), pp. 56–71.
2 For the centrality of slavery to the geopolitics and international political economy up until the American Civil War, see Rafael de Bivar Marquese and Tâmis Peixoto Parron, "Internacional escravista: política da Segunda Escravidão", *Topoi*, 12 (July–December 2011), pp. 97–117.

having to submit to debt bondage and various forms of criminal sanction for breach of contract.[3]

In this article, I focus on controversies regarding conditional manumission to explore the legal and social ambiguities between slavery and freedom that prevailed in nineteenth-century Brazilian society. In doing so, I suggest that the sharp distinction between slavery and freedom is an ideological construct that makes it difficult for us to re-imagine the experience of Africans and their descendants that were enslaved in Brazil and elsewhere. Furthermore, the tale of slave emancipation as a watershed event in the history of humanity prevents us from seeing the legacy of slavery and the burden of so-called "freedom" past and present that workers in so many parts of the world have had to bear until today. After all, as was the case during the times of Atlantic slavery, the logic of present-day world capitalist interactions continues to rely on the fact that somewhere, out of sight and out of mind, there are lives that are unworthy and expendable, available to be put to labor under very harsh conditions.

A couple of further introductory remarks are in order to situate readers regarding the history and historiography of Atlantic slavery and slave emancipation in general, and in Brazil in particular, as well as to clarify further my argument regarding conditional manumission in the more general historical landscape sketched above. Brazil was the last country in the Americas to abolish slavery, doing so in 1888, thus after the United States, which achieved it in 1865, and Cuba, in 1886. It did so after a long, protracted legislative process, which had landmark laws in 1850 (abolition of the African slave trade), 1871 (a law declaring free the offspring of slave mothers born thereafter), 1885 (freedom for sexagenarian slaves) and, finally, full abolition on 13 May 1888. The abolition decree did not determine any compensation to slave owners, neither did it establish or was followed by public policies devised to aid the approximately 700,000 people, then freed, in the transition to their new condition.

---

3 The literature on the subject is vast and growing; see, for instance, Robert J. Steinfeld, *The Employment Relation in English & American Law and Culture, 1350–1870* (Chapel Hill, NC [etc.], 1991); Amy Dru Stanley, *From Bondage to Contract: Wage Labor, Marriage, and the Market in the Age of Slave Emancipation* (Cambridge, 1998); Douglas Hay and Paul Craven (eds), *Masters, Servants, and Magistrates in Britain and the Empire, 1562–1955* (Chapel Hill, NC [etc.], 2004; Marcel van der Linden, *Workers of the World: Essays Toward a Global Labor History* (Leiden, 2008); Alessandro Stanziani, "Introduction: Labour Institutions in a Global Perspective, from the Seventeenth to the Twentieth Century", *International Review of Social History*, 54 (2009), pp. 351–358; Marcel van der Linden and Prabhu Mohapatra (eds), *Labour Matters: Towards Global Histories. Studies in Honour of Sabyasachi Bhattacharya* (New Delhi, 2009); Marcel van der Linden (ed.), *Humanitarian Intervention and Changing Labor Relations: The Long-term Consequences of the Abolition of the Slave Trade* (Leiden, 2011).

The historiography of slave emancipation in the Americas has been slow to recognize some key commonalities regarding emancipation processes in different countries. A brief comparison between the United States and Brazil may help to bring the subject and the argument of this article into sharp relief. Apparently, the two cases could not offer a more striking contrast: in the former country, a violent civil war and an abrupt ending to slavery; in the latter, a long and protracted process that spanned almost four decades until abolition. However, a common thread connects both histories: worlds of slavery and "free" labor coexisted for a long period in both countries, and the interplay of these different labor regimes configured much of the legal contradictions and social conflicts that shaped the experience of people of African descent, slave and free.

It is common to conceive of the process of slave emancipation in the United States as consisting of two very distinct phases.[4] The "first emancipation", associated with the repercussions of the American Revolution, consisted of gradual abolition laws that provided for the freedom of the children of those enslaved, normally when they reached a certain age in adulthood. The states of Pennsylvania, Rhode Island, Connecticut, New York, and New Jersey enacted such statutes between 1780 and 1804. This so-called "first emancipation" established the division and the sectional conflict that led to the American Civil War, thus bringing about the second, "revolutionary" emancipation, in 1865, which was such a dramatic event that it tends to obliterate somewhat the previous process of emancipation. Furthermore, the history of the conflict between the "free-labor" North and the "slave-labor" South appears to make difficult the proper appreciation of how the two processes coexisted and connected.

For example, the confirmation of the right of recapture of allegedly fugitive slaves by the Supreme Court in 1842 (based upon the Fugitive Slave Law of 1793) and the enforcement of the Fugitive Slave Law of 1850 in the northern states made clear how vulnerable was the freedom of people of African descent also in the North. As Steven Hahn says in his very insightful essay that I draw upon here, "as slaves disappeared officially in the states of what we call the North [as a result of first emancipation], they were appearing [there] unofficially as fugitives from the states of the South". Hahn concludes that it makes more sense to think of a picture "in which slavery – for the duration of the antebellum period – was national rather than sectional, in which freedom for African Americans was

---

[4] For what follows in this paragraph, see Steven Hahn, *The Political Worlds of Slavery and Freedom* (Cambridge, MA [etc.], 2009), chs 1 and 2.

highly contingent [...] and in which abolition and antislavery [...] were struggling, with successes and failures, to limit the prerogatives of slaveholders".[5]

In the case of Brazil, the politics of domination over slaves depended upon masters achieving a finely tuned balance between physical punishment and the positive incentive of manumission. However difficult, it seems that manumission was a meaningful possibility for Brazilian slaves, a hope renewed periodically by the experience of seeing a partner manumitted and by the observation of the significant presence, in the general population, of free and freed people of African descent, many of them heirs of freedoms obtained in previous generations. As I argued in a preceding article published in this journal,[6] nonetheless, the worlds of slavery and freedom were one and the same world of labor exploitation and control – as was also the case, however differently, in the United States. Going in a similar direction, Rebecca Scott and Jean Hébrard have pointed out in a recent study that the precariousness of freedom was, as long as slavery still existed, a shared experience for free and freed people of African descent in the Americas.[7] In Brazil, they were often enslaved illegally, received conditional manumission, had their freedoms revoked, were arrested on suspicion of being fugitive slaves, and so on.

There are three intertwined senses in which I conceive of conditional manumission as a politics of ambiguity in the context of Brazilian slave emancipation. First, regarding the realm of lived experience, masters and conditionally manumitted slaves were often unsure of what conditional manumission entailed in terms of expected behavior, prerogatives, and obligations. Therefore, they struggled to define it in daily relations, in situations often exposed at length in civil and criminal court cases.[8] This is an aspect of the question not approached in depth here. Second, conditional manumission was a legal conundrum, a difficult challenge to judicial authorities engaged in interpreting its meanings with regard to the status of children of conditionally manumitted mothers, to obligations of rendering service, to alleged motives that allowed it to be revoked, to inheritance rights, and so forth. Third, and this follows from the two previous observations, historical actors appropriated conditional manumission differently, interpreting

---

5 *Ibid.*, p. 13; see also, on "the precarious terrain of northern freedom", Ira Berlin, *Generations of Captivity: A History of African-American Slaves* (Cambridge, MA [etc], 2003), pp. 234–236.
6 Chalhoub, "The Precariousness of Freedom in a Slave Society".
7 Rebecca Scott and Jean Hébrard, *Freedom Papers: An Atlantic Odyssey in the Age of Emancipation* (Cambridge, MA [etc], 2012).
8 I analyzed some cases in Sidney Chalhoub, *Visões da liberdade: uma história das últimas décadas da escravidão na Corte* (São Paulo, 1990), pp. 122–142.

its ambiguous and uncertain nature according to circumstances and struggles about emancipation and the shaping of labor relations in its aftermath.

Figure 1. *Revista Illustrada*, 12th year, no. 466 (Rio de Janeiro, 30 September 1887), detail on p. 4.⁹ Translation of cartoon text: "While in parliament they make speeches and do not decide anything, blacks run away very quickly. The planters are not able to stop them."

The final crisis of slavery in Brazil involved episodes of massive slave flight from coffee plantations – perhaps one should not hesitate to call it "a general strike"[10] – apparently motivated or intensified, in part, by the government's plan to enact a law that would declare abolition together with the obligation of two, three, or more years of further service by freed people. The idea appeared a way of turning the then widely practised strategy by planters (of granting conditional manumission to their slaves in the hope of guaranteeing their forced labor for more years) into an official policy. However, in the spring and summer of 1887–1888, roughly from September to April, slaves "voted" against the projected law, "conditional manumission" for all, with their feet.

---

9 The *Revista Illustrada* was perhaps the most famous illustrated periodical published in the city of Rio in the nineteenth century. It acquired great prominence during the abolitionist campaign in the 1880s. Angelo Agostini (1843–1910), an Italian artist who had probably arrived in Brazil in 1859, founded it in 1876 and was its director for the next thirteen years. For a detailed study of Agostini's life and art, see Marcelo Balaban, *Poeta do lápis: sátira e política na trajetória de Angelo Agostini no Brasil imperial (1864–1888)* (Campinas, 2009).
10 Steven Hahn draws inspiration from W.E.B. Du Bois, who described the Southern slaves' flight towards freedom and service to the Federal army during the Civil War as a "general strike"; see Hahn, *The Political Worlds of Slavery and Freedom*, ch. 2, entitled "Did We Miss the Greatest Slave Rebellion in Modern History?". For the reference to Du Bois' idea of a "general strike", see pp. 106–110.

Slavery and freedom

An important characteristic of slavery in Brazil was that it depended heavily on the slave trade to continue to exist. In this sense, it offers a sharp contrast with slavery in the United States. From the 1560s to 1850, more than 4 million and 800,000 enslaved Africans were shipped to Brazil; in contrast, from the seventeenth century to 1808 about 450,000 enslaved Africans arrived in North America. Therefore, ten times more Africans went to Brazil than to the USA. It is also remarkable that 42 per cent of the total number of Africans taken to Brazil arrived there in the first half of the nineteenth century (more than 2 million people).[11] Recent historiography calls the period "second slavery": decline in the British and French Caribbean; expansion in Cuba, Brazil, and southern USA.[12] As a consequence, when this intense slave trade was ended by the mid-century, Brazilian slavery was very "Africanized", so to speak.[13] In the coffee-growing areas of the provinces of Rio de Janeiro and São Paulo, it was common to have approximately 80 per cent of the slave labor force in the plantations composed of African-born people.[14] Rio de Janeiro, the capital of the Brazilian Empire (1822–1889), had a population of 266,000 people in 1849; more than 110,000 inhabitants were slaves, or 41.2 per cent of the total population (this was the largest urban slave population in the Americas at any time; just as a point of contrast, there were 15,000 slaves in New Orleans in 1860). About 60 per cent of the 110,000 slaves living in Rio were Africans.[15]

Throughout the first half of the nineteenth century, although there was no national census in the whole period, slaves constituted about 30 to 40 per cent of the total population of Brazil, according to contemporary estimates. In 1872, when the first national census took place, 22 years after the cessation of the

---

[11] Data compiled from www.slavevoyages.org, accessed on 6 September 2010.
[12] Tomich, *Through the Prism of Slavery*, pp. 56–71.
[13] Robert Slenes, "'*Malungu, ngoma vem!*': África coberta e descoberta no Brasil", in Nelson Aguilar (ed.) *Mostra do Redescobrimento: Negro de Corpo e Alma – Black in Body and Soul* (São Paulo, 2000), pp. 212–220; Robert Slenes, *Na senzala, uma flor: esperanças e recordações na formação da família escrava – Brasil sudeste, século XIX* (Rio de Janeiro, 1999).
[14] Ricardo Salles, *E o Vale era o escravo. Vassouras, século XIX. Senhores e escravos no coração do Império* (Rio de Janeiro, 2008), p. 200; Ricardo Pirola, *Senzala insurgente: malungos, parentes e rebeldes nas fazendas de Campinas (1832)* (Campinas, 2011), p. 63. According to Pirola, considering only adult slaves, Africans represented 93 per cent of the slave population in Campinas, province of São Paulo, in the 1830s.
[15] Chalhoub, *Visões da liberdade*, pp. 186–187; for comprehensive studies of urban slavery in Rio, see Mary Karasch, *Slave Life in Rio de Janeiro: 1808–1850* (Princeton, NJ, 1987) and Luiz Carlos Soares, *O 'Povo de Cam' na capital do Brasil: a escravidão urbana no Rio de Janeiro do século XIX* (Rio de Janeiro, 2007).

African trade, slaves constituted 15 per cent of the population – that is, about 1.5 million people in a total population of 10 million.[16] The slave population had decreased sharply beginning in 1850, due to the cessation of the slave trade, high mortality rates (a cholera epidemic in 1855–1856 was particularly devastating among slaves), low birth rates, and significantly high manumission rates. In the 1850s through the 1870s, a slave labor force for coffee plantations was guaranteed by means of an intense internal trade that shifted bonded people from smaller to larger properties, from the interior to plantation areas nearer the coast, and from the north and south of the country to the provinces of Rio de Janeiro and São Paulo.[17]

Relatively high manumission rates meant that there was always a significant number of free and freed people of color in the Brazilian population. Thus, according to the census of 1872, 73.7 per cent of blacks and *pardos* (people of mixed blood) living in Brazil were free.[18] In the United States, in 1860, no more than 11 per cent of the population of African descent was free, which includes data from the northern states, where slavery had officially disappeared and 99 per cent of the colored population was registered as free.[19] Therefore, in the case of Brazil, it is somewhat misleading to think of a sharp contrast between slavery and post-emancipation. Although abolition came only in 1888 and still liberated about 700,000 captives, at all times a significant number of persons achieved freedom in Brazilian society, thus also giving rise to a large population of freeborn people of color.

Heavy dependence on the African trade to maintain and expand the slave labor force in the plantations posed a serious political problem for the Brazilian government in the decades following Independence (obtained from the Portuguese in 1822). Under pressure from the British, the government enacted a law to abolish the African trade in November 1831. However, the trade continued illegally until the early 1850s, resulting in approximately 750,000 Africans being smuggled into the country and enslaved in the period. The legacy of two decades of the contraband slave trade was manifold, ranging from challenges to the security of slave property thus acquired to a widespread practice of illegal enslave-

---

[16] Nelson de Castro Senra, *História das estatísticas brasileiras* (Rio de Janeiro, 2006), I, pp. 418–419, 423; for the first census see Diretoria Geral de Estatística, *Recenseamento geral do Brazil de 1872*, I: Quadros gerais. Recenseamento da população do Imperio do Brazil a que se procedeu no dia 1° de agosto de 1872 (Rio de Janeiro, 1876).
[17] Robert Slenes, "The Brazilian Internal Slave Trade, 1850–1888: Regional Economies, Slave Experience, and the Politics of a Peculiar Market", in Walter Johnson (ed.), *The Chattel Principal: Internal Slave Trades in the Americas* (New Haven, CT [etc.], 2004), pp. 325–370.
[18] Senra, *História das estatísticas brasileiras*, p. 423.
[19] Berlin, *Generations of Captivity*, pp. 278–279.

ment that threatened and rendered vulnerable the liberty of free and freed people of African descent in general.[20]

The cessation of the slave trade brought new challenges to the politics of domination under Brazilian slavery. Traditionally, the control of Brazilian slaves had relied heavily on the combination of constant new African arrivals with the occurrence of relevant rates of access to manumission. Therefore, the continuation of the slave trade guaranteed the replacement of a labor force that had its numbers constantly reduced by manumission, appalling death rates, and relatively low birth rates. The end of the African trade left the children born of slave mothers as the only remaining source of bonded people in the country. The reproduction of slavery by means of the bondage of children born of slave wombs was a common characteristic of modern slavery in Western societies and made the politics of slave emancipation a heavily gendered subject everywhere. New World regimes adopted the ancient Roman rule of assigning to the child the civil status of the mother probably as a consequence of the growing importance of the nuclear family as a property-owning entity, thus making it necessary that the masters' offspring by slave women be excluded from any inheritance claims, except by manumission and express recognition of paternity by the master.[21]

The principle that the condition of the child followed the mother's acquired different political meanings depending on time and place. Abolitionist movements in the nineteenth century dwelt extensively on the subject of the separation of mothers and children. The theme was inevitable as mothers became essential in the construction of national ideologies, key figures in the education of males to be invested with political rights and power to lead the nation. The preoccupation with the education of women and their influence on children made the routine separation of slave mothers and their children as a result of everyday business transactions pertaining to slavery a horror to inspire more than a handful of romantic poets and fiery politicians. Gradual emancipation legislation based on the idea of slave mothers giving birth to free children could be found in

---

[20] Beatriz Mamigonian, "O direito de ser africano livre: os escravos e as interpretações da lei de 1831", in Silvia Lara and Joseli Mendonça (eds), *Direitos e justiças no Brasil. Ensaios de história social* (Campinas, 2006), pp. 129–160; *idem*, "O estado nacional e a instabilidade da propriedade escrava: a lei de 1831 e a matrícula dos escravos de 1872", *Almanack*, 2 (2011), pp. 20–37; Chalhoub, "The Precariousness of Freedom in a Slave Society"; *idem*, *A força da escravidão: ilegalidade e costume no Brasil oitocentista* (São Paulo, 2012).
[21] Gwyn Campbell, Suzanne Miers, and Joseph Miller, "Women in Western Systems of Slavery: Introduction", *Slavery & Abolition: A Journal of Slave and Post-Slave Studies*, 26 (2005), p. 169.

several countries – as for example in the Moret law in Cuba in 1870 and the Free Womb law in Brazil in 1871.[22]

The end of the slave trade in the 1850s seems to have brought with it a sharp politicization of the theme of children born of slave mothers who had received conditional manumission (*statuliberi*, as they were described, resorting to the expression present in legal codes pertaining to ancient Rome). Although, as already mentioned, the rate of manumission in Brazil was relatively high in comparison with other contemporary slave societies, recent studies show that in the various samples collected, from different locations and periods, typically 30 to 40 per cent of freedoms were granted conditionally. Freedom might be dependent on a master's death, on a master's daughter marriage, on continued faithful service for a number of years, etc.[23] Let us suppose that a slave woman was granted a letter of manumission upon the condition of continuing to serve her master faithfully for a number of years. After the letter was granted, perhaps even entered into a notary public record book, and before the years of service were fulfilled, the slave woman became pregnant and gave birth to a child. Was the child, born to a conditionally manumitted woman, slave or free? Riddles of this type provoked much debate in Brazil in the 1850s and 1860s.[24] Following such controversies, in jurisprudence and in legal cases, allow us to gain insights into struggles about how to define important concepts pertaining to non-slavery spheres of labor, such as the idea of contract labor, as well as into the expectations of masters,

---

[22] Camillia Cowling, *Conceiving Freedom: Women of Colour, Gender, and Abolition of Slavery in Havana and Rio de Janeiro* (Chapel Hill, NC, 2013); Joseph Dorsey, "Women Without History: Slavery and the International Politics of *partus sequitur ventrem* in the Spanish Caribbean", *Journal of Caribbean History*, 28 (1994), pp. 165–207; Jessica Millward, "'That All Her Increase Shall Be Free': Enslaved Women's Bodies and the Maryland 1809 Law of Manumission", *Women's History Review*, 21 (2012), pp. 363–378.

[23] Studies about manumission in Brazil are numerous, and growing steadily. See, for instance, regarding conditional manumission, Peter Eisenberg, "Ficando livre: as alforrias em Campinas no século XIX", in *idem, Homens esquecidos: escravos e trabalhadores livres no Brasil, séculos XVIII e XIX* (Campinas, 1989), pp. 255–314; Manolo Florentino, "Sobre minas, crioulos e a liberdade costumeira no Rio de Janeiro, 1789–1871", in *idem* (ed.), *Tráfico, cativeiro e liberdade. Rio de Janeiro, séculos XVII–XIX* (Rio de Janeiro, 2005), pp. 331–359. For recent surveys of the literature on Brazilian slavery that show the centrality of the theme of manumission, see Hebert Klein and Francisco Vidal Luna, *Slavery in Brazil* (New York, 2010), especially ch. 9; Robert Slenes, "Brazil", in Robert Paquette and Mark Smith, *The Oxford Handbook of Slavery in the Americas* (Oxford, 2010), pp. 111–133; Jean Hébrard, "L'Esclavage au Brésil. Le Débat Historiographique et ses Racines", in *idem* (ed.), *Brésil: Quatre Siècles d'Esclavage. Nouvelles Questions, Nouvelles Recherches* (Paris, 2012), pp. 7–63; Herbert Klein and João Reis, "Slavery in Brazil", in José Moya (ed.), *The Oxford Handbook of Latin American History* (Oxford [etc.], 2011),pp. 181–211.

[24] For a previous discussion of this issue with different analytical purposes, see Chalhoub, *Visões da liberdade*, pp. 122–130.

employers, and workers during times of deep changes and uncertainties in labor relations.

Conditional manumission and labor contracts

During the nineteenth century, there was no civil code in Brazil, nor was there a "black code" or any other specific body of laws pertaining to slavery. Ordinary laws, Portuguese ordinances dating from colonial times, and different legal codes pertaining to ancient Rome regulated legal issues in relation to bondage.[25] The strong relevance of ancient Roman codes for Brazilian slavery may have been a consequence of the importance of manumission in both slave societies and the problem of dealing with different forms of transition to freedom and integration of freed persons into society.[26] Yet, manumission in ancient Greek and Roman contexts, and the ways of dealing with the liberation of certain individuals and their process of integration into the polity, happened in societies that would continue to operate as slave-based societies.[27] Resort to Roman law in legal debates regarding slavery in the 1850s and 1860s in Brazil, nonetheless, was embedded in the struggles pushing towards emancipation. Thus, for instance, the subtleties concerning the uncertain status of people who had received conditional manumission acquired new political meanings beginning in the 1850s, however traditional had been the practice of thinking Brazilian slavery in terms of Roman law.

In 1867, within an international context of increasing isolation of the remaining slave regimes in the aftermath of the defeat of the South in the American Civil War, a Brazilian lawyer, J. Caroatá, decided to organize a compilation of court decisions and other documents pertaining to questions of Brazilian slavery that

---

[25] Keila Grinberg, *O fiador dos brasileiros: cidadania, escravidão e direito civil no tempo de Antonio Pereira Rebouças* (Rio de Janeiro, 2002); Mariana Paes, *"Sujeitos da história, sujeitos de direitos: personalidade jurídica no Brasil escravista (1860–88)"* (Master's thesis in Law, Universidade de São Paulo, 2014).

[26] However, a recent study did not find any resort to Roman codes in slavery-related civil suits in eighteenth-century Minas Gerais; Fernanda Pinheiro, "Em defesa da liberdade: libertos e livres nos tribunais do Antigo Regime português (Mariana e Lisboa, 1720–1819)" (Doctoral dissertation in History, Universidade Estadual de Campinas [UNICAMP], 2013).

[27] For groundbreaking comparative views on ancient Roman and US slavery see: Moses I. Finley, "Between Slavery and Freedom", *Comparative Studies in Society and History*, 6 (1964), pp. 233–249; idem, *Ancient Slavery and Modern Ideology* (London, 1980); see also Marcus Wood, *The Horrible Gift of Freedom: Atlantic Slavery and the Representation of Emancipation* (Athens, OH [etc.], 2010), pp. 44–50.

had been highly controversial.²⁸ His explicit aim was to collect materials that would be useful to lawyers and judges who had to deal routinely with slavery and appeals for freedom in court. Furthermore, he argued that the decisions gathered were "regulated by moral principles that [...] conceded ample prerogatives and advantages in favor of freedom".²⁹ In other words, Caroatá recognized from the outset the political motivation of his efforts, which was to forward the cause of slave emancipation. Although the volume addressed twenty-six different legal questions, the first of them, and the one most lengthily documented, occupying about one-quarter of the whole book, concerned the condition of children born of slave women who had been granted conditional manumission.

Among the documents offered on the subject, there appeared the debates held in the Institute of Brazilian Lawyers (Instituto da Ordem dos Advogados Brasileiros, IAB) from October to December, 1857.³⁰ Some members of the Institute, such as Caetano Soares and Perdigão Malheiro, argued forcefully that the children of conditionally manumitted slave mothers were born free. They started with the assumption that the slave who had been granted conditional liberty became free from that moment onwards, irrespective of the limitations imposed on his or her freedom due to the obligation of rendering further services. Therefore, given the Roman principle of *partus sequitur ventrem,* the offspring of conditionally freed women (*statuliberi*) were born of free wombs.

The question was framed at the Institute in a way that presented a further complication. The imaginary master who granted freedom to a slave woman had done so in a last will and testament, therefore bequeathing her services as a conditionally freed person to a third party upon his death. The members of the Institute had to decide whether the third party enjoying the services of the *statuliber* became the proprietor of the fruits of the reproductive labor of the woman, inasmuch as the fruits of trees and the offspring of animals belonged to those who had formal temporary rights over them. Here again, both Soares and Malheiro found precedent in Roman law to maintain that, in contrast to the cases of plants and animals, the children of *statuliberi* slaves were not fruit, so they did not become the property of those with usufruct rights to the women's services. In addition, differently from the situation of their mothers, whose labor force belonged temporarily to the third party who had usufruct rights over them, the children were

---

28 J.P.J. da S.C. [Caroatá], *Apanhamento de decisões sobre questões de liberdade, publicadas em diversos periodicos forenses da Corte* (Bahia, 1867).
29 *Ibid.,* p. 4. All translations from Portuguese are mine.
30 *Ibid.,* pp. 12–37; for a detailed study of these debates and others regarding emancipation in the IAB, see the excellent book by Eduardo Spiller Pena, *Pajens da Casa Imperial: jurisconsultos, escravidão e a lei de 1871* (Campinas, 2001).

not under the obligation of rendering services – that is, they were *ingênuos*, or perfectly free, from the moment of their birth.[31]

Soares and Malheiro found a formidable adversary in the President of the Institute, Teixeira de Freitas, perhaps the most respected interpreter of Roman law in the country at the time. The President suggested that Soares and Malheiro had not based their opinion on the rigorous interpretation of Roman law, but rather on the application of tenets derived from natural law that could not apply to a society in which slavery still existed. The fact that slavery continued to exist in Brazil was to be lamented; however, seeking to rule a slave society according to legal principles that were incompatible with it seemed contradictory and pointless. Freitas analyzed the Roman legal text that served as the source for the contention that the children of *statuliberi* women did not become the property of a third party that had usufruct rights to their services. According to him, the purpose of the legal text cited was to defend the idea that the children belonged to the proprietor, or to his heirs, not to the third party who was enjoying the woman's services for a period. In other words, either Soares and Malheiro did not know what they were talking about, or they had purposefully distorted the meaning conveyed in a legal source that did not uphold the right to freedom of the children of *statuliberi* women. The exchange promptly turned sour, with Teixeira de Freitas arguing that, according to Roman law, the *statuliberi* remained in bondage for as long as there was a pending condition regarding their freedom; consequently, the children of conditionally manumitted women were slaves because their status followed that of their mothers.[32]

The nature of conditional manumission became a central aspect of the debates that followed. Teixeira de Freitas thought that manumission was a donation, a unilateral act originating exclusively from the master's will. Therefore it seemed incorrect to think of so-called conditional manumission as truly involving a condition because "a condition depends on an uncertain fact, on chance or on the will of man; in the case at hand the slave exercises no will";[33] that is, the services had to be performed regardless of his or her decision to do so. In other words, the obligation to render services meant the continuation of bondage itself. He proceeded to say that slavery could not be properly compared with other labor

---

31 Caroatá, *Apanhamento*, pp. 12–13, 17. Legally, in nineteenth-century Brazil, the offspring of free and freed women were called *ingênuos* (as opposed to the offspring of bonded women, who were slaves). According to the Constitution of 1824, *ingênuos*, regardless of color, could have access to political rights when they came of age and if they met the income requirements established by the Constitution. After the Free Womb Law (1871), the word *ingênuos* was commonly used to refer to the thereafter freeborn children of slave women.
32 Caroatá, *Apanhamento*, pp. 14–17.
33 Ibid., p. 17.

Figure 2. Caetano Soares. *Instituto dos Avogados Brasileiros;* http://www.iabnacional.org.br/article.php3?id_article=2031& var_recherche=escravos

regimes. Referring to the law of 1837 that regulated labor contracts for supposedly free workers in Brazil, Freitas argued that laborers entered into such contracts knowing that there were obligations to fulfill and that breach of contract would entail indemnification and penal sanctions. In contrast, slaves, including the *statuliberi*, could not refuse to perform services, nor were there applicable sanctions or compensation to deal with the situation. In sum, because the *statuliberi* had no space for choice, conditional manumission could not be compared to a labor contract that workers entered into voluntarily.[34]

Apparently aware that continuing the discussion on the terrain of Roman law did not seem promising for their purposes, Soares and Malheiro attempted to distance themselves from the idea that they proposed to solve the problem by merely seeking the right precedent in ancient codes.

Although slavery continued to exist and property rights associated with it had to be dealt with, the institution had been undergoing a process of change. If, according to Roman law, the *statuliberi* remained slaves of the heirs until the fulfillment of the condition established in the last will and testament, then, necessarily, the children born of conditionally manumitted mothers had to be considered slaves. The strict application of this principle meant that the children were in a worse position than their mothers, for *statuliberi* mothers had freedom ensured within a given time, while the children did not have a foreseeable hope of becoming freed. The situation seemed cruel and contradicted the present state of civilization; actually, Caetano Soares implied that the ideas of Teixeira de Freitas would have made perfect sense if he were living in ancient Rome.[35]

Malheiro and Soares then returned to the question, which Freitas had previously raised, of whether conditional manumission could be compared to a labor contract. They argued that the obligation to render services did not in itself mean a state of bondage. For instance, it would be absurd to consider as slaves the *colonos* – free agricultural laborers – hired under the contractual conditions established in the law of 1837. Furthermore, if the *statuliberi* did not enter into the new situation of their own initiative, judicial or notarial officials did so on their

---

[34] *Ibid.*, pp. 18–20. This contrast between slavery and labor contracts highlighted by Freitas at the same time also implied a proximity between them, especially in the case of conditional manumission: both of them involved a high degree of obligation. Peter Eisenberg had noticed this similarity between conditional manumission and labor contracts; Eisenberg, "Ficando livre", *passim*. Henrique Espada Lima has been studying systematically the "rental service contracts" made by freed persons to pay for their freedom. These contracts were made within the realm of the law of 1837 and, later, of the law of 1879; see, for example, Henrique Espada Lima, "Freedom, Precariousness, and the Law: Freed Persons Contracting out their Labour in Nineteenth-Century Brazil", *International Review of Social History*, 54 (2009), pp. 391–416. See also Marília Ariza, "Ofício da liberdade: contratos de locação de serviços e trabalhadores libertandos em São Paulo e Campinas (1830–1888)" (Master's thesis in History, Universidade de São Paulo, 2012).
[35] Caroatá, *Apanhamento*, p. 20.

behalf, thus assuring them the benefit of the contractual relation pertaining to conditional manumission.

Malheiro and Soares maintained that Teixeira de Freitas believed that all workers under obligation to render services had to be conceived of as in bondage. They deemed such a conception an error originating in a refusal to see the distinction between the slave as property and the slave as someone able to perform labor. These two things were not the same, as was clear from the fact that a proprietor could have a legal title to a slave and still grant to someone else the right to enjoy the labor such a captive was able to provide. Conversely, a person could be nominally free, such as an agricultural laborer hired under the law of 1837, and still have to perform labor under a contract that established criminal sanctions for its breach. In sum, since they conceived of labor relations originating in conditional manumission as not being the continuation of bondage, Soares and Malheiro defended the position that in the new, civilized world in the making, a person could be both nominally free and subjected to forms of compulsory labor.[36] This was a contention that would be taken up again in the future, under different political circumstances, to defend the postponement of the abolition of slavery, or, more precisely, to enact an abolition law that would subject freed people to further years of compulsory labor, as we shall see.

Slaves go to court

In presenting his selection of judicial controversies regarding the status of children of conditionally manumitted women, J. Caroatá did not choose to offer them chronologically, or according to their length. Instead, he opened the section with the reasons alleged by a solicitor, on behalf of the *pardo* Aquilino, in a civil suit in which it was argued that he had been born free because his mother had been born the daughter of a conditionally manumitted woman (that is, Aquilino's grandmother).[37] In this case, then, the justification for freedom originated in events two generations back in time. Caroatá's decision to begin his compilation with such a document may not have been accidental. In fact, had he followed a mere chronological order or reasoned according to the importance of the characters involved, he would have begun the volume with the debates in the Institute of Brazilian Lawyers. On the one hand, his editing decision may suggest the importance of the presence of slaves in court struggling for freedom in order to understand the

---

[36] *Ibid.*, pp. 20–30.
[37] *Ibid.*, pp. 5–10.

outcome of juridical controversies regarding slavery at the time. On the other hand, the long period which elapsed between the fact that originated the alleged right to freedom and Aquilino's actually going to court to claim such a right suggests the limits and difficulties bonded people had to deal with in appealing for justice.[38]

Freedom suits found in Brazilian archives are often lengthy documents that may contain hundreds of pages if they include appeals to higher courts. Such was the case with the *preto* (black) Pompeu, who filed his initial petition for freedom with a local judge in Rio in August 1860, having to wait for a final decision until July 1863.[39] "Pompeu said, through his guardian *(curador)*", as was the usual way of opening such texts, that he had a right to freedom because his mother, Lauriana, had given birth to him and to his siblings after having received conditional manumission from her master. Lauriana had the obligation "to serve only for as long as her liberator lived, and she would become absolutely free from the day of his death".[40] Lauriana's master had died in 1842 and she had been free since then; Pompeu, however, remained in bondage and lived now in another household. The curator argued that Pompeu should have been deemed free together with his mother, beginning on the day of her master's death.

The judge decided to take the slave away from his alleged proprietor's house for the duration of the court proceedings and to put him under "deposit", as was said, with a citizen indicated by the judge. The curator appended a certified copy of the conditional letter of manumission granted to Lauriana. He had obtained the certified copy of the letter of liberty from another appeal for freedom, filed by Pompeu's siblings against their supposed proprietors. One of the persons who testified on Pompeu's behalf mentioned that his mother, Lauriana, still lived in the company of her former mistress's family – more precisely, with the former mistress's son-in-law. The son-in-law, Pedro do Couto, acted as curator on behalf

---

38 Letícia Graziele Basílio de Freitas, "Escravos nos tribunais: o recurso à legislação emancipacionista em ações de liberdade do século XIX" (B.A. thesis in History, UNICAMP, 2012). Available online: http://www.bibliotecadigital.unicamp.br/document/?code=00094242 5&opt=1.

39 O preto Pompeu (plaintiff), and João Araújo Rangel (defendant), petition for freedom, n. 2665, maço 923, galeria A, Arquivo Nacional do Rio de Janeiro [hereafter, ANRJ]. I have analyzed this story before in Chalhoub, *Visões da liberdade*, pp. 123–127. For *Visões da liberdade* I had found only the proceedings pertaining to the lower court (2a. Vara Cível); very recently, I found the appeals to the higher court (Tribunal da Relação da Corte), which contain, at the beginning, a transcript of the proceedings in the lower court; microfilm copy, AN 84.0.ACI.096, made from the originals belonging to the Arquivo Nacional and deposited at the Arquivo Edgard Leuenroth, UNICAMP.

40 Lower-court proceedings (2a. Vara Cível), leaf 3, front side; the quoted passage reads as follows in Portuguese: "a servir somente durante a vida de seu libertador, e ficaria absolutamente livre, desde o dia em que ele falecesse".

of both Pompeu and his siblings in the two civil suits seeking to free Lauriana's children.[41]

Lauriana was then in her fifties, and it seems that the family she had served for her whole life decided to go to court to seek the freedom of her children. Nonetheless, we may hypothesize that the family itself had originally held her children as slaves and sold or dispersed them through inheritance. We will probably never know how Lauriana managed to obtain the support of her former master's family to seek the freedom of her offspring. We may suspect that decades of seemingly faithful service and subjection to labor exploitation had done the trick, together with the vulnerability suggested by the enslavement of her children and the fact that she continued dependent on and living with the seigneurial family in old age.[42]

However, Pompeu probably had his own reasons to struggle for freedom at that particular time. He had become a valuable slave. When he was nine or ten years old, his master had made him an apprentice tailor. He seemed to be also appreciated as a page, setting tables and serving family meals. Lately, he had learned to work as a coachman. Pompeu filed his petition for freedom when there appeared to be much business speculation around him in the lively slave market of the Empire's capital. João Rangel, the defendant in the petition for freedom, adopted as his first line of defense the allegation that he had just bought the young man, mentioning the names of two previous proprietors of Pompeu, therefore arguing that the freedom suit had to be filed against the person who had sold the slave to him. He gave details of the transaction and appended a letter received from the previous owner that included information on the expectations Pompeu had himself. João Rangel was looking for a slave to work for him as a coachman. Doctor Gonzaga Bastos learned of his need and offered Pompeu to him. The two men talked, negotiated the price, and agreed that Rangel as a potential buyer would have Pompeu examined by a medical doctor.

---

41 In the lower-court papers, the initial petition of the plaintiff and accompanying documents run from leaves 3 to 10, both sides of each leaf; the copy of the letter of manumission is on leaves 8 and 9. Pedro do Couto appears as one of the persons authorized to file on Pompeu's behalf on leaf 10. The witness who mentions Pedro do Couto as Lauriana's former mistress's son-in-law is Edwiges Godinho, born in Rio de Janeiro, thirty years old, widow, illiterate, "vive de seus bens" (that is, of income derived from her properties); testimonies appear in sequence beginning on leaf 44.

42 The practice of reducing to slavery the children of slave women who were freed but remained dependent on the master's family seemed relatively common. For other cases, see, for example, Odorico (plaintiff), petition for freedom, Juízo Municipal da Segunda Vara do Rio de Janeiro, no. 1, caixa 523, galeria C, 1862, ANRJ; Teresa Maria da Hora (plaintiff), petition for freedom, Tribunal da Relação do Rio de Janeiro, no. 8118, caixa 2, 1869–1872, ANRJ.

It is not possible to know whether Rangel also tested the slave's skills as a coachman, although this was often the case in such transactions in Rio at the time. In any case, the seller made it clear that, despite his other skills, Pompeu insisted that he wanted to work as a coachman and this was the reason given to sell him – Doctor Bastos did not have a carriage. Pompeu could keep the brand-new boots and coat that Doctor Bastos had recently bought him, although the latter would go without buttons because those had the doctor's initials. The price of the transaction was high. João Rangel complained that, although he had already paid the total amount, Doctor Bastos had not given him the documents proving his ownership of Pompeu and the payment of due taxes on slave property. Therefore, Rangel said that he had decided to start legal proceedings against Doctor Bastos, to recover the amount paid and return the slave to him, when he learned of Pompeu's petition for freedom.[43]

The story is fascinating in its details and complexities. On the one hand, it suggests the vulnerability of bonded people who received conditional manumission. Their situation was very uncertain, especially in the case of freedoms promised in last will and testaments and in letters of manumission by *causa mortis* – that is, those in which the donation of liberty depended upon the master's death – because they could be revoked in practice at any time by the proprietor, sometimes unceremoniously by just selling the captive.[44] Furthermore, as was the case with Lauriana, it seemed common to see conditional manumission as the continuation of bondage until the fulfillment of the condition, entailing that the children of *statuliberi* women remained in slavery. The threat of revocation of freedom probably ensured the faithfulness and dependence of the captive; in addition, it may explain the careful strategic calculation involved in choosing the time to go to court and struggle for freedom. On the other hand, it would be wrong to suppose that slaves regarded passively the unfolding of family arrangements, business transactions, and court cases that decided their fate. Lauriana found ways of obtaining allies in her former master's family. Pompeu had learned many of the skills implied in urban slavery in Rio at the time, skills which might be labelled as "political", so he had made himself valuable to his masters and managed to let them know of his expectations. In any case, as the legal battle that followed suggests, the general political context of the 1860s, with

---

[43] The expectations and anxieties regarding their sale often led slaves to revolt, commit crimes, and file petitions for freedom. For several such cases, documented in civil and criminal trial records, see Chalhoub, *Visões da liberdade*, especially ch. 1.

[44] Despite the wealth of studies on manumission in Brazilian slavery, as was mentioned above, works focusing on the experience of conditional manumission are still rare. For a recent study which seeks to analyze the masters' perspective as it appears in last will and testaments, see Alessandra Pedro, "Liberdade sob condição: alforrias e política de domínio senhorial em Campinas, 1855–1871" (Master's thesis in History, UNICAMP, 2009).

slave emancipation increasingly on the agenda, helps to understand why Lauriana and Pompeu had then a better chance of achieving their aims.⁴⁵

Besides alleging that the petition for freedom should have been addressed to Pompeu's previous owner, instead of to himself, João Rangel also argued, predictably, that the *statuliberi* were not freed until the fulfillment of their conditions. In other words, Lauriana remained in slavery when she gave birth to Pompeu, so the boy was a slave. Challenged to defend this argument further on several occasions in the following years, Rangel's lawyers tried two related paths. First, they proposed a careful reading of the letter of liberty granted to Lauriana in order to determine what had been the will of her master. The letter said in one passage that Lauriana should "be [or remain] a captive only during the life" of the master, supposedly meaning that the master thought of her as a slave for as long as he lived.⁴⁶ Second, they sought to define the freedom conceded to Lauriana as *causa mortis*. According to this reasoning, the intention of Lauriana's master had been to let the *crioula* (a black slave born in Brazil) know that "if she continued to serve him well, she would become free upon his death".⁴⁷ The strategy for slave control made explicit here could be effective only if the master retained the right to revoke the promised freedom as he wished. This situation seemed quite different from that of freed persons already in full possession of their freedoms, who theoretically could only have their liberties revoked if they showed ingratitude to former masters.⁴⁸

---

45 The participation of slaves in the country's legal culture has been an important theme in the historiography of Brazilian slavery for almost three decades; for early examples, see Silvia H. Lara, *Campos da violência: escravos e senhores na capitania do Rio de Janeiro, 1750–1808* (Rio de Janeiro, 1988); Chalhoub, *Visões da liberdade*; Hebe Mattos, *Das cores do silêncio: os significados da liberdade no sudeste escravista – Brasil, século XIX* (Campinas, 2013; 1st edn, 1995); Keila Grinberg, *Liberata – a lei da ambiguidade* (Rio de Janeiro, 1994). For a volume that gathers several of the most important Brazilian authors in the field and offers a very useful analysis of the state of the art in its introduction, see Silvia H. Lara and Joseli M. Mendonça (eds), *Direitos e justiças no Brasil. Ensaios de história social* (Campinas, 2006). Also, the studies of Rebecca Scott have been very important: *Slave Emancipation in Cuba: the Transition to Free Labor 1860–1899* (Princeton, NJ, 1985); *Degrees of Freedom: Louisiana and Cuba after Slavery* (Cambridge, MA, 2005); Scott and Hébrard, *Freedom Papers*. See also Alejandro de la Fuente, "Slave Law and Claims-Making in Cuba: the Tannenbaum Debate Revisited", *Law & History Review*, 22 (2004), pp. 339–369.
46 Lower-court proceedings (2a. Vara Cível), leaf 35; the quoted passage reads as follows in Portuguese: "somente seja cativa durante a vida dele outorgante".
47 Lower-court proceedings (2a. Vara Cível), leaf 35; the quoted passage reads as follows in Portuguese: "que se bem o continuasse a servir, por sua morte ficaria liberta". Allegations of the defendant in the lower-court volume begin on leaves 21, then 34; in the higher-court volume, there are allegations beginning on leaves 31 and 70.
48 Although masters retained the right to revoke manumissions (conditional or not) until the law of 1871, some freed people were more vulnerable to re-enslavement than others; see Chalhoub, "The Precariousness of Freedom in a Slave Society", pp. 418–420.

Pompeu's defenders replied that Rangel's lawyers had interpreted the cited passage of Lauriana's letter of liberty out of context. To begin with, the document carried a title, which was "deed of conditional liberty" *(escritura de condicional liberdade)*, to emphasize from the beginning that the donation of freedom occurred at the very moment of formalizing it. The assumption of a conditional letter of manumission was that the grantee would exercise her or his judgment to fulfill the obligation there stated; the outcome depended on his or her will, meaning that the person "was released from the position of a slave". The liberty thus granted was not *causa mortis*, but *intervivos* – that is, it became immediately effective. Of course, it could be revoked by ingratitude, as could all manumissions until the law of 1871 prohibited such a possibility, but Lauriana's freedom had never been revoked and this was not a point under consideration. Although Pompeu's defenders added other, procedural, reasons to argue that the liberty granted Lauriana was *intervivos*, the thrust of their argument was the contention that the condition imposed on the grantee destroyed the fiction of the slave as a thing, bestowing upon her or him the capacity to reason and decide on a course of action. In this the argument resembled the one presented by Perdigão Malheiro and Caetano Soares at the Institute of Brazilian Lawyers in 1857, for they deemed conditional manumission a form of labor contract because it depended on the will of the person being freed.

Pompeu's lawyers and solicitors did not cite the debates of 1857 in their petition for freedom, neither did they compare conditional manumission to a labor contract. However, the sentence passed by the local judge, Luiz Alvares de Azevedo Macedo, in November 1861, to be confirmed twice in higher courts, recalled in part the politically charged atmosphere of the 1857 debates at the Institute. After summarizing the allegations of each party, the judge said that he based his decision on the provisions of law as well as "on the humanitarian principles derived from the enlightenment of the century". He proceeded to say that João Rangel's argument that the petition should have been directed against Pompeu's previous master did not make sense because Rangel exercised effective "possession and dominion over the object" – that is, the slave – when Pompeu went to court. Next, he agreed with Pompeu's defenders regarding the freedom of the children born of conditionally manumitted slave mothers. Furthermore, he did so with an embattled tone, dismissing the reasoning of Rangel's lawyers as "sophistic".

The content of the judicial sentence seemed so obviously politicized that Rangel's lawyers included a protest against it in their appeal to the higher courts. They said that the local judge had reached his decision "upholding the desired emancipation", using "an academic style instead of a forensic one" – meaning that the politicization of the subject pertained to lawyers' professional associations and schools of law, not to the courtrooms. In fact, a lawyer named Alvares de Azevedo attended the debates at the Institute in 1857; furthermore, a member named Luiz Alvares de Azevedo Macedo participated in the editorial committee of the periodical published by the Institute and was the institution's secretary. Therefore, it seems that this very same person, who had closely followed the 1857 debates, served also as judge in Pompeu's petition for freedom.[49]

The arguments presented in Pompeu's case and the sentence of the local judge, who very likely had also attended the debates in 1857, suggests the continuity of political meanings commonly associated with conditional manumission into the 1860s – namely, that defenders of slave emancipation seized upon it when struggling for their cause. The situation would begin to change as early as 1871, during the debates leading to the Free Womb Law.

The politics of ambiguity

The politicization of slave motherhood and conditional manumission, issues that converged on the question of the condition of children born to conditionally manumitted women, was a central aspect of debates that led to the slave emancipation law of 1871 (also called the Free Womb Law). Perdigão Malheiro may be credited with having forwarded the cause by a speech in the Institute of Brazilian Lawyers on 7 September 1863.[50] He argued that property of slaves was illegitimate and that it contradicted natural law. In the past, enslavement occurred as a consequence of the master's will, imposed by coercion or violence. In the present, it had become a result of the legislators' arbitrariness. Bondage passed from one generation to another, in perpetuity, by heredity, based on the Roman principle *partus sequitur ventrem*. Mentioning several examples of countries that had abol-

---

49 I failed to write down the name of the judge when I read the lower-court proceedings in the mid-1980s; the transcription of the sentence and the name of the judge appear in the higher-court volume, leaf 28. For the confirmation of the presence of a lawyer called Alvares de Azevedo in the 1857 debates at the Institute of Brazilian Lawyers, see Caroatá, *Apanhamento*, p. 31. For Luiz Alvares de Azevedo Macedo as a member of the editorial committee of the periodical published by the Institute and as the institution's secretary see, respectively, *Revista do Instituto da Ordem dos Advogados Brasileiros*. Ano II, Tomo II, n. 4, October to December 1863, p. 163 and Ano II, Tomo II, n. 3, July to August 1863, p. 121.

50 A.M. Perdigão Malheiro, "Illegitimidade da propriedade constituída sobre o escravo – Natureza de tal propriedade – Justiça e conveniência da abolição da escravidão; em que termos", *Revista do Instituto da Ordem dos Advogados Brasileiros*, Ano II, Tomo II, n. 3, July to August 1863, pp. 131–152.

ished slavery during the nineteenth century, he suggested that the Brazilian parliament enact a bill declaring free the offspring of slave women.

Figure 3. Perdigão Malheiro. *Instituto dos Avogados Brasileiros;* http://www.iabnacional.org.br/article.php3?id_article=2059

He proceeded to recite the hymn of freedom according to the usage of the times: slave emancipation would allow the country "to join the great intellectual and moral movement of the nineteenth century, [...] advancing towards civilization", achieving the "extermination" of an institution that caused "the degradation of the people, the depravation of customs, the backwardness of industry", and so forth.[51]

Perdigão Malheiro also returned to the theme of the *statuliberi* in his massive study of Brazilian slavery published in 1866–1867. Perhaps still brooding over Teixeira de Freitas's contention that he had not mastered Roman law, he presented a detailed account of the problem in Roman codes. He sought to demonstrate that there had been an "evolution" regarding the subject in ancient codes. At first, the law deemed the *statuliber* fully a slave of the heir for as long as there was a pending condition on his or her freedom. Later, there appeared "a preponderance of liberty", with the prohibition of torture and whippings against conditionally manumitted slaves and the admission of their pleading in judicial cases. Nevertheless, as Perdigão Malheiro admitted, the children born of *statuliberi* slave mothers continued always to be considered slaves of the heirs.[52]

Perdigão Malheiro proceeded with his "work of reconstruction" of the legal aspects regarding conditional manumission by seeking to specify what happened when a master freed a slave. Traditionally, jurists conceived of manumissions as donations, but he thought such a view to be mistaken. In manumission, what is the object being donated? Who is the beneficiary? Enslavement had not been a "donation" to the slave; neither could freedom be seen in this way. "The truth of the matter" was that the act of conceding freedom meant that the master "renounced the dominion and power he exercised (against natural law) over the slave, restoring the natural state of freedom in which all men are born". Slavery belonged to the realm of positive law, contradicting the natural rights of slaves; therefore, it did not make sense to think of masters "donating" freedom to their captives.[53]

Then what happened when a slave received conditional manumission? It could be alleged that the slave's "natural state of manhood" remained suspended until the fulfillment of the condition. Malheiro stated that such an opinion resulted from "confusion", from refusal to abandon "the terrain of fictions" that the institution of slavery had created. According to him, upon receiving a conditional manumission a slave "is promptly restored to his natural condition of a

---

51 Perdigão Malheiro, "Illegitimidade da propriedade constituída sobre o escravo", p. 151.
52 Idem, *A escravidão no Brasil: ensaio histórico, jurídico, social*, 2 vols (Petrópolis, 1976); for the passage mentioned, see I, pp. 114–117.
53 Idem, *A escravidão no Brasil*, I, p. 118.

man and a person", despite the fact that the full enjoyment of liberty remained postponed. His imaginary opponent appeared again to say that it seemed absurd that someone repossessed his or her natural freedom and continued devoid of it, depending upon a certain period of time or a particular event to become fully free. Perdigão Malheiro explained that he considered the situation of conditionally manumitted individuals to be similar to that of minors, "who depended upon a certain event or a period of time to be emancipated and thus enjoy full civil rights and liberties".[54]

It is noteworthy that, in contrast to the debates of 1857, conditional manumission is not compared to a labor contract here, with the accompanying rhetoric of people able to reason and to decide on a given course of action – regardless of the notion that the choices to be made available consist of new forms of unfree labor. The approximation of conditionally manumitted persons to minors seems to underline instead their unpreparedness for freedom, thus echoing in the Brazilian context a central theme of passages from slavery to post-emancipation societies also present elsewhere.[55] Therefore, it seems paradoxical (but, at second view, perhaps not surprising) that Perdigão Malheiro changed his mind about the idea of pursuing gradual emancipation by means of freeing the children born of slave women. For reasons that are not clear and may include a petty revenge for not having been invited to become a minister of state, he opposed the Free Womb Law (1871).[56]

Interestingly, opponents of the law, representatives of the coffee economy prominent among them, adopted the view that the *statuliberi* must be considered free at the moment they received the promise of freedom. They did so with the intention of garnering political support against the bill through the spread of fear among planters. One of their arguments was that, since the bill established an emancipation fund which could eventually benefit every captive, the law would entail the recognition that all bonded people became *statuliberi*, just awaiting the fulfillment of a condition (enough funds for slave property indemnification) to achieve full freedom. The consequence of this would be a situation in which plantation slaves could not be disciplined and punished as slaves any more, nor could they be subjected to commercial transactions and other property deeds pertaining to slavery.

---

54 *Ibid.*, p. 120.
55 See, for instance, the "Introduction" in Frederick Cooper, Thomas Holt, and Rebecca Scott, *Beyond Slavery: Explorations of Race, Labor, and Citizenship in Postemancipation Societies* (Chapel Hill, NC [etc.], 2000), pp. 1–32.
56 Sidney Chalhoub, *Machado de Assis, historiador* (São Paulo, 2003), pp. 186–187.

The argument appeared again during the political debates that would result in the law of 28 September 1885, which freed slaves who reached the age of sixty. Opponents of the bill alleged that it meant attributing to all existing slaves the condition of *statuliberi*. In other words, every slave would have a right to freedom to be achieved after a period of time – that is, when he or she became sixty years old. The parliamentary opposition would then take up the arguments present in Perdigão Malheiro's book to say that conditionally manumitted slaves were already free, and therefore they could not be subjected to property transactions pertaining to slavery. In turn, defenders of the bill would refer to the 1857 debates to cite Teixeira de Freitas and maintain that the *statuliberi* continued in full bondage until the fulfilment of the condition established for manumission. As is clear from a comparison of political discourses regarding conditional manumission in the 1860s and 1880s, the same legal arguments had acquired completely different political meanings.[57]

Perhaps still more surprising is the manner in which the same legal controversies reappear in September 1887, in the wake of the social crisis and disorganization of labor relations in the coffee plantations, including the widespread slave flight mentioned at the beginning of this article, that would lead to abolition in May of the following year.[58] The parliament was in its final sessions of the year when the crisis of slavery became the focus of heated debates in the Senate. Antonio Prado, a prominent senator of the Conservative Party and a representative of coffee planters from the province of São Paulo, seems to have turned against his own constituents: slaves in Campinas, a major coffee-growing area in the province of São Paulo, had been running away from rural properties in massive numbers. Planters sent a petition to the Chamber of Deputies, there presented by Andrade Figueira, a deputy from the province of Rio de Janeiro and prominent defender of slavery, complaining that they had not been receiving proper assistance from the provincial and imperial authorities to maintain discipline in the slave quarters. Antonio Prado brought the theme to the Senate floor,

---

57 For the discussion on the *statuliberi* in 1871 and 1885, see Eduardo Pena, *Pajens da Casa Imperial*, ch. 3; for an in-depth study of the 1885 law and its application, Joseli Mendonça, *Entre a mão e os anéis: a lei dos sexagenários e os caminhos da abolição no Brasil* (Campinas, 1999).

58 My account of events in September 1887 is based on the reading of the *Gazeta de Notícias*, a daily paper published in Rio de Janeiro. Because discussions in the Senate became the focal point of the political crisis regarding slavery at that particular moment, the *Gazeta* is an essential source. The periodical published the proceedings of the Senate and commented extensively on what happened there. It opposed the conservative cabinet then in power. For a detailed study of slave resistance in the province of São Paulo in the 1880s, including the massive slave flights beginning in 1887 and continuing until abolition, see Maria Helena Machado, *O plano e o pânico: os movimentos sociais na década da Abolição* (Rio de Janeiro [etc.], 1994).

asking that the conservative cabinet inform parliament about what the President of the province of São Paulo had been doing to restore "public order on the occasions of massive flights of slaves from the plantations in the county of Campinas".[59] Antonio Prado's main purpose was to suggest that planters in Campinas should not be waiting for the government to muster the necessary forces to guarantee slave discipline. It was no longer possible to achieve that by the force of the military or police. Planters had to understand that they needed to deal with the situation by themselves and with a different strategy.

Figure 4. *Revista Illustrada*, 12th year, no. 468 (Rio de Janeiro, 22 October 1887), p. 4.[60] Translation of cartoon text: "According to telegrams from *O Paiz* [a daily paper in Rio] and other newspapers in this Court, 150 enslaved people left several plantations in Capivary (province of São Paulo) and walked to the capital. In Itú [a town in the interior of the province of São Paulo] 10 policemen attempted to arrest them; there was a serious conflict, in which the police force was badly defeated."

According to Antonio Prado, many slave owners in the province of São Paulo had successfully prevented massive flights from their properties by granting conditional manumission to their slaves. These freedoms were given upon the condition of continued service for a period of time – it appears that Prado himself recommended three years. Examples of such concessions of freedom abounded at that particular time, announced with self-interested pomposity in daily papers and saluted by journalists and readers with what seems to be, retrospectively, a rather hypocritical sense of moral worth. The idea was that the promise of freedom would restore the authority of masters in a moment of crisis in labor relations and instill in slaves the sentiment of gratitude, thus increasing the likeli-

---

59 Section entitled "Diario das Camaras", *Gazeta de Notícias*, 18 September 1887, p. 1.
60 On p. 3 of the same issue, there is an article about this episode, and the title is "Greve de escravizados" ["A strike by enslaved people"].

hood that they remain on the plantations while the imperial government decided what to do.

Actually, conditional manumission appeared to inspire many of the proposals presented in the parliament during the turbulent month of September 1887. Senators and deputies drafted several different bills that seem remarkable for what they had in common: the imperial government should enact a law declaring the emancipation of all slaves, who nonetheless would have the obligation to serve their masters for two, three, or five more years. Furthermore, the parliament should urgently pass legislation against vagrancy, thereby creating legal means to force all "free" people to perform forms of labor deemed acceptable or desirable.[61]

Politically, the decline of slavery seemed increasingly irreversible in September 1887. The tipping point may have been the news that Joaquim Nabuco, a famous abolitionist, had been elected to return to parliament as a deputy for the province of Pernambuco. Nabuco defeated a minister of the ruling conservative cabinet in the elections, compelling the minister to resign his post.[62] The outcome of the elections in Pernambuco dramatized the increasing political isolation of the president of the cabinet, Cotegipe, who resisted any suggestion that he should act promptly to abolish slavery while it was perhaps still possible to do so in a controlled manner. This is why a conservative senator such as Antonio Prado became critical of the cabinet: it was the perception that postponing the abolition of slavery meant losing control of events. Perhaps he believed that conditional manumissions granted by private masters, followed by an emancipation bill that required freed persons to render three more years of forced labor, would suffice to detain the massive flight of slaves from coffee plantations. Alternatively, slave labor did not matter much to him any more. By September 1887, Antonio Prado and coffee planters close to him had put in place a system of subsidized immigration that had already started to bring thousands of Italians to the province of São Paulo.[63]

---

61 See, for instance, two different bills proposed by senators Taunay and Godoy, section entitled "Elemento Servil", *Gazeta de Notícias*, 25 September 1887, p. 1. A similar combination of slave resistance, proprietors' grants of conditional manumission, and discourses on the alleged vagrancy of freed people appeared in the province of Bahia in the months before abolition; see Walter Fraga Filho, *Encruzilhadas da liberdade: histórias de escravos e libertos na Bahia (1870–1910)* (Campinas, 2006), especially chs 3 and 4.
62 For a good-humored and ironic comment on the repercussions of Nabuco's electoral victory, see the section entitled "Chronica", *Gazeta de Notícias*, 18 September 1887, p. 1.
63 Michael Hall, "Os fazendeiros paulistas e a imigração ", in Fernando Teixeira da Silva *et al.* (eds), *República, liberalismo, cidadania* (Piracicaba, 2003), pp. 153–161.

Meanwhile, in the very same eventful month of September 1887, members of the Institute of Brazilian Lawyers (IAB) returned to the subject of the condition of the *statuliberi*. More precisely, they discussed whether the law of 1885 had made every person still enslaved in the country a *statuliber*, which naturally led again to the question of what conditional manumission really meant. At this point, it is unnecessary to reintroduce the arguments there presented – they followed the patterns established in the 1850s. It suffices to say that, on 1 September, José da Silva Costa read a report on the subject, approved almost unanimously by his peers, saying that in the case of the *statuliberi* "the limitations imposed by the law do not destroy freedom, inasmuch as contingency does not eliminate essence".[64] However shallow the philosophical formulation, supported of course by plenty of citations from Perdigão Malheiro's book, it seemed clear that at this political juncture resorting to the debate in the Institute in 1857 meant support for the view that abolition should be preceded by a transitional period in which freed people would continue to render compulsory labor. The emphasis here is on the supposed freedom pertaining to the condition of the *statuliberi*. It seems that most members of the Institute, eight months before further events would lead to full abolition, sought to preclude the possibility of a "radical" (as was said) solution to the problem – that is, the enacting of further legislation on the subject, such as a bill abolishing slavery altogether, without the payment of a monetary indemnification to masters or the rendering of further services by freed people.

The dissonant voice at the Institute on this occasion was Baptista Pereira, who published a pamphlet, dated 30 September 1887, criticizing Silva Costa's piece and his peers' approval of it.[65] Resorting to the authority of Teixeira de Freitas regarding Roman legal precedent and to the debates preceding the law of 1885, he argued that it made no sense to seek freedom in the condition of the *statuliberi*. There existed no such thing as a transitional or intermediary state between slavery and freedom. Quoting Seneca, he deemed the *statuliber* the *monstrum* that revealed the horrific and painful truth – a slave remained a slave until freedom came without further requirements or procrastinating clauses. Given the present situation, the only choice left to legislators was "to resolve the problem radically" by simply abolishing slavery.[66]

---

[64] *Gazeta de Notícias*, 17 September 1887, p. 1. The text appeared soon thereafter; see José da Silva Costa, "Das relações juridicas dos sujeitos à condição de servir, especialmente após a promulgação da Lei n. 3270 de 28 de Setembro de 1885", *Revista do Instituto dos Advogados Brazileiros*. Tomo XI, 1887, pp. 10–52 (includes his reply to a colleague who criticized his text, as we shall see).
[65] J. Baptista Pereira, *Da condição actual dos escravos, especialmente após a promulgação da lei n. 3270 de 28 de Setembro de 1885* (pamphlet) (Rio de Janeiro, 1887).
[66] *Ibid.*, pp. 33–34.

Thus, we come to a moment in which the political turmoil and the disorganization of labor relations provoked by massive slave flights from coffee plantations made more apparent the political appropriations of the meanings of slavery and freedom. As the crisis deepened in the following months, resulting in the allegedly "radical" solution that Antonio Prado and the members of the Institute sought to avoid – abolition without monetary indemnification to proprietors or further services by freed people – decades of social and legal subtleties rooted in the structural ambiguities of conditional manumission seemed to vanish from the political imagination. "Slavery" and "freedom" – or slave labor and free labor – became two opposing, contrasting states, impossible to conceive of as dialectically coexistent given the belief in a supposed law of human evolution that assumed a sure march from one to the other. This retrospective view of past events makes it difficult for us to see spaces of ambiguity and perhaps freedom within slave societies. More importantly, it helps to render invisible the reproduction of bonded labor in modern capitalist societies.

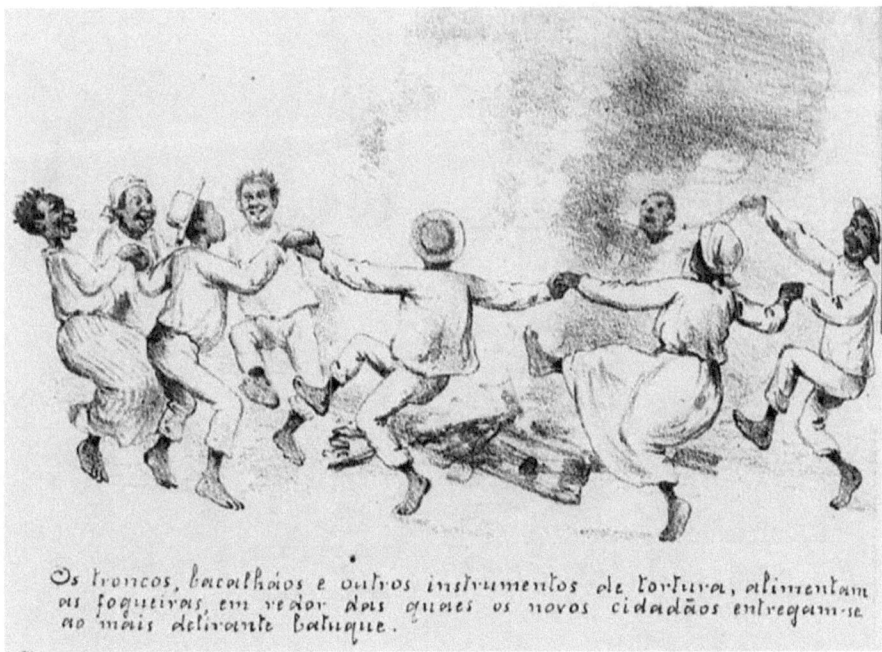

Figure 5. *Revista Illustrada,* 13th year, no. 00499 (Rio de Janeiro, 2 June 1888), p. 4.
Translation of cartoon text: "The stocks, whips, and other instruments of torture now feed the bonfires around which the new citizens dance the most delirious *batuque.*"

Figure 6. *Revista Illustrada,* 13th year, no. 00499 (Rio de Janeiro, 2 June 1888), cover page. Translation of cartoon text: "The planters and the newly freed. What! Yesterday lots of whiplashes to work, and today only money and adulation. Ha! Ha!"

Furthermore, the centrality of conditional manumission in the final crisis of slavery in Brazil reveals a great deal about the expectations of planters for the immediate aftermath of emancipation. They struggled to attain two main objectives: first, they wanted continued dependence and faithfulness on the part of ex-slaves, the maintenance of their "moral authority", as they used to say; second, if there was to be a legally regulated labor market, contracts had to restrict the mobility and the autonomy of workers. What actually happened afterwards depended on a number of factors and varied widely according to different regions of the country.

In the coffee-producing regions of São Paulo, (racist) resentment was further exacerbated by the experience of massive slave flight on the eve of abolition (the "general strike" mentioned above), the availability of impoverished Italian peasants in the global labor market, and the capacity of provincial grandees to organize and subsidize European immigration, resulting in the exclusion of ex-slaves from social and economic opportunities in the post-emancipation period.[67] Elsewhere, the picture that has been emerging slowly in historical studies is more nuanced and diverse.

There were old coffee areas in the province of Rio that suffered heavy economic losses and desolation; others, dedicated mainly to food production, allowed for some access to land and the growth of small properties;[68] and there seems to have occurred significant migration of people of African descent to capital cities.[69] More importantly, with the exception of immigrants in sharecropping and labour service arrangements (the *colonato*) in the province of São Paulo, and of some sectors of the labor force in major cities,[70] the labor market continued mostly unregulated for decades to come, with informal arrangements and

---

[67] Michael Hall, "The Origins of Mass Immigration in Brazil, 1871–1914" (Ph.D. dissertation, Columbia University, 1969); Verena Stolcke and Michael Hall, "A introdução do trabalho livre nas fazendas de café de São Paulo", *Revista Brasileira de História*, 6 (1983), pp. 80–120; George Reid Andrews, *Blacks and Whites in São Paulo, Brazil, 1888–1988* (Madison, WI, 1991); Luiz Aranha Corrêa do Lago, *Da escravidão ao trabalho livre, Brasil, 1550–1900* (São Paulo, 2014).

[68] Ana Rios and Hebe Mattos, "Para além das senzalas: campesinato, política e trabalho rural no Rio de Janeiro pós-Abolição", in Olívia Cunha and Flávio Gomes, *Quase-cidadão: histórias e antropologias da pós-emancipação no Brasil* (Rio de Janeiro, 2007), pp. 55–78; Hebe Mattos, *Ao sul da história: lavradores pobres na crise do trabalho escravo* (Rio de Janeiro, 2009); idem, *Das cores do silêncio,* part IV; for the region of the Recôncavo, in Bahia, see Fraga Filho, *Encruzilhadas da liberdade,* chs 6 to 9.

[69] For the case of Rio de Janeiro, there is a very detailed study of internal migration and racial inequalities after abolition: Samuel Adamo, "The Broken Promise: Race, Health, and Justice in Rio de Janeiro, 1890–1940" (Ph.D. dissertation, University of New Mexico, 1983).

[70] Maria Cecília Velasco e Cruz, "Da tutela ao contrato: 'homens de cor' brasileiros e o movimento operário carioca no pós-abolição", *Topoi,* 11 (2010), pp. 114–135.

paternalist strategies of control predominating over contracts and formal labor rights.[71] Thus the ambiguities of "freedom" and "unfreedom" by no means ended with abolition but continued in different guises – until today.

---

[71] See Ângela de Castro Gomes and Fernando Teixeira da Silva, "Os direitos sociais e humanos dos trabalhadores no Brasil: a título de apresentação", in *idem* (eds), *A Justiça do Trabalho e sua história: os direitos dos trabalhadores no Brasil* (Campinas, 2013), pp. 14–16.

Prabhu P. Mohapatra
Regulated Informality
Legal Constructions of Labour Relations in Colonial India
1814–1926[1]

The point of departure for this essay is the contemporary decline of public presence of labour in our society and implications this has for reconstruction of labour relations on the one hand and the reshaping of the wider public sphere on the other. The decline of public presence of labour, thereby meaning the precipitous decline in political power of the organised labour movement, does not need to be laboured here – two indicators will suffice for the present. First is the great decline in industrial disputes initiated from the side of workers and the trade unions (i.e. strikes and man-days lost due to it) since the last two decades, to such an extent that today lockouts greatly overwhelm strikes in the statistics of industrial disputes. Second, it does not need a psephologist to point out that the great industrial centres of India such as Kanpur, Mumbai, Jamshedpur, Calcutta which regularly sent up eminent trade unionists, labour leaders and militants of the labour movement as parliamentary representatives are today strongholds of right-wing parties. Paradoxically this has occurred at a time when the numerical preponderance of wage earners in India is no longer a matter of debate. What explains this precipitous decline of presence of labour in contemporary public life alongside the massive expansion in numbers of wage earners?

A key explanation of this trend commonly given out is that organised labour movement has been rapidly overwhelmed by the massive expansion in the so-called informal sector. Today the so-called informal sector labour force constitutes 93 per cent of the total labour force in India. However, this begs the question – how has the informal sector expanded and why has it remained unorganised? This leads us to the crucial role of the State in constructing labour relations in contemporary India. Currently we are witness to a massive campaign to withdraw the existing protective legislations affecting the 7 per cent organised labour force. It is argued that State protection to the tiny but vocal minority of workforce has perforce contributed to the expansion of the unorganised sector and by deregulation of the labour market (the so-called second generation reforms) in fact, the unorganised sector labour could benefit with increased employment and income.

---

[1] This article was first published under the same title in Sabyasachi Bhattacharya and Jan Lucassen (eds.), *Workers in the Informal Sector. Studies in Labour History 1800–2000*. New Delhi: Macmillan India 2005. Reprinted with permission.

This argument rests on, in my view, a fallacious identification of informal sector with absence of State regulation.

The history of State intervention in labour relations in India is commonly traced back to the late colonial period (1926) with the legal enactment recognising the Trade Union. It is assumed that prior to this date, a state of laissez-faire prevailed as far as relations between capital and labour were concerned. Further, by focusing on State legislations since 1926, it is again assumed that history of informal labour relations is of relatively recent vintage. Contrary to this common understanding, in this essay I investigate the genealogy of contemporary informal labour relations well into the early nineteenth century colonial India. My aim in this essay is to delineate the processes by which labour relations were constructed by colonial State action, especially through legislative intervention in nineteenth century colonial India. I will argue that in the process of such construction, labour relations were deeply impressed by pervasive informality, which has shaped subsequent developments in the post-independence India.

It might appear paradoxical that the informalisation process that I describe appears to be the result of State action, since by definition informal sector is marked by absence of or minimisation of State regulations. This definition of informalisation, (and cognate terms) stressing its distance from State regulation has had a singular success in the burgeoning literature on informal sector since 1970s. It is for instance shared widely by both the so-called 'miserabilist' and 'evolutionist' perspective on the informal sector – the former view denouncing informal sector as low wage sector of last resort and the latter celebrating its dynamism and vigour.[2]

This formulation of the issue of informality, informalisation or informal sector emerges primarily on two counts: first due to the identification of informal sector with self-employment and secondly because of the commonly held conception of informal sector as an underground or illicit sector. When wage employment and wage relations in the informal sector is at all taken into consideration it is conceived primarily as occurring in the absence of labour laws

---

[2] See for instance, the original formulation of the informal sector conception in ILO's 'Employment, incomes and equity: A strategy for increasing productive employment in Kenya', ILO, Geneva, (1972) and Keith Hart's essay 'Informal income opportunities and urban employment in Ghana', *Journal of Modern African Studies*, (1973) that uncorked the informal genie. A particularly strong elaboration of the celebration of absence of State intervention is to be found in de Soto, H., Ghersi, E., and Ghibellini, M., (1986) *El Otro Sendero. El Barranco*, Peru: Instituto Libertad y Democracia; De Soto, H. (1989) *The Other Path: The invisible revolution in the Third World*, New York. As regards the so-called miserabilist view see Paul E. Bassinger, The ILO and the Informal Sector: An Institutional History', ILO, Geneva, (2000), which traces the mutation of the informal sector concept from an original positive connotation.

or outside the purview of State regulations. Following from this is the commonsensical formulation that informal labour relations are in effect due to excessive State regulation of the labour market. In this view, the State appears as an external agent regulating what is otherwise a spontaneous relation between employers and employees (capital and labour). Regulation then appears as transaction costs that both employees and employers would naturally seek to avoid. Informal labour relations and State regulation then appear as opposed to each other while at the same time the relation between capital and labour appear as natural and spontaneously generated by the market.

Apart from the ahistorical nature of this conception (since informal relation between capital and labour appears as a timeless natural form rather than a historically specific structure of relation subject to change) it also is in some sense self-contradictory. There is no substantive definition of informal relations except as negation of formal relations and any historical exploration of the informal labour relations has to begin by explaining the emergence of formal structures of regulation. Therefore, a circular reasoning is involved in explaining informality in terms of absence of regulation. (Informal will always follow or emerge along with the formal – then how is the whole prehistory of the formal to be explained – what preceded formal relations?)

The way out of this circularity can be found in Marx's critique of classical liberal position premised on the absolute separation between the labour process on the one hand and the political realm of State and law on the other. By showing the intimate links even the common basis of both in the relation of exploitation of labour, Marx effected a theoretical short circuit between the realm of private domination to which the labour process is continuously relegated by classical liberal thought and the domain of public regulation and the State. It is the correlation between these two domains, which allows us to think of the fundamental ways in which the State was involved in the creation and regulation of the 'spontaneous and natural' character of informal relations of labour and capital.

In order to explicate the position outlined above I shall begin by stating the following propositions pending their historical demonstration which follows in the subsequent sections:

(a) First, the significant difference is not so much between the informal, natural and spontaneous relation between labour and capital and the world of formal and State regulation as between different modes of regulation implied in informal and formal relations. And the difference is no longer in the absence of regulation on one hand and the full presence of regulation in the other but between the tendency towards *privatisation of* regulation in one case and the tendency for greater public regulation in the other. It must be added here that once we adopt this proposition both formal and informal relations are no longer a self-sustained whole but imply a combination of different forms of regulations.

(b) Second, more important than the distinction between the 'formal and informal sector' or modes of regulation, etc., is the distinction between the realm of juridical freedom and contract and the domain of production where despotism of capital reigns. So formal equality can always coexist with informal domination. Marx characterised the former, i.e. the realm of contract as that of liberty and equality and Bentham the latter realm, hidden abode of production as where the buyer of labour power struts about and following him is the seller of labour power with a meekness that shows that he has come to sell his own hide.

(c) Third, it is important to take into account the role of law, which ensures not just the appearance of equality in the public domain and domination in the private, but also creates the very division of public and private.

With this wider perspective on legal regulation I propose to study the process by which privatisation of regulation of labour was constructed by colonial State action.

Informal labour relations in Indian labour historiography

Before I move on to the more substantive part of the paper I will take issue with the ways in which informal labour relations have been conceptualised in the historiography of labour in India. To begin with, it must be conceded that practically all of the written works on labour history have concentrated on the large industries and mines and plantations: very little is known of the vast majority of workers who worked in smaller workshops, handicrafts, domestic industries (or the whole range of occupations in informal sector). The focus on 'large' and 'modern' industries has also occluded knowledge about labour relations predating the late nineteenth century – establishment of cotton mills in Bombay, jute mills in Calcutta and the beginning of the railways in the 1850s have been conventionally held to mark the beginning of modern India's industrialisation. Despite some excellent studies on various aspects of labour control, labour protest, relation between nationalism and labour movement, etc., not enough is known of the emergence and operation of the legal framework of regulation of labour relations.

What then are the main ways in which informal labour relations have been framed in Indian historiography?

Two issues that regularly crop up in often opposed standpoints in labour history: (a) the relative importance of the 'indigenous' conditions and modes of regulation of labour and the formal procedural and legal forms of regulation enunciated by the colonial State, and (b) the distance between legal regulation and its implementation on the ground. Two main standpoints can be discerned here. Professor Peter Robb in a wide ranging (and often rambling) survey of labour history of India has insistently focused on the Indian 'continuities' in regulation of labour in colonial India.[3] In his estimation three elements of what he terms 'Indian' relations of production were pre-eminent – first the pervasive presence of intermediaries exercising effective control of labour (jobbers, maistries, and babus), second the persistence of 'indigenous beliefs and expectations' of labourers forming the 'core of repeated behavior ... by definition stronger than other transient forms' (meaning thereby caste and religious identities segmenting the labour market), and third persistence of personal ties of dependence engendered by localised matrix of social power (which are replicated in the 'modern industrial settings'). Pitted against this formidable 'internal' structures of control, regulatory modes introduced by 'capital' and 'colonial State' based on abstract principles of market discipline and English Law has had little chance of success. Colonial State regulations were not merely externally imposed categories; they also were forced by circumstances of Indian relations of production to partake of elements of Indian society. There was thus a yawning gap between the legal regulation and its enforcement – the law did little to change the ways labour was managed or the 'informal coercion' on the ground. Thus, Professor Robb not surprisingly concludes, 'colonial and capitalist influences were *surprisingly marginal* ... in their impact on South Asian consciousness and behaviour.'[4] His view on continuities of indigenous – now equated with 'informal' – mode of regulation of labour across the colonial State appears as a reaction to the idea of colonialism and colonial State marking a sharp break with earlier social forms of regulation and to a certain post modern and post colonial studies trend that gave undue weight to the impact of the colonial State. Instead, we have here a colonial State struggling against and being overwhelmed by indigenous and informal modes of control.

---

[3] Peter Robb, 'Introduction: Meanings of Labour in Indian Social Context', *Dalit Movements and the Meanings of Labour in India* (Delhi: Oxford University Press, 1993).
[4] Ibid., p. 66.

Starting from an opposing standpoint from (what was still) within the Marxist perspective, Professor Dipesh Chakrabarthy posed the question as to how far abstract rule-governed relationship embodied in bourgeois legal thought found expression in the modes of regulation of workers of jute mills in Calcutta in the early twentieth century.[5] He found pervasive presence of middlemen and a workforce steeped in hierarchical culture controlled more by personalised authority than impersonal rule bound procedures. This informal mode of labour control he locates in the pre-capitalist cultural milieu in which the enterprise and the labour force operated. So he concluded that since the crucial ingredient of egalitarian culture was missing in Indian labour relations, class solidarity and working-class consciousness failed to emerge.

The congruence of viewpoints on informal mode of labour control from opposed standpoints is striking and the reason is that, both these viewpoints adopt an abstract ideal typical schema of transition to which Indian developments never approximate. But by concentrating on the 'Indian cultural context' to explain the persistence of 'informal modes of regulation' what has been missed out are key areas of innovation and transformation wrought in labour relations under colonial capitalism.[6]

Michael Anderson, historian of labour law of India, in his important survey of the legal framework of regulation in 19th century India was struck by the absence of any systematic juridical ideation on labour.[7] There was he argued a powerful tendency to occlude the issues of labour subsuming it under the overarch-

---

[5] Dipesh Chakrabarthy, *Rethinking Working Class History,* (Delhi: Oxford University Press, 1989).
[6] Recent historiography on labour has moved away from this perspective substantially. Rajnarayan Chandavarkar's work on Bomabay labour and Chitra Joshi's work on Kanpur focus on the management strategy and workers' agency, respectively, to explain the so called 'informal labour relations' within the factories.The link between the factory sector and the informal sector rather than their absolute separation is also argued in their work. Rajnarayan Chandavarkar, *The Origins of Industrial Capitalism in India: Business Strategies and the Working Classes in Bombay 1900–1940,* (Cambridge University Press, 1989) and Chitra Joshi, *Lost Worlds: Indian Labour and its Forgotten Histories,* (Delhi: Permanent Black, 2003). For a strong argument emphasizing the discontinuity in modes of labour control across the colonial divide and the role of colonial State in altering labour relations and weakening the pre-colonial patterns of labour mobility and solidarities see Prasannan Parthasarathy, *The Transition to a Colonial Economy: Weavers, Merchants, and Kings in South India 1720–1800,* (Cambridge: Cambridge University Press, 2001). For a nuanced argument that poses the problem of continuity and change across the colonial divide in labour relations in terms of compatibility of pre-colonial and colonial regulatory modes see Ravi Ahuja, 'Labour Relations in Early Colonial India, Madras 1750–1800' in: *Modern Asian Studies,* Vol. 37, No. 2, October 2002.
[7] Michael Anderson 'Work Construed: Ideological Origins of Labour Law in British India' in: Peter Robb (ed.) *Dalit Movements and the Meaning of Labour in India,* op. cit.

ing image of a putative organic social order, labour if conceptualised at all was through the lens of land, caste and family ingredients of a pre-colonial framework of regulation. Over the nineteenth century only episodically did labour emerge as a distinct sphere deserving of State regulation around specific conjunctures where State legislation was demanded on moral and political grounds (such as on issue of slavery, or debt bondage, etc., or under specific needs of particular groups of European employers or under international pressures). What Anderson finds surprising is the 'stubborn refusal of the legal establishment to recognise worker welfare a object of State concern'. Thus legal recognition of labour remained 'haphazard and ad hoc' lacking in a coherent social vision?[8] Colonial labour policy if it existed at all, was mired in the contradiction between an ideology of free labour and legal paternalism. This adhocism gave way after the 1920s when a more systematic labour legislation process emerged as a result of war, Russian revolution and the need to contain the challenge posed by the labour movement.

While I am in sympathy with the elements of Anderson's nuanced position on the character of colonial legal regulation in the nineteenth century I also have serious problems with his framework which identifies formal regulation of labour only with 'worker welfare', the absence of which signified an 'incoherent social vision'. An alternative narrative of legal development in colonial India will make it elear that regulation of labour was not just episodic but in many ways much more pervasive than figures of 'legal enforcement or disputes' may indicate. In so far as the legal rhetoric of welfare was concerned, colonial labour policy had it in ample measure, one could even say that it was the wedge that allowed the State to unleash particularly harsh repressive direct regulation of labour. Finally, a major flaw in the framework is not dissimilar to what we have seen earlier as the dominant tendency in labour historiography in general – it lies in the rather stark opposition and mutual exclusion posited between 'abstract formal law' and 'informal modes of control'. Given the pervasive presence of the latter the former appears as mere gloss – regulation then becomes either a 'mask' or un-implementable.

---

8 Ibid., p. 91.

Legal construction of labour relations in colonial India – criminalisation of free labour

How did the colonial State view the issue of regulation of labour in the nineteenth century?

Focusing for the moment on the statutory modes of labour regulation we may distinguish four interrelated strands within it emerging in three different temporal conjunctures. The first is a set of regulations dating from the early nineteenth century (the earliest one located by me are in the year 1814) ending in 1859–60 with the promulgation of the Indian Penal Code and an important piece of legislation, the Workmans Breach of Contract Act or Act XIII of 1859. The coverage of these sets of regulations varied but they affected a wide range of labouring activities including domestic labour, contract labour, skilled artisans and also in some instances the disguised labour forms such as contract cropping practised for cultivation of indigo.

A second interrelated legislative process was linked to the grand design of legal codification beginning with the Indian Law Commission in 1837 under Macaulay and ending in the 1880s with the last Law Commission (the 4th one). This legal codification drive came to a halt in the 1880s in the face of opposition both within India and in Britain to create a superordinate body of substantive and procedural law that was often at great variance with ground reality. Within this grand design, there was an attempt to place regulation of labour relations which would have transcended the piecemeal legislation on labour. However, this attempt failed as colonial labour policy lurched between 'civil' and 'criminal' conception of labour contract and finally ground to a halt with the rejection of a comprehensive draft Master and Servants Law in 1879. Exploration of the reasons for the hesitation and ambiguity inherent in the codification drive of the colonial State will throw important light on the process of colonial State intervention in shaping labour relations. I have however not attempted to do that in this paper.

The third strand of labour regulation consisted of a body of exceptional legislation directed specially at the plantation labour in Assam. Beginning in the 1860s, these extraordinary legislative efforts aimed at a comprehensive regulation of both the long distance mobilisation of labour force and its control at the place of work. The history of the making of these laws will throw light on the interaction between state regulation and informal management of labour. This exceptional legislation came to an end in 1926 along with abolition of all the legal vestiges of the Penal Contract laws initiated since 1860.

A fourth strand of legislation which began with the Indian Factory Act of 1881 is conventionally taken as the origin of formal labour regulation – a series of such Acts derived primarily from the British Acts sought to regulate employment of women and children in large factories, hours of work and some safety measures for protection of workers which had begun to dot the landscape of Indian cities by the late nineteenth century. This legislative initiative which was rather ineffective till the end of the war began to gather momentum in the 1920s when a slew of labour legislations were added focusing primarily on large industries in the factory sector. These legislations emerging from a different context and having a different set of aims, and covering in the main the large industrial establishments ultimately provided the sinews of a 'non-criminalised' mode of control of labour. This legislation is excluded from the purview of the paper.

Early labour legislation 1814–1860

The first issue to occupy the colonial State in the earliest stages of its rule was that of Indian slavery. It is now accepted that the main impetus for the debate on Indian slavery was in response to the growing abolitionist sentiment in Britain and the terms in which the debate was carried on were borrowed from that context. Various regulations prohibited the sale and trafficking in human beings in India the first one being Regulation X of 1811 which prohibited importation of slaves into British India. However, a key element in this debate was the conceptualisation of free labour in opposition to those who were enslaved. British attitude to slavery threw into sharp relief their adherence to the contractarian ideology and the free labour model. Yet the irony of this formulation (innate as it was in the contractarian form itself) was that theoretically there was nothing to prevent the most blatant form of servitude after one gave 'voluntary consent' to such a contract.[9] Contractarian ideology based on the model of free labour had become the dominant model of British attitude towards juridical free labour and provided the one element of the 'legal culture of work' (a term I have borrowed from legal

---

9 Gyan Prakash provides evidence of the peculiar legal formulation by which the early colonial judicial officers enforced contracts of servitude (often of 90 years or more generally sixty years duration) since they were 'voluntarily entered into', while disallowing sale and purchase of chattel slaves. Gyan Prakash, *Bonded Histories: Geneologies of Labour Servitude*, (Cambridge: Cambridge University Press, 1990). The East India Company continued to hold slaves till late 1830s in Malabar. Dharma Kumar, *Land Caste in South India*, (Cambridge: CUP, 1965). For an illuminating insight into the contradictions of contractarian ideology specially with regard to slave contracts, see Carole Pateman, *The Sexual Contract*, (Polity Press, 1988).

historian Chris Tomlins) that the British introduced in India.[10] However, what is interesting is the other element of the legal culture of work that was simultaneously introduced into India, that which criminalised breach of contract by the workmen. Supported by a long-standing legal tradition by which masters regularly prosecuted servants for refusal to work before Justices of Peace in both industrial and rural counties of England the Master and Servants laws formed very much a part of the 'legal cultural baggage' that the British carried with them. No less than 109 statutes have been discovered in England from 1278 onwards the most famous being the Statute of Labourers of 1349 and the Statute of Artificerers of 1562. It might be recalled that during the late eighteenth century, a particularly strong draught of penal legislation was introduced in England.[11] The application of these principies in India did not have to wait long. The earliest legislation that I have found dates to 1814 April as a Calcutta by-law. Enacted at the behest of sundry English manufacturers, coach makers, cabinet makers and furnishers and other traders, the by-law sought to curb the persistent habit of the native labourers and their contractors of abandoning work after having agreed to perform them at a certain rate or wage. Worse still, they often took and demanded advance as is 'customary' and failed to complete the task. They, it was further alleged, refused to begin work at the time required by the employers and frequently took holidays. 'The Hindus follow the Mussalmans to their festival and the Mussalmans the Hindus to theirs'. Since there was no redressal in the Petty Causes Court, and the Supreme Court being too expensive, the manufacturers of Calcutta demanded that Justices of Peace apprehend the defaulter punishing them with two months imprisonment on the model of the Merchant Seaman's Act, which was regularly used in Calcutta by the masters of the ships in apprehending deserting seamen.[12] Unfortunately we do not have enough information about the use of this by-law; however, its replication in subsequent laws, sometime ad verbatim, indicates a fairly successful career.

The first workman and journeyman's by-law of 1814 April was followed by a special by-law on domestic servants which similarly punished recusant servants

---

10 Christopher L. Tomlins, 'Freedom Bound: Migration Servitude and the Legal Culture of Work in Early British America', in D. Hay and P. Carven (ed.) *Master, Servants and Magistrates: Britain and the Empire 1562–1955*, (University of North Carolina Press, Chapel Hill, 2004).

11 There is now a growing body of literature on the enormous impact the Master and Servants statutes enacted in Britain had on the legal conception of labour relations all over the Empire. See for instance the pioneering work of Doug Hay and Paul Craven in Hay and Craven (ed.), op cit. Also see Robert Steinfield, *Invention of Free Labour: The Employment Relations in English and American Law and Culture, 1350–1870*, (University of North Carolina Press, 1991).

12 Bengal Judicial (Criminal) Consultations No. 36 of 14 April 1814 (West Bengal State Archives).

who left their master's employ in 1814 November.¹³ In 1816, another by-law explicitly punished combination among worker and journeymen to raise wages or conspiracy to do so.¹⁴ In 1819 the Bengal Regulation VII was enacted which punished breach of contracts by workers and artificers in the rural areas of Bengal where by this time a fair number of European planters, and landowners as well as merchants had settled. Imprisonment of one month and two months on repeating the offence was prescribed for deserting workers. This also applied to domestic servants who deserted without notice. Magistrates were given summary powers of the Justice of Peace. The Bengal initiative was followed in Bombay where a similar regulation criminally punishing breach of contract was promulgated in 1827. Interest from Madras and Malabar was also strong from where demands for regulation of domestic servants, workers on plantation, etc., came up regularly from European manufacturers and planters. With the setting up of the Indian Law Commission in 1837 under Macaulay, this provisional penal regulation making was stopped pending the discussion and promulgation of the great Indian Penal Code.

The draft Penal Code of 1837 dampened the fervour of the European population since Macaulay refused to support criminal prosecution of domestic servants as practised by the European households in the Presidency towns. It might be noted that in England domestic servants were not criminally prosecuted for breach. Macaulay was following the English precedent and was against legal innovation in this regard. It is then that we find several representations made by European officials as to the great difficulty they find in controlling breach of contract by the domestic servants. Among some of the most frequently committed misdemeanours were 'leaving the employ of masters suddenly without arranging for substitutes' or leaving the master's food uncooked, clothes unwashed and coachmen tending to their own dogs and such rather than the master's horses, wet nurses exposing children to danger, the cleaners of toilets (mehatars) leaving their master's privy dirty, etc. A further misdemeanour regularly practised by the servants apparently was their combining to prevent other servants from taking up employment in their former master's house (from which they had been dismissed or had left on their own).¹⁵ The European household was critically dependent on the native servant for its reproduction for both their material and symbolic domination of the subject population. The demand for bolstering of already extensive

---

13 Bengal Judicial (Criminal) Consultations No. 51–55, 13 December 1814 (West Bengal State Archives).
14 Bengal Judicial (Criminal) Consultations No. 36, 6 December 1816 (West Bengal State Archives).
15 Legislative Consultations No. 6–10 November 1838 (National Archives of India hereafter NAI).

powers of chastisement they possessed by legal curbing of servant's wilful behaviour (such as running away without informing), kept on coming up even after the colonial State, following Macaulay, hesitated and finally decided to not enact any special criminal breach Act for domestic servants.

The making of Act XIII of 1859 or the Workman's Breach of Contract Act

In the 1850s the thinking as regards labour was concerned had become as follows: while mere breach of contract was to be not punished criminally and only civil procedure was to be followed, certain exceptional situations could be imagined where they could be criminally prosecuted, as, abandoning of disabled by their nurse, or of English ladies by palanquin bearers or more commonly when workers deserted after receiving advances. While the debates over the making of the Indian Penal Code carried on for the best part of 23 years, it was often not possible to keep on hold the demand for specific Acts to meet the needs of particular interest groups. The by-laws of Calcutta governing manufacturer and labourer relations was suspended because of changes in municipal and policing functions of local bodies and Justices of Peace. In 1852, the Police Act took away policing functions of the Justices of Peace. In the absence of any new enactment, it seems the relation between manufacturers and labourers was again thrown into some confusion.

It is in this context that the Calcutta Tradesman's Association, the premier body of European merchants and traders, sent a petition to the government's legislative council in July 1858 demanding that a simple criminal breach of contract law be enacted to prevent workers from deliberately breaking their contracts of engagement after receiving advances from employers as there was no law to prevent such act and the workers knew that civil procedure would be impossible for recovery of advances. 'Knowing the inability of the masters, the workers regularly abandon contract or higher wages and also combine to raise their wage demand, which they have to perforce accept.'[16] The tradesmen demanded simple summary procedure for prosecution so that the worker could be brought back to perform his work or repay his advances failing which he would imprisoned. The select committee of the legislative department readily accepted the argument that the taking of advances and failure to perform the contract could be seen as 'tinged with fraudulence'. So, while penal provision may not be applied to mere breach of contract fraudulence qualified for its application. According to the law,

---

16 Papers connected with Act XIII of 1859, in Legislative 1859 (NAI).

on complaint by a master that a workman, journeyman or artificer had taken advance and agreed to work on a contract on terms specified either orally or in written form and had failed to perform the contract, would be ordered by a magistrate to perform the unfinished work, or repay the advance as required by the employer and failure to do either will be punished with imprisonment not more than three months. In the first instance the law was enacted for the Presidency towns but could be extended to any part of the country by the orders of the·government. The Act was very quickly extended in 1863 to Assam and before that to all parts of Madras, and by the 1870s, to almost all parts of India. Till the time it was finally abolished in 1926, Act XIII of 1859 remained in a sense the master contract governing employment relations in colonial India (the issue of special labour legislation for plantation is taken up later). Before I discuss the extent to which Act XIII fulfilled the functions of regulating employment relations, let me recapitulate the major findings of this study of early labour legislation.

Certain features, which marked the process of introduction of this body of legislation and its impact, may be noted. First we must note the urban context and early manufacturing activities associated with private European merchants who were the main initiators of the legislative control of labour. They were very much steeped in the 'legal culture of work' of England where workers were regularly prosecuted and imprisoned for breach of contract. I must repeat that to the British officials or manufacturers these were not at all contrary to their belief in the non-interference of State in matters of private regulation of the contract. The appeal to public authority was precisely to very clearly acknowledge the private nature of the contract and the absolute power the masters held in determining its terms. So these first set of initiatives in the formation of criminal breach of contract provisions of law were efforts in the direction of privatising labour regulations based on the ultimate power of the State to criminally prosecute the 'offending' worker. In this regard at least this was a clear and startling legal innovation in the Indian context.

A second feature which makes its appearance in these legal enactments is the reference to the pervasive practice of taking of advances by the native labourers which was often described as 'customary'. It seemed also that these customary advances were not so much a British imposition (to tie down labourers) as an absolutely necessary compromise in face of workers' demand. What the manufacturers often resented was that the workers could succeed in getting their terms and even then refuse to fulfil their contract. It was the practice of free exit from the contract, which the manufacturers wanted to curb with State help by criminalising this practice. In the early period at least the legislations were again very clearly designed to curb the customary and traditional power. By criminalising a customary form of worker resistance to bad conditions of employment, the penal contract legislation also managed to change the signs that surrounded the advance system. Once signifying worker power and their ability to control their conditions of employment, advances quickly became employers' weapon to tie down workers to low wage or subnormal working conditions. In no small measure, criminalisation of free labour initiated in 1814 was instrumental in this change of sign marking the advance system.

Regarding the coverage and application of Act XIII it is difficult to make any estimation since its use was 'informal' and only with the coming up of a criminal prosecution could one say that the law had been used. Because of summary procedures adopted, even that information is missing from court and judicial records. However, when the Act was sought to be abolished, a certain amount of information about its usage and effectiveness, etc., was known. This information is briefly summarised here. These details have been taken from a set of government papers in 1920–26 which enquired into the question of abolition of the Act XIII.[17]

1. Act XIII was used in practically all cases where extensive system of advance payments existed. To that extent, from being an Act exclusively utilised by Europeans, it had acquired a larger clientele by the 1920s. The most extensive use of this Act seems to have been in the government PWD department undertaking large projects of public works through contract labour imported from a long distance. It was mainly the labour contractors who utilised this Act. It was thus reported to have been extensively used in the construction of New Delhi between 1914–22, in the making of Sucker barrage in Sind in the 1920s, in practically all irrigation works in the Central Provinces and UP, in the making of canal colonies in Punjab, etc. In the Central Provinces where an irrigation work was being constructed by 2500 workers, nearly a third were imprisoned for refusal to work, in Punjab, in Jhelum and Montgomery canal colony it was widely used with figures reaching up to an annual average prosecution of 7000 persons between 1907–15. An official in Punjab noted that mere threat of prosecution under the Act and getting a group of labourers handcuffed from their home in south Punjab was enough for the recalcitrant group to trudge back to their employers in the canal colony.
2. The Act was used in almost all-urban centres in small workshops and factories but the only statistical evidence is available of Madras in 1921–22, already at the very end of the career of the law. From the very brief account it seems that the law was used extensively in about 42 trades. The most important

---

[17] Home (Judicial) File No. 168 of 1922, Home (Judicial) File No. 400 of 1923 and Home (Judicial) File No. 336 of 1924. See also Revenue and Agriculture (Emigration) July 1922 A Prog No. 3–14 (NAI).

trades in so far as prosecutions are concerned are as follows: (a) weaving, (b) silver and goldsmithery, (c) cigar and small cigarette (*bidi*) making, (d) brass smithery, (e) steel trunkmaking in which roughly 40 per cent of all cases were recorded. On an average the advances were two months' wages of these artisans and workers. A few master weavers also seem to have used this Act in India.

3. Large mills and factories do not seem to have utilised the provisions of this Act to a great extent because there was not much use of advance in these concerns. The only exception to this was Ahmedabad where the Ahmedabad Millowners' Association strongly deprecated the abolition of Act XIII on the ground that their members used this Act to prevent the imported workers from running away. However, excepting this reference it is elear that Act XIII was the 'Informal Sector Act' par excellence.

4. Some interesting insights as to the effectiveness of the Act are as follows: The operation of the Act had not in any way reduced the practice of advance, in fact, the Act operated on the basis of the advance system. However, in spite of the Act, the practice of bargaining through the advance by a specific skilled group of workers seems to have continued up to the 1920s. This was reported in the case of the brick moulders in Punjab who apparently specialised in moving from place to place seeking higher advances from competing employers especially during the large-scale building of canal colonies.[18]

5. While the actual use of the Act may have been limited in number of prosecutions, etc., it is quite possible that its effectiveness was never really in the actual prosecutions under the Act as in the threat of its use. Thus, an interesting observation by a lawyer employer of Simla:

> As an employer of labour on a small scale I have never really earnestly used the Act direcdy against any one, however their existence in the statute book and a mere reference to the Act often has considerably smoothened away difficulties and has acted wholesomely on the employed who are often tempted by outside elements.

Irrespective of the extent of its use as evidenced in its prosecution there is no doubt that the central presumptions of the criminal breach of contract agreements seem to have pervaded the general work culture which gave an absolute power to set the terms of employment to the employer, normalised State intervention on behalf of the employer to curb the mobility of labour. Its effect on

---

[18] Tirthankar Ray's account of advance system in carpet making in Punjab in 'Outline of an History of Labour in Traditional Small-Scale Industry in India,' mimeo, VVGNLI Research Studies Series, 2000, V.V. Giri National Labour Institute, pp. 25–27.

the advance system is particularly important as the criminalisation of advance helped in curbing and regulating one important customary power of the workers. We can only speculate as to the impact of the Act on wage levels, but if the curbing of advance system is anything to go by, it is more than possible that the law acted to depress wage levels below the normal market clearing rates. This will become clearer in the following discussion on the history and use of penal contract legislation in the tea plantations of Assam which by 1920 was the largest single employer of wage labour in India.

Special labour legislation in Assam

Capital and labour shortages till the end of the 1850s though in existence from 1839 continually plagued tea plantations when a speculative boom in 1860 led to the rapid opening up of gardens and importation of thousands of labourers through native recruiting agencies. 'Tea mania' as it was called, ended in 1865 with a series of bankruptcies and mergers of old gardens and takeovers by managing agency houses. A leaner tea industry was launched on a path of steady growth aided by large importation of indentured labourers recruited through State regulated agencies, from the central Indian uplands and the congested districts of the Gangetic plains. A significant change was introduced in the recruitment and employment of labour in the tea industry in 1882, when the government deregulated emigration and strengthened penal sanctions by a special labour legislation. No less than a million persons (including children) were imported into Assam in the next twenty years under indenture as tea acreage and production and exports experienced spectacular growth. Acreage more than doubled while production tripled as India ousted China as the largest exporter of tea in the world market. What is interesting however is that this expansion took place under conditions when tea prices had slumped to half the level of 1880s by the beginning of the 1900s. After a decade of stagnation and slump the war years saw another surge in the growth of production and acreage.[19]

A second feature of the plantation complex in Assam was the remarkably stable nominal wage level, the so-called statutory minimum wage remained constant for over about seventy years when the indenture system was in operation. It was Rs 5 a month in Assam for adult male labour. This, of course, was the wage of indentured labour yet it was this wage that also determined over the long term

---

[19] See Rana P. Behal and Prabhu P. Mohapatra, 'Tea and Money versus Human Lives: The Rise and Fall of the Indentured System in Assam', *Journal of Peasant Studies, 1992.*

the wages of free labour. This stable wage rate of a bound labour force was crucial for the phenomenal growth of production and consequent profits in favourable years, as it was essential for tiding over prolonged slumps for the plantations. This was one of the effects of the deployment of special penal sanctions of indenture law, which by immobilising a substantial section of the labour force allowed planter control over the labour market as a whole.[20]

The other main effect of the penal contract labour system was, of course, to discipline the labour force over and above the 'discipline' of the labour market. As it happened, the main argument for importation of labour was the alleged absence of a local labour market which could impose the normal market discipline on the labourers. It was argued by the planters and their supporters in the colonial officialdom that in the absence of a normal labour market, the local labourers, i.e. recently freed slaves and the local Assamese demanded exorbitant wages and in any case were not prepared to work regularly on the plantations.[21] At the same time when once imported labour was made available, the planters were the first to demand that the operation of labour market be curtailed. They now argued that what was needed was not just labour in sufficient quantity but 'reliable' labour that did not 'wander about' testing the market. In other words, the planters now demanded a labour force bound to the employer for sufficiently long terms. This then was the origin of the institution of penal contract in the plantations in Assam. The colonial State obliged by introducing a series of special labour laws and institutionalised a system of 'voluntary servitude' that remained in place for nearly a century. A brief review of the origins and evolution of the penal sanctions and their incorporation in the special ordinances and legislations enacted over time would throw light on the paradoxical process by which the contract institutionalised a form of servitude.

In Assam, the legislation of penal contract followed the previous trajectory for the other Criminal Breach of Contract Acts noted earlier. Between 1840–61 there seems to have been *laissez faire* as regards both recruitment and employment of labourers, the period being marked by spluttering growth of tea acreage and production. Labourers were brought in with agreements to labour for three years though there was no legal enforcement of the contracts, simply because there was no statute in place. It was the wave of expansion during the tea mania between 1860

---

20 Walter Rodney, *A History of the Guyanese Working People, 1881–1905*, (London and Baltimore: John Hopkins Press, 1981) p. 34. In Assam statutory wages were Rs 5.50 for those under special labour laws in the last two years of their indenture. Attempts to raise the statutory minimum wages by 10 per cent in 1901 was resisted fiercely by the planters.

21 See the initial reactions of planters and officials as to the absence of suitable labour in Assam in P. Griffiths, *A History of Indian Tea Industry*, pp. 73, 101–103.

and 1865 that saw the first legislation to regulate recruitment and employment. Occasioned apparently by the massive mortality among the labourers recruited by Indian contractors who were paid a price per head and as 'all parties considered their duty and responsibility discharged when the living are landed and the cost of the dead are adjusted' the colonial State intervened to enforce registration of labourers and sanitary regulations en route to Assam in 1863.[22] It was the combined effect of death and large-scale desertions which led to the institution of indenture contracts in Assam. Between 1863 and 1866, of the 85,000 workers transported to Assam, 35,000 had died or deserted the plantations. From 1861 onwards, planters often had recourse to the newly enacted India Penal Code of 1860, Section 492, which allowed for prosecution of defaulting labourers who had been conveyed over a long distance at the employer's cost. The problem was that maximum penalty under the Act was one month's imprisonment and prosecution terminated the contract. Planters complained that deserting workers willingly courted imprisonment to get out of the contract. Citing instances of immigration ordinances in overseas colonies, planters demanded full scale penal provisions.[23] In January 1863, the Workman's Breach of Contract Act XIII of 1859 was extended to Assam which allowed the planters to prosecute deserting workers who had received an advance. Originally enacted for the Presidency towns of British India, Act XIII enabled magistrates to order performance of the contract from workers who had received an advance payment and had reneged on their contract. This Act too was not considered adequate by the planters as the contract could be terminated with prosecution and imprisonment of a maximum of three months and there was some uncertainty whether the passage cost constituted an advance.

So in 1865, Act VI of 1865 was passed in the Bengal Council which conceded the planter, demand for penal contract and allowed extensive powers of private arrest.

It also allowed for first time contracts of three years with a statutorily fixed minimum wages, a nine hour working day, and a government inspector of labour empowered to cancel the contracts on ill-treatment of the labourers. The most important provisions of the Act were those related to breach of contract by the

---

[22] Statement of Objects and Reasons' prefixed to the Act III of 1863 of Bengal Council in Government of India (GOI), Legislative Department 'A' Proceedings No. 28–36 April 1865 (National Archives of India).

[23] For planters' complaints, 'Reports on the Working of Act III of 1863', in GOI, Legislative Department, A Prog. No. 30–38, November 1865. The report clearly demonstrates that planters had resorted to large-scale illegal detention of labourers during 1861–64 and initiated private powers of arrest. Among several suggestions for penal provisions some planters demanded flogging by the government of recalcitrant labourers, a special emigration police to stop desertion and repeated prosecution and return of the labourer to the plantation.

labourers. Desertion was to be punished with imprisonment, as was refusal to work or unlawful absence from work and significandy, planters or any person authorised by them were given powers to arrest absconders without warrant. For the Act to be operative the contract had to be executed before a magistrate in the recruiting districts rather than in the district where labour was to be performed. Thus, time expired labourers (i.e. those who had already finished a term of contract) or local labourers could not execute the contract under the Act; they were either employed without any penal contract or as became the common practice were contracted under Act XIII of 1859 (Workman's Breach of Contract Act). In 1873, recruitment outside the Act but employment without penal contract was allowed under Bengal Act VII of 1873. This innovation was hardly ever used as planters were firmly in favour of a long-term penal contract system.

Between 1865 and 1882, recruitment of labourers was government regulated while a fairly wide-ranging penal contract system came into existence. In 1882, due to persistent complaints from the planters about high cost of recruitment and inadequate penal powers, the colonial State substantially deregulated emigration and strengthened penal powers. Under Act I of 1882, the duration of the contract was increased from three to five years and could now be signed before a magistrate in the labour districts rather than in the recruiting districts. Further it allowed local labour contracts of similar duration which effectively increased the hold of the planters over time expired labourers. Limitations on the powers of private arrest were slackened further and endorsements and extensions of indenture for unlawful absence from work were made simpler. Deregulated labour recruitment and strengthened penal powers were the basis on which massive importation of labour and subsequent expansion of tea industry took place. The opposition to deregulated recruitment and penal sanctions emerged strongly during this period largely focused on abuses of recruitment. In 1893 the period of labour contract under the Act was reduced to four years and the maximum period of local labour contract (used mainly for time expired labourers) to one year. The main effect of these changes was that the planters increasingly used Act XIII of 1859 now to bind time expired labourers instead of Act VI as it relieved them from the duties of maintaining registers or accounting for their mortality, etc., which was required under Act VI. Till the beginning of the twentieth century, in Assam, two sets of penal contract laws were widely used. New recruitment was largely under the special labour legislation (Act I of 1882 as modified in 1893) while Act XIII was used mainly for old labourers.[24]

---

24 There was significant difference within Assam as to the extent of use of these two Acts. In the more accessible Surma Valley, Act XIII was predominantly used for both new and old labourers while in the more remote Brahmaputra Valley, Act VI was the clear favourite.

During a period of acute crisis marked by overproduction, high mortality of labour, increased cost of recruitment and rising incidence of labour disturbances – between 1901 and 1908 – there were substantial changes wrought in the penal contract system. Government was forced to intervene and bring recruitment again under regulation in 1901 when a new Act (Act VI of 1901) was passed. Penal powers were substantially reduced in 1908 when private power of arrest was withdrawn from all over Assam. That was a signal for rapid changeover from Act VI to Act XIII all over Assam as without the key provision for private arrest Act VI was thought to invite only more government interference. Finally in 1915 the special labour legislation itself and the system of recruitment under it were completely withdrawn. After 1915 till 1926, planters employed labourers largely under Act XIII of 1859 which Act was modified first in 1920 and finally abolished in 1926.

In this account of penal labour legislation in Assam certain features stand out. First, the formative period of the legislation coincides with phases of rapid expansion of the plantations, i.e. 1865–1901. The primary function of the legislation was to restrict an increase in the wages, that a burgeoning demand consequent on expansion would normally have led to. A second function of the legislation was to immobilise the labourer, thereby regulating competition among the individual planters themselves. Operation of the penal labour contract was thus crucial in fuelling expansion of plantations. Further, long-term penal contracts of five years' duration, ensured predictability and control over labour costs during the period. The most important function of the penal legislation was however in ensuring 'labour discipline' that is to deter the ever-present possibility of workers withdrawing their labour power.

Use and enforcement of Penal Contract Law in Assam

Prosecutions in Assam under the Special Labour Acts (Act I of 1882 and Act VI of 1901) were extremely low. Absolute number of prosecutions increased from about 500 a year in early 1880s to 1,428 in 1895 after which it declined steadily – the rate of prosecutions followed largely the absolute number of labourers under the Act. As a proportion, prosecutions were on the average only 0.65 per cent of the labour force under the Act and never higher than 1 per cent. Convictions as a proportion of prosecution was on the other hand pretty high – 80 per cent on the average and 75 per cent of convictions ended in imprisonment. Under Act XIII, the absolute numbers of prosecutions were always lower than those under Act I and Act VI till the last years of 1890s after which prosecutions under it increased rapidly as those under Act VI declined rapidly. Even so the rate of prosecution remained always much below 1 per cent of the total numbers employed under the Act.[25]

Indenture laws in Assam at first blush seem to have had a rather underused machinery of enforcement given the relatively low prosecution rates. This was reflected too in the composition of the offence. Between 1882 and 1908, no less than 95 per cent of all convictions were for desertion. The bulk of the other offences were for enticement of labourers to desert the services of their employers and were used largely against leaders of groups of workers who were arrested while attempting to leave the plantation. Further, what is interesting is the complete absence of any offence related to actual performance of work in the Assam laws (e.g. refusal to begin work, neglect to amend work or disobeying orders of overseer, etc.).

Privatised enforcement

Low rates of prosecution and absence of convictions for performance of work might suggest that the indenture laws were relatively less important for labour discipline in Assam, or were not rigidly enforced. Do they indicate that the labour regime on the plantations in Assam was relaxed? On the contrary, I would argue that the labour regime on the tea plantations was extremely brutal and intense. What however marked the Assam labour regime was what I would call a privatisation of the enforcement of contract, i.e. there was far greater involvement of private planter power in disciplining of the labour. This was not a result of the persistence of practices in contravention of the legal provisions of indenture but rather flowed directly from the provisions of the indenture law.

The keystone of the penal contract system in Assam was the provision of private power of arrest granted to the planters. It was introduced right from the beginning in the earliest indentured law in Assam in Act VI of 1865. Initially the provision was introduced as a concession to the planters to combat desertions in the 1860s and as a consequence of the absence of sufficient number of magistrates in the remote parts of the province. Yet even before the Act was passed, planters seemed to have set up their own establishment for detaining and capturing absconders. This blatantly illegal form of labour control was legalised by the granting of private power of arrest to the planters. The sympathetic commissioner of Assam had compared the position of the planter in Assam to that of a master of a ship in high seas and had recommended magisterial powers for the plant-

---

25 Prabhu P. Mohapatra, Assam and West Indies: Immobilising Plantation Labour', in D. Hay and P. Craven (ed.), *Master, Servants and Magistrates Britain and the Empire 1562–1955*, op. cit.

ers.²⁶ The horrible excesses including practice of severe corporal punishment by the planters were brought to light in a commission established subsequent to the passing of the 1865 Act and led to some limitations on the right to private arrest in the Act of 1873.²⁷

Planters were allowed to arrest without warrant an absconder if found beyond ten miles of the nearest magistrate. This limitation was relaxed further in the interest of the planters to a five-mile limit in Act VI of 1882 and remained in place till it was withdrawn in 1908. The private power of arrest was exercised not just by the planter but by any person authorised by him. Legally it was applicable only to those labourers who were indentured under the special labour legislation. In 1904, the commissioner of Assam was shocked to discover ferry masters, boatmen and station masters in railway stations exercising the power of arrest at the behest of the planters.²⁸ Private power of arrest could be exercised only by an elaborate private machinery of watchdogs, watchmen and informers, etc. 'Coolie catching' culture had been part and parcel of the recruitment of labour but under the penal contract became part of the labour regime. This apparatus was not merely used to prevent 'absconding' but was turned inward in the regulation of the labour relations on the plantation itself in compelling labourers to work or in punishing short work and other breaches of contract. It was the existence of this private machinery of labour control that obviated the recourse to indenture law except when in prosecuting deserters.²⁹ Even in the case of desertion the number

---

26 Letter of Commissioner of Assam to Secy. GOB, 6 October 1864 in ibid.
27 *Papers Regarding Tea Industry in Bengal*, p. XXII. Several planters openly admitted that they practised flogging to compel workers to adhere to the contract and some even suggested that they would cease to do so if the government took over the practice of corporal punishment. See letters *of* W. Stoddart, C. Eglinton and A.R. Spier, managers of tea estates in Assam and Cachar in ibid., pp. 45, 151–152.
28 'Coolie is detained at every ferry he comes to; he cannot obtain a ticket and I have lately discovered that the station masters are subsidised by the planters to arrest on suspicion in their interests. Managers exercise their power of arrest whether the coolie is under Act VI, under Act XIII or under no Act at all.' Bampfylde Fuller, Chief Commissioner of Assam to Curzon, Governor-General 2 September 1903, and 4 January 1904, Curzon Collection MSS Eur. F 111/204 in India Office Library (IOL).
29 One planter had already in the early stages of the institution of penal contract indicated the futility of exclusive reliance on courts to enforce discipline. 'At the present time if we were to send every coolie that ought to be punished before a magistrate, about one-third of our coolies would be in court daily as complainants, prisoners and witnesses.' The same planter had suggested that planters be allowed to legally institute fines for minor offences rather than be forced to send the coolie to the court. Letter of C.A. Alexander to Deputy Commissioner Cachar in *Papers Relating to Tea Industry in Bengal*, p. 148.

of persons who were arrested and brought back to the plantation without being prosecuted was numerous and never entered the statistics.[30]

Superficially the low rates of prosecution were trumpeted about as an index of satisfactory labour relations on the plantations. This privatisation of enforcement of contract resulted in blurring the limits of legality. Though planters were forbidden to physically assault labourers on pain of severe fines and other punishments, there were several instances of such acts with probably only the worst cases ever being found out during the late nineteenth century. Protests by the emergent nationalist intelligentsia against arbitrary exercise of power by the planters were dismissed by the colonial State as exaggerated. The prevalent idea within the officialdom was that, 'the tea planter as master of a large and irregular labour staff must enforce discipline by occasional severe measures which need not be looked into too closely, because these are substantially just and for the general good of the coolies.' A typical official attitude regarding use of private methods of discipline by the planters was exemplified by the Deputy Commissioner of Darrang. While reporting on complaints of frequent caning of labourers on the plantation he wrote:

> As a rule the coolie is not caned unless he has committed some offence for which the punishment would be far more severe if he were tried and convicted before a court of law ... and the coolie as a rule is not an undue sufferer from these illegal actions.[31]

Yet flogging was common in the 1870s as admitted by many managers themselves and even in 1894, a delegation of tribal headmen from the recruiting districts witnessed a young woman being flogged for having wrongly plucked four leaves instead of three in her basket. Another official wrote that the labourers themselves exaggerated when they designated every form of 'punishment however mild and done for coolies' good, *as fatak* (literally meaning confinement or jail). The wide currency of the term '*fatak*' among the labourers to designate both the form of punishment as well as the plantation system and penal contract system as a whole was reported in 1904 by the chief commissioner of Assam. The power of private arrest was applied not only to the new recruits under the indenture Act but was used against time expired and Act XIII labour too, providing the planters the power to immobilise practically the whole labour force.[32]

The penal contract in Assam I have argued was enforced largely through private agencies, which accounts for the low recourse to the provisions of penal

---

30 *Assam Special Report*, paras 238 and 239.
31 Ibid., p. 239.
32 Fuller to Governor-General in GOI Emig. A Prog. Nos. 12–14 December 1904.

law itself. But I must repeat that this privatisation of enforcement was not a deviation from the norms of penal contract or indenture law, rather it was a direct consequence of the provisions in the law itself namely that of the private power of arrest without warrant. The main effect of the penal contract legislation was, of course, in putting down wage levels but it acted too in allowing extremely unhealthy gardens to retain their labour force thus in effect increasing the mortality rates as labourers were prevented from fleeing these gardens. Elsewhere I have argued that indenture system and penal contract legislation were substantially transformed between 1901 and 1908 when the high cost of cheap labour plunged the industry into an acute crisis of overproduction and declining profits. Penal contract and the power of private arrest was now considered by the colonial State as the most important cause of the high cost of recruitment and low natural reproduction of the labour force which plagued Assam. It had ensured low living wages but the tendency towards overexploitation of the labour force resulted in high mortality and labour resistance in the form of desertion and increasingly violent protests, riots and disturbances.[33] The last vestiges of the special laws were abolished in 1915 and the penal contract system that remained in force in the plantations was only based on the Act XIII which as I have noted earlier was finally abolished in 1926.

In this paper I have tried to explain that the major forms in which informalisation of regulation of labour relations occurred in India in the nineteenth century and early twentieth century was through a tendency towards privatisation of modes of regulation. I have explained too that this happened with the active intervention of the State. I have also argued that the main effect of this informalisation process can be charted out in the tendency towards depression of wage levels for bulk of the workers in India. The relation of this mode of informalisation with the emergence of State-based regime of industrial relations beginning from the 1880s but more stridendy in the late colonial period deserves a separate exercise. But it might not be too wide off the mark, if we imagine that the system of regulation based on criminalisation of free labour backed by privatised power of enforcement cast a long shadow on the subsequent developments in the industrial relations system in India.

---

33 Behal and Mohapatra, 'Tea and Money versus Human Lives', pp. 156–158, 168–170.

Alessandro Stanziani
The Legal Status of Labour from the Seventeenth to the Nineteenth Century

Russia in a Comparative European Perspective[1]

Introduction

Since the eighteenth century at least, comparatives analyses of labour institutions and labour conditions in Russia have been made as if the boundary between free and unfree labour were ahistorically and universally defined. Free labour in "the West" is thus contrasted with serf labour in Russia and "eastern Europe". We intend to call that view into question and to show that serfdom was never officially institutionalized in Russia, and that the rules usually invoked to justify that opinion were actually intended not to "bind" the peasantry but to identify noble estate owners, as distinct from nobles in state service or the "bourgeoisie". However, it is a matter not only of legal definitions. We shall study the ways in which the tsarist administration, nobles, and peasants themselves made use of courts of law in order to contest ownership titles and, on that basis, the obligations and legal status of peasants and workers. Great changes had occurred in their legal status before the official abolition of serfdom in 1861, in outcomes that were rather similar to those which had been recently achieved in the "second serfdom" in Prussia, Lithuania, and Poland.[2] In turn, that means that such labour contracts and institutions were not the opposites of so-called "free labour" contracts and institutions, which placed many more constraints on workers than is usually acknowledged.

---

[1] This article was first published under the same title in *International Review of Social History*, 54 (2009), pp. 359–389 doi:10.1017/0020859009990307 © 2009 Internationaal Instituut voor Sociale Geschiedenis, published by Cambridge University Press, reproduced with permission. I should like to thank my colleagues David Moon (University of Durham), Elise Kimerling Wirtschafter (California State Polytechnic University, Pomona, CA), and Kenneth Pomeranz (University of California, Irvine, CA), and two anonymous referees for their valuable suggestions. I should like also to record my special thanks to the editorial board of the IRSH for their help and valuable comments.

[2] Edgar Melton, "Population Structure, the Market Economy, and the Transformation of *Gutsherrschaft* in East Central Europe, 1650–1800: The Cases of Brandenburg and Bohemia", *German History*, 16 (1998), pp. 297–327; William Hagen, *Ordinary Prussians: Brandenburg Junkers and Villagers, 1500–1840* (Cambridge, 2002).

To prove the point, since the link between the Master and Servants Acts and indenture has already been explored,[3] we shall pay particular attention to the presumed "French exception". France is still considered the only country in the West to have abolished service, as synonymous with wage labour, and punishment for breach of contract as a crime at the end of the eighteenth century – Britain, the United States, and Germany followed a century later. We intend to put that assertion to the test, focusing on French *engagés* (indentured workers) and rural labourers, both of which categories were subject to heavy legal constraints during the nineteenth century.

Our work is based on both archive and published sources. We have made use of Russian archives, mostly archives of ancient Russia (RGADA) and local archives in Moscow (TsGIAM), including decisions of local courts of law. To those must be added the impressive collection of Russian laws, decrees, and case law,[4] which gives us the opportunity to capture the almost incredible number of rules concerning our subject, their connection with rules governing the nobility and family, and the main legal decisions adopted by the high courts and the senate in Russia. French archives, both national and local, and French case law, as well as British and American legal judgments on questions about labour, servants, and the colonies, have been explored equally fully. Further, we have made extensive use of published Russian, French, and English sources from the eighteenth and nineteenth centuries and of the huge bibliography on this topic available in all those countries.

---

[3] Robert Steinfeld, *The Invention of Free Labor: The Employment Relation in English and American Law and Culture* (Chapel Hill, NC, 1991).

[4] *Polnoe sobranie zakonov Rossiiskoi Imperii* [Full Collection of Laws of the Russian Empire], henceforth *PSZ*, three series: I: 1649–1825, 46 vols (St Petersburg, 1830); II: 1825–1881, 55 vols (St Petersburg, 1830–1884); III: 1881–1913, 33 vols (St Petersburg, 1885–1916).

Rules of serfdom

The historiography of Russian serfdom has focused mainly on its origin (in the state,[5] or landowners), and its profitability,[6] rather than on the interplay between its legal rules and economic activity. The most remarkable contributions are those of Hoch, Wirtschafter, Melton, and Moon, who have effectively revisited the simplistic definition and functioning of Russian "serfdom".[7] Serfdom's dynamics and rules have been questioned; it has been suggested that serfdom was never

---

5 J. Blum, *Lord and Peasant in Russia: From the Ninth to the Nineteenth Century* (New York, 1964); A. Gershenkron, *Economic Backwardness in Historical Perspective* (Cambridge, MA, 1962); Olga Crisp, *Studies in the Russian Economy before 1914* (London, 1976); R. Portal, "The Industrialization of Russia", in H. Habakkuk and M. Postan (eds), *The Cambridge Economic History of Europe from the Decline of the Roman Empire*, VI, Part 2: *The Industrial Revolutions and After: Incomes, Population and Technological Change* (Cambridge, 1965), p. 51; A. Kahan, "Capital Formation During the Period of Early Industrialization in Russia, 1890–1913", in P. Mathias and M. Postan (eds), *The Cambridge Economic History of Europe from the Decline of the Roman Empire*, VII, Part 2: *The Industrial Economies: Capital, Labour, and Enterprise* (Cambridge, 1978), pp. 265–275; R. Bartlett, "Serfdom and State Power in Imperial Russia", *European History Quarterly*, 33 (2003), pp. 29–64; Richard Hellie, *Enserfment and Military Change in Muscovy* (Chicago, IL, 1971); P. Kolchin, *Unfree Labor: American Slavery and Russian Serfdom* (Cambridge, 1987); M.L. Bush (ed.), *Serfdom and Slavery: Studies in Legal Bondage* (Manchester, 1996); and Daniel Field, *The End of Serfdom: Nobility and Bureaucracy in Russia, 1855–1861* (Cambridge, MA, 1976).
6 P. Struve, *Krepostnoe khoziaistvo. Issledovaniia po ekonomicheskoi istorii Rossii v XVIII i XIX vv* [The Serf Economy: Studies on the Economic History of Russia, Eighteenth to the Nineteenth Century] (St Petersburg, 1913); I.D. Koval'chenko, *Russkoe krepostnoe krest'ianstvo v pervoi polovine XIXth v.* [The Russian Serf Peasantry during the First Half of the Nineteenth Century] (Moscow, 1967); Ian Blanchard, *Russia's Age of Silver: Precious Metal Production and Economic Growth in the Eighteenth Century* (New York, 1989); David Moon, *The Abolition of Serfdom in Russia, 1762–1907* (London, 2001); T.K. Dennison, "Did Serfdom Matter? Russian Rural Society, 1750–1860", *Historical Research*, 79:203 (2003), pp. 74–89; Edgar Melton, "Proto-Industrialization, Serf Agriculture and Agrarian Social Structure: Two Estates in Nineteenth-Century Russia", *Past & Present*, 115 (1987), pp. 73–81; idem, "Enlightened Seignorialism and its Dilemmas in Serf Russia, 1750–1830", *Journal of Modern History*, 62 (1990), pp. 675–708; and Steven Hoch, *Serfdom and Social Control in Russia: Petrovskoe, A Village in Tambov* (Chicago, IL, 1986). See too E. Domar and M. Machina, "On the Profitability of Russian Serfdom", *The Journal of Economic History*, 44 (1984), pp. 919–955.
7 Hoch, *Serfdom and Social Control in Russia*; Melton, "Enlightened Seignorialism and its Dilemmas", and idem, "Proto-Industrialization, Serf Agriculture and Agrarian Social Structure"; Elise Kimerling Wirtschafter, *Structures of Society: Imperial Russia's "People of Various* Ranks" (DeKalb, IL, 1994); Elise Kimerling Wirtschafter, *Social Identity in Imperial Russia* (DeKalb, IL, 1997); Moon, *Abolition of Serfdom*; idem, "Reassessing Russian Serfdom", *European History Quarterly*, 26 (1996), pp. 483–526; idem, *The Russian Peasantry, 1600–1930: The World the Peasants Made* (London, 1996).

officially introduced[8] and that it was much more a set of practices than a true system.[9] We are keen to extend research in the same direction by analysing the rules defining the legal status of actors and assessing their implementation.

We shall show that the rules never spoke of "serfs" but rather aimed to identify people entitled to transmit "immovable" property. In fact, Russian and Western historiography from the twentieth century to today considers *krepostnoe pravo* as the equivalent in the Russian language of the word "serfdom", just as *krepostnye liudi* has been translated as "serfs". That translation might be correct, but one problem is that the expression *krepostnoe pravo* did not appear in Russian texts until the years preceding the reforms of 1861. If we consider official Russian texts from the sixteenth to the middle of the nineteenth century, we find no *krepostnoe pravo* nor *krepostnye liudi* (people subject to a *krepost'*, a deed) but only *krest'iane* (peasants) and the rural population.

The limitation of the mobility of peasants has to be viewed in that context, for although not a goal in itself, such limitation did affect relationships between different groups of landowners and the state.[10] The Muscovite state did precisely that in 1550, when the *Sudebnik* (law reports) incorporated and widely applied the provisions originally intended (1455–1462) only for monastery peasants, which consisted in limiting their mobility.[11] The rules were thus appropriated by the state and broadened to include the entire peasantry in relation to a particular operation, namely the attempt by Muscovite leaders to establish a land register.

Throughout the sixteenth and seventeenth centuries, several rules were adopted which had the effect of limiting peasant mobility; however, those rules actually aimed to establish a cadastre in order to improve tax income and military conscription, but also to settle arguments over estates to which there were various claimants, including different categories of noble, the crown, the Church, and monasteries. In other words, among the Muscovite elites claims to land and conflicts over them were at the root of rules concerning the cadastre and, only

---

8 Bartlett, "Serfdom and State Power in Imperial Russia"; Wirtschafter, *Structures of Society*, and idem, *Social Identity in Imperial Russia*.
9 Examples of this can be found in Hoch, *Serfdom and Social Control in Russia*, and Dennison, "Did Serfdom Matter?".
10 Cadastre documents *(Pistsovye knigi)* are largely available in RGADA in a large number of collections, including f. 1239, op. 3, ch. 17, 69–72, 74, 76, 86–87 (cadastres of Moscow district, 1674–1681); f. 396, op. 2, ch. 5 (1616–1732), Smolensk, and several other districts; fonds 1209 (prilozhenie arkhiv prezhnikh votchinnykh del, 1565–1692), op. 1, ch. 1–3, op. 2, ch. 1–2, op. 16–72.
11 Daniel Kaiser, *The Growth of the Law in Medieval Russia* (Princeton, NJ, 1980), provides a detailed analysis of the different editions of the *Sudebnik* (1550, 1589, and 1606).

implicitly, peasant mobility.[12] The provisions meant that peasants could move from central "black earth" lands to state or court lands, if they felt so inclined, and there is no doubt that many peasants moved freely about Russia and that the government took measures to ensure they had the right to do so. Until the first half of the seventeenth century, it was assumed that the restriction was temporary; by the 1630s landlords even came to enjoy the right to allow their peasants to move, as expressed in a document they signed (the *otpusknaia gramota*).[13]

These measures were dictated not only by the taxation and military requirements of the state,[14] which were linked to Russian territorial expansion,[15] but overlapped with a significant redefinition of the relationships between social groups and that state, especially the value of land ownership as a social and political marker.[16] The Russian elites welcomed the requests of the provincial nobility to legitimize their properties, for the elites could thereby secure an important ally in their fight against the *boiare*. The delimitation of properties and the increasingly strong link between land ownership and the obligations of the resident population formed the point at which the interests of the state and those of small landowners intersected. The process was by no means simple, however, as is evidenced by the numerous legal disputes and petitions drawn up by noble families against other claimants to their properties, whether other nobles, merchants, *boiare*, or others.[17] The position was complicated even more by the fact that landowners were ready to keep runaway peasants and that the state was unable to enforce the relevant rules. In other words, limitations to peasant mobility were part of a wider game being played by opposing Russian elites.

The alliance between the state and the provincial and lesser nobility was supposed to offer a solution, new rules on runaways being adopted in exchange

---

12 Henry Eaton, "Cadasters and Censuses of Muscovy", *Slavic Review*, 26 (1967), pp. 54–69; the most complete list of published sixteenth and seventeenth cadastral records is in S.V. Voznesenskii, *Materialy dlia bibliografii po istorii narodov SSSR XVI–XVIIvv* [Materials for a Bibliography on the History of the People of the USSR, Sixteenth to the Seventeenth Century] (Leningrad, 1933).
13 Hellie, *Enserfment and Military Change in Muscovy*, p. 108.
14 W.C. Fuller, *Strategy and Power in Russia, 1600–1914* (New York, 1992); and Carol S. Leonard, *Reform and Regicide: The Reign of Peter III of Russia* (Bloomington, IN, 1993).
15 Moon, *Abolition of Serfdom*; Blum, *Lord and Peasant in Russia*, Dennison, "Did Serfdom Matter?"; Hellie, *Enserfment and Military Change in Muscovy*, and *idem, Slavery in Russia: 1450–1725* (Chicago, IL, 1982); P. Perdue, "Military Mobilization in Seventeenth and Eighteenth-Century China, Russia, and Mongolia", *Modern Asian Studies*, 30 (1996), pp. 757–793.
16 Moon, "Reassessing Russian Serfdom"; P.A. Zaionchkovskii, *Otmena krepostnogo prava v Rossii* [The Abolition of Serfdom in Russia], 3rd edn (Moscow, 1968).
17 R. Crummey, "Sources of Boyar Power in the Seventeenth Century", *Cahiers du Monde Russe*, 34:1–2 (1993), pp. 107–118.

for landowners' acceptance of a cadastre. However, that agreement proved to be ineffective as different state administrations were unable to cooperate in achieving a cadastre, returning runaways, and punishing owners whose claims were illegitimate. To that must be added the lack of cooperation among landowners, who continued to retain peasants who were on the move – "runaways". This is where the famous *Ulozhenie* of 1649 comes in; according to many interpretations, Russian, Soviet, and Western alike, it marked the final adoption of the servile regime *(krepostnoe pravo)* in Russia and thereby the central role of the state in the process.[18] Yet, if we read that document carefully, we find that it contains nothing concerning the organization of work on the estates.[19] We find instead, in chapter 11 of the document, a section devoted to the trial of runaway peasants. The document mentions peasants and the rural population, but not serfs. The thirty-four articles making up its eleventh chapter define the rules governing runaways, which is to say peasants.

"Peasants" meant individuals, with or without land, who were members of any rural community, who were said to have moved outside their own rural districts without the permission of the landowner or the local public authority in order to settle in another rural district or place themselves under the authority of cities, monasteries, and so on. It refers to members of rural communities with obligations towards either private landowners or the state, or towards their rural community.[20] In other words, like the other documents discussed earlier, the 1649 *Ulozhenie* aimed not so much to "bind" the peasantry as to grant state certification of the property rights of nobles over the land, and only on that basis to transfer property along with the population residing on it. Nobles were, therefore, able to demand payment of credit, work service, and the like, from rural inhabitants. However, exactly as they did before, peasants continued to sign "settlement contracts"[21] with landlords, in which they identified the conditions and terms of their

---

18 Hellie, *Enserfment and Military Change in Muscovy.*
19 Blum, *Lord and Peasant in Russia,* pp. 262–265; A. Man'kov, *Razvitie krepostnogo prava v Rossii vo vtoroi polovine XVII veka* [The Development of Serfdom in Russia during the Second Half of the Seventeenth Century] (Leningrad, 1962).
20 A new Russian edition *(Sobornoe ulozhenie 1649 g.)* and commentaries was published in 1987 under the supervision of A. Man'kov. For an English translation see Richard Hellie, *Muscovite Society* (Chicago, IL, 1967); idem, *The Muscovite Law Code (Ulozhenie) of 1649* (Irvine, CA, 1988); "The Law Code of 1649" and "Muscovite-Western Commercial Relations", in Thomas Riha (ed.), *Readings in Russian Civilization,* 2nd edn (Chicago, IL, 1969), pp. 154–172.
21 Hellie, *Enserfment and Military Change in Muscovy,* p. 144; E.I. Kamentseva, "Usloviia zakreposhcheniia novoporiadchikov" [The Conditions of Enserfment of New Settlers], *Trudy moskovskogo gosudarstvennogo istoriko-arkhivnogo instituta,* 7 (1954), pp. 129–154.

engagement. The contracts provided landlords with titles over peasants for use in case they ran away.

The question to be answered concerns the extent to which the provisions contributed to solving the long-term questions of land ownership and social status in Russia, and in particular the unfair competition between hereditary nobles with their practice of keeping "runaways" on the one hand, and the sharp conflicts between nobles in government service and hereditary nobles on the other hand, as well as the conflict between nobles and merchants. The available sources reveal a clear attempt by the state to enforce rules,[22] but as litigation recorded among landowners and between landowners and urban merchants plainly shows, the legal definition of those who had the right to own and transfer populated estates was not made clear.

As a consequence, throughout the eighteenth century, differing rules were adopted to assess claims. Those rules took a clear position, determining the definition of "hereditary nobles". From the mid-1730s until the early 1760s, a number of decrees limited the numbers of those entitled to own and transmit inhabited estates. Servants, servants in monasteries,[23] soldiers and the lower administrative levels, the clergy, merchants, urban guilds, Cossacks, and *raznochintsy* (people of various ranks) were all prohibited from acquiring or transferring inhabited estates and from establishing *krepost'* relationships.[24] Finally, in 1762, factory owners were prohibited from buying and transferring estates with either urban or rural workers.[25]

In short, from the mid-sixteenth century until the last quarter of the eighteenth century Muscovite, Russian, and Imperial Russian rules of land ownership did not refer to serfs but mostly aimed to define who was entitled to own and then dispose of populated estates and, as a consequence of that entitlement, who could retain runaways. Attempts by nobles to limit access to land and status by

---

22 On peasant mobility, see Hellie, *Enserfment and Military Change in Muscovy*, pp. 142 ff.; Daniel Morrison, *"Trading Peasants" and Urbanization in Eighteenth Century Russia: The Central Industrial Region* (New York [etc.], 1987); E.I. Indova, "Rol' dvortsovoi derevni pervoi poloviny XVIII v. v formirovanii russkogo kupechestva" [The Role of the Village Court during the First Half of the Eighteenth Century in the Formation of a Russian Bourgeoisie], *Istoricheskie Zapiski*, 68 (1961), pp. 189–210, a French translation of which has appeared as "Les activités commerciales de la paysannerie dans les villages du tsar de la région de Moscou (première moitié du XVIIIe siècle)", *Cahiers du monde russe*, 5 (1964), pp. 206–228. Several examples of this can be found in RGADA, fond 294, op. 2.
23 *PSZ* (I), VIII, n. 5633. Blum, *Lord and Peasant*, pp. 358–362, on the debates and various drafts of these laws: RGADA, fond 342, op. 1, delo 37, part 2.
24 *PSZ* (I), XII, nn. 9332, 9367.
25 *PSZ* (I), XV, n. 11490; XVI, n. 11638.

other groups, such as service elites and the bourgeoisie, were constantly mitigated by the ambivalent approach of the state elite, which wished to allow, yet at the same time also restrict, access by the nobility, in order to win support for reform and ensure social stability.

That equilibrium changed during the final quarter of the eighteenth century, when "entitled" nobles seemed to become more and more interested in selling properties to non-noble elites, to present a loan as a sale or vice versa, mainly for tax reasons, but also in response for instance to financial difficulties or conflicts within the family.[26] Of course, other nobles and the tsarist elites were opposed to such practices, for both sociopolitical and economic reasons. Nonetheless, in 1836, nonhereditary nobles were confirmed in their right to own inhabited estates, though not to transfer them.[27] Those provisions were followed by an increasing number of disputes among nobles, service nobles and hereditary nobles, and between nobles and the administration. According to the statistics of the Ministry of Justice, in 1845 alone 6,400 requests for confirmation of the title of "noble" were submitted, only half of which were validated.[28]

From that perspective, the rules paved the way to a closer focus on a legal definition of "illegal bondage". All transactions made between nobles and people who were not entitled to possess populated estates were illicit, and gave rise, therefore, to illegal possession and illegal bondage. A law in 1833 prohibited any new bondage, even if the parties agreed to it.[29] Limitations imposed on the mobility of peasants residing on an estate owing to a debt to a non-noble were also forbidden.[30] Several other rules followed during the first half of the nineteenth century, which in fact precipitated a broader process in which administrative and legal condemnation of bondage opened the way to large-scale administrative and judicial "emancipation".

---

[26] The High Chamber (senate) records several of those cases in 1816; *Arkhiv gosu- darstvennogo soveta*, 5 vols (St Petersburg, 1869–1904), IV, vyp. 1, ch. 2, pp. 253–258.
[27] *PSZ* (II), XI, n. 9203.
[28] *Otchet ministerstva iustitsii za 1845* (St Petersburg, 1846), p. xix.
[29] *Svod zakonov*, IX, art 546 (1833).
[30] Wirtschafter, *Structures of Society*, p. 81.

Changing legal status: administrative procedure or court proceedings

The ways in which economic and social actors appropriate legal rules have been the subject of a huge number of studies in sociology, economics, history, and anthropology, and, of course, among legal scholars. In social and economic history, the same approach has been developed for different countries and different periods, and Russian studies too have recently developed similar methods of analysis.[31] However, it is widely accepted that peasants had but few legal rights in eighteenth-century Russia; indeed, some scholars consider that to have been true right up to the legal reforms of 1864.

Their arguments require a serious assessment. In fact, recourse to the law for capturing social and economic assets depends on the distribution of legal rights, as well as on legal procedures and on the precise wording of laws. In particular, it is true that peasants had no right of recourse to the law against their masters, but that situation had begun to change even before 1864, with the institution of peasant courts in the 1770s. Those courts were certainly limited in their scope and effect, as they were controlled by landlords. At the same time, the difficulties faced by peasants in challenging their masters generally related to physical punishment and the organization of labour, which we shall examine in the next section. Legal rights on estates were easier to mobilize not only for other nobles or merchants, but also sometimes for peasants, with the encouragement of others who might have been interested in a particular estate. In fact, many laws were passed during the first half of the nineteenth century to facilitate administrative changes to the legal status of peasants. They were reforms that responded simultaneously to particular claims and worries at a given moment and to a more general attitude on the part of Russian elites. Political stability, economic efficiency, paternalistic

---

[31] The rapidly growing bibliography includes: Wirtschafter, *Structures of Society*; idem, *Social Identity in Imperial Russia*; and Virginia Martin, *Law and Custom in the Steppe: The Kazakhs of the Middle Horde and Russian Colonialism in the Nineteenth Century* (Richmond, 2001). Most of the available literature on legal action in Imperial Russia focuses on the post-1864 period: Richard Wortman, *Development of a Russian Legal Consciousness* (Chicago, IL, 1976); William Wagner, Marriage, *Property and Law in Late Imperial Russia* (Oxford, 1994); Jane Burbank, *Russian Peasants Go to Court: Legal Culture in the Countryside, 1905–1917* (Bloomington, IN, 2004); Peter Solomon (ed.), *Reforming Justice in Russia, 1864–1994: Power, Culture, and the Limits of Legal Order* (Armonk, NY, 1997); and E.A. Pravilova, *Zakonnost' i prava lichnosti: administrativnaia iustitsiia v Rossii, vtoraia polovina XIX v. –oktiabr' 1917* [Legality and the Rights of the Person: Administrative Justice in Russia, in the Second Half of the Nineteenth Century to October 1917] (St Petersburg, 2000).

criticism of serfdom, and the particular economic interests of the state or some of the nobility all played a part, to different degrees, in reform.[32]

In general, the matter of rules and their implementation consisted in transferring peasants belonging to private estates to the legal category of state peasants. After the seventeenth century, peasants on noble and private estates had been distinguished from state peasants.[33] State peasants had certain obligations only to the state, for example to pay an annuity, usually in money, sometimes in kind. They were also obliged to perform work of common interest, which is usually mentioned to justify the existence of forced labour and serfdom in this category. At the same time, state peasants could work in cities in trade and industry, provided they had the required documents.[34] Catherine II even included representatives of state peasants in her legislative commission assigned to define the rights and obligations of the main social groups.[35] In 1842, state peasants were freed from any obligation towards the state, apart from tax.

Starting from that premise, we can study the rules allowing a peasant from a private estate to be reclassified as a state peasant. A first reform was adopted by Alexander I, who ascended the throne in 1801 and gave the impression of being willing to introduce far-reaching reforms. In 1801 he allowed merchants, townspeople, and state peasants to own unpopulated estates, which he intended as a partial breaking up of the nobles' monopoly of landownership. In 1803, a decree

---

32 Moon, *Abolition of Serfdom in Russia*; Blum, *Lord and Peasant in Russia*; Hoch, *Serfdom and Social Control in Russia*; Robert E. Jones, *The Emancipation of the Russian Nobility, 1762–1785* (Princeton, NJ, 1973); and D. Saunders, *Russia in the Age of Reaction and Reform, 1801–1881* (London [etc.], 1992).

33 On this difference, see V.I. Semevskii, *Krest'ianskii vopros v Rossii v XVIII i pervoi polovine XIX veka* [The Peasant Question in Russia in the Eighteenth to the First Half of the Nineteenth Century], 2 vols (St Petersburg, 1888); idem, *Krest'iane v tsarstvovanie Imperatritsy Ekateriny II* [The Peasantry under the Reign of Catherine II], I, 2nd edn (St Petersburg, 1903 [first published 1881]), II (St Petersburg, 1901); I.I. Ignatovich, *Pomeshchich'i krest'iane nakanune osvobozhdeniia* [Private Landlords' Peasants on the Eve of Emancipation], 2nd edn (Moscow, 1910), 3rd edn (Leningrad, 1925); D.I. Raskin, "Ispol'zovanie zakonodatel'nykh aktov v krest'ianskikh chelobitnykh serediny XVIII veka. (Materialy k izucheniiu obshchestvennogo soznaniia russkogo krest'ianstva)" [The Appeal to Legal Acts in Peasant Petitions in the Mid-Eighteenth Century, in Materials for Studies of the Social Consciousness of Russian Peasantry], *Istoriia SSSR*, 4 (1979), pp. 179–192; M.A. Rakhmatullin, *Krest'ianskoe dvizhenie v velikorusskikh guberniiakh v 1826–1857 gg* [Peasant Movements in the Grand Russian Provinces, 1826–1857] (Moscow, 1990).

34 N.M. Druzhinin, *Gosudarstvennye krest'iane i reforma P.D. Kiseleva* [State Peasants and the Reform of P.D. Kiselev] (Moscow, 1958). See too Struve, *Krepostnoe khoziaistvo*.

35 *Sbornik imperatorskogo russkogo istoricheskogo obshchestva* [Collected Essays of the Russian Historical Society], X (St Petersburg, 1872), pp. 285–288; Isabel de Madariaga, *Russia in the Age of Catherine the Great* (London, 1981), p. 139; Moon, "Reassessing Russian Serfdom", and idem, *The Abolition of Serfdom in Russia*.

created the *svobodnye khlebopashtsy*, free farmers who at the discretion of the landowner were exempt from any obligation to him, apart from those obligations arising from the attribution to peasants of plots of land belonging to the overall owner. Those agreements were legally binding on both peasants and landowners.[36]

The influence of German and Russian intellectuals, as well as pressure from some among the noble elites, encouraged the reforming attitudes of the tsars, in particular Alexander, who was pushed to adopt that provision by Count Rumyantsev. Rumyantsev had sought permission to free some of his serfs and sell land to them, and the agreeable answer to his request became the basis for broader reform. This provision by Alexander was supposed to lead to an improvement in agriculture while being advantageous to estate owners, and according to the estimates of Hoch and Augustine, between 1833 and 1855 alone 58,225 people were emancipated on the basis of it,[37] a figure that rose to 114,000 male peasants between 1803 and 1855. However, despite several attempts to go further, Alexander did not adopt other reforms of the same kind. The Napoleonic wars and opposition by some groups of nobles and high-ranking officials seem to have played a role in his change of heart.[38]

The next tsar too, Nicholas I, spent some time in projecting reforms before adopting concrete rules. They occurred in the broader realm of Kiselev's reforms between 1838 and 1842, which radically modified the conditions of state peasants. Peasants' general and professional education was taken into account, while their fiscal burden and the obligations toward the state were no longer assessed per head, but in conformity with the value of each individual peasant's land or income from non-agricultural activities.[39]

Kiselev ordered a general enquiry into agriculture and the peasantry; its final report concluded that the labour of peasants with no statutory obligations to landowners was more productive than coerced labour. However, on the basis of that report, Kiselev and Nicholas I maintained that the present difficult situation of agriculture and the extent of coerced labour was the result of the fact that some landowners had abused their power and had extended the power of their patronage over the peasantry. Limitation of those abuses thus became a precondition

---

[36] *PSZ* (I), XXVII, n. 20620 (20 February 1803).
[37] S. Hoch and W. Augustine, "The Tax Censuses and the Decline of the Serf Population in Imperial Russia, 1833–1858", *Slavic Review,* 38 (1979), pp. 403–425.
[38] Moon, *Abolition of Serfdom in Russia*, p. 42; S.V. Mironenko, *Samoderzhavie i reformy: politicheskaia bor'ba v Rossii v nachale XIX v.* [Autocracy and Reforms: Political Struggle in Russia in the Early Nineteenth Century] (Moscow, 1989).
[39] Druzhinin, *Gosudarstvennye.*

for deeper reforms. At the same time, it was argued that peasants should not be freed from their illegal bondage without being given the opportunity to acquire their own land. In fact, as the reforms experienced in the Western borderland had proved, freedom without land would lead to a clear worsening of the peasants' circumstances and thence to social and political instability.

Accordingly, in 1842 a new decree was adopted. It was conceived as the direct descendant of the 1803 decree, but with the major difference that the contractual agreement between an estate owner and peasants would not be left to the free will of the former but would be regulated by law. If the peasants involved did not redeem the value of the land, estate owners would retain the right of full patrimonial ownership of it and the peasants would receive plots for their use. A particular category of peasant was created; they were the peasants with an obligation *(obiazannye krest'ianie)* towards noble landowners who fitted neither the category of private estate peasants in the strict sense *(pomeshchichie krest'iane)* nor that of servants *(dvornye liudi)*.

As with previous rules, this new decree referred specifically to peasants, private peasants, and rural inhabitants, but not to "serfs", who would be subject to other legal rules *(uslovnoe pravo)*; peasants no longer had any general obligations towards landowners, except those concerning the plot received when the contract with the property owner was signed.[40] Peasants concluded contracts with landowners based on the size of their allotment and the level of their obligations. From the adoption of the new law until 1858, a total of 27,173 male peasants, and their families, were affected by the decree.[41] In 1841, peasants whom private nobles had allotted freely to monasteries or charitable institutions were also reclassified due to the prohibition on the ownership and transfer of serfs by those institutions.[42] About 8,900 people were thus transferred to the category of state peasants, and the institutions to which they belonged were compensated by the state.[43]

Tsar Nicholas did not cease his reforms; in 1844, two new laws facilitated the reclassification of *dvornye liudi* (servants); the first one freed their masters from any responsibility for the payment of their taxes, while the servants freed were subject neither to military service nor taxation until the next revision. The

---

[40] *PSZ* (II), XVII, n. 15462.
[41] Hoch and Augustine, "Tax Censuses and the Decline of the Serf Population", p. 410.
[42] *PSZ* (II), XVI, n. 14669, 19 June 1841.
[43] Hoch and Augustine, "Tax Censuses and the Decline of the Serf Population", fn. p. 410; N. Mel'nitskii, *Sbornik svedenii o voennoe-uchebnykh zavedeniiakh v Rossii* [Collection of Figures on the Military Establishments in Russia], 4 vols (St Petersburg, 1857–1860), II, part 3, pp. 187, 217; part 4, pp. 52, 119; part 5, p. 141.

second law facilitated a change in legal status in cases in which a landowner mortgaged his estate to certain credit institutions. According to a study at the time, in 1851 alone 11,000 *meshchane* (merchants) from 11 provinces were said to have benefited from those rules, having been previously the peasants of private owners.[44] About 19,000 working peasants attached to private factories were freed between 1840 and 1851, and during the same period many mines had recourse to "temporary workers" *(nepremennye* or *urochnye rabotniki)*, who were registered as private peasants at the time of the eighth revision. The facts were denounced years later and a court decision was made only for the ninth revision in 1851. At that time, 53,900 men working in the mines were transferred to state estates as peasants.[45] All those rules gave rise to a reclassification of private peasants into other categories, and thereby erased their obligations towards their landlords.

Administrative emancipation sometimes occurred for other reasons. As we have seen, under tsarist law mortgaged estates put up for auction were especially targeted. State and noble elites agreed that indebted landowners must be helped in order to prevent their lands from falling into the hands of "speculators" and bourgeoisie. To that end, along with the state itself, local peasants were granted priority in acquiring such lands. In 1847, the peasants from auctioned estates could buy land and purchase their own freedom to move.[46] That same year, however, the state Ministry of Estates, set up in 1838, was obliged to buy private estates put up for auction. As a result, 178 estates were taken over between 1838 and 1855, with a population of about 58,275 serfs consequently transferred to the state. Beginning in 1842, the same ministry also began taking over estates belonging to "isolated peasants" *(odnodvorcheskie krest'iane)*. Until 1858, about 8,000 peasants were taken over by the state in that way. In 1845, the administration in charge of feeding horses in the province of Voronezh bought the estate of Count Orlov, with its 6,562 inhabitants, who became state peasants. The "public treasury" *(udel)* also took over estates: between 1831 and 1860 it bought 52 estates in the provinces of Simbirsk and Orel, with about 25,000 inhabitants. In all, between 1833 and 1858 alone, the legal status of 343,575 male peasants changed owing to mass emancipations by the state: they ceased to be private estate peasants and became state peasants and sometimes *meshchane*.

---

44 P. Keppen, *Deviataia reviziia: issledovanie o chisle zhitelei v Rossii v 1851 goda* [The Ninth Census: Study of the Number of Inhabitants in Russia in 1851] (St Petersburg, 1857), pp. 6–7, 21, 62, 88, 95, 100, 127, 142–144, 152–159.
45 P.G. Ryndzinskii, "Vymiralo li krepostnoe krest'ianstvo pered reformoi 1861g.?" [Were Serfs Really Disappearing Before the Reform of 1861?], *Voprosy istorii*, 7 (1967), pp. 54–70.
46 Wirtschafter, *Social Identity in Imperial Russia*, p. 121.

General and administrative law regarding emancipation had a cumulative effect not only on mortgaged estates, but also on the terms of succession. Thus, two new laws adopted in 1836 and 1839 stipulated that if a landowner left no heirs, or no heirs who could legitimately own serfs, the peasants would become state peasants, whereas the servants could register in cities as *meshchane*.[47] In 1841, a new law prohibited the succession of landless nobles or landless owners of peasants. Consequently, between 1841 and 1858 the number of landless nobles dropped from 17,700 to 3,633 and their serfs from 62,000 to 12,045, a dramatic fall even taking into account the possibility that some of the serfs had been sold to other nobles.[48]

The voluntary redemption of peasants' obligations and thus a change in legal status by the master was already provided for in the seventeenth and eighteenth centuries. It is, however, difficult to estimate the number of those redemptions as no systematic, province-by-province studies are available, although notarial archives *(krepostnye knigi)* and estate archives provide useful information. The impression given by the huge mass of archives is that voluntary acts of redemption accelerated during the nineteenth century in response to both tax support and legal simplification as provided by the tsarist rules.[49] According to estimates at the time, the ninth revision of 1851 held in 12 provinces *(guberniia)* resulted in a change in the legal status of 11,000 *meshchane*.[50] Though not cumulative, relatively detailed data on those individual acts was collected by the tsarist authorities between 1860 and 1868; they cover 25 volumes and give a wealth of information on the state of the population in Russia's provinces and in its empire.[51] These acts were part of the paternalistic relationships proper to the system; they set an example for the mass of peasants to engage in cordial relations with their landowners with a view to their possible emancipation. The pace of those acts accelerated during the nineteenth century in response to incentives from the authorities and the compensation guaranteed to noble landowners.[52]

However, changing legal status also resulted from the increasing number of legal proceedings brought by peasants themselves against their masters. Until the 1770s, there were no special courts in Russia for peasants, who were forced to apply to nobles and their courts to request emancipation, which considera-

---

[47] *Svod zakonov*, IX, art. 462–463 (1857); *PSZ* (II), XI, n. 9203 (1836); XIV, n. 13012 (1839).
[48] Hoch and Augustine, "Tax Censuses and the Decline of the Serf Population", p. 420.
[49] Notarial archives in RGADA, fonds 615, op. 1; fonds 1253 and 1274.
[50] Keppen, *Deviataia reviziia*, pp. 6, 7, 21, 88, 95–100, 127, 142–144, 152, 159.
[51] Glavnyi General'nyi Shtab, *Materialy dlia geografii i statistiki Rossii, sobrannye ofitserami general'nogo shtaba* [Materials for the Geography and Statistics of Russia, Collected by the Officers of the General Headquarters], 25 vols (St Petersburg, 1860–1868).
[52] *PSZ* (II), XI, n. 9203.

bly reduced attempts to initiate proceedings. The situation changed in 1775 with the introduction of peasant courts, accompanied by a clear-cut legal separation between ownership of things and rights over human beings. Throughout the nineteenth century, those issues were frequently the subject of court rulings. Peasants themselves were sometimes able to demonstrate in court that the landowner, or master, concerned was not entitled to own the estate.[53] Proceedings brought by peasants became so numerous that between 1837 and 1840 the senate actually decided to put a stop to cases involving serfs still living with their masters.[54] Overall, between 1833 and 1858 the senate recorded 15,153 cases of illegal bondage, while the provincial courts dealt with 22,000 cases of this type.[55] Naturally, these positive outcomes should not obscure the difficulties confronting peasants who tried to bring proceedings against a noble or someone claiming to be noble. The rulings of local courts often differed considerably, and several judges considered peasant petitions inadmissible and even refused to grant them the right to appeal.[56] A number of cases of corruption of judges by noble landowners were also recorded. Finally, the investigations of proceedings went slowly and it often took ten years to reach a conclusion.[57]

To sum up, like a number of other historians of Russia (Wirtschafter, Hoch, and Moon particularly), it is our contention that the abolition of serfdom in Russia cannot be traced to a single act (the emancipation statute of 1861) but has to be seen as a long-term process, started no later than the turn of the nineteenth century. At the same time, we go further and add another dimension, by examining the way in which rules actually defined the main social actors and the use those groups or individuals made of the rules. In our perspective, the opposition between "reforms from above" and bottom-up processes does not make sense insofar as the rules were adopted and implemented by different actors, with different interests. In other words, there is no "real life" beyond rules in as much as rules are not only "reference books" but shape the psychological and practical horizons and expectations of socioeconomic players.

---

53 TsGIAM, fond 54 (Moskovskoe gubernskoe upravlenie), 1783–1917, op. 1, for example 56, 284, 966, 1509. Several other cases can be found in *Deistviia Nizhegorodskoi gubernskoi uchenoi arkhivnoi komissii*, several booklets, 1890s.
54 RGIA, f. 1149, op. 2, delo 90; Wirtschafter, *Structures of Society*, p. 84.
55 *PSZ* (II), XX, n. 19283; XXII, n. 20825, RGIA, fond 1149, op. 3, delo 125. See too Hoch and Augustine, "Tax Censuses and the Decline of the Serf Population".
56 RGIA, fond 1149, op. 2 delo 20. In particular, the lack of documentation was one of the most widespread arguments for rejecting petitions; Wirtschafter, *Structures of Society*, pp. 79, 119.
57 In particular, the law of 1847, in PSZ (II), XXII, n. 20825; Wirtschafter, *Structures of Society*, p. 84.

In particular, serfdom and enserfment were never defined as such in tsarist legal rules. A large part of the peasant population was initially limited in its movements by contractual rules, which were then transformed into conditions of status. The rules defined the limitations on peasant movement resulting from their obligations to noble landowners or to the state, and represented a form of servitude but not the *serf de la glèbe*. The legal definition always retained its contractual and status aspects, however, which allowed it to be distinguished from slavery in the strict sense, by likening it to long-term forms of indenture, as with the status of certain miners in Scotland for example. The specific feature of "serfdom" relationships in Russia was that they referred not to bilateral relationships between nobles and peasants or between peasants and the state, but to a multilateral classification process involving craftsmen and peasants, noble landowners, *meshchane*, tsarist administrative directors, and judges. All that meant that the legal rights of peasants were limited, compared with those of elites, but also that they were not completely non-existent, as the changes in their legal status testify.

That has implications for our interpretation of the reforms of 1861 and the long-term trend for the Russian peasantry. At the time of the 1861 reforms, peasants on private estates made up about half the total peasantry; of those, fewer than a half – in fact about 37 per cent of the whole population – were still required to provide *corvées*.[58] Consequently, the end of "coerced labour" affected barely a quarter of all Russia's peasants. The obligations on landowners of this sizeable portion of the Russian population were transformed; what had become a genuine status was turned into chronic indebtedness to the state. From that perspective, the reforms of 1861 have to be seen in a broader context made up of several reforms implemented over a century and a half, and in any case aiming not to abolish "serfdom" so much as to change forms of power and hierarchies in the countryside. In particular, the reforms dealt with the legal entitlement of estate owners on the one hand, and forms of bondage on the other.

The reforms of 1861 did not mark a caesura, in that "serfdom" did not exist as such before, and legal constraints on peasant mobility and peasant labour did not disappear after 1861. In particular, the obligations on peasants to work did not disappear in 1861, although they continued to become less onerous, as they had during the first half of the century. Before that date, labour as a service defined the legal status and obligations of peasants and manufacturing serf workers towards estate owners. Undue statutory labour services were linked to the entitlement of the estate owner and the civil status of the peasant. After 1861,

---

58 Koval'chenko, *Russkoe krepostnoe krest'ianstvo v pervoi polovine 19th v.*; Hoch and Augustine, "Tax Censuses and the Decline of the Serf Population".

temporary obligations remained in force until they might be redeemed, while, on the industrial labour market, labour was mostly conceived as a service, and criminal penalties regulated any breach of contract by the worker. Consequently, despite the view still widespread in comparative analyses of forced labour, we would claim that Russia does not constitute an exception in the global history of emancipation, where the usual pattern was a gradual ending of coerced forms of labour rather than their sudden abolition.[59] The question that prompts then concerns the specificity of the Russian path. We shall consider that first in relation to other areas experiencing the "second serfdom" and then in relation to the legal status of labour elsewhere in Europe.

The legal status of labour in the eighteenth and nineteenth centuries: a comparative approach

The conclusions we have reached for Russia are quite similar to those recently advanced for Brandenburg and Bohemia. In contrast to the traditional orientations of historiography, the period from 1650 to 1800 saw a fundamental transformation in *Gutsherrschaft* and its legal relations well before the reforms of the early nineteenth century.[60] In Brandenburg, villagers were not designated as "serfs" but rather as "subjects" *(Untertanen)*.[61] Forms of personal serfdom (*Leibeigenschaft*) did exist in German east Elbia, but, still, the term "unlimited labour services" actually entailed specific limits and numerous disputes related to those occurred in law courts between peasants and landlords as early as in the seven-

---

[59] On this, see *inter alia* Martin Klein (ed.), *Breaking the Chains: Slavery, Bondage, and Emancipation in Modern Africa and Asia* (Madison, WI, 1986); and P.C. Emmer (ed.), *Colonialism and Migration: Indentured Labour Before and After Slavery* (Dordrecht, 1986). A full bibliography on emancipation can be found in Rebecca Scott, Thomas Holt, Frederick Cooper, and Aims McGuinness, *Societies after Slavery: A Select Annotated Bibliography of Printed Sources on Cuba, Brazil, British Colonial Africa, South Africa and the British West Indies* (Pittsburgh, PA, 2004).
[60] Edgar Melton, "The Decline of Prussian *Gutsherrschaft* and the Rise of the Junker as Rural Patron, 1750–1806", *German History*, 12 (1994), pp. 334–350; *idem*, "Population Structure, the Market Economy, and the Transformation of *Gutsherrschaft*"; William Hagen, "Village Life in East-Elbian Germany and Poland, 1400–1800", in Tom Scott (ed.), *The Peasantries of Europe: From the Fourteenth to the Eighteenth Centuries* (London, 1998), pp. 145–190; and Sheilagh Ogilvie, "Communities and the 'Second Serfdom' in Early Modern Bohemia", *Past & Present*, 187 (2005), pp. 69–119.
[61] William W. Hagen, *Ordinary Prussians: Brandenburg Junkers and Villagers, 1500–1840* (Cambridge, 2002).

teenth century. The subjection of village farmers did not restrict their right to hold and transmit property, contract marriages, nor take action in courts of law.

That is to say that the translation of *Untertanen*, which really means "subject", as "serf" is misleading; the dependency the terms described was not a personal attribute but rather a consequence of occupying a farm from which unpaid labour service could be claimed.[62] The enlightened autocracy of Frederick II (1740–1786) took steps to abolish hereditary subjection in villages, widen the rural commoners' access to royal appellate courts, limit noble enclosure of village land, reduce labour services, and register the manorial obligations of villages in legally enforceable contracts.[63] The very fact that the law sanctioned heavy dependence of peasants on landlords was not inconsistent with the raising of legally "free" villages, something which was true not only of Brandenburg but also of other regions in east central Europe. For example, half of peasant households in late sixteenth-century Poland kept farm servants.[64] In Schleswig-Holstein, Mecklenburg, Swedish Pomerania, and Lusatia severe forms of personal dependency were widespread,[65] and the line separating the free from the subject farmers began to blur, especially where, as in Brandenburg-Prussia, commutation payments increasingly eclipsed the value of labour services.

As in Russia, the government encouraged changes in the legal status of peasants.[66] Legal intervention was important during the last quarter of the eighteenth century and it was not rare to find peasants taking their cases to the appellate court in Berlin.[67] In turn, that in itself gives further confirmation of the specific access to capitalism in the eastern Elbe region, where both proto-industry and peasants' multiple activity as well as the Junkers' "commodification" found in the evolving institutional environment a crucial resource.[68] At least from the point

---

[62] *Ibid.*, pp. 36–37.
[63] Hagen, "Village Life in East-Elbian Germany and Poland", p. 149.
[64] Robert Frost, "The Nobility of Poland-Lithuania, 1569–1795", in Hamish Scott (ed.), *The European Nobilities in the Seventeenth and Eighteenth Centuries*, II, Northern, Central and Eastern Europe, (London, 1995), pp. 183–222; Hagen, "Village Life in East-Elbian Germany and Poland"; *idem*, "Capitalism and the Countryside in Early Modern Europe: Interpretations, Models, Debates", *Agricultural History*, 62 (1988), pp. 13–47.
[65] Hagen, "Village Life in East-Elbian Germany and Poland", p. 175.
[66] Hartmut Harnisch, "Bäuerliche (Ökonomie und Mentalität unter den Bedingungen den ostelbischen Gutsherrschaft in den letzten Jahrzehnten vor Beginn der Agrarreformen", *Jahrbuch für Wirtschaftsgeschichte*, 24:3 (1989), pp. 87–108.
[67] Idem, *Kapitalistische Agrarreform und Industrielle Revolution* (Weimer, 1989).
[68] Terence J. Byres, *Capitalism from Above and Capitalism from Below: An Essay in Comparative Political Economy* (London, 1996); Shearer David Bowman, *Masters & Lords: Mid-19th-Century US Planters and Prussian Junkers* (New York, 1993); Peter Kriedte, *Peasants, Landlords and Merchant Capitalists: Europe and the World Economy, 1500–1800* (Cambridge, 1983).

of view of legal categories and practices, the notion of "second serfdom" has to be revisited, exactly as had been done with medieval serfdom after Marc Bloch's seminal paper in 1921. Bloch warned against the use of the word "serf" and the expression *serf de la glèbe*. He showed in particular that the concept was absent in the Middle Ages and, indeed, only enjoyed success after Montesquieu's *De l'Esprit des lois* in 1748. From that point of view, the *serf de la glèbe* was used to identify a largely stylized feudal system and to oppose it to an equally stylized liberal economic system.[69]

If all that is true, we might ask to what extent this heritage of labour as service migrated into the industrial notion and legal definition of labour. During the first half of the nineteenth century, patrimonial courts strongly sanctioned farm labourers who moved without their landowner's permission.[69][70] Prior to initial unification, Germany adopted rules similar to those in the French civil code, distinguishing the renting of work from the renting of service.[71] Most contracts emphasized service, and therefore the selling of "labour time", rather than the results of the work itself.[72] In keeping with that approach, significant criminal sanctions were provided for in the labour law of the main German states, in Prussia, and then in the Reich. In the 1845 Law on Industry, the criminal sanctions concerning labour were justified, exactly as they were in Great Britain, in terms of the freedom of economic activity and of contracts. More specifically in Prussia, employers treated unpunctual attendance as a withholding of labour power whose loss could be calibrated and precisely counterbalanced. That not only graduated the fine, it also gauged the value of the time lost.[73] The attention devoted to time was consistent with the notion of labour as service – work time was a continuous process of converting labour power into an output.

In Germany, major reforms took place at the turn of the twentieth century, linked to the emergence of the welfare state, the "social question" in public debate, and the rise of socialism. Criminal sanctions were repealed in 1869, but

---

[69] Marc Bloch, "Serf de la glèbe. Histoire d'une expression toute faite", *Revue historique*, 36 (1921), pp. 220–242.
[70] Monika Wienfort, "Administration of Private Law or Private Jurisdiction? The Prussian Patrimonial Courts, 1820–1848", in Willibald Steinmetz (ed.), *Private Law and Social Inequality in the Industrial Age: Comparing Legal Cultures in Britain, France, Germany and the United States* (Oxford, 2000), pp. 69–88.
[71] A. Supiot, *Critique du droit du travail* (Paris, 2002); V. Sims, "Good Faith in Contract Law: A Comparative Analysis of English and German Law" (unpublished Ph.D. dissertation, University of Cambridge, 2002).
[72] Richard Biernacki, *The Fabrication of Labor: Germany and Britain, 1640–1914* (Berkeley, CA, 1995).
[73] *Ibid.*, p. 113.

only for wage-earners in the industrial sector; they were maintained for domestics and agricultural labourers until the early twentieth century. With regard to labour, the new civil code adopted in 1896 bore only a superficial resemblance to previous codes and to the French model. The worker's loyalty corresponded to the employer's obligation to "take care" of his workers. The "new" labour contract shifted from contract and tort law to the law of persons, but in any event labour was still viewed as a service; technical rules and workshop regulations therefore remained important.[74] The change in labour from contract to status, from contractual freedom to social protection, took place while the link between labour and service provision was maintained.[75]

Was that link between labour and service specific to "central" and "eastern" Europe, or was it widespread in other European countries too? In view of those elements, and contrary to any common view, it would be difficult to compare Anglo-Saxon "free labour" to guilds and other types of constraint in France and Germany. Thus, from the sixteenth to the nineteenth century, rules on runaways were adopted not only in the colonial Americas for slaves and indentured workers, but also in Great Britain, where runaway workers, journeymen, and so on were submitted to quite similar rules under the Master and Servants Acts and the Statute of Artificers of 1562. Apprenticeship, advances in wages and raw materials, and also simple master-servant relations justified such provisions. From the sixteenth to the end of the nineteenth century, in Britain and Europe, free labour was, despite the existence of a contract, considered the "property" of the employer and a resource for the whole community to which the individual belonged.[76]

In Britain, the Statute of Labourers of 1350-1351 was enacted two years after the contract clause of the ordinance of labourers had been put in place.[77] The Statute of Artificers and Apprentices, adopted in 1562, controlled apprenticeship until 1814. The reform of 1814, usually presented as the rise of liberal market control, especially of labour, had no effect on the contractual aspects of the labour relationship. From the 1720s and throughout the nineteenth century, a number of laws were adopted to strengthen criminal sanctions in the event of breach of contract, especially by the worker, and penalties were laid down for

---

[74] S. Simitis, "The Case of the Employment Relationship: Elements of a Comparison", in Steinmetz, *Private Law and Social Inequality in the Industrial* Age, pp. 181–202.
[75] S. Simitis, "Juridification of Labor Relations", in G. Teubner (ed.), *Juridification of Social Spheres* (Berlin, 1987), pp. 113–161.
[76] Steinfeld, *Invention of Free Labor,* especially ch. 3; M. Postan, "The Chronology of Labour Services", *Transactions of the Royal Historical Society,* 20 (1937), pp. 169–193.
[77] Steinfeld, *Invention of Free Labor,* p. 30; Ann Kussmaul, *Servants in Husbandry in Early Modern England* (Cambridge, 1981).

those who refused a job.[78] On the whole, work-related criminal sanctions were reinforced between 1720 and 1850, being combined in the Master and Servants Acts. Wage-earners were considered domestic servants and were above all supposed to provide a service.[79] The labour of servants was usually conceived as a master's property.

All the same, one has to be careful when defining "servants". Like many lawyers, MacPherson refers to all forms of wage labour,[80] while Peter Laslett limits it to domestic servants.[81] Indeed, as Steinfeld has demonstrated, the word "servant" took on multiple meanings at different times, and the labour relationship did not consist of a single homogeneous legal status. For example, between the fourteenth and sixteenth centuries contemporaries limited the word "servant" to particular wage workers who resided with their master, so labourers and artificers were excluded from its meaning. However, from the sixteenth century onwards, "servant" was increasingly used to define any sort of wage-earner and thus included journeymen, artificers, and other workmen.[82] Confusingly, from the late eighteenth century, domestic servants were excluded by judicial decision from the scope of master and servants statutes, at least in England, although in the colonies they were usually included.[83] Special varieties of contract existed for mining, where an annual "bond" was in use, and shipping, where seamen s labour agreements were widespread.

The criminal measures accompanied the emphasis placed on contractual free will as a foundation of the labour market. Criminal sanctions were provided for because labour was free and the worker freely agreed to them. The measures were also applied to journeymen, unskilled workers, and in general whenever short-term contracts to improve output were involved. Insubordination or failure to comply with workshop production rules were also presented as a breach of contract without notice and as such were liable to criminal sanctions.[84] In other

---

78 D. Hay and N. Rogers, *Eighteenth-Century English Society: Shuttles and Swords* (Oxford, 1997); D. Hay, "Master and Servant in England: Using the Law in the Eighteenth and Nineteenth Centuries", in Steinmetz, *Private Law and Social Inequality in the Industrial Age*, pp. 227–264.
79 S. Deakin and F. Wilkinson, *The Law of the Labour Market: Industrialization, Employment, and Legal Evolution* (Oxford, 2005), p. 45.
80 C.B. Macpherson, *The Political Theory of Possessive Individualism: Hobbes to Locke* (Oxford, 1962).
81 Peter Laslett, *The World We Have Lost* (New York, 1965).
82 Steinfeld, *Invention of Free Labor*, pp. 17–22.
83 P. Craven and D. Hay, "The Criminalization of 'Free' Labour: Master and Servant in Comparative Perspective", *Slavery and Abolition*, 15:2 (1994), pp. 71–101.
84 D.C. Woods, "The Operation of the Master and Servants Act in the Black Country, 1858–1875", *Midland History*, 7 (1982), pp. 93–115; G. Barnsby, *Social Conditions in the Black Country, 1800–1900* (Wolverhampton, 1980).

words, application of criminal law to labour was aimed at reducing both turnover and supervision costs.[85] Monetary or raw material investments made by the employer were used to further justify such sanctions against wage-earners who left their jobs.[86] Increasingly harsh labour laws were in fact applied; as recent quantitative and qualitative analyses show, between 1750 and 1875 the rules governing labour and the interpretations of the courts became more unfavourable towards wage-earners.[87] At the same time, the master and servants laws reflected the concerns of the central state about social and political stability. The penal clauses and wage-recovery elements of the law were deeply embedded in poor law policy, the control of vagrancy, and the setting of wages.[88] In contrast, until 1844 employers were never threatened with imprisonment for breach of contract.[89]

Even if the poor law system of hiring was abolished in 1844, it was not until 1875 that criminal sanctions concerning labour contracts were abolished too and, even then, genuine measures to protect labour were not adopted until the next century,[90] including those pertaining to occupational industrial accidents.[91] It was not before the mid-nineteenth century that a general theory of contract employment informed new legislative activity. It is only in the decisions of the early twentieth century that the courts can first be seen applying the contractual

---

[85] Michael Huberman, *Escape from the Market: Negotiating Work in Lancashire* (Cambridge, 1996).
[86] Woods, "Operation of the Master and Servants Act"; M.R. Freedland, *The Contract of Employment* (Oxford, 1976); D. Galenson, "The Rise of Free Labor: Economic Change and the Enforcement of Service Contracts in England, 1351–1875", in J. James and M. Thomas (eds), *Capitalism in Context: Essays on Economic Development and Cultural Change in Honor of R.M. Hartwell* (Chicago, IL, 1994), pp. 114–137.
[87] Hay, "Master and Servant in England". See also Craven and Hay, "Criminalization of 'Free' Labour".
[88] Hay, "Master and Servant in England", p. 80.
[89] Douglas Hay, "England, 1562–1875: The Law and its Uses", in Douglas Hay and Paul Craven (eds), *Masters, Servants and Magistrates in Britain and the Empire, 1562–1955* (Chapel Hill, NC, 2004), pp. 59–116, 67.
[90] Huberman, *Escape from the Market*; Robert Steinfeld, *Coercion, Contract, and Free Labor in the Nineteenth Century* (Cambridge, 2001), p. 72; Deakin and Wilkinson, *Law of the Labour Market*; Steinmetz, *Private Law and Social Inequality in the Industrial Age*; S.F.C. Milsom, *A Natural History of the Common Law* (New York, 2003); M.R. Freedland, *The Personal Employment Contract* (Oxford, 2003).
[91] On the evolution of Britain's rules on workers' health, see P.W. Bartrip and S. Burman, *The Wounded Soldiers of Industry: Industrial Compensation Policy, 1833–1897* (Oxford, 1983); P.W. Bartrip, *Workmen's Compensation in Twentieth Century Britain: Law, History and Social Policy* (Aldershot, 1987); and E.P. Hennock, *British Social Reform and German Precedents: The Case of Social Insurance, 1880–1914* (Oxford, 1987).

model, which they had developed for the middle classes, to industrial workers too, as well as to agricultural labourers and domestic servants.[92]

Thus, the long-term movement of labour and its rules in Great Britain hardly confirms the traditional argument that early labour freedom in the country supported the industrial revolution. On the contrary, the latter was accompanied by increasingly tough regulations and criminal sanctions with regard to workers. The removal of criminal sanctions from the individual employment relationship in the 1870s was soon followed by the first legislative interventions of the welfare state, beginning with the Employers' Liability Act of 1880. Before that time, the idea of contract of employment as a mechanism for expressing reciprocal obligations of employers and employees had developed only for professional and managerial workers. Indeed, this distinction ceased only when collective bargaining and social legislation extended their influence over the employment relationship.[93]

The process is particularly clear in the legal history of the indenture contract. As Steinfeld has brilliantly demonstrated, indentured servitude has been considered primarily a form of contractual freedom. Under colonial and later state statutes related to servants, masters could recover runaway servants, were authorized to administer corporal punishment, and could withhold their consent to their servants marrying.[94] In political imageries, although not in law, indenture ceased to be considered a form of free contract at the same moment as "serfdom" was clearly identified in the "East". In fact, indenture was at the same time fully embedded in the legal culture of the Master and Servants Act and not so far removed from forms of coerced labour in Russia. At the same time, its evolution was linked to that of criminal penalties in labour contracts. By perhaps the mid-eighteenth century the contracts of ordinary native-born adult workers could no longer be enforced by recourse to criminal law, but the contracts of white imported indentured servants still could, although by the 1830s those contracts too were no longer likewise enforceable. Only minors and black people continued to be exposed to criminal sanctions, and those practices regarding black people were not eliminated until the beginning of the twentieth century.[95]

At the same time, the legal provisions interacted with the economic features of indenture. From that perspective, one can distinguish a first phase, from the

---

[92] Deakin and Wilkinson, *Law of the Labour Market*, p. 80.
[93] *Ibid.*, p. 107.
[94] Steinfeld, *Invention of Free Labor*, p. 11. See also Richard Brandon Morris, *Government and Labor in Early America* (New York, 1946), and David Galenson, *White Servitude in Colonial America: An Economic Analysis* (Cambridge, 1981).
[95] Steinfeld, *Coercion, Contract, and Free Labor*.

seventeenth century until 1830, from a second phase, which lasted from the nineteenth and into the twentieth century. The first phase mostly involved some 300,000 indentured Europeans, occurred when slavery was still in place, and was organized mainly by merchants. Indentured labour went to tobacco plantations, and into manufacturing. The second phase involved 2.5 million non-Europeans, mostly Indians and Chinese but also including Japanese, Africans, and Pacific islanders, and indentured workers were employed in sugar production and manufacture. Unlike the first phase, they barely entered the "free" world at the end of their contract and retained their "unfree" engagement.[96] However, within this common European, if not quite global, link between labour and service, France seems to be a partial exception, not so much as regards the notion of labour, but in the lack of criminal sanctions against breach of contract.

A French exception?

In fact, in France, the notion of a work contract, and hence that of a "wage-earner" as we know it today, did not exist until the end of the nineteenth century. In eighteenth-century France, labour was considered a lease.[97] Jurisprudence gave no definition of wage as there was no clear difference in status between hiring out labour and hiring out a commodity.[98] The case of domestic servants was different because they were engaged for a longer period, usually a year or more, and their wage was the price of their engagement; the law at the time often considered their position akin to slavery.[99] In that context, the act of apprenticeship was analogous to the primordial alienation of natural liberty.[100]

Agricultural labourers were not necessarily journeymen, but were often engaged as servants and as such they were supposed to complete a given task,

---

[96] David Northrup, *Indentured Labor in the Age of Imperialism, 1834–1922* (Cambridge, 1995); and Galenson, *White Servitude in Colonial America*. See also Michael L. Bush, *Servitude in Modern Times* (Cambridge, 2000), and Hugh Tinker, *A New System of Slavery: Export of Indian Labour Overseas, 1830–1920* (London, 1974).
[97] Jean Domat, *Les lois civiles dans leur ordre naturel* (1st edn, 1697), reprinted in *Œuvres* (Paris, 1835), I. R. Pothier, *Traité du contrat de louage* (Paris, 1861).
[98] M. Sonenscher, *Work and Wages: Natural Law, Politics and the Eighteenth-Century French Trades* (Cambridge, 1989), p. 70.
[99] *La domesticité est une sorte d'esclavage*, Encyclopédie méthodique, Jurisprudence, IX (Paris, 1789), p. 15. On this see Sara Maza, *Servants and Masters in Eighteenth-Century France: The Uses of Loyalty* (Princeton, NJ, 1983), and Jean-Pierre Gutton, *Domestiques et serviteurs dans la France de l'Ancien Régime* (Paris, 1981).
[100] Sonenscher, *Work and Wages*, p. 75.

such as the year's harvest.[101] As in Russia and other countries in modern times and in the nineteenth century too, supervision was the biggest difficulty in the organization of labour in agriculture. The problems of supervising and motivating servants were compounded by the possibility that the servants could leave. As Philip Hoffman has stressed, historians have ignored such mobility in the early modern countryside, largely because demographers have noted the tendency of peasants to marry in their home villages. Various contractual arrangements sought to address the problem, with for example some tasks, such as some types of harvesting, being payable through piecework rates, while honesty and assiduousness could be rewarded with a wage raise.[102] Most important, as in Russia, in modern France between the sixteenth and eighteenth centuries year servants and labourers had the right to move, with no penalties nor fees to pay – apart from in the period around St Martin's Day (11 November), between the end of the great labours of the autumn and the beginning of winter.[103]

As in Britain, in France indentured labour in the colonies (*engagés*) developed on the basis of the ordinary free labour contract. Indentured workers were subject to criminal sanctions, for instance "desertion" applied not only to convicts, but to ordinary indentured workers too, and the contracts of indentured individuals could be sold on. During the seventeenth and eighteenth centuries indentured labour targeted the Antilles and Canada,[104] with 5,200 indentured servants leaving from La Rochelle alone for the Antilles between 1660 and 1715. However, that is far less than the estimated 210,000 servants and indentured emigrants leaving the British Isles to work in the New World colonies between 1630 and 1700.[105]

The French Revolution abolished slavery, but only for a few years; its ultimate abolition came about only in 1848 and, even after that date, coerced labour was in use widely in the colonies, while indentured labour saw a revival. The contracts of *engagés* for Réunion, for example, included *corvées* and limited the length of the working day to between nine and ten hours, but the individual *engagé* was

---

[101] Jean-Marc Moriceau, "Les Baccanals ou grèves des moissonneurs en pays de France (seconde moitié du XVIIIe siècle)", in Jean Nicolas (ed.), *Mouvements populaires et conscience sociale* (Paris, 1985), pp. 420–433.
[102] Philip T. Hoffman, *Growth in a Traditional Society: The French Countryside, 1450–1815* (Princeton, NJ, 1996), pp. 45–46.
[103] Ibid., p. 47.
[104] Louise Dechêne, *Habitants et marchands de Montréal au XVIIe siècle* (Paris, 1974); Gabriel Debien, *Les engagés pour les Antilles, 1634–1715* (Paris, 1952); and Frederic Mauro, "French Indentured Servants for America, 1500–1800", in Emmer, *Colonialism and Migration*, pp. 83–104.
[105] Galenson, *White Servitude in Colonial America*.

supposed to be at the master's full disposal.[106] Such provisions were not necessarily "illegal" because, although the French Revolution suppressed lifetime engagement, it did not abolish the notion of labour as service. Instead of a work contract, there were two contracts provided for by the civil code: the *louage d'ouvrage* – renting of work in the sense of a piece of work or completed task – and the *louage de service* – the renting of "service".

The first type of contract considered the worker as an independent artisan who provided his own tools and was expected to produce a certain result within a certain time, while by contrast the second covered the provision of a "service" for a certain amount of time, and was a legacy of the relationship between service and domesticity characteristic of the *ancien régime*.[107] When the renting of work was involved, the contract was often a written one, and the owner could terminate it by compensating the contractor. In the case of an accident, the employer had no objective liability, only a liability for negligence. However, when the renting of service was involved, the employer was the real contracting authority if the question of his liability arose in the event of an accident.[108] The contract would most probably have been oral, and whereas the employer's word would have been sufficient for legal purposes, the wage-earner had to provide written proof. In any case, whether renting of work or renting of service was concerned, in accordance with the principle of contractual freedom, a judge was not allowed to intervene in setting wages.[109] In that context, labourers were considered most often as people rented for service and their task was relatively unimportant compared to the time span of their renting.[110] However, that well-understood legal and economic classification was not always respected, and so it was possible that labourers might be engaged for a certain task over a certain period. That was then de facto *louage*

---

[106] Hubert Gerbeau, "Engagées and Coolies on Réunion Island: Slavery's Masks and Freedom's Constraints", in Emmer, *Colonialism and Migration*, pp. 209–236.

[107] A. Cottereau, "Droit et bon droit. Un droit des ouvriers instauré, puis évincé par le droit du travail", *Annales*, 57 (2002), pp. 1521–1560.

[108] F. Gueugnon, M.C. Revol, and E. Serverin, *Une analyse sociologique de jurisprudence : la réparation des accidents de travail, 1840–1913* (Lyons, 1983).

[109] Cass. Civile, 12 December 1853, Sirey, *Recueil générale des lois et des arrets* (1854), I, 133.

[110] For local labour relations and customs during the revolutionary period: AN (National Archives) F 12 1516 to 1544; AN F 10 451-2. Parliamentary reports on local customs in 1848 are in *AN C844–958*; parliamentary enquiry of 1870 is in *AN C 1157–61*. For nineteenth-century collections of local customs, see for example: *Usages locaux ayant force de loi dans le département de la Meuse* (Bar-le-Duc, 1900); I. Bertrand, *Usages locaux du département de la Haute-Loire* (Le Puy, 1865); A. Dumay, *Usages locaux du département de la Côte d'Or* (1884); R. Mosse, *Les usages locaux de l'arrondissement d'Orange* (Orange, 1914); J.M.P. Limon, *Recueil des usages locaux en vigueur dans le finistère* (Quimper, 1852); and H. Watrin, *Département de l'Eure-et-Loire: usages des quatre arrondissements et notions de droit usuel* (Chartres, 1910).

d'ouvrage, even if it was not admitted as such, being in fact practised to escape the legal constraints of de jure *louage d'ouvrage*.

Day labourers were especially widespread in the Midi and Mediterranean area, in Alsace-Lorraine, in Île-de-France, and Picardy. In 1862 day labourers were estimated to comprise about half of the four million wage-earners in agriculture. Thirty years later the number of day labourers had fallen to 1.2 million, mostly as a result of the sharp decline between 1862 and 1892 in the number of labourers possessing small farms.[111] In turn, servants (*domestiques*) accounted for an increasing proportion of hired people in agriculture. Their contracts were supposed to last about a year, or sometimes six or eight months, in which their circumstances were different from those of domestic servants, who were engaged for far longer periods. According to most local customs, servants were "subject to the will of the master", who owned as his property all the labour time of the servant during the entire period of service. The servants' *gage* (not "wages") thus took the form of a lump sum.

The value of the *gage* and tasks were the most common subjects of litigation, as labourers and servants quite often threatened to go to court, though they rarely did so. However, when they did, they had a good chance of winning their case. Rural employers then accused justices of the peace of being "on the side of labourers and servants",[112] just as industrial employers accused *prud'hommes* of "sitting with workers".[113] Any breach of contract for "serious reasons" – which might range from illness to insubordination, which included "unkindness" – was punished by civil penalties. That was one of the major outcomes of the Revolution and a sharp difference between France and everywhere else in the nineteenth century. Even if most wage-earners were servants, they were no longer subject to criminal sanction in labour disputes. That does not mean that criminal rules disappeared from labour regulation.

Labour relations and labour mobility were regulated by specific controls connected to the workbook *(livret ouvrier)*. That record was kept by the employer and served a twofold purpose: from the standpoint of the public authorities, it was used to guarantee public order and keep track of workforce movements; from the employer's point of view, it served to control the workforce and protect the

---

111 Jean-Luc Mayaud, "Salariés agricoles et petite propriété dans la France du XIXe siècle", in Ronald Hubscher and Jean-Claude Farcy (eds), *La moisson des autres* (Paris, 1996). pp. 29–56.
112 Yvonne Crebouw, "Droit et obligations des journaliers et des domestiques, droits et obligations des maîtres", in Hubscher and Farcy, *La moisson des autres*, pp. 181–200.
113 Cottereau, "Droit et bon droit".

employer from poor conduct on the part of wage-earners and other employers.[114] Indeed, in order to be taken on, a wage-earner had to present his workbook along with proof of discharge from his previous employer. That discharge was provided only if the wage-earner was not indebted, through an advance on wages, or in the case of bespoke workers, through an advance on raw materials. Such workers received raw materials from their employer; the discharge prevented the untimely departure of those workers or fraud in relation to raw materials.[115]

At the same time, the *livret* also constituted an instrument to control relationships between employers, particularly the possibility of one employer "poaching" workers from another. Without the approval of the first employer, as evidenced from the *livret*, no transfer could take place without that potentially leading to a legal dispute.[116] Disputes often fell within the scope of unfair competition. The notion of poaching was thus linked to apprenticeship. Employers did not want to waste their investment in training their workers, so discharge letters served to curb worker mobility and encourage agreements between employers. The letters testified to the worker's debt to his employer, whether in the form of an advance on wages, an apprenticeship contract, or the rental of tools or machines, and had to be signed and countersigned by all the employers involved.[117]

The situation changed slowly over the course of the century. Beginning in the 1840s, new labour legislation was enacted, first with regard to child labour, then working hours and working conditions in general.[118] On the other hand,

---

114 *Répertoire Dalloz*, XXVII, p. 397, n. 1 (1852); rapport Bertrand sur le projet de loi du 26 juin 1854, *Dalloz* (1854), p. 119.

115 Henri Bernard, *Le Livret ouvrier* (Paris, 1903); Jean-François Germe, "Le livret ouvrier: mobilité et identification des salaries", in Robert Salais and Laurent Thévenot (eds), *Le travail. Marchés, règles, conventions* (Paris, 1986), pp. 357–370; Jean-Pierre Le Crom, "Le livret ouvrier au XIXe siècle entre assujettissement et reconnaissance de soi", in Yvon Le Gall, Dominique Gaurier, and Pierre-Yannick Legal (eds), *Du droit du travail aux droits de l'humanité. Études offerts à Philippe-Jean Hesse* (Rennes, 2003), pp. 91–100; J. Le Goff, *Du silence à la parole* (Paris, 2004), p. 59; A. Dewerpe, "En avoir ou pas? A propos du livrer ouvrier", paper presented at the conference, "Time and Labor Constraints in France and Japan", held at the Maison Franco-Japonaise, Tokyo, June 2007.

116 Cour de Douai, Sirey, *Recueil générale des lois et des arrets* (1874), II, 184; *Dalloz* (1874), II, 114.

117 C. Sabel and J. Zeitlin (eds), *World of Possibilities: Flexibility and Mass Production in Western Industrialization* (Cambridge, 1997), and especially the essay by A. Cottereau, "The Fate of Collective Manufacturers in the Industrial World: The Silk Industries of Lyons and London, 1800–1850", pp. 75–152; G. Gayot, *Les draps de Sedan (1640–1870)* (Paris, 1998); A. Cottereau, "Industrial Tribunals and the Establishment of a Kind of Common Law of Labour in Nineteenth-Century France", in Steinmetz, *Private Law and Social Inequality in the Industrial Age*, pp. 203–226.

118 C. Lemercier, "Apprentissage", in A. Stanziani (ed.), *Dictionnaire historique de l'économie-droit, XVIIIe–XXe siècles* (Paris, 2007), pp. 23–34; and Y. Lequin, "Apprenticeship in Nine-

contractual relationships in the strict sense evolved much more slowly. The "total subordination" of servant to master and the unequal penalties they faced in cases of breach of contract had been under attack since the middle of the century, but attempts to change the civil code failed. The argument raised by employers associations was the same as that used in relation to other forms of subordination and coerced labour, including indenture, namely the "voluntary" character of the engagement. However, that argument would become outdated, and important changes would occur. The growing importance of trade unions, particularly after the repeal of the law against "coalition" in 1864 and the law on associations of 1884, the strong competition of the city in the rural urban market,[119] and the reorientation of jurisprudence all contributed to the increasing identification of labour employment with renting of service.[120]

Such a shift would not have been possible without the activity of the other branch of labour competition – "coalitions". Coalitions were forbidden in 1791, with the official aim of preserving competition in the labour market,[121] an attitude that prevailed in both public debates, economic thought, and jurisprudence right up to the mid-nineteenth century.[122] The notion of coalition as a crime would be eliminated only in 1864. The main supporters of repealing the law against coalition maintained that the criminalization of coalition was a burden not only on workers, but on employers too, who suffered from a lack of coordination. The offi-

---

teenth-Century France: A Continuing Tradition or a Break with the Past?", in Steven Laurence Kaplan and Cynthia J. Koepp (eds), *Work in France: Representations, Meaning, Organization, and Practice* (Ithaca, NY, 1986), pp. 457–474; Steven L. Kaplan and Gilles Postel-Vinay, "L'apprentissage: un destin?", *Le Gnomon*, 126 (2000), pp. 23–24; *Revue d'histoire moderne et contemporaine*, dossier "Apprentissages, XVIe–XXe siècles", 40:3 (1993); Olivier Tholozan, "Le débat parlementaire de 1851 sur le contrat d'apprentissage ou la liberté contractante acclimatée", *Cahiers de l'IRT*, 9 (2001), pp. 207–222; J. Freyssinet, "Hétérogénéité du travail et organisation des travailleurs", fascicule 3, La révolution industrielle, IRES Working Papers, January 2005.

119 Yvonne Crebouw, *Salaires et salariés agricoles en France des débuts de la Révolution aux approches du XXe siècle* (Paris, 1986).
120 Cottereau, "Droit et bon droit".
121 AN BB 24, 100–115: coalition ouvrières à Darnetal, Seine-Inférieure, en septembre 1830; BB 24, 195–218: coalitions d'ouvriers à Paris, le 1e septembre 1840, contre l'introduction de machines anglaises; BB 24 327–347: coalitions et troubles à Lyon, bris de machines et métiers, fin février 1848.
122 "Le commerce et le monopole. Nouvelle lettre de M. Jobard en réponse à des observations de M. Joseph Garnier", *Journal des économistes*, 11 (15 January 1855), pp. 100–105; "Les vingt questions de M. Jobard sur la concurrence, suivies de vingt réponses par M. Joseph Garnier", *Journal des économistes*, 12 (1855), pp. 247–256; "Chronique économique", *Journal des économistes*, 2nd series, 125 (May 1864), pp. 321–323; "Des moyens de remédier aux abus des coalitions", *Journal des économistes*, 75 (March 1872), pp. 477–486.

cial attitude was widely supposed to encourage political extremism.[123] Once the crime of coalition had been abolished, the question arose of the link between coalitions and the manner in which contracts were made. Was it lawful for a union to press an employer into dismissing a worker who had been freely employed? The Cour de Cassation decided that the defendant (the union) was liable for damages to the plaintiff, the court apparently seeing the union's threat as a legal means directed towards an illegal end.[124]

That is to say that in France, the emergence of the general idea of unfair competition was possible only at the moment when competition on the labour market gained a new dimension, when criminal punishments for coalition were abolished and the new labour contract replaced the old *louage d'ouvrage* and *louage de service*. That turning point took place in a context marked by the emergence of the welfare state. The protection of labour as an instrument to defend capitalism against the rise of socialism was confirmed at the turn of the century and culminated first in the official recognition of trade unions (1884), then in the suppression of the *livret ouvrier* (1890), and finally in the law on industrial accidents (1898), which required employers to pay part of the premiums for wage-earners' insurance. Those elements converged in the labour code of 1910,[125] which defined the labour contract as a contract of subordination, as we know it today. The specification of causes for dismissal or grounds for breach of contract, the central political role played by trade unions, and the very definition of subordination were therefore turn-of-the-century inventions.

To sum up, the "French exception" was more limited than has usually been asserted. Eighteenth-century rules included lifetime engagement and service; criminal penalties for breach of contract were reduced, but during most of the nineteenth century they persisted for workers' coalitions and indentured labourers.

---

[123] E. Ollivier, *Commentaire de la loi du 15 mai 1864 sur les coalitions* (Paris, 1864), pp. 52–53.
[124] Cassation civile, 22 June 1892, Sirey, *Recueil générale des lois et des arrets* (1893), I, 42. This case was discussed on appeal by Chambéry's Cour d'Appel, which upheld the ruling of the first tribunal (14 May 1893, Sirey, *Recueil générale des lois et des arrets* (1893), II, 139; *Dalloz* (1893), II, 191). See also the ruling by the Cour de Cassation on 9 June 1896, *Dalloz* (1896), I, 582. For a discussion of this case, see Vernon Palmer, "A Comparative Study (From a Common Law Perspective) of the French Action for Wrongful Interference with Contract", *American Journal of Comparative Law*, 40 (1992), pp. 297–342.
[125] C. Didry, *Naissance de la convention collective* (Paris, 2002).

Conclusion

Between the sixteenth and the end of the nineteenth century, the barrier between freedom and bondage was not only moveable and negotiable, it also thought of differently from how we are used to thinking of it today. In fact, in modern times and until the end of the nineteenth century, labour was submitted to serious legal constraints, usually justified by reference to the "debt" or the "deed" the worker, or the peasant, had contracted with both master and community. Such things encompassed apprenticeship, wage advances, land, raw materials and seeds, and so on. "Runaways" included not only slaves and indentured workers but "serfs", servants, and apprentices too, and all of them could find themselves subject to criminal as well as civil penalties. They were neither "free economic actors" choosing their status as entrepreneurs or workers in the "neoclassical" sense, nor were they "proletarians" in the Marxist sense.

In reality, in most "Western" countries labour was similar to service and wage conditions resembled those of domestic servants, with numerous constraints imposed on work mobility. The material and living conditions of "free" workers and servants were not necessarily better than those of "serfs," although the difference lay in the scope lowly people had to seize the law and use it to improve their situation. In fact, France was the first country to repeal criminal sanctions against workers and to make "labour" fundamentally different from "service". However, that "exception" held good much less for rural labourers and indentured workers in the colonies, and was partially nullified by an interdiction of workers' coalitions. In turn, Britain experienced a long-term tradition of master-servant relations crossing the boundaries of the medieval, modern, and contemporary periods. Once again, free and unfree forms of labour were much more in concert than in opposition; the close link between the status of servants and that of indentured labourers confirms the point.

At the opposite end of the scale, in Russia and Poland, landlords exploited existing rules in order to create an informal market for "serfs". Even if legal constraints on labour were harsher there than in Britain or in France, peasants and workers were not entirely deprived of legal rights, and they did manage to exploit their legal protection in the courts. In Russia, changes of legal status occurred on a huge scale before the official emancipation of 1861.

Throughout the period studied here, free and unfree forms of labour were therefore much less in opposition than in action side by side, and many forms of unfree labour were actually still considered "free" engagements. At a global level, in Europe and its colonies, in Russia, and in Asia, the institutional and economic dynamics from the seventeenth to the end of the nineteenth century, which saw agrarian, consumption, commercial and the first industrial revolutions, to say nothing of the proto-industrial dynamics they witnessed, were therefore most firmly based upon this peculiar classification of labour and labour institutions. It was only at the turn of the twentieth century that the idea of labour as service definitely collapsed, criminal penalties disappeared, and coercion became incompatible with the new notion of the labour contract, at least in Europe and the United States. By contrast, Russia, Asia, and the European colonies would experience new forms of heavy and widespread bondage.

The End of Wage Labour?

Michael Denning
Wageless Life*

Under capitalism, the only thing worse than being exploited is not being exploited. Since the beginnings of the wage-labour economy, wageless life has been a calamity for those dispossessed of land, tools and means of subsistence. Expelled from work, the wageless also became invisible to science: political economy, as Marx noted in the earliest formulations of his critique of the discipline, 'does not recognize the unemployed worker': 'The rascal, swindler, beggar, the unemployed, the starving, wretched and criminal workingman – these are figures who do not exist for political economy but only for other eyes, those of the doctor, the judge, the gravedigger, and bum-bailiff, etc; such figures are spectres outside its domain.'[1] These days, Marxism – more often seen as an example of political economy than as its critique – and other labour-based analyses face the same objection. Understandings built upon wage labour cannot, we are told, account for the reality lived by the most numerous and wretched of the world's population: those without wages, those indeed without even the hope of wages. Bare life, wasted life, disposable life, precarious life, superfluous life: these are among the terms used to describe the inhabitants of a planet of slums. It is not the child in the sweatshop that is our most characteristic figure, but the child in the streets, alternately predator and prey.

In face of this situation, neither of the classic Marxist designations for the wageless – the reserve army of labour or the lumpenproletariat – seems adequate. For some, only a theory of citizenship and exclusion from it, or rights and their absence, can capture this reality: to speak of labour is to speak of the already enfranchised. Others have turned to a biopolitics or necropolitics of bare existence. Neither of these alternatives is persuasive. Though the struggle for social and cultural inclusion as well as political citizenship is vital in a world of *sans-papiers*, too often the theoretical battles over citizenship and human rights remain caught in fantasies of sovereignty. On the other hand, the rhetoric of life and death sometimes has a false immediacy, seeing a state of exception or emergency in what is unfortunately a state of normality. To speak repeatedly of bare

---

* This article was first published in New Left Review 66 (2010), pp. 79–97.
1 Karl Marx and Frederick Engels, *Collected Works*, New York 1975ff (hereafter MECW), Volume 3, p. 284. This essay was originally written as part of the Yale Working Group on Globalization and Culture. I would like to thank the other members for their suggestions and criticisms, and Achille Mbembe for his response to an earlier text at the Wits Institute for Social and Economic Research, University of the Witwatersrand, South Africa, 22 February 2006.

life and superfluous life can lead us to imagine that there really are disposable people, not simply that they are disposable in the eyes of state and market.

Moreover, bare life is not without practical activity. A critical account of living and making a living under capitalist imperatives must, I believe, begin not from the accumulation of capital but from its other side, the accumulation of labour. They are, dialectically, the same: as Marx put it, 'Accumulation of capital is therefore multiplication of the proletariat.'[2] But to approach the issue from the point of view of capital is, as Hegel and Marx might put it, one-sided. A number of contemporary critics of political economy have noted this imbalance. Michael Lebowitz argues that Marx's book on capital was meant to be accompanied by one on wage labour; in *The Limits to Capital*, David Harvey describes 'Marx's rather surprising failure to undertake any systematic study of the processes governing the production and reproduction of labour power itself' as 'one of the most serious of all the gaps in Marx's own theory'.[3]

In what follows, I will suggest that we need a similar reversal regarding wage labour. Wageless life has almost always been seen as a situation of lack, the space of exclusion: the unemployed, the informal. I do not claim to solve this semantic problem: my own working vocabulary – the wageless – is a parallel construction. However, I want to insist that we decentre wage labour in our conception of life under capitalism. The fetishism of the wage may well be the source of capitalist ideologies of freedom and equality, but the employment contract is not the founding moment. For capitalism begins not with the offer of work, but with the imperative to earn a living. Dispossession and expropriation, followed by the enforcement of money taxes and rent: such is the idyll of 'free labour'. In those rare moments of modern emancipation, the freed people – from slavery, serfdom and other forms of coerced labour – have never chosen to be wage labourers. There may be a 'propensity to truck, barter and exchange one thing for another', as Adam Smith put it, but there is clearly no propensity to get a job.

Rather than seeing the bread-winning factory worker as the productive base on which a reproductive superstructure is erected, imagine the dispossessed proletarian household as a wageless base of subsistence labour – the 'women's work' of cooking, cleaning and caring – which supports a superstructure of migrant wage seekers who are ambassadors, or perhaps hostages, to the wage economy. These migrations may be short in distance and in interval – the daily streetcars or buses from tenement to factory, apartment block to office, that will come to be called 'commuting' – or they may be extended to the yearly proletarian globe-hopping

---

[2] Karl Marx, *Capital*, vol. 1, Harmondsworth 1976, p. 764.
[3] Michael Lebowitz, *Beyond* Capital: *Marx's Political Economy of the Working Class*, New York 2003; David Harvey, *The Limits to Capital*, Chicago 1982, p. 163.

of seasonal workers by steamship, railroad and automobile, as well as the radical separation of airborne migration linked by years of remittances and phone calls. Unemployment precedes employment, and the informal economy precedes the formal, both historically and conceptually. We must insist that 'proletarian' is not a synonym for 'wage labourer' but for dispossession, expropriation and radical dependence on the market. You don't need a job to be a proletarian: wageless life, not wage labour, is the starting point in understanding the free market.

Emergence of unemployment

In this essay, I want to explore the lineaments of wageless life over the past century by offering a genealogy of two key representations which not only name and seek to regulate it, but draw a dramatic line between its conceptions in capitalism's imperial metropoles and its periphery: the figures of unemployment and the informal sector. The former was the founding trope of twentieth-century social democracy, invented in the midst of the great economic crises which gripped the industrial capitalisms of the North Atlantic and reverberated across their colonial territories. It displaced a host of earlier conceptions of the poor, the idle and the dangerous, and became a central part of state and popular discourse through the next century, particularly during the moments of mass unemployment: the Great Depression of the 1930s and the Great Recession of the 1970s. On the other hand, the term 'informal sector' was coined in the early 1970s to reckon with the mass of wageless life in the newly independent Third World, which seemed to escape the categories of employment and unemployment alike. It too displaced earlier conceptions – perhaps most notably that of the lumpenproletariat figured by Frantz Fanon's *Wretched of the Earth* – and continues to be part of official and unofficial discourse.

An older institutional history might say that the welfare state was created in response to unemployment: the spectre of the unemployed returns with every depression and recession, as illustrators and photographers try to represent the absence of work in icons ranging from Victorian cartoonist Tom Merry's 'The Meeting of the Unemployed' to Dorothea Lange's 'White Angel Breadline'. But a more recent biopolitical history suggests that the emerging social state invented unemployment in the process of normalizing and regulating the market in labour.[4] The word itself emerged just when the phenomenon became the object

---

4 Biopolitical readings of unemployment are in a way the product of the intellectual upheaval triggered by the third wave of mass unemployment; two landmark texts both date from 1986:

of state knowledge production in the long economic downturn of the 1880s and 1890s. The term was first used in English in 1887, when the chief of Massachusetts's Bureau of Labor Statistics, Carroll D. Wright, attempted to count the unemployed, triggering a statistical practice that became central to the modern state, and by the following decade was in common use. The earliest theoretical treatment, the 1895 article 'The Meaning and Measure of "Unemployment"' by the liberal economist J. A. Hobson (best known for his influential analysis of imperialism), set the agenda for a century of debate: how does one define and measure it? The French word for unemployed, *chômeur*, dates from the same era, and the German equivalent, *Arbeitslosigkeit*, was rarely used before the 1890s. Indeed, as John Garraty, the author of the still-standard *Unemployment in History*, points out, Marx himself did not use the expression. In *Capital*, as well as in the passage from the 1844 manuscripts quoted earlier, Marx writes of *die Unbeschäftigten* – the not-busy, the unoccupied in one English translation – rather than *die Arbeitslosen*, the contemporary term for the unemployed.[5]

The modern notion of unemployment depended on the normalization of employment, the intricate process by which participation in labour markets is made ordinary. As employers make rules, workers insist on customary practices, while courts, legislatures and factory inspectors set standards. 'The creation of a normal working day [ein *Normalarbeitstag*]', Marx argued, 'is, therefore, the product of a protracted civil war, more or less dissembled, between the capitalist class and the working class.' Indeed, he insisted that: 'in place of the pompous catalogue of the "inalienable rights of man" comes the modest Magna Carta of a legally limited working day.'[6]

Normalizing employment made possible the normalization of unemployment in at least three senses. First, to be unemployed was to lose one's usual employment – and indeed the first forms of unemployment protection came from trade unions that tried to maintain the going wage rate by offering members out-of-work benefits. In his discussion of unemployment and government William Walters proposes that 'the status of "out-of-work" was actually invented by trade unionism'. The second form of normalization arose as the wageless began to meet and march as the unemployed. The canonical starting point is the famous Feb-

---

Robert Salais, *L'invention du chômage: histoire et transformations d'une catégorie en France des années 1890 aux années 1980*, Paris 1986, and Alexander Keyssar, *Out of Work: The First Century of Unemployment in Massachusetts*, Cambridge 1986. See also Christian Topalov, *Naissance du chômeur: 1880–1910*, Paris 1994. A more recent study that draws on this work is William Walters, *Unemployment and Government: Genealogies of the Social*, Cambridge 2000.

5 John Garraty, *Unemployment in History*, New York 1978, pp. 109, 4; J. A. Hobson, 'The Meaning and Measure of "Unemployment"', *Contemporary Review* 67, March 1895.

6 Marx, *Capital*, pp. 303, 307.

ruary 1886 London riot. A Tory-led Fair Trade League had called a meeting of the unemployed in Trafalgar Square that attracted 20,000 jobless building- and dock-workers; when the Social Democratic Federation led part of the crowd down Pall Mall, windows were smashed, shops were looted and London, according to *The Times*, was in a panic. Similar demonstrations continued and grew through 1887, culminating that November in Bloody Sunday, the protest against coercion in Ireland, in which police attacked demonstrators and three were killed.[7]

Finally, unemployment was integrated into the work of turn-of-the-century theorists such as Hobson and William Beveridge, who argued that it was not a matter of individual depravity or idleness but was a normal and unavoidable aspect of industrial society. 'Personal causes, no doubt, explain in a large measure who are the individuals that shall represent the 10 per cent "unemployed"', Hobson argued, 'but they are in no true sense even contributory causes of "unemployment"'. These analyses built on the earlier notion that capitalism created a reserve army of labour, a concept often taken to be distinctively Marxist since it appears in *Capital's* discussion of capitalism's relative surplus population. However, Marx was simply adopting the rhetoric of the British labour movement. Radicals, particularly the Chartists and Fourierist associationists, imagined the new factory workers as great industrial armies, and this common trope led the Chartist leader Bronterre O'Brien to write of a reserve army of labour in the *Northern Star* in 1839. The young Engels picked up that image in *The Condition of the Working Class in England in 1844*, and Marx would invoke the metaphor occasionally, distinguishing between the active and reserve armies of the working class. By the end of the nineteenth century, it was part of the common sense understanding of unemployment: by 1911, even the Massachusetts Bureau of Statistics of Labor could conclude that, 'however prosperous conditions may be, there is always a "reserve army" of the unemployed'.[8]

Risk and relief

This normalization of unemployment was the basis for the great social-democratic techniques that sought to contain the spectre of wageless life. The first

---

7 Walters, *Unemployment*, p. 18. See also Gareth Stedman Jones, *Outcast London*, New York 1984, pp. 291–6. In his letters Engels was very critical of the SDF's 'bunkum about social revolution'. His characterization of their procession as merely comprised of 'idlers, police spies and rogues' is one of the classic passages on the lumpenproletariat; MECW 47, pp. 407, 408.
8 Hobson quoted in Walters, *Unemployment*, p. 32. See also Stedman Jones, *Languages of Class*, Cambridge 1983, p. 159. Massachusetts Bureau quoted in Keyssar, *Out of Work*, p. 72.

moment was characterized by an initial conceptualization of unemployment as an insurable risk, an accident like illness, fire, theft or death. This was the basis of Britain's National Insurance Act of 1911, the first government programme of its kind. Imitating Bismarck's regime of welfare provision, the Asquith government created a state-managed fund to insure workers against unemployment. However, the logic of insurance fails in cases of collective disaster, when there are too many accidents all at once. And thus it was the mass unemployment during the Great Depression of the 1930s that made clear the limits of such safety-nets. A new generation of unemployed movements emerged, usually led by young communist militants, such as the Comités des Chômeurs in France or the Unemployed Councils in the United States, where a third of the population was out of work. The most celebrated street processions and eviction protests were in these industrial heartlands – the 1930 Wall Street riot, the Ford hunger march two years after, the Lille-to-Paris hunger march in late 1933 – but there were similar demonstrations in the colonies as well, such as the 1933 hunger march in Jamaica.

The subsequent Keynesian reconceptualization of unemployment as an economic indicator subject to national macroeconomic fine-tuning became the basis for the post-WWII welfare states, which imagined a full-employment economy. For two decades, it appeared as if mass unemployment was a thing of the past. However, the Great Recession of the 1970s in Europe and North America marked the return of the spectre of wageless life, now under the sign of redundancy – the permanent shuttering of plants as entire regions underwent an Industrial Counterrevolution. A new wave of movements arose, particularly in France in the winter of 1997–98. As in the 1930s, deindustrialization is often understood to be a First World phenomenon, but, as we will see, it took place in rust belts around the globe like Ahmedabad, the Manchester of India.

But for some theorists, deindustrialization marked the end of unemployment as a political and conceptual tool. Among those arguing that we had reached the end of work was Ulrich Beck, the German theorist of neoliberalism's risk society, who pointed to the shift from a 'uniform system of lifelong full-time work organized in a single industrial location, with the radical alternative of unemployment, to a risk-fraught system of flexible, pluralized, decentralized underemployment, which, however, will possibly no longer raise the problem of ... being completely without a paid job.'[9] Neoliberal economists insisted that involuntary joblessness did not even exist; unemployment was either a choice for the marginal utility of leisure, or a temporary blockage of the labour market caused by high wages made too sticky by union monopoly and the state's minimum wage.

---

9 Ulrich Beck, *Risk Society*, London 1992, p. 143.

It is also worth noting the great weakness of the social-democratic normalization of employment and unemployment. It constituted a normal subject: the wage earner. As a result, much of capitalism's multitude was unrecognizable to a labour movement that had been reconstituted by state apparatuses into an employment movement, the agent of wage-earners divided into collective-bargaining units. Across society, there were many who lived outside typical employment and unemployment – women working in their own households, deindustrialized and disinvested communities without wages, those subjected to racial codes, even wage-earners in officially unrecognized industries and workplaces (in the US, for example, domestic, agricultural and academic workers not covered by the National Labor Relations Board). As a generation of feminist critics of the welfare state argued, this led to a gendered and unjust bifurcation of social security. Working-class households and neighbourhoods were divided between the independent, characteristically male, subjects of social insurance, and the dependent, characteristically female, subjects of social relief. One arm of the state apparatus insured and secured the normative male breadwinner against the risk of involuntary unemployment; another arm tested the ways and means of women raising children, before doling out a stigmatized relief. If the social-democratic conception of unemployment broke with the nineteenth-century rhetoric of the Poor Laws by understanding it as systemic rather than individual, as a waste of social labour rather than a malingering of the idle and dissolute, it also drew a stark and ideological line across the working multitude.

Favelas and bidonvilles

If unemployment dominated the imagination of the capitalist states of the West, it was not to be the governing concept in the development discourse of the post-colonial states. Here the spectre of wageless life in the sprawling shanty towns *and favelas* of Asia, Africa and Latin America overwhelmed any clear divide between employed and unemployed. Wageless life was not a temporary accident that might be insured against, nor a macroeconomic failure of aggregate demand; it appeared to be the main mode of existence in a separate, almost autonomous, economy.

The idea of the informal sector emerged following two decades of extraordinary Third World migration to cities, in which the urban working population doubled between 1950 and 1970. Colonial and settler-colonial regimes, as well as the plantation economies of the Americas, had restricted and even criminalized migration to the city; thus many mid-century revolts were based on the insurgency of peasants and rural agricultural workers. But in the wake of national liberation, 'the poor', as Mike Davis put it, 'eagerly asserted their "right to the city", even if that meant only a hovel on its periphery'.[10] New forms of livelihood and struggle emerged out of the great squatter cities of the 1950s, and even before the development economists and sociologists had named the informal sector, filmmakers represented the wageless life of the new shanty towns in films that became paradigmatic for the rest of the century: Marcel Camus's *Black Orpheus* (1959), which launched the first World Music – *bossa nova* – out of a mythic romanticization of Rio's *favelas* during carnival; and Gillo Pontecorvo's *Battle of Algiers* (1966), which lastingly portrayed the anti-colonial Algerian revolution not as the peasant war it was but through the epic metonymy of the defeated urban insurrection of 1956–57.

The first great theoretical engagement with this new form of wageless life also came out of a reflection on the Algerian revolution: Frantz Fanon's revival of the nineteenth-century Marxist word 'lumpenproletariat' in *The Wretched of the Earth*. Coined by Marx in the 1840s as one of a family of terms – the lumpenproletariat, the mob, *i lazzaroni, la bohème,* the poor whites – it characterized the class formations of Second Empire Paris, Risorgimento Naples, Victorian London and the slave states of North America. In most cases, Marx even used the original language to suggest the historical specificity of these formations rather than the theoretical standing of the concept. For him, such expressions had two key connotations: on the one hand, of an unproductive and parasitic layer of society, a social scum or refuse made up of those who preyed upon others; on the other hand, of a fraction of the poor that was usually allied with the forces of order – as in the account of Louis Napoleon's recruitment of the lumpenproletariat in *The Eighteenth Brumaire*, or Marx's analysis of the slaveholders' alliance with poor whites in the US South.

In these formulations, Marx had two antagonists. First, he was combating the established view that the entire working class was a dangerous and immoral element. He drew a line between the proletariat and the lumpenproletariat to defend the moral character of the former. Second, he was challenging those – particularly his great anarchist ally and adversary Bakunin – who argued that criminals and thieves were a revolutionary political force.[11] By the mid-twentieth century, the concept of the lumpenproletariat had pretty much disappeared from socialist and Marxist discourse. However, its reinvention in *The Wretched of the Earth* to describe the entirely new urban populations of the Third World made

---

[10] Mike Davis, *Planet of Slums*, London 2006, p. 55.
[11] See Hal Draper, *Karl Marx's Theory of Revolution*, vol. 2, New York 1978, ch. 15 and appendix G: 'On the Origin of the Term Lumpenproletariat'.

it one of the key stakes in the theoretical debates of the 1960s and 1970s. The discussion of the lumpenproletariat comes primarily in the book's second essay, 'Spontaneity: Its Strength and Weakness', in which Fanon delineates the contradictions of the anti-colonial coalition, as urban nationalist militants turn to the peasant masses. He makes three powerful and controversial claims. The first is a sociological one about the emergence of a new dispossessed population, the people of *les bidonvilles*: 'Abandoning the countryside ... the landless peasants, now a lumpenproletariat, are driven into the towns, crammed into shanty towns and endeavour to infiltrate the ports and cities, the creations of colonial domination'; 'These men, forced off the family land by the growing population in the countryside and by colonial expropriation, circle the towns tirelessly, hoping that one day or another they will be let in.' Fanon resorts to biological metaphors: 'The shanty town is the consecration of the colonized's biological decision to invade the enemy citadels at all costs, and, if need be, by the most underground channels.' It is an 'irreversible rot', a 'gangrene eating into the heart of colonial domination'. 'However hard [this lumpenproletariat] is kicked or stoned it continues to gnaw at the roots of the tree like a pack of rats.'[12]

Secondly, Fanon, like Marx, argues that this lumpenproletariat is readily manipulated by the repressive forces of colonial order – if it is not 'organized by the insurrection, it will join the colonialist troops as mercenaries' – and gives examples from Madagascar, Algeria, Angola and the Congo. Thirdly, and most famously, against the accepted wisdom of both nationalist and communist movements, he insists that

> it is among these masses, in the people of the shanty towns and in the lumpenproletariat that the insurrection will find its urban spearhead. The lumpenproletariat, this cohort of starving men, divorced from tribe and clan, constitutes one of the most spontaneously and radically revolutionary forces of a colonized people ... These jobless, these species of subhumans, redeem themselves in their own eyes and before history.[13]

Birth of informality

Fanon's appropriation of the nineteenth-century term fuelled political debates throughout the 1960s. Virtually all the pioneering studies of labour in the Third World addressed his formulation: Pierre Bourdieu on work and workers in Algeria; Ken Post on the Jamaican labour uprisings of the 1930s; Charles van Onselen on

---

12 Frantz Fanon, *The Wretched of the Earth*, New York 2004, pp. 66, 81.
13 Fanon, *Wretched of the Earth*, pp. 87, 81–82.

everyday life on the Witswatersrand. Development economists and sociologists struggled to name the new reality that Fanon identified. In his landmark history of the economic development of the Third World, Paul Bairoch argued that 'concepts of unemployment and underemployment as they have been formulated in the West cannot be applied ... except in a very crude and approximate way.'[14] Working in a social-democratic tradition, the Jamaican economist W. Arthur Lewis developed an influential model of the colonial 'dual economy' in the early 1950s. By the mid-1960s, the Argentine Marxist economist José Nun's concept of the marginal mass had provoked an important debate.

The phrase that came to dominate official discourse – the 'informal sector' – was coined in the early 1970s by a British development economist, Keith Hart, who was studying the communities of Frafra migrants from northern Ghana living in the Nima shanty town on the northern outskirts of the old city of Accra. 'A very large part of the urban labour force is not touched by wage employment', Hart wrote. He went on to outline the forms of 'self-employment' that made up the means of livelihood of Nima slum-dwellers: 'the distinction between formal and informal income opportunities is based essentially on that between wage-earning and self-employment.' The term was quickly adopted by the International Labour Organization in a 1972 study of employment in Kenya. Twenty years later the ILO had developed standards for the statistical measurement of the informal sector, and there were distinct debates not only in Anglophone Africa, but also in South Asia and Latin America. The 'informal sector' became the master trope for representing wageless life in cities around the world. According to the ILO 'informal employment comprises one half to three-quarters of non-agricultural employment in developing countries': 48 per cent in North Africa, 51 per cent in Latin America, 65 per cent in Asia and 72 per cent in sub-Saharan Africa. Moreover, 'three types of non-standard and atypical work – self-employment, part-time work, and temporary work –omprise 30 per cent of overall employment in 15 European countries and 25 per cent of total employment in the United States.' By the end of the century, the informal economy (as it had been renamed) had been made visible not only in Accra and Nairobi but in Los Angeles and Moscow.[15]

In his essay on Accra, Hart launched the debate about informal wageless life that has continued ever since: 'It is generally understood that growing residual underemployment and unemployment in the cities of developing countries is "a

---

14 Paul Bairoch, *The Economic Development of the Third World since 1900*, Berkeley 1975, p. 165.
15 Keith Hart, 'Informal Income Opportunities and Urban Employment in Ghana', *Journal of Modern African Studies*, vol. 11, no. 1, March 1973, pp. 62, 68; Paul E. Bangasser, *The ILO and the Informal Sector*, ILO Employment Paper 2000/9, p. 10; and ILO, *Women and Men in the Informal Economy*, Geneva 2002, p. 7.

bad thing". But why should this be so? In what way precisely does this phenomenon constitute a *problem?*' His question might be seen as the beginning of the normalization of the informal economy. Earlier models of the dual economy had treated it as the 'bad' legacy of colonialism's incomplete modernization, a transitional moment on the way to formal employment and unemployment. These states had inherited colonial labour apparatuses that had tried to discipline and regularize casual work. And, indeed, the mid-century era of import-substitution industrialization did see the growth of formal-sector employment in Latin America and even in some parts of Asia and Africa; the emergence of new armies of organized industrial workers gave rise to the great labour uprisings of South Africa, Brazil and South Korea. However, by the 1970s the growth of such jobs had stalled, and the discourse that named the informal sector saw it as a normal – indeed under neoliberalism, expanding – sphere of economic activity, part of the logic of post-colonial capitalist accumulation.[16]

Just as the definition of unemployment in the late nineteenth century had depended on a new understanding of the economy, so the discovery of the informal sector depended on a sense of the state's formal wage-labour apparatuses, which set minimum wages and maximum hours and provided unemployment insurance and social security. It was not the size of the enterprise that characterized the informal sector, nor the form of the labour process, but its relation to the state. The central issue then becomes the strength or weakness of the state: for some, informal economies develop when states regulate too much, driving economic activity to an underground, unregulated, untaxed world; for others, they are a product of weak or failed states, unable to provide social protections to their citizens and enforce rules or collect taxes. Neoliberal critics of state regulation have tended to celebrate the entrepreneurial gusto of the informal sector, its micro-enterprises that need only micro-credit to thrive. Defenders of social democratic welfare states have advocated the formalization of the informal: the extension of social protections and representation in unions.

Organizing in Ahmedabad

At the same time as development economists like Hart were discovering the informal sector, the first major organization of informal-sector workers took shape.

---

16 Hart, 'Informal Income Opportunities', p. 81. See also Alejandro Portes and Kelly Hoffman, 'Latin American Class Structures: Their Composition and Change during the Neoliberal Era', *Latin American Research Review*, vol. 38, no. 1, February 2003.

In 1972, an activist in the Gandhian Textile Labour Association, Ela Bhatt, began to bring together the women head loaders and street vendors of the Gujarat mill town of Ahmedabad into a union, the Self-Employed Women's Association. She had been assigned to survey families affected by the closure of two major textile mills.

> While the men were busy agitating to reopen the mills ... it was the women who were earning money and feeding the family. They sold fruits and vegetables in the streets; stitched in their homes at piece-rate for middlemen; worked as labourers in wholesale commodity markets, loading and unloading merchandise; or collected recyclable refuse from city streets ... jobs without definitions. I learned for the first time what it meant to be self-employed. None of the labour laws applied to them; my legal training was of no use in their case.

'Ironically', she recalls three decades later, 'I first glimpsed the vastness of the informal sector while working for the formal sector.'[17]

Over the next thirty years, SEWA became a cluster of three types of membership-based organizations of the poor: first, a union – by 2004, the largest primary union in India – of a variety of informal trades – rag pickers, home-based *chindi* and garment stitchers, *bidi* rollers, vegetable vendors – bargaining with buyers, contractors and municipal authorities over piece-rates and pavement space; second, a coalition of dozens of producer co-operatives, producing shirt fabrics, recycling waste paper and cleaning offices; and third, several institutions of mutual assistance and protection, including a SEWA bank and health cooperatives, organized around midwives who were themselves part of the informal sector.

A key part of its history has been a struggle over representation. 'When someone asks me what the most difficult part of SEWA's journey has been', Bhatt writes,

> I can answer without hesitation: removing conceptual blocks. Some of our biggest battles have been over contesting preset ideas and attitudes of officials, bureaucrats, experts and academics. Definitions are part of that battle. The Registrar of Trade Unions would not consider us 'workers'; hence we could not register as a 'trade union'. The hard-working *chindi* workers, embroiderers, cart pullers, rag pickers, midwives and forest-produce gatherers can contribute to the nation's gross domestic product, but heaven forbid that they be acknowledged as workers! Without an employer, you cannot be classified as a worker, and since you are not a worker, you cannot form a trade union. Our struggle to be recognized as a national trade union continues.[18]

---

17 Ela Bhatt, *We Are Poor but So Many: The Story of Self-Employed Women in India*, Oxford 2006, p. 89.
18 Bhatt, *We Are Poor*, p. 17–18.

SEWA rejected the rhetoric of the informal sector that dominated official discourse: 'dividing the economy into formal and informal sectors is artificial', Bhatt argues, 'it may make analysis easier, or facilitate administration, but it ultimately perpetuates poverty': 'to lump such a vast workforce into categories viewed as "marginal", "informal", "unorganized", "peripheral", "atypical", or "the black economy" seemed absurd to me. Marginal and peripheral to what, I asked ... In my eyes, they were simply "self-employed".' Indeed the women street vendors who were among the first to build SEWA called themselves traders.[19]

This rhetoric of self-employment drew on the ideologies of the Gandhian wing of Indian trade unionism from which SEWA emerged, and it has been adopted by other organizations of wageless workers, notably the Durban-based South African Self-Employed Women's Union founded in the mid-1990s. However, in retrospect, it seems to have been a nominal place-holder, as SEWA took as one of its key tasks the representation of a world of wageless work which was invisible to the labour apparatuses of the state. When SEWA organized the women who stitched *chindi* – fabric scraps discarded by textile mills – into *khols* (quilt covers) in the late 1970s, they began by depicting them, in spite of their scepticism:

> in order to better understand the problems of *chindi* workers, we decided to conduct a survey in the seven *poles*, or streets, where most of the *khols* were stitched. Karimaben [one of the militant workers] had no patience for a survey. She complained, 'We all know exactly what the problem is. Let me tell you that I spend more on a *khol* than I earn from making it'.

Nonetheless, SEWA insisted on 'proceeding methodically and conducting a survey', reporting the findings to the *chindi* workers, and using them to fight for an increase in piece-rates both to *khol* traders and Labour Department officials. Surveys, Bhatt argues, 'have served SEWA well over the years. They help us gain a thorough understanding of the issues before taking any action, and the process helps us identify potential leaders in the community.'[20] These studies have given a much more complex view of the world of the self-employed. By 2004, SEWA's research had divided its members into more than eighty occupations in four main categories: street vendors and hawkers, home-based producers, labourers and service providers, and rural producers.[21] Table 1 shows

---

19 Bhatt, *We Are Poor*, pp. 18, 10, 11.
20 Bhatt, *We Are Poor*, p. 63.
21 Martha Alter Chen, *Self-Employed Women: A Profile of SEWA's Membership*, Ahmedabad 2006, p. 12.

Table 1. *SEWA Membership in Gujarat*

Year	Total	Vendors		Home workers		Labourers		Producers	
			% of total		% of total		% of total		% of total
1975	3,850	825	21	950	25	2,075	54	–	
1980	4,934	950	19	1,934	39	2,050	42	–	
1985	15,741	2,472	16	8,464	54	4,805	31	–	
1990	25,911	3,230	12	13,821	53	6,700	26	2,160	
1995	158,152	11,515	7	55,114	35	73,768	47	17,755	
2000	205,985	18,759	9	72,156	35	105,811	51	9,259	
2002	535,674	39,460	7	141,458	26	314,245	59	40,511	
2003	469,306	42,745	9	105,439	22	298,761	64	22,361	
2004	468,445	28,575	6	85,976	18	313,814	67	40,080	

Source: Chen, *Self-Employed Women*, p. 14.

the growth of each of these categories since the 1970s: notice how the most visible group – the street vendors who make up about two per cent of urban India – were a major part of the early SEWA, before dropping off proportionally.

After beginning in the cities, the organization of rural producers and agricultural labourers took off in the 1990s. Two-thirds of their members are not so much self-employed as what Jan Breman has called 'wage hunters and gatherers', casual labourers and service providers who work for others in the intricate disguises of contracted and piece-rate jobs.[22] A more specific breakdown in 2004 (Table 2, above) shows not only the variety of informal trades – from

---

[22] Jan Breman, *Wage Hunters and Gatherers: Search for Work in the Urban and Rural Economy of South Gujarat*, Delhi 1994.

Table 2. *SEWA Membership in Gujarat by Occupation, 2004*

Trade Group		% of total membership
Vendors & Hawkers	28,575	6
Fruit & vegetable	21,553	5
Utensils and old clothes	2,252	<1
Other	4,770	1
Home workers	85,976	18
Embroiderers	26,782	6
Garment makers	20,878	4
Bidi rollers	15,478	3
Agarbati rollers	8,928	2
Kite makers	2,576	1
Other	11,334	2
Labourers & Service providers	313,814	67
Agricultural labourers	227,345	49
Tobacco workers	20,421	4
Waster pickers	20,165	4
Casual day labourers	14,732	3
Construction workers	11,673	3
Cleaners	6,741	1
Contract factory workers	3,950	1
Head loaders	3,259	1
Other	5,528	1
Rural producers	40,080	9
Milk producers	14,247	3
Animal rearers	10,867	2
Small farmers	9,281	2
Gum collectors	1,425	<1
Salt makers	3,288	1
Other	972	<1
Total	468,445	

Source: Chen, *Self-Employed Women*, p. 16.

vegetable vendors, waste pickers to head loaders – but the overwhelming numbers of agricultural labourers.

Thus, organizations of workers in the so-called informal sector have mapped their world less by its relation to a formal state-regulated economy than by its workplaces, particularly the street and the home. When SEWA pioneered transnational alliances of informal-workers associations in the 1990s, they did so by creating StreetNet and HomeNet. Increasingly, the two key representations of informalized workers in both official discourse and popular culture are the street vendor and the home-based worker.

Wandering the market

What can we conclude from this genealogy of representations of wageless life? It seems clear that neither of the great twentieth-century terms – unemployment and the informal sector – remain adequate, not least because of their segregation to specific zones of the capitalist world system; even the scholarly literatures on them barely speak to each other. This sense of conceptual exhaustion also applies to their traditional Marxist analogues: the socialist adoption of Marx's 'industrial reserve army', and the anti-colonial adoption of Fanon's re-figuring of the lumpenproletariat. But what alternatives do we have?

As I suggested earlier, two types of metaphor seem to dominate our contemporary imagination. The first points to the insecurity of many kinds of contemporary work: we speak of casualization, informalization and the proliferation of temporary and precarious jobs. In 1999, the ILO – long a site of struggle over forms of representation of work, its 1996 convention on home-based work the product of a protracted battle led in part by SEWA – tried to cut across the formal-informal divide by characterizing such work as vulnerable, against which they called for decent work. This demand is both a retreat – a recognition that formal labour regulation does not touch the majority – and an advance – an argument for social protections and labour rights for the vulnerable. In the face of the many still-pompous invocations of inalienable human rights, one might note that we still await the modest Magna Carta of decent work.

A second metaphor goes further, suggesting that we have passed a historical watershed, the end of work as we have known it. Work, we are told, has lost its centrality to life; wageless life is workless, wasted life. Noting the dramatic break in popular discourse between the rhetoric of unemployment and that of redundancy, Zygmunt Bauman writes that '"redundancy" shares its semantic space with "rejects", "wastrels", "garbage", "refuse" – with *waste*. The destination of the unemployed, of the "reserve army of labour", was to be called back into active service. The destination of waste is the waste-yard, the rubbish heap'. 'The production of "human waste", or more correctly wasted humans ... is an inevitable outcome of modernization'; 'refugees, asylum seekers, immigrants' are 'the waste products of globalization'.[23]

Bauman's apocalyptic denunciation of our culture of waste is powerful, but it misses the mark for two reasons. First, in its overly glib linking of material waste and human waste, it repeats one of the oldest tropes regarding the wageless – that they are akin to garbage, rubbish. Such metaphors run throughout this literature: early on Hobson characterized unemployment as waste; Marx was not immune, referring to the lumpenproletariat as refuse in *The Eighteenth Brumaire*. And indeed there is a connection: for those without wages have long worked as scavengers. As I noted earlier, not only are waste pickers a significant part of SEWA, but many of their trades, like the *chindi* stitchers, were built out of the by-products of the textile industry. In March 2008, the first international conference of waste-pickers' organizations was held in Bogotá.

That globalization produces redundancy would be better understood not through the deceptively concrete image of wasted lives, but through Marx's two dialectically related concepts: the relative surplus population and the virtual pauper. The one is from *Capital;* the other from the *Grundrisse*. In the key chapter on 'The General Law of Capitalist Accumulation' in *Capital*, Marx views the problem from the vantage point of capital: 'it is capitalist accumulation itself that constantly produces, and produces indeed in direct relation with its own energy and extent, a relatively redundant working population, i.e. a population which is superfluous to capital's average requirements for its own valorization, and is therefore a surplus population.' He continues: 'this is a law of population peculiar to the capitalist mode of production; and in fact every particular historical mode of production has its own special laws of population'. Indeed, 'the relative surplus population exists in all kinds of forms. Every worker belongs to it during the time when he is only partially employed or wholly unemployed.' The industrial reserve army is thus merely one of these forms; in fact, as might be expected, Marx's specific examples of the relative surplus population are the most dated part of his analysis.[24]

The fundamental metaphor in Marx's account is that of opposing forces: it is not as if there are two kinds of workers, employed and unemployed, or two sectors of the economy, formal and informal; rather, there is a process in which 'greater attraction of workers by capital is accompanied by their greater repul-

---

23 Zygmunt Bauman, *Wasted Lives*, Cambridge 2004, pp. 12, 5, 66.
24 Marx, *Capital*, pp. 782,783–784, 794.

sion ... the workers are sometimes repelled, sometimes attracted again in greater masses'. The 'higher the productivity of labour, the greater is the pressure of the workers on the means of employment, the more precarious therefore becomes the condition for their existence, namely the sale of their own labour-power'. Intriguingly, almost the entire contemporary vocabulary – redundant, superfluous, precarious – can be found in this chapter.[25]

If the passage in *Capital* tells the story from the point of view of the accumulation of capital, the parallel passage in the *Grundrisse* begins from the point of view of living labour: 'It is already contained in the concept of the free *labourer*, that he is a *pauper*: a virtual pauper ... If the capitalist has no use for his surplus labour, then the worker may not perform his necessary labour'. Marx is not arguing that all workers are or will become beggars, as in the immiseration thesis often attributed to him. Rather, this is his account of bare life: since the exchange required for the means of living—the selling of labour-power—is accidental and indifferent to their organic presence, the worker is a virtual pauper.[26] Virtual paupers: this strange figure – which combines an almost lost word with one that has taken on entirely new connotations – will be my temporary resting place. In a letter written as he turned fifty, Marx wrote: 'half a century on my shoulders and still a pauper'. A century and a half on again, the spectre of wageless life still weighs upon us.

---

25 Marx, *Capital*, pp. 783, 794, 798.
26 Marx, *Grundrisse*, trans. Martin Nicolaus, New York 1973, p. 604. For an intermediate draft of this passage in the 1861–63 manuscripts, see MECW 30, p. 40.

Kathie Weeks
The Problem with Work[1]

> Though women do not complain of the power of husbands, each complains of her own husband, or of the husbands of her friends. It is the same in all other cases of servitude, at least in the commencement of the emancipatory movement. The serfs did not at first complain of the power of their lords, but only of their tyranny.
>
> JOHN STUAR MILL, *THE SUBJECTION OF WOMEN*

> One type of work, or one particular job, is contrasted with another type, experienced or imagined, within the present world of work; judgments are rarely made about the world of work as presently organized as against some other way of organizing it.
>
> C. WRIGHT MILLS, *WHITE COLLAR*

Why do we work so long and so hard? The mystery here is not that we are required to work or that we are expected to devote so much time and energy to its pursuit, but rather that there is not more active resistance to this state of affairs. The problems with work today – my focus will be on the United States – have to do with both its quantity and its quality and are not limited to the travails of any one group. Those problems include the low wages in most sectors of the economy; the unemployment, underemployment, and precarious employment suffered by many workers; and the overwork that often characterizes even the most privileged forms of employment – after all, even the best job is a problem when it monopolizes so much of life. To be sure, if we were only resigned to such conditions, there would be no puzzle. What is perplexing is less the acceptance of the present reality that one must work to live than the willingness to live for work. By the same token, it is easy to appreciate why work is held in such high esteem, but considerably less obvious why it seems to be valued more than other pastimes and practices.

That these questions are rarely posed within the field of political theory is also surprising. The lack of interest in representing the daily grind of work routines in various forms of popular culture is perhaps understandable,[2] as is the tendency among cultural critics to focus on the animation and meaningfulness of commodities rather than the eclipse of laboring activity that Marx identifies as the source of their fetishization (Marx 1976, 164–65). The preference for a level of

---

[1] This text was first published in Kati Weeks: The Problem with Work. Introduction, Durham & London: Duke University Press 2011, pp. 1–36.

[2] Indeed, as Michael Denning notes, it is by now "a commonplace to note our reluctance to represent work in our popular stories. A Martian who hijacked the stock of the average video store would reasonably conclude that humans spent far more of their time engaged in sex than in work" (2004, 91–92).

abstraction that tends not to register either the qualitative dimensions or the hierarchical relations of work can also account for its relative neglect in the field of mainstream economics. But the lack of attention to the lived experience and political textures of work within political theory would seem to be another matter.[3] Indeed, political theorists tend to be more interested in our lives as citizens and noncitizens, legal subjects and bearers of rights, consumers and spectators, religious devotees and family members, than in our daily lives as workers.[4] And yet, to take a simple example, the amount of time alone that the average citizen is expected to devote to work – particularly when we include the time spent training, searching, and preparing for work, not to mention recovering from it – would suggest that the experience warrants more consideration. Work is crucial not only to those whose lives are centered around it, but also, in a society that expects people to work for wages, to those who are expelled or excluded from work and marginalized in relation to it. Perhaps more significantly, places of employment and spaces of work would seem to be supremely relevant to the very bread and butter of political science: as sites of decision making, they are structured by relations of power and authority; as hierarchical organizations, they raise issues of consent and obedience; as spaces of exclusion, they pose questions about membership and obligation. Although impersonal forces may compel us into work, once we enter the workplace we inevitably find ourselves enmeshed in the direct and personal relations of rulers and ruled. Indeed, the work site is where we often experience the most immediate, unambiguous, and tangible relations of power that most of us will encounter on a daily basis. As a fully political rather than a simply economic phenomenon, work would thus seem to be an especially rich object of inquiry.

There are at least two reasons for the inattention to work within political theory that bear mentioning. The first of these is what I will call the privatization of work. As the pair of epigraphs above suggest, we seem to have a hard time grasping the power relations of both work and family systematically; we often experience and imagine the employment relation – like the marriage relation – not as a social institution but as a unique relationship. Certainly this can be explained in part by the institution of private property that secures the privacy

---

[3] Whereas work was once a phenomenon worthy of scrutiny, "contemporary political theory," Russell Muirhead observes, "has had more to say about pluralism, toleration, virtue, equality of opportunity, and rights than it has about the character of work" (2004, 14).
[4] In a review of sociological work on the intersection of work and identity, Robin Leidner concludes that despite the widespread interest in identity across the social sciences and the humanities, "relatively few contemporary theorists have put work at the center of their analyses of identity in late or post modernity" (2006, 424).

of the employment relation alongside the marriage relation. However, it should also be noted that this mode of privatizing work is not easily maintained: work has long occupied a somewhat vexed position in the private-public economy of liberalism. Thus, even though John Locke could establish the private character of work through both the natural right to property and its integration into the economy of the household, the state's role in defending property rights (and, since Locke's day, increasingly regulating and planning on property's behalf) threatens the status of work as a private relationship, exposing it, by the logic of Locke's scheme, to the purview of properly political power.[5] Work's place within the private-public division becomes even more troubled with the advent of industrialization; as work becomes identified with waged work and separated from the household, it could more easily seem – by comparison to that exemplary private sphere – relatively public. But there are additional mechanisms that secure what I am calling work's privatization. One is its reification: the fact that at present one must work to "earn a living" is taken as part of the natural order rather than as a social convention. Consequently, as C. Wright Mills observes (in one of the epigraphs above), we tend to focus more on the problems with this or that job, or on their absence, than on work as a requirement, work as a system, work as a way of life. Like the serfs who, as John Stuart Mill claims in the other epigraph, "did not at first complain of the power of their lords, but only of their tyranny" (1988, 84), we are better at attending to the problems with this or that boss than to the system that grants them such power. The effective privatization of work is also a function of the way the labor market individualizes work – never more so than today, with the enormous variety of tasks and schedules that characterize the contemporary employment relation. The workplace, like the household, is typically figured as a private space, the product of a series of individual contracts rather than a social structure, the province of human need and sphere of individual choice rather than a site for the exercise of political power. And because of this tethering of work to the figure of the individual, it is difficult to mount a critique of work that is not received as something wholly different: a criticism of workers. As a result of work's subordination to property rights, its reification, and its individualization, thinking about work as a social system – even with its arguably more tenuous private status – strangely becomes as difficult as it is for many to conceive marriage and the family in structural terms.

The second reason for the marginalization of work within political theory's configuration of the political could be attributed to the decline of work-based

---

[5] Workers could thus be represented by the figure of the servant, as in one famous passage from The Second Treatise on Civil Government, in which Locke insists that the labor that entitles an individual to private property includes "the turfs my servant has cut" (1986, 20).

activism in the United States. In the absence of a worker's party, and with the fickle and sometimes conflicting class alignments within and between the two major parties, electoral politics has rarely served as an adequate vehicle for work-centered activism. The power of union-based politics has also been curtailed by the sharp decline of union membership in the period since the Second World War. Many activists today seem to assume that, besides party-line voting and institutionalized collective bargaining, our best chance for exerting collective power lies in our purchasing power. Ethical buying and the consumer boycott as ways to effect corporate decision making thus rise to the forefront of the political-economic imaginary. Of course, the logic that informs these models of consumer politics is the same one that enables corporations to make the case that low prices for ever more worthy consumer goods is an adequate trade-off for low wages, outsourcing, union busting, and government make-work programs. To the extent that unionization and consumer organizing continue to represent not only two obviously important means, but often the *only* avenues for imagining a politics of work, we are left with few possibilities for marshaling antiwork activism and inventing postwork alternatives.

What amounts in all these instances to a depoliticization of work is precisely what I want to think through and challenge in this contribution to the political theory of work. The brief chapter summaries at the end of this introduction will outline the book's specific points of focus and lines of argument. But first, I want to concentrate on presenting the project's major theoretical lineages and dominant conceptual frames, not to preview the analyses to come so much as to account for their inspiration and explain the kinds of claims and assumptions they presuppose. In terms of theoretical resources, although Max Weber, Jean Baudrillard, and Friedrich Nietzsche will each have a critical role to play at some point in the analysis, the project draws most heavily, albeit selectively, on the fields of feminist theory and Marxist theory, as this introductory discussion will illustrate. I should note, however, that it is not only political theory's disregard for the politics of work that poses obstacles for this endeavor; as we will see, both feminism's and Marxism's productivist tendencies – their sometimes explicit, sometimes tacit pro-work suppositions and commitments – present problems as well. There are, nonetheless, a number of exceptional cases or even whole subtraditions within each of these fields that have much to offer antiwork critiques and post-work imaginaries. But rather than organize this introductory discussion around a rehearsal of the project's more specific theoretical debts, I want to structure it instead in relation to a selection of its key concepts. The analysis begins with two concepts that orient the undertaking and give it direction: the work society and the work ethic. It then proceeds to a series of conceptual pairings – including work and labor, work and class, and freedom and equality – through which I hope to flesh out the text's central themes and further clarify my concerns and intentions. Let me start by articulating some of the reasons why I find the topic of work so theoretically interesting and politically pressing. The concept of the work society is my point of entry into that discussion.

The work society

The shift in perspective that I would like to see more political theorists pursue – from state and government to political economy, from cultural products to the sites and relations of their production, from public spaces and marketplaces to workplaces – is reminiscent of something Marx proposed in an oft-cited passage at the end of part two of the first volume of *Capital*. As a way to describe the buying and selling of that very "peculiar" commodity labor power, Marx presents the story of two free, self-interested individuals, each an owner of property and both equal under the law, who enter into an exchange of equivalents: one consents to give the use of his or her labor power for a limited period of time, and in return, the other agrees to pay the first a specific amount of money. But to see what happens after the employment contract is signed, the analysis must then move to a different location, the site where this special commodity will be "consumed" by putting the seller of it to work. "Let us therefore," Marx proposes,

> in company with the owner of money and the owner of labour-power, leave this noisy sphere, where everything takes place on the surface and in full view of everyone, and follow them into the hidden abode of production, on whose threshold there hangs the notice "No admittance except on business." Here we shall see, not only how capital produces, but how capital is itself produced. (1976, 279–80)

By altering the focus of the study in this way, Marx promises, "the secret of profit-making" will be exposed (280). By changing the site of the analysis from a market-based exchange to wage-based production, the labor-process itself – that is, the activity of labor and the social relations that shape, direct, and manage it – will be revealed as the locus of capitalist valorization.

So what are the benefits of this vantage point? What do we see when we shift our angle of vision from the market sphere of exchange to the privatized sphere of production? As the language about revealing secrets suggests, part of what Marx seeks to accomplish by descending into this "hidden abode" is to publicize the world of waged work, to expose it as neither natural precursor nor peripheral byproduct of capitalist production, but rather as its central mechanism (the wage) and lifeblood (work). With this shift in perspective, Marxian political economy recognizes waged labor as central to the capitalist mode of production and claims it as the standpoint from which capitalism's mysteries can be uncovered and its logics laid bare. This recognition of the significance of work remains, I argue, as relevant now as it was when Marx wrote, and it is this observation that my deployment of the category of the work society is intended, in part, to underscore.

Waged work remains today the centerpiece of late capitalist economic systems; it is, of course, the way most people acquire access to the necessities of food, clothing, and shelter. It is not only the primary mechanism by which income is distributed, it is also the basic means by which status is allocated, and by which most people gain access to healthcare and retirement. After the family, waged work is often the most important, if not sole, source of sociality for millions. Raising children with attributes that will secure them forms of employment that can match if not surpass the class standing of their parents is the gold standard of parenting. In addition, "making people capable of working is," as Nona Glazer notes, "the central goal of schooling, a criterion of successful medical and psychiatric treatment, and an ostensible goal of most welfare policies and unemployment compensation programs" (1993, 33). Helping to make people "work ready" and moving them into jobs are central objectives of social work (Macarov 1980, 12), a common rationale for the prison system, and an important inducement to perform military service. Indeed, enforcing work, as the other side of defending property rights, is a key function of the state (Seidman 1991, 315), and a particular preoccupation of the postwelfare, neoliberal state.

But making public the foundational role of work is only part of what Marx achieves with this change in venue. In descending from the sphere of the market – which he satirized as "a very Eden" of equal rights, individual freedom, and social harmony (1976, 280) – into the privatized spaces of work, Marx seeks not only to publicize but also to politicize the world of work. That is to say, the focus on the consumption of labor seeks to expose the social role of work and, at the same time, to pose it as a political problem. Despite Marx's insistence that waged work for those without other options is a system of "forced labor" (1964, 111), it remains for the most part an abstract mode of domination. In general, it is not the police or the threat of violence that force us to work, but rather a social system that ensures that working is the only way that most of us can meet our basic needs. In this way, as Moishe Postone notes, the specific mechanism by which goods and services are distributed in a capitalist society appears to be grounded not in social convention and political power but in human need (1996, 161). The social role of waged work has been so naturalized as to seem necessary and inevitable, something that might be tinkered with but never escaped. Thus Marx seeks both to clarify the economic, social, and political functions of work under capitalism and to problematize the specific ways in which such world-building practices are corralled into industrial forms and capitalist relations of work. This effort to make work at once public and political is, then, one way to counter the forces that would naturalize, privatize, individualize, ontologize, and also, thereby, depoliticize it.

Work is, thus, not just an economic practice. Indeed, that every individual is required to work, that most are expected to work for wages or be supported by someone who does, is a social convention and disciplinary apparatus rather than an economic necessity. That every individual must not only do some work but more often a lifetime of work, that individuals must not only work but become workers, is not necessary to the production of social wealth. The fact is that this wealth is collectively not individually produced, despite the persistence of an older economic imaginary that links individual production directly to consumption.[6] Indeed, as Postone observes, "on a deep, systemic level, production is not for the sake of consumption" (1996, 184). The relationship may appear direct and incontrovertible, but it is in fact highly mediated: the goal of neither party in the work relation is consumption; one seeks surplus value, and the other income. The normative expectation of waged work as an individual responsibility has more to do with the socially mediating role of work than its strictly productive function (150). Work is the primary means by which individuals are integrated not only into the economic system, but also into social, political, and familial modes of cooperation. That individuals should work is fundamental to the basic social contract; indeed, working is part of what is supposed to transform subjects into the independent individuals of the liberal imaginary, and for that reason, is treated as a basic obligation of citizenship. (The fact that the economy's health is dependent on a permanent margin of unemployment is only one of the more notorious problems with this convention.) Dreams of individual accomplishment and desires to contribute to the common good become firmly attached to waged work, where they can be hijacked to rather different ends: to produce neither individual riches nor social wealth, but privately appropriated surplus value. The category of the work society is meant to signify not only the centrality of work, but also its broad field of social relevance (see, for example, Beck 2000).

---

6 Cultural representations of the world of work are not only relatively rare but are also often slow to change. Daniel Rodgers gives the example of the continuing use of a cartoon image of a blacksmith to represent workers in the context of an industrial economy in which very few such figures could be found (1978, 242). In the 1960s, James Boggs made a similar point about the problem of clinging to outdated economic imaginaries when he argued that to tell the postindustrial unemployed "that they must work to earn their living is like telling a man in the big city that he should hunt big game for the meat on his table" (1963, 52).

Gender at work

Another way to get at the extra-economic role of work that the concept of the work society is intended to evoke is through a further consideration of work's subjectification function, alluded to above. Work produces not just economic goods and services but also social and political subjects. In other words, the wage relation generates not just income and capital, but disciplined individuals, governable subjects, worthy citizens, and responsible family members. Indeed, given its centrality both to individuals' lives and to the social imaginary, work constitutes a particularly important site of interpellation into a range of subjectivities. It is, for example, a key site of becoming classed; the workplace is where, as Marx describes it, the seller of labor power who we are invited to follow into the hidden abode of production "becomes in actuality what previously he only was potentially, namely labour-power in action, a worker" (1976, 283). Class identities and relations are made and remade as some people are excluded from and others conscripted into work, by means of educational tracks and workplace training regimens, through the organization of labor processes and the interactions they structure, via the setting of wage levels, and in relation to judgments about occupational status. This process of subjectification is perhaps best understood in terms of a model not of passive construction but of active recruitment, often less a matter of command and obedience than one of inducement and attraction (West and Zimmerman 1991, 27–29). Along these lines, one can observe that some of the attractions of different forms of work are about joining a relatively advantaged class: becoming a member of the working class rather than the underclass, a middle-class rather than a working-class person, a salaried versus an hourly worker, a professional with a career as opposed to a working stiff and job holder. As a way to build on these logics a little further, let us turn to another dimension of this process of subject making and doing and consider work as a site of gendering.

To say that work is organized by gender is to observe that it is a site where, at a minimum, we can find gender enforced, performed, and recreated. Workplaces are often structured in relation to gendered norms and expectations. Waged work and unwaged work alike continue to be structured by the productivity of gender-differentiated labor, including the gender division of both household roles and waged occupations. But the gendering of work is not just a matter of these institutionalized tendencies to distinguish various forms of men's work and women's work, but a consequence of the ways that workers are often expected to do gender at work. Gender is put to work when, for example, workers draw upon gendered codes and scripts as a way to negotiate relationships with bosses and co-workers, to personalize impersonal interactions, or to communicate courtesy, care, professionalism, or authority to clients, students, patients, or customers.

And this is, of course, not limited to waged forms of work. As Sarah Fenstermaker Berk argues, unwaged domestic work too should be recognized for producing not just goods and services, but gender as well (1985, 201). As a result of these activities, work plays a significant role in both the production and reproduction of gendered identities and hierarchies: gender is re-created along with value.

As in the example of class identities noted earlier, gender identities are coordinated with work identities in ways that can sometimes alienate workers from their job and other times bind them more tightly to it. Whether it is the women informatics workers whose pink-collar status and dress code is, Carla Freeman argues, at once a disciplinary mechanism and a source of individual expression (2000, 2), or the specific model of blue-collar masculinity that made industrial work attractive to the working-class boys of Paul Willis's famous study (1977, 150), this gendering of labor – doing men's work or women's work, doing masculinity or femininity as part of doing the job – can also be a source of pleasure in work and serve to promote workers' identification with and investments in the job. This can extend to unwaged forms of labor too; consider, for example, the ways in which conforming to a gender division of household labor might be for some people welcome confirmations of gender and sexual identities and relations. "What is produced and reproduced," in the case of one such example, is thus "not merely the activity and artifact of domestic life, but the material embodiment of wifely and husbandly roles and, derivatively, of womanly and manly conduct" (West and Zimmerman 1991, 30). Sometimes doing gender might be treated as part of doing the job; at other times doing the job is part of what it means to do gender. As Robin Leidner observes in her study of routinized interactive service work, the "degree to which workers accept the identity implied by a job is therefore determined in part by the degree to which they can interpret the job as expressing their gender in a satisfying way" (1993, 194).

But there is more to this story. For an employee, it is not merely a matter of bringing one's gendered self to work but of becoming gendered in and through work. For an employer, it is not just a matter of hiring masculine and feminine workers and putting them to work, but of actively managing workers' gendered identities and relationships. Exploitable subjects are not just found; they are, as Michael Burawoy famously argues, made at the point of production (1979). Even at the level of specific workplaces, individual managers can to some degree fashion the exploitable subjects, including the specific kind of feminized or masculinized subjects they imagine that they have already hired (Salzinger 2003, 20–21). Of course, it is difficult to predict whether various jobs will be segregated by gender in this way, whether they will be considered suitable men's work or women's work, and which particular models of gender such workers will be expected to conform to. In the fast-food franchise that Leidner studied, cooking was understood by managers and workers alike as men's work when it could have just as easily been coded as a feminized activity. Though it is not always easy to foresee if jobs will become gendered – or, if so, which jobs will be treated as more or less appropriate for which specific ideal of gendered comportment – the occupational segregation that is part and parcel of the gender division of labor stands nonetheless as supposed empirical proof of the necessity of gender difference and hierarchy. Thus, as Leidner notes, "the considerable flexibility of notions of proper gender enactment does not undermine the appearance of inevitability and naturalness that continues to support the division of labor by gender" (1993, 196). In her study of gendered labor in the maquiladoras, Leslie Salzinger argues that it is precisely the combination of rigid gender categories with the malleability and variability of their enactments and meaning that explains the resilience of gender as a principle of human differentiation (2003, 25). In this sense, ironically, the tremendous plasticity of gender reinforces rather than undermines its naturalization.

Work values

The category of the work society refers not just to the socially mediating and subjectively constitutive roles of work but to the dominance of its values. Challenging the present organization of work requires not only that we confront its reification and depoliticization but also its normativity and moralization. Work is not just defended on grounds of economic necessity and social duty; it is widely understood as an individual moral practice and collective ethical obligation. Traditional work values – those that preach the moral value and dignity of waged work and privilege such work as an essential source of individual growth, selffulfillment, social recognition, and status – continue to be effective in encouraging and rationalizing the long hours US workers are supposed to dedicate to waged work and the identities they are expected to invest there. This normalizing and moralizing ethic of work should be very familiar to most of us; it is, after all, routinely espoused in managerial discourse, defended in the popular media, and enshrined in public policies. The ethic's productivist values are promoted on both the political Right and Left, from employers seeking the most able and tractable workers, and politicians intent on moving women from welfare to waged work, to parents and educators eager to prepare their children or students to embrace the values that might best ensure their future economic security and social achievement.

Let me be clear: to call these traditional work values into question is not to claim that work is without value. It is not to deny the necessity of productive activity or to dismiss the likelihood that, as William Morris describes it, there might be for all living things "a pleasure in the exercise of their energies" (1999, 129). It is, rather, to insist that there are other ways to organize and distribute that activity and to remind us that it is also possible to be creative outside the boundaries of work. It is to suggest that there might be a variety of ways to experience the pleasure that we may now find in work, as well as other pleasures that we may wish to discover, cultivate, and enjoy. And it is to remind us that the willingness to live for and through work renders subjects supremely functional for capitalist purposes. But before the work society can be publicized and raised as a political problem, we need to understand the forces – including the work ethic – that promote our acceptance of and powerful identification with work and help to make it such a potent object of desire and privileged field of aspiration.

Feminism has its own tendencies toward the mystification and moralization of work and has reproduced its own version of this famed ethic. Consider two of the dominant feminist remedies for the gender divisions and hierarchies of waged and unwaged work. One strategy, popular with at least some feminists of both the first and second waves, is to more or less accept the lesser value accorded to unwaged domestic labor and seek to secure women's equal access to waged work. Waged work would be women's ticket out of culturally mandated domesticity. While recognizing the importance of the ongoing struggle to secure equal employment opportunities for women, I want to argue that subjecting feminism's own idealization of waged work to critical scrutiny remains an important task as well. Confronting the present organization of waged labor and its values is especially urgent in the wake of the 1996 welfare reform debate and resulting legislation. Certainly the attack on poor women that was perpetrated in the name of the work ethic should inspire the reconsideration and reinvention of feminist perspectives on waged work – its ever-shifting realities and its long-standing values.

A second feminist strategy concentrates on efforts to revalue unwaged forms of household-based labor, from housework to caring work. Certainly making this socially necessary labor visible, valued, and equitably distributed remains a vital feminist project as well. The problem with both of these strategies – one focused on gaining women's entry into all forms of waged work and the other committed to gaining social recognition of, and men's equal responsibility for, unwaged domestic work – is their failure to challenge the dominant legitimating discourse of work. On the contrary, each approach tends to draw upon the language and sentiments of the traditional work ethic to win support for its claims about the essential dignity and special value of women's waged or unwaged labor.[7] How might feminism contest the marginalization and underestimation of unwaged forms of reproductive labor, without trading on the work ethic's mythologies of work? Feminists, I suggest, should focus on the demands not simply or exclusively for more work and better work, but also for less work; we should focus not only on revaluing feminized forms of unwaged labor but also challenge the sanctification of such work that can accompany or be enabled by these efforts.

The question is, then, how to struggle against both labor's misrecognition and devaluation on the one hand, and its metaphysics and moralism on the other hand. The refusal of work, a concept drawn from the autonomous Marxist tradition, will help to focus the analysis on the question of work's meaning and value. In contrast to some other types of Marxism that confine their critique of capitalism to the exploitation and alienation of work without attending to its overvaluation, this tradition offers a more expansive model of critique that seeks to interrogate at once capitalist production and capitalist (as well as socialist) productivism. From the perspective of the refusal of work, the problem with work cannot be reduced to the extraction of surplus value or the degradation of skill, but extends to the ways that work dominates our lives. The struggle against work is a matter of securing not only better work, but also the time and money necessary to have a life outside work. Although there are a number of important analyses of the most exploited forms of waged and unwaged work performed by workers both in the United States and beyond its borders, the larger systems of labor and especially the values that help sustain them are often insufficiently theorized, leaving one to conclude that all of our work-related goals would be met and the dominant work values justified if only such work were to resemble more closely the employment conditions at the middle and upper reaches of the labor hierarchy. The theory and practice of the refusal of work insists that the problem is not just that work cannot live up to the ethic's idealized image, that it neither exhibits the virtues nor delivers the meaning that the ethic promises us in exchange for a lifetime of work, but perhaps also the ideal itself.

---

[7] Taken together, the two strategies risk replicating the traditional choice between either valuing work or valuing family, in relation to which various "work-family balance" programs remain the most-cited – but, it seems to me, singularly inadequate – solution to the conflicts generated by the two spheres' competing claims on our loyalties.

Work and labor

Earlier I noted the difference between thinking systematically about work and thinking about this or that job. As a way to further clarify my concerns and intentions, I turn here to another distinction – the first of three additional conceptual pairs that I want to explore – that between work and labor. Although the division that I want to register between these categories is not a terminological one, I want to begin the discussion with a brief clarification about my use of the first term. In this book, the label "work" will refer to productive cooperation organized around, but not necessarily confined to, the privileged model of waged labor. What counts as work, which forms of productive activity will be included and how each will be valued, are a matter of historical dispute. Certainly the questions of whether or not various forms of productive activity – including some unwaged forms – will be recognized as work and at what rate they will be compensated have long been at the forefront of class, race, and gender struggles in and beyond the United States.

Which brings me to the relationship between work and labor: for the purposes of this project, I will use the terms interchangeably, thereby running roughshod over a distinction that is frequently, though inconsistently and variably, posed. For Hannah Arendt, to cite one notable theorist, the distinction between labor as the activity that reproduces biological life and work as the creation of an object world serves, among other things, to establish by way of comparison the singularity of a third category, action, as the definitively political activity of being in common (1958). Within the Marxist tradition, by contrast, it is perhaps more often labor – or, specifically, living labor – that figures as the more expansive category and valued practice. Conceived as a collective and creative human capacity harnessed by capital to the production of surplus value, living labor can yield both a critical standpoint from which the alienating and exploitative conditions of modern work can be critically interrogated and a utopian potential that can inform speculations about the revolutionary transformation of those conditions. By this account, the human capacity for labor may be hobbled by the organization of waged work, but as a collective creative potential, can also exceed them.

As far as the classic Arendtian approach to the categories is concerned, the distance it places between both labor and work on the one hand, and the legitimate business of the political on the other hand, renders it less useful for my purposes. As for the example from the Marxist tradition, while I recognize the power of the distinction it poses, I find it ill-suited to a critique that takes aim at both the structures of work and its dominant values. The trouble with the category of living labor deployed in this way as an alternative to work is, as I see it, that it is haunted by the very same essentialized conception of work and inflated notion of its meaning that should be called into question. To the extent that it is imbued in this way with the productivist values I want to problematize, it can neither provide the critical leverage necessary to interrogate the dominant ethic of work nor generate an alternative mode of valuation – a vision of the work society not perfected but overcome.[8] Consistent in this respect with Postone's antiproductivist Marxism, the ensuing analysis intends not to advance a "critique of capitalism *from the standpoint of* labor," but to pursue a "critique *of* labor in capitalism" (1996, 5). My refusal to distinguish between work and labor is thus a wager of sorts: by blocking access to a vision of unalienated and unexploited work in the guise of living labor, one that could live up to the work ethic's ideals about labor's necessity and virtues and would be worthy of the extravagant praise the ethic bestows, I hope to concentrate and amplify the critique of work as well as to inspire what I hope will be a more radical imagination of postwork futures.

In place of the opposition between labor and work, I will employ a number of other distinctions over the course of the argument to secure some critical insight into particular dimensions of work and to imagine other possibilities. These will include the distinction between work time and non-work time, between work and life, between time for what we are obligated to do and time for "what we will," or – to mark differences at yet another level of abstraction – between the category of antiwork used to signal the deconstructive moment of this critique of the work society, and the concept of postwork offered as a place holder for something yet to come.

Work and class

Whereas the distinction between work and labor will be suspended for the purposes of this analysis, the relationship between work and class is a link I want to maintain, if only obliquely. Class is, of course, a central category of Marxist political economy, as Marx makes clear in what follows the passage from *Capital* cited above. Consider the first thing we see when we accompany the two owners of property – in one case, money; in the other, labor power – as they descend from the Eden of market exchange where they meet to trade equivalents into the hidden abode of production where one party is set to work. "When we leave this sphere of simple circulation or the exchange of commodities," Marx writes, "a certain change takes place, or so it appears, in the physiognomy of our *dramatis personae*. He who was previously the money-owner now strides out in front as a

---

[8] Harry Cleaver offers a similar argument against the labor-work distinction (2002).

capitalist; the possessor of labour-power follows as his worker" (1976, 280). Where we had observed two equal individuals, each in possession of a commodity, who agree to make an exchange for the benefit of each, now we witness the inequality that separates the one who steps in front from the one who follows behind; with this shift of the locus of perception from the marketplace to the workplace, the existence of a social hierarchy based on class comes into sharp focus.

Despite the centrality of class in traditional Marxist analysis, work remains my privileged object of study and preferred terrain of political struggle. So let me say something about the relationship between work and class and what might be at stake in different formulations of its terms. There are at least two ways to approach the relationship between the categories: one draws a rather sharp distinction between them, whereas the other finds overlapping concerns. I will start with the first. The difference between the concepts is perhaps most starkly posed when work understood as a process is compared to class conceived in terms of an outcome – that is, as a category (whether explained by reference to ownership, wealth, income, occupation, or forms of belonging) designed to map patterns of economic inequality. To the extent that class is defined and measured in this way, as an outcome rather than an activity, then its utility for my purposes will be limited.

I am, of course, not the first to raise such concerns about this approach to the category of class. For example, the potential shortcomings of the concept have long been debated within Marxist feminism. The original "woman question" was, after all, generated by the disjuncture between the categories of gender and class, and the question this posed for the relationship between feminism and class struggle. But the trouble with class for second-wave feminists was not just that it might be inadequate to broader, extra-economic fields of analysis; the problem was that to the extent that class was conceived – as it typically was – as a gender- and race-blind category, its ability to register the contours of even narrowly economic hierarchies was limited as well. For some of the same reasons that I want to foreground the category of work over that of class, Iris Young once argued in favor of substituting the Marxist category of division of labor for class as a primary analytic of Marxist feminism. In this classic contribution to second-wave Marxist feminism, Young describes at least two advantages of this methodological shift. First, the division of labor has at once a broader reach than class and allows a more differentiated application. Not only can it be used to register multiple divisions of labor by class as well as by gender, race, and nation, but it can, as Young explains, also expose "specific cleavages and contradictions *within a class*" (1981, 51; emphasis added) – not just along the lines of gender, race, and nation, but also, potentially, of occupation and income. Thus the category of the gender division of labor, for example, enables a focus on gendered patterns of work "without assuming that all women in general or all women in a particular society have a common and unified situation" (55). Like the division of labor, the category of work seems to me at once more capacious and more finely tuned than the category of class. After all, work, including its absence, is both important to and differently experienced within and across lines of class, gender, race, and nation. In this sense, the politics of and against work has the potential to expand the terrain of class struggle to include actors well beyond that classic figure of traditional class politics, the industrial proletariat.

Consider too the second advantage noted by Young: "The category of division of labor can not only refer to a set of phenomena broader than that of class, but also more concrete." Unlike class, by her account, the division of labor "refers specifically to the *activity* of labor itself, and the specific social and institutional relations of that activity," proceeding thus "at the more concrete level of particular relations of interaction and interdependence in a society" (51). By this measure, whereas class addresses the outcome of laboring activity, the division of labor points toward the activity itself. Here too there are similarities between Young's interest in the category of division of labor and my focus on work: after all, work, including the dearth of it, is the way that capitalist valorization bears most directly and most intensively on more and more people's lives. This politics of work could be conceived as a way to link the everyday and sometimes everynight experiences of work – its spaces, relations and temporalities; its physical, affective, and cognitive practices; its pains and pleasures – to the political problematic of their present modes and codes of organization and relations of rule.[9] Although the category of class remains analytically powerful, I would argue that its political utility is more negligible. The problem is that while the oppositional class category of the industrial period – the "working class" – may accurately describe most people's relation to waged labor even in a postindustrial economy, it is increasingly less likely to match their self-descriptions. The category of the middle class has absorbed so many of our subjective investments that it is difficult to see how the working class can serve as a viable rallying point in the United States today. A politics of work, on the other hand, takes aim at an activity rather than an identity, and a central component of daily life rather than an outcome. Once again, the struggle over work in this respect has the potential to open a more expansive terrain than that of traditional class politics, insofar as the problem of work carries the potential to resonate, albeit in very different ways, across a number of income, occupational, and identity groups.

---

[9] The notion of "relations of rule" is adapted from Dorothy Smith's (far richer) category of "relations of ruling" (1987, 3).

The advantages of work over class extend beyond its breadth and tangibility. Crucial for Marx in his own privileging of labor as the point of entry into the materialist analysis of capitalist society – rather than beginning, for example, with political inequality or poverty – is the relationship between labor and agency that he assumes to be fundamental to anticapitalist politics. Thus in the *German Ideology*, Marx and Engels distinguish their materialist methodology not only from the idealism of the Young Hegelians but also from Feuerbach's "ahistorical" brand of materialism that may have recognized, to borrow another of Marx and Engels's formulations, "that circumstances make men" but not necessarily that "men make circumstances" (1970, 59). Materialism, as Marx and Engels understand it, is a matter not merely of the social construction of subjects but a matter of creative activity, of doing and making, the ontological trajectories of which are equally synchronic and diachronic. By focusing on laboring practices, or "living sensuous *activity*" (64), materialism as Marx and Engels conceive it is a matter not merely of the social construction of subjects but of creative activity, the capacity not only to make commodities but to remake a world. In this way, the focus on laboring practices, on the labor process and the relations of labor, can register the workers' power to act, in contrast, it seems to me, to their relative disempowerment that is registered in the economic outcomes the categories of class are often used to map and measure.[10]

So by at least one way of reckoning, class and work belong to different fields of analysis, and my project pursues the critical study of work instead of class analysis and antiwork politics as a substitute for class struggle. But there is another way to approach class that does not produce such a sharp contrast with the category of work and that yields a different and, I think, more compelling approach to this territory. The distinction between the two fields of analysis becomes rather less clear when class too is conceived in terms of a process rather than an outcome. Process notions of class disrupt the functionalism of static mappings of class formations by attending to the practices by and relations within which they are secured, re-created, and challenged.[11] If class is figured as a process of

---

[10] Here, it should be noted, the concepts of living labor and work are rendered more compatible if living labor is conceived not as an interior essence or normative standard, but as a potential for specifically political agency. In this way, the concept serves not as a critical lens so much as "a source of the auto-valorization of subjects and groups, as the creation of social cooperation," as the potential to construct alternatives (Negri 1996, 171). See also Jason Read's similar approach to the category (2003, 90–91).

[11] Different but compatible approaches to class as process include Joan Acker's revisiting of class from a feminist perspective (2000), Stanley Aronowitz's insistence on a class theory that places the emphasis on social time over social space (2003), and William Corlett's model of "class action" as a process of labor's self-determination (1998).

becoming classed, it may be that work – including struggles over what counts as work – could be conceived as a useful lens through which to approach class; in this way, the struggle against work could be a terrain of class politics.

But let me add one caveat: rather than conceiving class groupings and relations as the ground of antiwork politics, as that which provides its fuel and organizational form, it might be better to think of them as what might emerge from these efforts. By this reading, class formation, or what the autonomist tradition calls class composition, is best conceived as an outcome of struggles rather than their cause. The particular composition of the working class that might emerge from this politics of work – that is, the collectivities that might coalesce around its issues and the divisions that might develop in the interstices of antiwork struggles and in relation to postwork imaginaries – remains an open question. To the extent that the concerns it raises carry the potential to cut across traditional class divisions, a politics against work might serve to de-constitute the field of working-class politics and reconstitute it in a different, perhaps more expansive, way.

So in the end, I am not saying that we should stop thinking about class, but rather that focusing on work is one politically promising way of approaching class – because it is so expansive, because it is such a significant part of everyday life, because it is something we do rather than a category to which we are assigned, and because for all these reasons it can be raised as a political issue. By this account, work is a point of entry into the field of class analysis through which we might be better able to make class processes more visible, legible, and broadly relevant and, in the process, perhaps provoke class formations yet to come.

Freedom and equality

Whereas my analysis ignores the difference between work and labor and, in the end, defers the question of the precise relationship between work and class, it presumes the significance of another distinction, the one between freedom and equality. To get a sense of how this pair of concepts is conceived for the purposes of this project, let us return yet again to Marx's description of what we see when we descend with the owners of money and labor power from the realm of market exchange to the realm of production. To recall our earlier discussion of the passage, accompanying the change of venue is a visible change in the physiognomy of the dramatis personae: we see the money owner stride out in front as capitalist, while the possessor of labor power follows behind as worker. "The one," Marx continues, "smirks self-importantly and is intent on business; the other is timid and holds back, like someone who has brought his own hide to market and now has nothing else to expect but – a hiding" (1976, 280; translation modified). Whereas we had, as noted above, witnessed the formal equivalence of contractors in the labor market, in the realm of work we discover hierarchy. As the conclusion of the passage suggests, however, it is not only inequality that is revealed, with the capitalist striding in front and the worker following behind, but subordination, with the former smirking and self-important and the latter timid and holding back. In other words, the critical analysis of work reveals not only exploitation but – as the reference to the violence of a hiding serves to amplify – domination.[12]

The domination and subordination experienced at work is not merely incidental to processes of exploitation. Carole Pateman's analysis of the employment contract is illuminating on this point. By her account, the problem with the labor contract is not just a function of the coerced entry that is ensured by the absence of viable alternatives to waged labor, nor is it only a matter of the inequality that is produced as the result of the contract's terms. To translate this into a Marxist vocabulary, the problem can be reduced neither to forced labor nor to exploitation. Rather, we need to pay more attention to the relationship of dominance and submission that is authorized by the waged labor contract and that shapes labor's exercise. Exploitation is possible, Pateman notes, because "the employment contract creates the capitalist as master; he has the political right to determine how the labour of the worker will be used" (1988, 149). This relation of command and obedience, the right of the employer to direct his or her employees that is granted by the contract, is not so much a byproduct of exploitation as its very precondition.

Marx too would seem to be quite clear that the problem with work cannot be reduced to the terms of its recompense, but rather extends into the very heart of the wage relation and the labor process it commands. That is why he insists on describing the program of raising wages as only *"better payment for the slave"* (1964, 118). To focus narrowly on outcomes rather than processes, and on inequality and not also on unfreedom, is to impoverish the critique of capitalism. Marx muses about a comparably inadequate approach in "Critique of the Gotha Program": "It is as if, among slaves who have at last got behind the secret of slavery and broken out in rebellion, a slave still in thrall to obsolete notions were to inscribe on the programme of the rebellion: Slavery must be abolished because the feeding of slaves in the system of slavery cannot exceed a certain low maximum!" (1978, 535).

---

12 A relationship that might have been captured by a quantitative logic, measured by the distance between the one in front and the one behind, is revealed as something that must be grasped also in qualitative terms, as attitude, affect, feeling, and symbolic exchange.

I am thus interested in adding to the critique of the exploitative and alienating dimensions of work a focus on its political relations of power and authority, as relations of rulers and ruled. My inspiration for this, it should be noted, is not only these readings of Marx, but certain strands of 1970s feminism. A commitment to freedom in conjunction with or beyond equality was what distinguished the more radical sectors of the early second wave of US feminism from liberal feminists of the time. Refusing to honor the "do not enter" sign on the door leading to the so-called private terrains of the family, marriage, and sexuality – a sign meant to ban political judgment of relations that were thought to be governed only by the exigencies of nature or prerogatives of individual choice – the radical elements of the movement sought not women's assimilation into the status quo but a sweeping transformation of everyday life.[13] The goal was not, to use the vocabulary of the day, women's mere equality with men, but women's liberation. What precisely they were to be liberated from and to were, of course, matters of lively debate, but the language of liberation and the project of conceiving a state of freedom beyond equality did serve to open a broader horizon of feminist imagination and indicate new agendas for action.

In addition to 1970s women's liberation, about which I will have more to say below, another resource for this project comes from recent work in political theory that affirms freedom as an important feminist goal. The work of Wendy Brown and Linda Zerilli is particularly valuable for its efforts to take up "the project of feminism in a freedom-centered frame" (Zerilli 2005, 95). Freedom is understood in these accounts beyond the liberal model of an individual possession, something that emanates from the sovereign will and guards its independence such that, to quote a familiar formulation, "over himself, over his own body and mind, the individual is sovereign" (Mill 1986, 16). Instead, freedom is seen as a practice, not a possession, a process rather than a goal. Whether it is drawn from the simultaneously creative and destructive qualities of the will to power in Brown's Nietzschean analysis, or from the inaugural and disordering capacities of human action in Zerilli's Arendtian account, freedom emerges in these texts as a double-sided phenomenon. It is depicted, on the one hand, as an antidisciplinary practice – that is, to use Brown's formulation, as "a permanent struggle against what will otherwise be done to and for us" (1995, 25). But there is more to it: freedom is also a creative practice, what Zerilli describes as a collective practice of world building and Brown characterizes in terms of a desire "to participate in shaping the conditions and terms of life," a longing "to generate futures

---

[13] Indeed, as one radical feminist famously declared, with a combination of daring and grandiosity not uncommon to 1970s feminism, "if there were another word more all-embracing than revolution we would use it" (Firestone 1970, 3).

together rather than navigate or survive them" (1995, 4). Freedom thus depends on collective action rather than individual will, and this is what makes it political. Though freedom is, by this account, a relational practice, it is not a zero-sum game in which the more one has, the less another can enjoy. Freedom considered as a matter of individual self-determination or self-sovereignty is reduced to a solipsistic phenomenon. Rather, as a world-building practice, freedom is a social – and hence necessarily political – endeavor. It is, as Marx might put it, a species-being rather than an individual capacity; or, as Zerilli contends, drawing on an Arendtian formulation, freedom requires plurality (2005, 20). Thus Arendt provocatively declares: "If men wish to be free, it is precisely sovereignty they must renounce" (1961, 165). Freedom in this sense demands not the absence of power but its democratization.

Although political theorists like Brown and Zerilli are helpful in elaborating a notion of freedom that can serve as a central analytic and principle of political aspiration, political theory in general, as noted above, has not attended sufficiently to work. Work has been relatively neglected not only as a practice productive of hierarchies – a scene of gendering, racialization, and becoming classed – but as an arena in which to develop and pursue a freedom-centered politics. Yet at the same time, as Michael Denning reminds us, "the workplace remains the fundamental *unfree* association of civil society" (2004, 224). It is the site of many of the most palpable and persistent relations of domination and subordination that people confront, even if these are not conventionally perceived as potentially alterable enough to be regarded as properly political matters. If, as I maintain, a political theory of work should address the problem of freedom, a political theory of freedom should also focus on work. My interest, then, is in developing a feminist political theory of work that could pose work itself – its structures and its ethics, its practices and relations – not only as a machine for the generation of inequalities, but as a political problem of freedom.[14] Linking the previous distinction between class and work to this conceptual pair might help to clarify my concerns in this respect. Rather than a politics of class focused primarily on issues of economic redistribution and economic justice – particularly a politics that seeks to alter wage levels to redraw the map of class categories – the politics of work I am interested in pursuing also investigates questions about the command and control over the spaces and times of life, and seeks the freedom to participate in shaping the terms of what collectively we can do and what together we might become. If what I am calling a "politics of class outcomes" lodges its central

---

14 Here I obviously part company with more orthodox Arendtian – let alone Nietzschean – analyses that would exclude work from the proper business of the political.

complaint against the inequalities of capitalist society, the politics of work that I would like to see elaborated would also levy a critique at its unfreedoms.[15]

Marxist feminism redux

Although I draw on a variety of sources, the version of 1970s feminism that has been of particular importance to this effort to theorize work in these terms is Anglo-American Marxist feminism.[16] As an attempt to map capitalist political economies and gender regimes from a simultaneously anticapitalist and feminist perspective, the tradition in its heyday was committed to investigating how various gendered laboring practices are both put to use by, and potentially disruptive of, capitalist and patriarchal social formations.[17] Three focuses of this literature are especially relevant to my interests here: publicizing work, politicizing it, and radically transforming it. However, the efforts in all three of these areas require some prodding and pushing if they are to be of use to this project in this moment. The category of the refusal of work introduced above will be used to do some of this prodding and pushing, serving as a tool with which to reconfigure each of these focuses by providing certain correctives and additions.

The Marxist – or, as some prefer to call it, socialist feminist – tradition is an inspiration for this project first and foremost because of its focus on labor, both as

---

[15] To be sure, to affirm the value of this latter agenda focused on freedom is not to discount the ongoing importance of the former committed to equality.

[16] I will generally use the label "Marxist feminism" to describe a wide variety of feminisms, including my own, despite the fact that I sometimes draw on sources more typically identified (and often even self-identified) as socialist feminist. The distinction between Marxist feminism and socialist feminism is not always clear. Often they are distinguished by period, with Marxist feminism preceding the development of socialist feminism, and the latter described as a synthesis of Marxism and radical feminism developed in the 1970s. The term "socialist" is also sometimes used as a way to designate a more expansive and inclusive project, one committed to political-economic analysis, but not necessarily to Marxism per se. I prefer the term "Marxist feminism" for two reasons: first, because my own work and many of its points of reference, including the domestic-labor and wages for housework literatures, are indebted to Marxist theoretical traditions; and second, because I am skeptical about the contemporary relevance of the term "socialist," a point I will expand upon below.

[17] The late 1960s to the early 1980s marks the period of Marxist feminism's maximum influence within US feminist theory. Today the project lives on, often under other labels, and explores, among other things, how the present organization of both waged and unwaged work – including current instances of the class, gender, race, and transnational divisions of labor – are implicated in the construction and maintenance of class, gender, racial, and national differences and hierarchies.

a point of entry into the critical analysis of capitalist patriarchy and as a key site of political action. "Socialist feminism," as one analyst summarizes it, "means paying consistent attention to women *in our capacity as workers,* and in all our variety" (Froines 1992, 128). Perhaps its most significant contribution to the critical theory of work in the 1970s was the expansion of the category. Feminists insisted that the largely unwaged "reproductive" work that made waged "productive" work possible on a daily and generational basis was socially necessary labor, and that its relations were thus part and parcel of the capitalist mode of production. What had been coded as leisure was in fact work, and those supposedly spontaneous expressions of women's nature were indeed skillful practices. In their efforts to adapt Marxist concepts and methods to new concerns, these feminists usefully troubled the tradition's definition of work. Nancy Hartsock describes this by way of an addendum to Marx's story about the owner of money and the owner of labor power. To return to that passage one final time, if after descending with the capitalist and worker into the realm of waged work we were then to follow the worker home, into yet another hidden abode of production, we might observe another change in the dramatis personae:

> He who before followed behind as the worker, timid and holding back, with nothing to expect but a hiding, now strides in front, while a third person, not specifically present in Marx's account of the transactions between capitalist and worker (both of whom are male) follows timidly behind, carrying groceries, baby, and diapers. (Hartsock 1983, 234)

By following the worker not only from marketplace to workplace, but also from the place of employment to the domestic space, we find evidence not only of class hierarchy, but of specifically gendered forms of exploitation and patterns of inequality. By descending into the even more hidden, even more fiercely privatized space of the household, we see men and women who may be formally equal under the law transformed through the gender division of labor into relatively privileged and penalized subjects. Thus, Marxist feminists in the 1970s explored the means by which gender hierarchies deliver unwaged women workers to the domestic mode of reproduction while also ensuring a cheaper and more flexible secondary or tertiary waged labor force. These feminists debated the exact value to capital of women's unwaged domestic labor and exposed the hyperexploitation of women wage earners around the globe. And they studied the interconnections among the family, the labor market, waged and unwaged labor processes, and the welfare state. As we will see, in fact, many of their insights into the conditions of women's labor under Fordism will prove to be more widely applicable to the forms of work typical of post-Fordist economies. By extending these efforts to publicize, politicize, and transform work into the field of domestic labor, feminists usefully complicated and upped the ante of all three projects. What might have at first appeared to be a simple addition to Marxist analyses has in fact required a vast rethinking of its concepts and models, its critical analyses and utopian visions.

Whereas many of these texts are helpful for their emphasis on work, the tradition's productivist tendencies, which it shares with some other versions of Marxist theory, prove more troublesome. As we have already noted, feminism has managed to reproduce its own version of the work ethic, whether in the process of defending waged work as the alternative to feminine domesticity in both liberal feminism and traditional Marxism, or through efforts to gain recognition for modes of unwaged labor as socially necessary labor. Feminism, including much of 1970s Marxist feminism, has tended to focus more on the critique of work's organization and distribution than on questioning its values. The autonomous Marxist tradition is thus useful in this instance insofar as it simultaneously centers its analytical apparatus on work and disavows its traditional ethics. Central to that tradition is not only the analytical primacy accorded to the imposition of work as fundamental to the capitalist mode of production, but also the political priority of the refusal of work – a priority recorded in the call not for a liberation *of* work but a liberation *from* work (see Virno and Hardt 1996, 263). The refusal of work is at once a model of resistance, both to the modes of work that are currently imposed on us and to their ethical defense, and a struggle for a different relationship to work born from the collective autonomy that a postwork ethics and more nonwork time could help us to secure. As a simultaneous way to insist on work's significance and to contest its valuation, the Marxist feminist literature on wages for housework – with roots in an Italian feminism that was, as one participant observed, "characterized, with more emphasis than in other countries, by the *leitmotif* of 'work/rejection of work'" (Dalla Costa 1988, 24) – will be of particular importance to my project in this respect.

Thus work is not only a locus of unfreedom, it is also a site of resistance and contestation.[18] This brings me to the second element of the Marxist feminist literature that I have found instructive: the commitment to work's politicization. Marxist feminists focused not only on exploited workers but, to cite one of these authors, also on subjects that are "potentially revolutionary" (Eisenstein 1979, 8). Within this body of literature, one can find an attention both to structures of domination and to the possibilities for critical consciousness, subversive practices, and feminist standpoints that might be developed in their midst. This investment in constructing collective political subjects on the basis of, or in relation to, work

---

[18] Both Marxists and feminists, as Barbara Ehrenreich explained her understanding of the socialist feminist project in 1976, "seek to understand the world – not in terms of static balances, symmetries, etc. (as in conventional social science) – but in terms of antagonisms" (1997, 66).

practices, relations, and subjectivities remains for me an aspect of this literature with the most relevance to contemporary feminism. Harking back to the example of a Marxism that conceived the industrial proletariat as a revolutionary class less because it had nothing to lose but its chains than because it had the power to create a new world, many of these authors concentrate on the ways that feminized modes of labor – marginalized by, but nonetheless fundamental to, capitalist valorization processes – could provide points of critical leverage and sites of alternative possibility.

This more capacious understanding of work also entailed a transformation of what might be recognized as a terrain of anticapitalist politics, pushing beyond orthodox Marxism's industrial model of productive cooperation that centered on the factory, in which the Proletariat was once imagined as the singularly revolutionary subject, to a more expansive set of sites and subjects. The focal point of analysis for this expanded political terrain might best be described as the contradiction between capital accumulation and social reproduction.[19] Capital requires, for example, time both to "consume" labor power and to produce (or reproduce) it, and the time devoted to one is sometimes lost to the other. The competing requirements of creating surplus value and sustaining the lives and socialities upon which it depends form a potential fault line through capitalist political economies, one that might serve to generate critical thinking and political action. Under the conditions of Fordism, for example, this meant that capital was dependent on a family-based model of social reproduction, one that was in some respects functional to its purposes but was in other ways a potential hindrance to its hegemony. Thus we find in a body of management literature and practice that spans the Fordist and post-Fordist periods an expressed need to locate and preserve some kind of balance between work and family – a relationship that many feminists, on the contrary, struggled to expose as a product of normative imposition rather than natural proclivity and a site of flagrant contradiction rather than mere imbalance.

But just as Marxist feminism's critical study of work was limited, at least for the purposes of this project, by its productivist propensities, so too the focus on locating and cultivating revolutionary possibilities in relation to work was sometimes compromised by a susceptibility to functionalist logics. The temptation of functionalism is, of course, not peculiar to feminist theory. Indeed, its presence at some level reflects a methodological and political choice: whether to con-

---

[19] Perhaps the contemporary literature that most directly addresses social reproduction as a feminist analytic, in this case on the terrain of political economy, comes out of Canada. For some good examples, see Bakker and Gill (2003), Bezanson and Luxton (2006), and Luxton and Corman (2001).

centrate on how social systems persist over time, or to highlight the ways that they can and do change. Foucault explains it this way: because of the instability and unpredictability generated by the "agonism" of power relations on the one hand and the "intransitivity of freedom" on the other hand, there is always the option "to decipher the same events and the same transformations either from inside the history of struggle or from the standpoint of the power relationships" (1983, 223, 226) – a pair of options between which his own work could be said to oscillate. This same methodological distinction marks a long-standing division within the Marxist tradition as well. Thus, for example, although they both offer systematic mappings of capitalist logics and social formations, Marx's *Grundrisse* approaches the analysis more from the point of view of crisis and conflict, whereas *Capital* tells the story from the perspective of capital's appropriative and recuperative capacities.

To return to the case of 1970s Marxist feminism, the residues of functionalist logics show up in what is, I would argue, a limited understanding of social reproduction. In fact, there are at least two related problems with the analyses from a contemporary perspective. First, whereas these authors arguably succeeded in developing more-complete accounts of the relationship between production and reproduction typical of Fordist political economies than were available elsewhere at the time, these accounts are no longer adequate to the project of mapping post-Fordism. In the classic texts from this period, production and reproduction were associated according to the logic of a dual-systems model with two different spaces: the waged workplace was the site of productive labor, and the household was the site of unwaged, reproductive labor. Reproductive labor in these accounts usually included the forms of unwaged work through which individuals met their daily needs for food, shelter, and care and raised a new generation to take their place.[20] However, under the conditions of postindustrial, post-Fordist, and post-Taylorist production, the always vexing exercise of distinguishing between production and reproduction – whether by sphere, task, or relationship to the wage – becomes even more difficult. The dual-systems model, always problematic, is thereby rendered even more deficient.

The second reason why the older models are no longer tenable brings us to the issue of their functionalism. Here is the problem: when reduced, as it tends to be in these analyses, to a familiar list of domestic labors, the category of social reproduction cannot pose the full measure of its conflict with the logics and processes

---

[20] "Social reproduction can thus be seen to include various kinds of work – mental, manual, and emotional – aimed at providing the historically and socially, as well as biologically, defined care necessary to maintain existing life and to reproduce the next generation" (Laslett and Brenner 1989, 383).

of capital accumulation. The specific problems that this more limited notion of reproduction serves to highlight – the invisibility, devaluation, and gendered division of specifically domestic labors – could, for example, be responded to (but not, of course, remedied) through an expanded reliance on marketized versions of such services. As the refusal-of-work perspective suggests, the problem with the organization of social reproduction extends beyond the problems of this work's invisibility, devaluation, and gendering. Although I want to register that domestic labor is socially necessary and unequally distributed (insofar as gender, race, class, and nation often determines who will do more and less of it), I am also interested in moving beyond the claim that if it were to be fully recognized, adequately compensated, and equally divided, then the existing model of household-based reproduction would be rectified. A more expansive conception of social reproduction, coupled with the refusal of work, might be used to frame a more compelling problematic. What happens when social reproduction is understood as the production of the forms of social cooperation on which accumulation depends or, alternatively, as the rest of life beyond work that capital seeks continually to harness to its times, spaces, rhythms, purposes, and values? What I am in search of is a conception of social reproduction – of what it is we might organize around – that can pose the full measure of its antagonism with the exigencies of capital accumulation, a biopolitical model of social reproduction less readily transformed into new forms of work and thus less easily recuperated within the present terms of the work society.

The third aspect of the Marxist feminist tradition that I want to acknowledge here is its commitment to thinking within a horizon of utopian potential, that is, in relation to the possibility of fundamental transformation (Feminist Review Collective 1986, 8). Work is not only a site of exploitation, domination, and antagonism, but also where we might find the power to create alternatives on the basis of subordinated knowledges, resistant subjectivities, and emergent models of organization. At least some of this literature focuses on both antiwork politics and postwork imaginaries. This model of utopian politics that can "make the creation of prefigurative forms an explicit part of our movement against capitalism" and challenge the "politics of deferment" that would postpone such innovations to some distant future after "the revolution" is something that I think feminist theory should embrace (Rowbotham, Segal, and Wainwright 1979, 147, 140). The problem with these visions of radical social change from a contemporary perspective is that they were most often conceived of as variations on a theme named socialism, even if some called for "a new kind of socialism" or a socialist revolution that would be equally feminist and antiracist.[21] Today, however, it seems unlikely that socialism can serve as a persuasive signifier of a postcapitalist alternative. There are at least three kinds of problems with the term. At one level, there is the problem of the name itself: it has been some time since the language of socialism could resonate in the United States as a legible and generative utopian vocabulary (even though it continues to serve occasionally as a viable dystopia for the Right). But it is not just a matter of the label; it is about the content of the vision, which has traditionally centered on the equal liability to work together with a more equitable distribution of its rewards. As a certainly more just version of a social form that is nonetheless centered on work, it gestures toward a vision of the work society perfected, rather than transformed.

Beyond the obsolescence of the label and the commitment to work it affirms, there is a third problem with the legacy of socialism. Whereas the Marxist feminist – or, more specifically in this instance, the socialist feminist – tradition was willing to affirm the value of utopian speculation about a radically different future, the use of the label "socialism" often nonetheless seemed to assume that this future could be named and its basic contours predetermined. In this respect – here I anticipate an argument that I will develop in chapter 5 – socialist feminists would seem "to know too much too soon." There are advantages, I claim, to morepartial visions of alternatives, fragments or glimpses of something different that do not presume to add up to a blueprint of an already named future with a preconceived content. I will use the label "postwork society" not to anticipate an alternative so much as to point toward a horizon of utopian possibility, as it seems preferable to hold the space of a different future open with the term "post" than to presume to be able to name it as "socialist."

In summary, my project can thus be said to begin with a historical tradition of Marxist feminism that often focused on the category of class, the ideal of equality, the problem of domestic labor, and the socialist struggle for more and better work, which I would like to redirect by way of the sometimes rather different commitments and imaginaries referenced by the categories of work, freedom, social reproduction, life, the refusal of work, and postwork. I will thus use work as a point of entry into the territory of class politics; freedom to supplement and redirect an anticapitalist political theory also committed to equality; the refusal of work to confront work's overvaluation; the field of social reproduction as part of a struggle to wrest more of life from the encroachments of work; and postwork

---

21 That is, in terms of "the new forms of organization and relations between people which we define as socialism" (Berkeley-Oakland Women's Union 1979, 356), but also sometimes in the more expansive terms of what another group identified as socialist, feminist, and antiracist revolution (Combahee River Collective 1979, 366).

utopianism to replace socialism as the horizon of revolutionary possibility and speculation.

Chapter overviews

The questions raised and points of focus elaborated above are meant to set the stage for the specific arguments pursued in the remaining chapters. One way to approach the overall structure of the discussion that follows is to separate it into two parts: a first part, encompassing chapters 1 and 2, that concentrates on the diagnostic and deconstructive dimensions of the critical theory of work; and a second part, including chapters 3, 4, and 5, that focuses on the prescriptive and reconstructive aspects of the project. Whereas "refusal" is the animating category of the first part, "demand" anchors the analysis in the second part. The argument thus proceeds from the refusal of the present terms of the work society to demands for remedies and for the imagining of alternative futures.

As noted above, the work ethic is at the center of the political theory of and against work that I want to begin to elaborate. A critique of work that seeks to challenge its dominance over our lives must take on the ethical discourse that gives work its meaning and defends its primacy. The first two chapters seek to develop a critical account of the work ethic and to explore some of the theoretical resources through which it might be interrogated. Chapter 1 concentrates on the nature and function of the work ethic in the United States. In what may be a fitting departure for a text so often indebted to Marxist resources, the analysis in chapter 1 draws on one of that tradition's most famous critiques, Max Weber's *Protestant Ethic and the Spirit of Capitalism*. Tracing the continuities and shifts in the work ethic over the course of its different incarnations – first as a Protestant ethic, and later as an industrial and then a postindustrial ethic – the analysis seeks to map the recent history of the work ethic and to raise questions about its future. Today when neoliberal and postneoliberal regimes demand that almost everyone work for wages (never mind that there is not enough work to go around), when postindustrial production employs workers' minds and hearts as well as their hands, and when post-Taylorist labor processes increasingly require the self-management of subjectivity so that attitudes and affective orientations to work will themselves produce value, the dominant ethical discourse of work may be more indispensable than it has ever been, and the refusal of its prescriptions even more timely. The analysis thus attempts to account not only for the ethic's longevity and power, but also its points of instability and vulnerability.

Chapter 2 explores some theoretical tools with which we might exploit some of these openings. Drawing on Jean Baudrillard's critique of productivism, the chapter explores the limitations of two familiar paradigms of Marxist theory, labeled here "socialist modernization" and "socialist humanism," and then concentrates on an explication of autonomist Marxism's theory and practice of the refusal of work. The critical review of the two earlier models presents an opportunity to confront the pro-work assumptions and values that remain stubbornly embedded within a number of theoretical frameworks, including some Marxist discourses, as well as instructive contrasts to the very different commitments animating the more recent example of autonomist Marxism. As a refusal not of creative or productive activity, but of the present configuration of the work society and its moralized conception of work, the refusal of work serves as a methodological center of gravity and ongoing inspiration for the models of analysis and speculation that occupy the subsequent chapters. The critical practice at the heart of the refusal of work, as I read it here, is at once deconstructive and reconstructive – or, as the autonomists might describe it, a practice of separation and process of self-valorization – an analysis that is committed at once to antiwork critique and postwork invention.

In keeping with this dual focus of the refusal of work, chapter 3 marks a shift in the project from the critical charge I just described to the task of constructing possible alternatives, from the development of an antiwork critique to the incitement of a postwork political imaginary. More specifically, the argument shifts at this point from a focus on the refusal of work and its ethics to the demands for a guaranteed basic income (chapter 3) and for a thirty-hour work week (chapter 4). The category of the utopian demand (a category I explore in more detail in chapter 5) is one of the ways I want to conceive the relationship between antiwork analysis and postwork desire, imagination, and will as they figure in the practice of political claims making. Utopian demands, including demands for basic income and shorter hours, are more than simple policy proposals; they include as well the perspectives and modes of being that inform, emerge from, and inevitably exceed the texts and practices by which they are promoted. Assessments of their value thus need to be attentive to the possibilities and limits of both their structural and discursive effects.

But first: why single out these demands? Certainly there are any number of demands for change worth exploring, proposals that could affect tangible improvements in the present conditions of work.[22] The demand for a living wage is an obvious example; across the United States, campaigns for living-wage

---

[22] Although since it is less a demand for change than a demand for the enforcement of existing policies, it is important to note that even demanding the enforcement of the wage and hours laws

reform have mobilized impressive levels of political activity and achieved significant victories. I focus on the demands for basic income and shorter hours for two reasons. First, like the demand for living wages and others, they represent important remedies for some of the problems with the existing system of wages and hours. A guaranteed and universal basic income would enhance the bargaining position of all workers vis-à-vis employers and enable some people to opt out of waged work without the stigma and precariousness of means-tested welfare programs. A thirty-hour full-time work week without a decrease in pay would help to address some of the problems of both the underemployed and the overworked. The second reason for focusing on these demands – which I think distinguishes them from many other demands for economic reform, including the demand for a living wage – is their capacity not only to improve the conditions of work but to challenge the terms of its dominance. These demands do not affirm our right to work so much as help us to secure some measure of freedom from it.[23] For the purposes of this project, I am interested in demands that would not only advance concrete reforms of work but would also raise broader questions about the place of work in our lives and spark the imagination of a life no longer so subordinate to it – demands that would serve as vectors rather than terminal points.[24]

Chapter 3 begins with a rereading of the 1970s movement for wages for housework, the most promising dimensions of which, I argue, have been poorly understood. This instance of Marxist feminist theory and practice is particularly relevant to this project because of its roots in the autonomist tradition and for its commitment to, and distinctive deployment of, the refusal of work. Building on some of this literature's unique analyses of the gendered political economy of work, its mode of struggle against the organization of domestic work, and its treatment of the feminist political practice of demanding, I go on to propose a rationale for a different demand: the demand for a guaranteed basic income. I argue that this demand can deliver on some of the potential of wages for housework while being more consistent with conditions in a post-Fordist political economy. Drawing on a framework gleaned from the wages for housework literature, the demand for basic income can do more than present a useful reform; it can serve both to open

---

already on the books would make an enormous difference, especially to the lives of low-wage workers. See Annette Bernhardt et al. (2009).

23 Another example is the demand for universal healthcare without any ties to employment, although that demand's critique of work per se might be less direct than the critiques posed by the demands for basic income and shorter hours.

24 The demand for less work, as Jonathan Cutler and Stanley Aronowitz explain it, is unusual in its capacity to position workers to make further demands: "No other bargaining demand simultaneously enhances bargaining position" (1998, 20).

a critical perspective on the wage system and to provoke visions of a life not so dependent on the system's present terms and conditions.

This particular understanding of what a demand is and what it can do guides the analysis in chapter 4 of another demand, this one for shorter hours. The chapter explores the demand for a six-hour day with no decrease in pay as at once a demand for change and a perspective and provocation, at once a useful reform and a conceptual frame that could generate critical thinking and public debate about the structures and ethics of work. In contrast both to those who defend a reduction of hours at work in order to expand family time, and to those who fail in their articulation of the demand to address the intimate relationship between work and family, the case for shorter hours developed here focuses on expanding our freedom not only from capitalist command but also from imposed norms of sexuality and traditional standards of proper household composition and roles. Taking aim at, rather than appropriating, normative discourses of the family, the demand for shorter hours is conceived here as a demand for, among other benefits, more time to imagine, experiment with, and participate in the relationships of intimacy and sociality that we choose. This account thus understands the movement for shorter hours in terms of securing the time and space to confront and forge alternatives to the present structures and ethics of both work and family.

Whereas the demands for basic income and shorter hours usefully point in the direction of a critical politics against and beyond work, they could be easily dismissed as utopian. Chapter 5 investigates the case against utopia and, drawing on the work of Ernst Bloch and Friedrich Nietzsche, attempts a response. Rather than rehearse the arguments made in other chapters about why these demands are in fact realistic proposals, chapter 5 pursues another tack. Provisionally accepting the judgment that they are utopian, the discussion explores instead what a utopian demand is and what it might be able to do, arguing that only through a more complicated understanding of the utopian dimensions of these demands can we appreciate their efficacy. To establish the general credentials and specific possibilities and limitations of the demand as a utopian form, the analysis explores its relation to other, perhaps more familiar, utopian artifacts, including the traditional literary and philosophical utopia and the manifesto. The conception of the utopian demand that emerges from this account emphasizes not only its capacity to advance significant reforms, but also its potential as a critical perspective and force of provocation that can incite political desires for, imagination of, and mobilization toward different futures.

The brief epilogue attempts to both reflect on the previous arguments and address some topics that they neglected. I begin with two points of clarification. First, my preference for politics over ethics as the terrain of antiwork struggle and postwork speculation raises a question about the relationship between politics and ethics that the analysis presumes. Also meriting discussion is a second relationship, between the project's radical aspirations to remake a life outside of work and its comparatively moderate demands. This seeming incongruence between ambitious ends and modest means warrants an elaboration of the relationship between reform and revolution that informs the project. In the final section, I take another step back from the material to consider one way to bring the two demands together as part of a broader political effort to defend life against work, the colloquial version of which could be described as "getting a life." The rubric of life against work is, I propose, both capacious and pointed enough to frame a potent antiwork politics and fuel a postwork imagination.

In the epigraph above, C. Wright Mills laments the fact that we measure the satisfaction of jobs only against the standard of other jobs: "One type of work, or one particular job, is contrasted with another type, experienced or imagined, within the present world of work." That is to say, "judgments are rarely made about the world of work as presently organized as against some other way of organizing it" (1951, 229). I want to make a case for the importance of a political theory of work and specifically, a political theory that seeks to pose work as a political problem of freedom. Beyond any particular claim or category – beyond any of the specific arguments about the role of the work ethic in sustaining the structures and cultures of work, the legitimacy of basic income, the need for shorter hours, or the utility of utopian thought – the project is meant to raise some basic questions about the organization and meaning of work. The assumptions at the heart of the work ethic, not only about the virtues of hard work and long hours but also about their inevitability, are too rarely examined, let alone contested. What kinds of conceptual frameworks and political discourses might serve to generate new ways of thinking about the nature, value, and meaning of work relative to other practices and in relation to the rest of life? How might we expose the fundamental structures and dominant values of work – including its temporalities, socialities, hierarchies, and subjectivities – as pressing political phenomena? If why we work, where we work, with whom we work, what we do at work, and how long we work are social arrangements and hence properly political decisions, how might more of this territory be reclaimed as viable terrains of debate and struggle? The problem with work is not just that it monopolizes so much time and energy, but that it also dominates the social and political imaginaries. What might we name the variety of times and spaces outside waged work, and what might we wish to do with and in them? How might we conceive the content and parameters of our obligations to one another outside the currency of work? The argument that follows, then, is one attempt to assess theoretically and imagine how to confront politically the present organization of work and the discourses that support it.

References

Acker, Joan. 2000. "Revisiting Class: Thinking from Gender, Race, and Organizations." *Social Politics* 7 (2): 192–214.
Arendt, Hannah. 1958. *The Human Condition*. Chicago: University of Chicago Press.
Arendt, Hannah. 1961. "What Is Freedom?" In Hannah Arendt, *Between Past and Future: Eight Exercises in Political Thought*. New York: Viking.
Aronowitz, Stanley. 2003. *How Class Works: Power and Social Movement*. New Haven: Yale University Press.
Bakker, Isabella, and Stephen Gill, eds. 2003. *Power, Production, and Social Reproduction: Human In/security in the Global Political Economy*. Houndmills, England: Palgrave Macmillan.
Beck, Ulrich. 2000. *The Brave New World of Work*. Translated by Patrick Camiller. Cambridge: Polity.
Berk, Sarah Fenstermaker. 1985. *The Gender Factory: The Apportionment of Work in American Households*. New York: Plenum.
Berkeley-Oakland Women's Union. 1979. "Principles of Unity." In *Capitalist Patriarchy and the Case for Socialist Feminism*, edited by Zillah Eisenstein, 355–361. New York: Monthly Review Press.
Bernhardt, Annette, et al. 2009. "Broken Laws, Unprotected Workers: Violations of Employment and Labor Laws in America's Cities." http://nelp.3cdn.net/319982941a5496c741e9qm6b92kg.pdf.
Bezanson, Kate, and Meg Luxton, eds. 2006. *Social Reproduction: Feminist Political Economy Challenges Neo-Liberalism*. Montreal: McGill-Queen's University Press.
Boggs, James. 1963. *The American Revolution: Pages from a Negro Worker's Notebook*. New York: Monthly Review Press.
Brown, Wendy. 1995. *States of Injury: Power and Freedom in Late Modernity*. Princeton: Princeton University Press.
Burawoy, Michael. 1979. *Manufacturing Consent: Changes in the Labor Process under Monopoly Capitalism*. Chicago: University of Chicago Press.
Cleaver, Harry. 2002. "Work Is *Still* the Central Issue! New Words for New Worlds." In *The Labour Debate: An Investigation into the Theory and Reality of Capitalist Work*, edited by Ana C. Dinerstein and Michael Neary, 135–148. Aldershot, England: Ashgate.
Combahee River Collective. 1979. "A Black Feminist Statement." In *Capitalist Patriarchy and the Case for Socialist Feminism*, edited by Zillah Eisenstein, 362–372. New York: Monthly Review Press.
Corlett, William. 1998. *Class Action: Reading Labor, Theory, and Value*. Ithaca: Cornell University Press.
Cutler, Jonathan, and Stanley Aronowitz. 1998. "Quitting Time: An Introduction." In *Post-Work: The Wages of Cybernation*, edited by Stanley Aronowitz and Jonathan Cutler, 1–30. New York: Routledge.

Dalla Costa 1988. "Domestic Labour and the Feminist Movement in Italy since the 1970s." *International Sociology* 3 (1): 23–34.
Denning, Michael. 2004. *Culture in the Age of Three Worlds*. London: Verso.
Ehrenreich, Barbara. 1997. "What Is Socialist Feminism?" In *Materialist Feminism: A Reader in Class, Difference, and Women's Lives*, edited by Rosemary Hennessy and Chrys Ingraham, 65–70. New York: Routledge.
Eisenstein, Zillah. 1979. "Developing a Theory of Capitalist Patriarchy and Socialist Feminism." In *Capitalist Patriarchy and the Case for Socialist Feminism*, edited by Zillah Eisenstein, 5–40. New York: Monthly Review Press.
Feminist Review Collective. 1986. "Editorial." In "Socialist-Feminism: Out of the Blue." Special issue, *Feminist Review* 23 (1): 3–10.
Firestone, Shulamith. 1970. *The Dialectic of Sex: The Case for Feminist Revolution*. New York: Farrar, Straus and Giroux.
Foucault, Michel. 1983. "The Subject and Power." In Hubert L. Dreyfus and Paul Rabinow, *Michel Foucault: Beyond Structuralism and Hermeneutics*, with an afterword by Michel Foucault, 2nd ed., 208–226. Chicago: University of Chicago Press.
Freeman, Carla. 2000. *High Tech and High Heels in the Global Economy: Women, Work, and Pink-Collar Identities in the Caribbean*. Durham: Duke University Press.
Froines, Ann. 1992. "Renewing Socialist Feminism." *Socialist Review* 22 (2): 125–131.
Glazer, Nona Y. 1993. *Women's Paid and Unpaid Labor: The Work Transfer in Health Care and Retailing*. Philadelphia: Temple University Press.
Hartsock, Nancy C. M. 1983. *Money, Sex, and Power: Toward a Feminist Historical Materialism*. Boston: Northeastern University Press.
Laslett, Barbara, and Johanna Brenner. 1989. "Gender and Social Reproduction: Historical Perspectives." *Annual Review of Sociology* 15: 381–404.
Leidner, Robin. 1993. *Fast Food, Fast Talk: Service Work and the Routinization of Everyday Life*. Berkeley: University of California Press.
Leidner, Robin. 2006. "Identity at Work." In *Social Theory at Work*, edited by Marek Korczynski, Randy Hodson, and Paul Edwards, 424–463. Oxford: Oxford University Press.
Luxton, Meg, and June Corman. 2001. *Getting By in Hard Times: Gendered Labour at Home and on the Job*. Toronto: University of Toronto Press.
Macarov, David. 1980. *Work and Welfare: The Unholy Alliance*. Beverly Hills: Sage.
Locke, John. 1986. *The Second Treatise on Civil Government*. Amherst, N.Y.: Prometheus.
Marx, Karl. 1964. *The Economic and Philosophic Manuscripts of 1844*. Translated by Martin Milligan. New York: International Publishers.
Marx, Karl. 1976. *Capital: A Critique of Political Economy*. Vol. 1. Translated by Ben Fowkes. New York: Vintage.
Marx, Karl. 1978. "Critique of the Gotha Program." In *The Marx-Engels Reader*, 2nd ed., edited by Robert C. Tucker, 525–541. New York: W. W. Norton.
Marx, Karl, and Friedrich Engels. 1970. *The German Ideology, Part One*. Edited by C. J. Arthur. New York: International Publishers.
Mill, John Stuart. 1986. *On Liberty*. Amherst, N.Y.: Prometheus.
Mill, John Stuart. 1988. *The Subjection of Women*. Indianapolis: Hackett.
Mills, C. Wright. 1951. *White Collar: The American Middle Classes*. New York: Oxford University Press.
Morris, William. 1999. "Useful Work Versus Useless Toil." In William Morris, *William Morris on Art and Socialism*, edited by Norman Kelvin, 128–143. Mineola, N.Y.: Dover.

Muirhead, Russell. 2004. *Just Work*. Cambridge: Harvard University Press.
Negri, Antonio. 1996. "Twenty Theses on Marx: Interpretation of the Class Situation Today." Translated by Michael Hardt. In *Marxism beyond Marxism*, edited by Saree Makdisi, Cesare Casarino, and Rebecca E. Karl, 149–180. New York: Routledge.
Pateman, Carole. 1988. *The Sexual Contract*. Stanford: Stanford University Press.
Postone, Moishe. 1996. *Time, Labor, and Social Domination: A Reinterpretation of Marx's Critical Theory*. Cambridge: Cambridge University Press.
Read, Jason. 2003. *The Micro-Politics of Capital: Marx and the Prehistory of the Present*. Albany: State University of New York Press.
Rodgers, Daniel T. 1978. *The Work Ethic in Industrial America*: 1850–1920. Chicago: University of Chicago Press.
Rowbotham, Sheila, Lynne Segal, and Hilary Wainwright. 1979. *Beyond the Fragments: Feminism and the Making of Socialism*. London: Merlin.
Salzinger, Leslie. 2003. *Genders in Production: Making Workers in Mexico's Global Factories*. Berkeley: University of California Press.
Seidman, Michael. 1991. *Workers against Work: Labor in Paris and Barcelona during the Popular Fronts*. Berkeley: University of California Press.
Smith, Dorothy E. 1987. *The Everyday World as Problematic: A Feminist Sociology*. Boston: Northeastern University Press.
Virno, Paolo, and Michael Hardt. 1996. "Glossary of Concepts." In *Radical Thought in Italy: A Potential Politics*, edited by Paolo Virno and Michael Hardt, 261–264. Minneapolis: University of Minnesota Press.
West, Candace, and Don H. Zimmerman. 1991. "Doing Gender." In *The Social Construction of Gender*, edited by Judith Lorber and Susan A. Farrell, 13–37. Newbury Park, Calif.: Sage.
Willis, Paul. 1977. *Learning to Labor: How Working Class Kids Get Working Class Jobs*. New York: Columbia University Press.
Young, Iris. 1981. "Beyond the Unhappy Marriage: A Critique of Dual Systems Theory." In *Women and Revolution*, edited by Lydia Sargent, 43–69. Boston: South End.
Zerilli, Linda. 2005. *Feminism and the Abyss of Freedom*. Chicago: University of Chicago Press.

Rina Agarwala
Reshaping the social contract
Emerging relations between the state and informal labor in India[1]

Since the late 1990s, a literature designed to examine the variable effects of "globalization" has grown exponentially in the social sciences.[2] Within this literature, several scholars have bolstered the significance of globalization by arguing that the economic policies and the social forces that integrate national economies are undermining the traditional role of the state in determining local outcomes (Castells 1997; Held et al. 1999; Teeple 2000). In particular, ruthless competition in the global marketplace is said to exacerbate pressures on governments to ensure economic survival by reducing costly interference in capital production (Harvey 1990; Held et al. 1999; Hyman 1992; Tilly 1995). Issues concerning labor protection have comprised a prime target area for such reduced government intervention in recent years.

These trends raise a pressing question: how have such changes affected state-labor relations? As states pull back on earlier levels of direct welfare provision and rhetoric, and they no longer hold employers accountable for the welfare of their employees, the proportion of informally employed workers who do not receive secure wages or benefits from either the state or their employer is increasing the world over (Benton 1990; Kundu and Sharma 2001; Portes and Schauffler 1993). Informal workers represent one of the poorest and most marginalized populations of the liberalization era. Yet little is known about their social and political location in the liberalized economy. What strategies are these workers using to improve their livelihood? What new institutions and relationships, if any, are they forging among state, capital, and labor as a response to the recent changes in structures of production? How do we conceive of the "state" and of "society" in the current era?

This study begins to address these questions using an in-depth examination of informal workers' organizations in India, the largest democracy in the world. The informal sector consists of economic units that produce goods and services

---

[1] This articles was first published under the same title in *Theory and Society*, Vol. 37, No. 4 (Aug. 2008), pp. 375–408 DOI 10.1007/s11186-008-9061-5 © Springer Science + Business Media B.V. 2008, reproduced with permission of Springer.
[2] I use the term "globalization" to encompass the myriad of economic, social, political, cultural, and technological changes that are taking place to increase interdependence, integration, and interaction across national boundaries. As Charles Tilly writes, "Ideally, globalization means an increase in the geographic range of locally consequential social interactions" (Tilly 1995: 1).

legally, but engage in operations that are not registered or regulated by fiscal, labor, health, and tax laws.[3] Thus the primary difference between informal and formal workers is that the latter are protected and regulated under state law while the former are not (Portes et al. 1989). Informal workers include the self-employed (such as Street vendors or trash pickers), employees in informal enterprises, and contractors who work for formal enterprises through sub-contractors. Self-employed workers include those who hire or do not hire employees. Informal workers may work at home, on the employers' site, or in a third site, such as a sub-contractor's workshop.

Although informal workers are often featured in passing in the recent globalization literature, in-depth studies on the social and political lives of informal workers remain scant. Latin American and African scholars have provided some important exceptions (Beneria and Roldan 1987; Cross 1998; Grasmuck and Espinal 2000; Gugler 1991; Macharia 1997). In India, studies on the informal sector primarily focus on its definition and measurement.[4] The few case studies that examine informal workers' politics in India are consistent with the Latin American and African studies that show their organizing activities improve working conditions (Carr et al. 1996; Chowdhury 2003; Sanyal 1991; Sharma and Antony 2001). Still little is known about specific organizing strategies, and almost none of the studies has connected informal workers' experiences to the theoretical literature on state-labor relations in the current era.

Informal workers' organizational strategies can provide important insights into new forms of institutionalism that develop in the current system of little state regulation over capital and blurred employer-employee relations. For decades, industrialized workers fought to enter into an institutional structure that provided some play for collective interests; this institutional structure formalized workers' identity and status through legislation designed to protect them against employer exploitation. Their efforts, while laudable, have affected only a minority of the world's workers.[5] Now, due to the industrial restructuring of the

---

[3] Although debates abound on how to define the informal sector, this definition, which is drawn from Portes et al. 1989, has been accepted in much of the literature (see Cross 1998; De Soto 1989; Portes 1994). To operationalize this definition, I use the worker-based definition of informal work that was endorsed by the 17th International Conference of Labor Statisticians (ICLS) in 2003 and utilized by the National Sample Survey of Employment and Unemployment (NSS) in India in 1999.

[4] Kulshreshtha and Singh 1999; Kundu and Sharma 2001; Mahadevia 1998; Oberai and Chadha 2001; Sundaram 2001; Unni 1999.

[5] This is a narrow claim, specific to worker-protection. Collective action by industrialized workers has, of course, benefited the mass population in arenas such as suffrage and citizenship (see Collier and Mahoney 1997; Rueschemeyer et al. 1992).

1980s and 1990s, even the small global share of formally protected workers is diminishing. These changes have brought scholarship of labor movements to a critical juncture by questioning traditional mobilization strategies and institutions that rely on formal state protections and employer accountability. Although informal and formal workers share the same ultimate goal of attaining a social wage that embodies an expanded notion of citizenship, informal workers, who by definition are tied to the state in a starkly different way from formal workers, must form alternative institutions to attain their goals. Informal workers' organizations, therefore, not only offer an important corrective to the existing literature on the state and labor, which focuses almost exclusively on formal workers (Badie and Birnbaum 1983; Rudolph and Rudolph 1987), but they also offer significant insights into institutional structures that are relevant to a growing share of the world's workers.

In addition, an examination of contemporary informal workers' movements, as distinct from formal workers' movements, raises important questions about the nature of democracy in the current era. State policies designed to decentralize structures of production in the name of global competitiveness have distanced the state from labor by filing down state regulation and protection for workers. Informal workers' organizations provide a ready lens into workers' efforts to re-exert their voices into development dialogues and to reestablish their connections with the state. These organizations serve as an important instance of what Patrick Heller (2000: 488) eloquently calls a "consultative arena located in the interstices of state and society where 'everyday' forms of democracy either flourish or founder. Equally essential to understanding democratic politics in the era of globalization is analyzing what Supriya Roy Chowdhury (2003) calls "the politics of dissent." Informal workers' organizations represent key new spaces of struggle among critics and "change agents" of the emerging new economy (Chowdhury 2003).[6]

In contrast to the recent globalization literature that claims a diminishing role for the state and the increasingly unprotected worker, the experiences of informal workers in India suggest the continuing power of both states and workers in shaping the current phase of economic and political transition. Changes in state policies have forced informal workers in India to alter their strategies; rather than demanding employers for workers' benefits, they are making direct demands on the state for welfare benefits. To attain state attention, they are using the rhetoric of citizenship rights. To mobilize the dispersed, unprotected workforce, unions are

---

6 In addition to formal and informal labor movements in India, there is a growing group of radical, leftist political movements that address labor issues, such as the Naxalites. Much of their activities to date have focused on rural labor.

organizing at the neighborhood level without disrupting production. As I argue below, incorporating these experiences into conventional models of state-labor relations, lends insight into a *reformulated* model that explains the important ways in which informal workers' mobilization strategies are creating new institutions that alter the relationship between state and labor. In return for their unregulated labor and their political support, informal workers are demanding state recognition for their work and state provision for their social consumption needs. This emerging social contract bestows informal workers with a degree of social legitimacy, thereby dignifying their discontent and bolstering their status as claim makers in their society.

Background

Existing literature on globalization and labor tends to focus less on changing forms of state-labor relations and more on the impact that reduced state intervention in certain areas of capital production has had on labor and industrial relations. On one hand, reductions in state power, it is still argued in Washington D.C. and elsewhere, will enable capital accumulation and ultimately benefit labor through greater economic and social development (Krueger 1990; Williamson 1993).[7] In his inaugural address as the 40th President of the United States in 1981, Ronald Reagan launched the era of neoliberalism by famously claiming that "reversing the growth of government" would "reawaken this industrial giant [i.e., the US economy]."[8] He promised to make government "work with us, not over us; to stand by our side, not ride on our back" (Reagan 1981). Since 1981, leaders throughout the world have followed Reagan's lead by instituting policies that reduce the percentage of government-owned assets and spending on welfare and facilitate greater private capital investment. Increasingly, such policies focusing on the domestic arena have been accompanied by efforts to reduce barriers to capital flows in the international arena. In terms of labor, the World Bank, a significant influence on domestic government policy, focused its 1995 *World Development Report* on workers noting, "Countries with rigid labor laws [protecting

---

[7] See Stiglitz 2003 for an in-depth look at how this argument came to dominate the policies of the World Bank and the International Monetary Fund (IMF) during the 1990s.

[8] I define "neoliberal reforms" as the set of policies designed to decrease government control regimes and facilitate investment and capital formation. Policies to this end have included the de-licensing of industries, de-reservation of the public sector, easing of competition controls, decreasing import tariffs, deregulating interest rates, easing the interstate movement of goods, opening capital markets, and reforming labor laws.

workers] also tended to have higher unemployment rates" (World Bank 1995).[9] A decade later, the Bank continued to urge less government intervention by showing that the ability to "hire and fire" workers was a major factor in increasing a country's attractiveness to domestic and foreign businesses (Andrews 2005). Reduced government enforcement of costly labor protection regulations, so the argument goes, will ultimately benefit both capital and labor by ensuring greater employment in a highly competitive market.

Scholars writing from a different perspective emphasize not just employment per se, but the increasing vulnerability and degradation of current forms of work. These scholars argue that the eclipsing of the state's role in the economy due to the forces of liberalization and globalization has harmed labor by undermining their ability to make demands on the state and on employers. Focusing on recent economic pressures, some scholars argue that liberalization policies, such as lifting industry subsidies, trade and quota regulations, and license restrictions, push firms to be more competitive by minimizing production costs, increasing labor flexibility, and spatially dispersing their Capital (Hyman 1992; Sassen 1994; Zolberg 1995). To meet these needs, states are pulling back on their role as labor protectors by enabling firms to retrench formally employed workers and hire informal workers instead. By definition the state does not require firms to extend benefits, minimum wages, or job security to informal workers. Other scholars focus on the politics of liberalization and globalization, arguing that the increased ease with which labor, investments, and information now travel has enabled international institutions and transnational corporations to avoid state regulations on the stock and flow of goods and people. This has weakened the power of national states to enforce legislation designed to ensure employers protect their labor force (Castells 1997; Held et al. 1999; Tilly 1995). Additionally, normative perceptions on the government's role in the economy have changed. More states are contracting their public welfare services to the private sector, shifting the state's role to that of a facilitator. As states retreat from their traditional role as protectors of formal labor, so *this* argument goes, work is becoming increasingly insecure and degraded.

Regardless of the conclusions emerging in this literature, the underlying assumption in most studies is that the state's diminishing role in labor protection translates into a weaker relationship between the state and labor. Given the deep and significant relationships that have been forged between workers and their states since the early 1900s, the prospect of a diminished relationship between the state and labor can have profound consequences on the institutions of indus-

---

9 Note the two exceptions the World Bank makes in terms of government interference in labor policy are on issues concerning child labor and gender discrimination.

trial relations, as well as on broader notions of democracy and citizenship. It is this prospect, therefore, rather than its impact, that demands more in-depth analysis.

Current examinations on the weakening relationship between state and labor are unsatisfying on several counts. First, they place a disproportionate emphasis on the *quantity* of state involvement. Less state intervention in labor protection is analyzed as either beneficial or harmful to labor; in both cases the relationship between state and labor is viewed as diminishing. As Fred Block (1994) insightfully argues in his "new paradigm" of the state's role in the economy, far greater analytical leverage can be gained by examining the changing *qualitative* nature of the nexus between state and society. In both theory and practice, Karl Polanyi (2001 [1944]) famously warned against "disembedding" the economy from state forces. The state is always implicated in capitalist production relations, because it sets the ground rules within which business and labor compete for state attention. Moreover, the state must remain active in reproducing labor as a "fictitious commodity" (Block 2001). Reformulating existing models of state-labor relations to focus less on the quantity of state involvement in the economy, and more on its qualitative nature enables a more dynamic and nuanced analysis of changing forms of state involvement in the current global economy.

Second, the direction of impact in the existing literature appears to flow in one direction only: from the state to labor. Recent state actions that have absolved employers of responsibility for protecting their workforce are said to either (1) benefit labor by ensuring greater employment opportunities or (2) undermine labor by increasing their degradation, vulnerability, and disempowerment. Scholars have long demonstrated that the arrow of impact can also flow in the other direction; organized workers have played an instrumental role in shaping transformative events, modern societies, and institutions (Collier and Collier 1979; Collier and Collier 1991; Heller 1999; Moore 1966; Rueschemeyer et al. 1992; Thompson 1966; Tilly 1978). Yet recently, scholarship and the media have shown a growing skepticism of the intentions and the ability of workers' movements to improve people's living conditions today.[10] As Beverly Silver (2003: 1) begins her award-winning account of workers' movements since 1879, "During the last two decades of the twentieth century, there was an almost complete consensus in the social science literature that labor movements were in a general and severe crisis." Scholars of Western Europe and the United States (Tilly 1995; Western 1995), Eastern Europe (Crowley and Ost 2001; Przeworski 1991), and the

---

10 Recently, some notable exceptions have emerged to analyze new movements among immigrant workers and service workers in the US (see Fine 2006; Milkman 2006).

newly industrializing countries of East Asia (Deyo 1989) point to declining union density and public influence as evidence of the so-called labor movement crisis.

In large part, it is the growing informal sector that is held responsible for undermining existing labor movements and thus enabling the weakened relationship between the state and labor. As an alternative to state support for labor, for example, scholars highlight governments in traditional welfare states (Castells 1997; Held et al. 1999; Tilly 1995) and in formerly socialist states (Lee 1999; Stark and Bruszt 1998) that are promoting the informal sector as a safety-net for workers who cannot find jobs in the formal sector. In developing countries, Hernando De Soto (1989) celebrates the growing informal sector as a creative way to avoid Latin American States' mercantilist regulations. Implicit in these arguments is that informal workers cannot organize to demand the state or the employer for improved benefits. Informality disperses the site of production through home-based work, complicates employer-employee relationships through multiple sub-contracting arrangements, atomizes labor relationships by eliminating the daily shop floor gathering of workers, and undermines workers' bargaining power by denying them legally protected job security. Thus the growing number of workers operating in these very circumstances as a result of reduced state intervention is viewed as an affront to the relevance of labor organizations. As Arandarenko (2001: 169) writes, "The informal economy is undoubtedly the most important buffer against class opposition in Serbia."

As I illustrate below, however, conditions of informal employment today do not preclude a priori workers' organization and interaction with the state. Rather, part of the reason for the perceived unidirectional impact from state to labor can be attributed, not to the growth of the informal workforce, but to the flawed conceptualization of the state and of society as independent, static entities. Re-conceptualizing the state and society as inter-dependent and dynamic entities that affect one another in a constant evolution can allow for a two-way arrow between state and labor. Scholars have shown how state changes to structures of production during the 1800s not only altered the composition of the working class, but also motivated the need to *remake* workers' movements in a way that redefined industrial relations (Voss 1993). During the 1980s, Charles Sabel and David Stark (1982: 440) argued that the planned economies of the Soviet Union, alongside struggles within the party apparatus, inadvertently created "the precondition for shop-floor power" through tight labor markets; labor's increased bargaining position, in turn, helped determine state investment policy. They reconceptualize class relations to emphasize "the ways the strong and the weak must depend on each other in order to pursue their separate ends" (Sabel and Stark 1982: 443). Similarly, recent state policies that aim to decentralize structures of production not only alter labor's choice set and the meaning of labor (to include unregulated, informal workers), but they also create conditions in which workers (even informal workers) redefine state's role in society. This re-conceptualization of the state and society as inter-dependent, dynamic entities broadens attention beyond just state attempts to undermine labor through informal employment, and includes alternative forms of labor movements that can, and indeed do, emerge in response to recent changes in state policies.

Finally, arguments on the weakening relationship between state and labor in the current era rely on experiences that emerged in only *some* contexts of factory-based production structures in the nineteenth century as the primary point of comparison. These accounts, however, are too narrow to describe all contexts. Implicit in much of the recent globalization literature, for example, is an assumption that prior to the 1980s and 1990s, socialist and labor parties pushed states to intervene against the interests of capital and in support of labor by holding capital responsible for labor's welfare. The recent era becomes a tipping point when such parties decline in power and state leaders alter their actions by reducing intervention in capital production, thereby undermining state relations with labor. Debates then center on how these changes in state action ultimately benefit capital and either indirectly benefit labor with increased employment or directly hurt labor by increasing their vulnerability.

This homogenous characterization of the pre-1980s state-labor-capital relationship, however, stands in sharp contrast to the range of relationships found in recent empirical scholarship. In Sweden, for example, Peter Swenson (2002) demonstrates how state policies on welfare benefits and minimum wages under social-democratic parties from the 1940s to the 1960s were strategically designed to benefit both capital and labor. Significantly, the state not only mediated the relationship between capital and labor, it also provided direct welfare benefits to labor, which in turn also benefited capital by limiting the realm in which capital had to compete for high-skilled labor. In the United States, Kim Voss (1993) argues that it was the US state's relative neutrality, in contrast to that of the French and British states, that ultimately enabled the highly organized US capitalists to crush the Knights of Labor. As Voss (1993: 204) explains, "The US state set the rules for industrial conflict and then generally absented itself from labor disputes"; when the US state did intervene, it was against the strikers. In India, Vivek Chibber (2003) argues that the newly independent Indian state in the **1950s** and **1960s** partnered with capital over labor, which not only harmed labor, but ultimately also harmed the long-term interests of capital. These diverse realities of both the nature of state-labor relations and the impact of these relations on labor and capital lend insight to the socially specific and historically contingent constraints under which states have always intervened in the muddy triangle of industrial relations. Incorporating these insights into analyses of current state-labor relations is essential to unearthing creative, new constellations of relations among state, labor, and capital that are emerging to accommodate the economic forces of globalization in the South today.

The case of India

This study brings the Indian experience into the global debate on the changing nature of state-labor relations. Throughout the 1980s, the Indian government took a drastic turn away from its earlier industrial policies, and began to decrease bureaucratic controls over industry, enable businesses to become more competitive, and promote business growth. In 1991, the Indian government announced its official policy commitment to liberalization reforms, which included an expansion of the deregulation efforts initiated in the 1980s, as well as increased privatization and the opening of the economy to international flows (Kohli 2006). India's 20-year experiment with economic reforms has altered the normative role of the state and labor, thereby making it an ideal location to begin a study on the changing relationship between the two.

As in many nations attempting to compete in the global market through the use of low cost, flexible labor, the government of India has begun to explicitly encourage informal employment although it operates outside the state's jurisdiction. Recent government reports, for example, stress the import role informal labor plays in ensuring the success of India's reforms (Ahluwalia 2002; Gupta 2002; NCL 2002). Today, 93 % of the national labor force and 82 % of the non-agricultural workforce are informally employed.[11] In other words, over 114 million non-agricultural workers in India are unregulated and unprotected by the state. Although the informal labor force in India has always been large, the number of households in self-employed and casual labor increased between 1991 and 2001, while households engaged in regular wage/salaried jobs decreased in the same time period (NSSO 2001). By the end of the 1990s, the informal sector was estimated to account for over 60 % of gross domestic product (Kulshreshtha and

---

11 In 2001, India became the second demographic billionaire after China. Forty-one percent of the Indian population, nearly 400 million people, is in the labor force. In recent years, scholars, activists, and government officials have achieved a near consensus that 93 % of the labor force is informally employed. Nearly 6 % of formal workers are in the public sector (NSSO 2001). Recently some scholars have argued that a more accurate picture would exclude India's massive agricultural workforce, which has never aimed to become formalized (see Satpathy 2004). The 82 % figure, which is limited to the non-agricultural workforce, was calculated by the author using the NSS 2000.

Singh 1999). In 2004, the Central Government appointed a high-profile commission to examine ways to further increase productivity in the informal sector. Second, India's formal democratic system, which ensures equal rights under constitutional law, has existed for nearly 60 years.[12] Set against a long history of stable democracy and vibrant political activity, India's economic reforms of the 1980s and 1990s allow us to isolate the impact of structural reform on workers' politics by comparing the periods before and after 1980.

Finally, India has had a rich history of labor organization. Today, India's union density among formal workers is comparable to that of developed nations.[13] Despite scholarly and activist claims that informal workers cannot organize, 8 % of informal workers in India's non-agricultural sectors (i.e., over 9 million workers) is unionized.[14] While formal workers' unions have received substantial attention in India, almost nothing is understood about India's informal workers' unions. Examining how informal workers organize provides an intriguing opportunity to understand these workers' impact on the state's liberalization agenda, especially in light of diminished state welfare responsibilities.

Data and methods

The data for this article are drawn from two sets of in-depth interviews conducted in India from 2002 to 2004. The first set was attained using a snowball technique and comprises nearly 200 Interviews with government officials, labor leaders, journalists and activists. They provided a necessary supplement to the dearth of secondary information on India's informal sector.

The second comprises 140 interviews with poor women workers who are members of an informal workers' organization. Labor organization and legislation has traditionally been industry-based in India. To account for variation due to differences in the circumstances of work, as well as the socio-economic characteristics

---

12 The exception was the State of Emergency between 1975 and 1977.
13 Union density is defined as the number of trade union members/paid employees. There is no internationally agreed upon definition of "paid employees." According to the most recent figures available at ILO, India's union density is 23 % (ILO 2004). According to the NSS 1999, India's union density is lower. If "paid employees" are defined as regular wage workers and casual workers, India's union density is 10 % for all workers and 21 % for non-agricultural workers. If the self-employed are included (along with regular wage workers and casual workers), union density is 6.5 % for all workers and 15 % for non-agricultural workers. (These figures have been calculated by the author.)
14 This figure has been calculated by the author using the NSS 1999.

of workers, I covered two industries: construction and *bidi*, a local Indian cigarette made of a rolled leaf and roasted tobacco. These two industries represent the most organized in India's informal workers' movement.[15] They both operate with private employers, a long chain of sub-contractors, and a vast majority of informal workers. Construction employs 11 % and *bidi* employs 3 % of India's non-agricultural workforce.[16] Urban construction workers tend to be migrants, while urban *bidi* workers tend to have fixed homes; those in urban areas congregate in particular slums. Although both industries are growing in terms of employment, urban *bidi* production is considered a "sunset" industry, while urban construction work is on the rise.[17]

Indian labor legislation is implemented at the state government level. To account for variations in economic policy and political leadership, I examined labor movements in both industries in each of three cities/states: Mumbai/Maharashtra, Chennai/Tamil Nadu, and Kolkata/West Bengal. These three cities share a deep history in India's labor and independence movement, and they represent the three birthplaces of India's largest trade unions. Today, however, their differences allow for a comparative examination of the state's role in influencing conditions for informal sector workers.

Finally, I examine seven informal workers' organizations. Six of the organizations are trade unions, registered under the Trade Union Act, and one is a nongovernmental organization (NGO), registered under the Trust and Societies Act. The *bidi* organizations tend to be unions that are affiliated to communist political parties; the construction organizations tend to be independent unions or NGOs. Twenty members of 1 *bidi* organization and 20 members of 1 construction workers' organization were interviewed in each city/state. In Kolkata, two construction organizations were included, because it is one of the few cities to have a politically affiliated construction workers' union, as well as an independent one. These interviews focus solely on women, because over 90 % of the lowest rung of workers in both sectors is composed of women contract workers. All interviewees earn between US$ 0.25 and US$ 2.00 per day, living below the international poverty line that relies on an income-based definition of poverty. These interviewees were chosen first from a stratified sample based on locality, and then

---

15 Note this is a study about variations and strategies among *organized* informal workers. While an examination of why informal workers are most organized in construction and *bidi* is important, it requires a comparison of organized vs. unorganized workers. Finding and accessing the latter, however, requires extensive resources, which were beyond the scope of this study.
16 Calculated by the author using the NSS 1999.
17 The *bidi* industry is under pressure from domestic and international campaigns against smoking. To reduce costs (from municipal taxes and fees), most *bidi* production has shifted to rural areas.

randomly from either the contractor's lists or the membership list (whichever was applicable) in a particular area. Some male workers who were not randomly selected were also interviewed. Finally, the leaders of each organization as well as employers in both industries were interviewed in all three cities.

Institutions of industrialization: a conventional model of state-labor relations

With the dawn of industrialization, workers responded to the resulting changes in structures of production by fighting to create an institutional structure that provided some play for collective interests. Significantly, these institutions tied workers with the state *through* an employer. By the early 1900s, organized workers in Germany, France, United Kingdom, United States, and the Scandinavian countries began successfully to hold their governments responsible for enacting and implementing policies that require employers formally to recognize and to protect their employees against exploitation (Badie and Birnbaum 1983; Collier and Mahoney 1997; Katznelson and Zolberg 1986; Rueschemeyer et al. 1992; Thompson 1966). Governing bodies, in turn, attempted to balance workers' interests against employers' demands for policies that maximized capitalist accumulation and minimized social disruptions. The result has been varying degrees of state-supported class compromise (Przeworski and Wallerstein 1982; Schmitter 1974). In the social democratic models of Scandinavia and Northern Europe, organized labor pressured states to hold employers responsible for providing workplace benefits to their employees. Labor also succeeded in attaining some universal welfare provisions from the state to all citizens.[18] Labor parties represented these interests at the state level. In the "economistic" model of the US, the National Labor Relations Act enabled organized labor in the private sector to pressure employers for employer-provided benefits. Direct, universal welfare provisions from the state, while extant, were less generous than those in Europe, and labor parties did not develop to the same extent. Despite the diverse results, workers in the early industrializing countries attained at the very minimum government recognition and protection and capital's accountability for wages, job security, and some health and retirement benefits. These victories became testimonies of a "modern" society; pre-capitalist relationships based on feudal ties

---

[18] As Peter Swenson argues, capital also supported these movements for compressed wages and universal, state-provided welfare policies, because they provided capital with a ceiling in labor market competitions (Swenson 2002).

between state rulers and society's masses were replaced with an institutional structure that tied together a representative state, a formally recognized and organized workforce, and a class of capitalists held legally accountable for their laborers (Hirschman 1977).

Underlying this institutional structure of the industrialization era is what I call a "conventional model of state-labor relations". As shown in Fig. 1, once workers succeed in attaining formal recognition and protection at the state level, interactive negotiations with regard to workplace benefits, such as minimum wages, holidays, bonuses, and job security, take place between formal workers organized into labor unions and employers. These two parties are tied to one another through a state-backed legal contract. Formal workers demand the state for the legal right to benefits that an employer can provide. In return for labor, the state holds employers responsible for formal workers' livelihood and welfare. In some cases, the state provides direct universal welfare provisions to all citizens. With regard to workplace benefits, however, the state serves as a mediator between employers and unions, enforcing the legal contract when necessary. This conventional model acknowledges that employers also hire informal workers. However, the model assumes that these informal workers have no relationship (direct or indirect) with the state, because by definition employers are not required to recognize them under any legal work contract. Only once informal workers become formally recognized under state law, and therefore legally accountable for by employers, are they expected to participate in modern labor institutions and join the triad of industrial relations.

As newly independent nations began to industrialize during the second half of the twentieth century, prescriptions from the left and right attempted to apply this conventional model of state-labor relations to developing country contexts. The earliest development scholars in the 1950s, later known as modernization theorists urged poor states to build political institutions that could absorb the growing diversity of social demands (Huntington 1968; Kuznets 1955). Walt Rostow (1960) famously envisioned a "final stage" of development where developing countries would follow in the footsteps of Western Europe, building governments that would protect the work benefits of their citizens through legal contracts that held employers responsible for their employees.

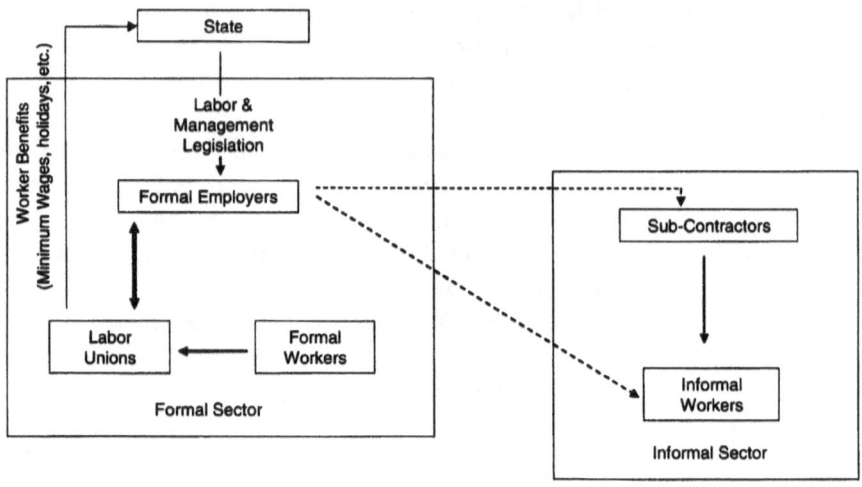

Fig. 1 Conventional model of state-labor relations

As part of this development vision, the predominantly informal labor force in poor countries was encouraged to join the modern, formal sector through rural urban migration (Lewis 1955). The unprotected, informal sector was predicted to decline as economies grew and more state-protected, formal sector jobs were created. In the meantime, J. Harris and M. Todaro (1970) argued, new migrants would bear "wait unemployment," remaining unemployed or doing odd, informal jobs in the city. In other words, informal workers were viewed as an expression of Karl Marx's notion of a reserve army of labor – a pre-capitalist entity separate from the proletariat, invisible to the modern state, and *temporarily* operating on the margins of modern institutionalism (Marx 1906).

Prior to the **1950s,** some intellectuals challenged this model by arguing that state-labor relations in poor countries could not be divorced from state-labor relations in rich countries. Formal workers in colonial states relied on the cheap, flexible, informal proletariat in the colonies to absorb the costs of labor reproduction in the modern, capitalist system (Lenin **1939;** Luxemburg **1951)**. During the **1970s,** dependency and world systems theorists argued that it was this reliance on and participation in the modern, capitalist world system that prevented labor in developing countries from establishing institutions that could push their states to hold capital accountable. Rather, the small capitalist class in poor countries propped up unstable, developing states that were unable to meet the welfare needs of the mass workforce. Through the weak and poor periphery state, local capital benefited from unequal trade relations with rich or core states. In turn, core states gained legitimacy by maintaining a protected workforce at home and accessing a cheap, flexible labor force abroad. The vast majority of labor in the periphery, therefore, remained unprotected by the state (Baran **1957**; Chase-Dunn and Rubinson **1977**; De Janvry and Garramon **1977**; Frank **1969**; Przeworski and Wallerstein **1982**).

As I illustrate in the following section, Indian scholars and activists failed to incorporate these insights on the interdependence between modern and so-called "traditional" sectors into analyses on local labor institutions. Instead, they reified modernizationist calls to replicate the institutions developed in Europe and the United States during the industrialization era. While the prescribed institutions did not develop to the same extent in India as they did in the Social-Democracies of Europe, they did reproduce the conventional model of state-labor relations, where a social contract between state and labor necessitates that capital is held legally accountable for its workforce. These state-labor relations defined Indian informal workers' location in the economy and in labor's institutional structures in important ways.

India's informal workers in the conventional model

India's labor movement began in the early 1900s under British colonialism and was instrumental in the nation's fight for independence. The Trade Union Act, which formally enabled workers to organize and demand protection from their employers, was enacted as early as 1926. Influenced by the Keynesian consensus in the West (Singer 1997), and the labor movement in its own nation, the independent Indian government in the 1950s expressed a commitment to workers' welfare – at least in rhetoric. In practice, however, unlike in Scandinavia, direct universal welfare provisions were not enacted by the state for all citizens in India. Rather, the 1947 Industrial Disputes Act emphasized collective bargaining and compulsory adjudication as the central method for Indian labor relations (Punekar 1948).[19]

It was in this context that Indian workers in the *bidi* and construction industries developed significant labor movements. The government was viewed by both movements as a third party that could serve as a mediator between labor and capital. Organized workers' interface with the state was at first confined to rallies designed to attain legislation that held employers accountable to their employ-

---

19 Much of the scholarship on Indian state-labor relations has focused on critiquing the state's bias in this System (see Ramaswamy 1988).

ees. The state's role in ensuring workers' rights through employers was prioritized over the state's role in providing welfare benefits directly to labor. To enact protective laws, organized workers sought representation in the government through left-oriented politicians and held strikes against employers.[20] By the early 1970s, these movements had succeeded in attaining some protective legislation. In 1966, the first national-level legislation to protect *bidi* workers (the *Bidi and Cigar Workers Conditions of Employment Act)* forced employers to provide minimum wages and work benefits (such as an annual bonus, maternity benefits, social security, and safe working conditions). In 1970, the *Minimum Wages Act of 1948* was extended to include the construction industry. In 1972, the *Contract Labor Regulation and Abolition Act* was passed to hold principal employers and sub-contractors responsible for providing casual labor with minimum wages and decent working conditions; this Act was to be applied directly to construction workers (Samant 1998).

Organized workers in both movements expected that once they attained state legislation that held employers accountable, they would locate the primary axis of their conflict and negotiation for workplace rights between their unions and their employers; interactions with the state would take place only when employer-employee negotiations failed. Not surprisingly, this approach limited union membership in both movements to formal workers – employed by private sector companies in the case of *bidi*, and by government projects in the case of construction. Unions recruited members in factories.[21] This focus on formal workers restricted the characteristics of union members in several ways. For example, by 1960, registered membership in both the construction and *bidi* unions was 98 % male (GOI 1960). Formal workers also tended to be literate; in the case of construction, they were usually also skilled (Chakrabarti 1998; Girija et al. 1988).

Within unions, leaders taught members to view provisions from employers as "workers' rights," implying a formal contract between capital and labor. In 1934, union leaders from India's first *bidi* association wrote, "It is the duty of the

---

[20] Each political party in India has its own federation of trade unions. To date, the largest, most revolutionary federations have been attached to India's two left wing political parties: the Communist Party of India (CPI)'s federation is called All India Trade Union Congress (AITUC), and the Communist Party of India-Marxist (CPI-M)'s federation is called Center for Indian Trade Unions (CITU). *Bidi* unions formed close ties to these parties during India's independence movement. While construction unions have operated more independently, the earliest construction union for informal workers was affiliated to CPI-M. Unions affiliated to right-wing and center parties have not made major gains in the *bidi* and construction industries. Note also that construction industry employers until the 1990s were largely state-owned.

[21] Although *bidi* manufacturing is not mechanized, the work-sheds in which employees sat to roll *bidis* together were referred to as "factories."

employers to the human laborers to provide them with sufficient wages for subsistence and to limit the working time... It is because the employers do not give a return in proportion to their labor expended at the workplace that the workers are forced to sweat like bullocks" (Isaac et al. 1998: 31). Drawing from the labor theory of value, workers demanded that capital provide fair returns for their work.

Since the contract was to be between labor and capital, the fair returns that workers demanded centered on what employers could provide, such as minimum wages, bonuses, and decent working hours. These provisions were considered sufficient to the broader goals of justice and human dignity. As Ram Ratnagar, General Secretary of All India *Bidi* and Cigar Workers Federation recalled, "At that time, our main demand was a minimum wage from the employer. We thought everything else could only follow from that."[22] Early guild associations in construction demanded employers for minimum wages and an annual holiday. As illustrated in a report written by the Construction Workers' Union in Tamil Nadu, during the 1950s and 1960s, the holiday was viewed as an opportunity to visit the temple, which would "confer recognition of the services of construction workers... thus giving them social recognition" (Girija et al. 1988: 94). By 1969, nearly 50 % of industrial disputes focused on minimum wages and bonuses (GOI 1970).

Significantly, this organizing model excluded the mass of workers in both **industries** that were, in fact, informally employed. To the extent that some unions addressed this group, they sought to bring them within the purview of the state-backed contract between capital and labor by formalizing them. In 1962, Sundar Navelkar, one of the earliest female lawyers in India and then a member of the Communist Party of India-Marxist, started the first construction workers' union for informal workers in Mumbai, Maharashtra. While the union's focus on informal workers was unique for the time, the union's organizing model and membership of literate men followed that of formal sector unions. The union fought to enact the National Contract Labor Act to limit capital's use of informal contract labor, which was considered an inferior option to regular, formal employment. The union also fought to ensure that employers provide the same working conditions to contract and regular workers through timely payment of wages and the provision of canteens, rest-rooms, drinking water, and first-aid boxes on the work sites. At the age of 83, Sundar recalled this early movement, "Workers learned they had a *right* to things. That was our greatest victory."[23] Meeting workers' "rights" was viewed as the responsibility of the employer.

Workers' collective action against capital in these early movements was militant and often violent. The first recorded strike in the *bidi* industry took place 1

---

22 Interview with Ram Ratnagar, July 1, 2003.
23 Interview with Sundar Navelkar, August 4, 2003. Emphasis in original.

month after the first *bidi* union was formed in 1934. For the next three decades, the strike served as the most popular form of workers' resistance. In 1951 alone, the Indian Government reported 120 registered strikes in the *bidi* industry; hundreds more took place on a spontaneous basis (GOI 1952). Even when strikes did not result in economic gains, they were heralded as a means to bolstering solidarity in both *bidi* and construction (Chauhan 2001; Isaac et al. 1998).

Despite these efforts, however, the apparent victories that formal workers attained in terms of state legislation and employer accountability soon boomeranged against them. To avoid being regulated, employers in both industries during the late 1960s hired even more informal workers that fell outside the jurisdiction of the new laws. These actions altered the demographics of the labor force in both industries. Unskilled women in construction were targeted to perform menial tasks, such as carrying bricks and cleaning and mixing cement (Vaid 1997). These women had not been actively involved in the labor movement, they were desperate for employment, and, most importantly, they were willing to work informally (Vaid 1999). On October 15, 1968 just months after the state of Kerala implemented the *Bidi Act*, the state's largest *bidi* company, Mangalore Ganesh *Bidi*, shut down all its factories, instantly laying off 12,000 workers (Isaac et al. 1998). Almost all *bidi* factories in the three cities covered in this study had closed down by the mid-1970s. In place of the largely male factory labor, *bidi* employers hired women who could manufacture *bidis* in their own homes. Subcontractors were used to veil the employer-employee relationship, so employers could not be held responsible for their workers under the *Bidi* Act.

As predicted by the conventional state-labor relations model, both movements became dormant once the labor force overtly shifted from a formal to an informal one. Informal workers' employers are not constant, often unknown, and not held legally responsible for their labor. These circumstances of informal employment made it impossible for unions organized under the conventional model to internet with the state by holding employers accountable to the newly-attained labor protection acts. As shown in Fig. 2, the number of registered industrial disputes fell after the early 1970s. Registered *bidi* disputes were sporadic between the 1950s and 1970s, but they generally maintained a high level. After 1967, however, they show a marked decline, and from 1973 onward, the Minister of Labor no longer even reported the number. Registered disputes in construction show a rising trend until 1970, after which they steadily decline. These trends mirror the aggregate picture of all industries at the national level shown in Fig. 3. As Sundar Navelkar lamented in an interview, "My attempt to bring workers' rights to informal workers failed."[24] Today, as the globalization literature

---

[24] Interview, August 4, 2003.

points out, changing state policies throughout the world are enabling even more firms to avoid labor protection legislation by hiring informal labor. Recent analyses rely on the conventional model to argue that such state actions are neutering the labor movement and thus undermining the state-labor relationship. The conventional model, however, provides a static snapshot of state-labor relations during the industrialization era and does not adequately explain how labor may respond when capital adjusts to avoid organized labor, and the state adjusts to protect capital. As the Indian experience illustrates, alternative institutions and new relationships between the state and labor can develop as both parties form a revised social contract that reformulates the nature of industrial relations in the current era.

A new institutionalism: reformulating state-labor relations

A closer look at the Indian case uncovers new forms of institutionalism that are developing to connect informal workers with the state, and helps inform a "reformulated model of state-labor relations" that is more relevant to the contemporary era (see Fig. 4). Significantly, the findings outlined below on Indian informal workers' organizational strategies are consistent regardless of industry-level variations in conditions of work and state-level variations in economic and political landscapes.[25] Unearthing these new patterns requires a challenge to the theoretical assumptions embedded in the recent globalization literature. To this end, I propose greater attention to (1) the qualitative nature of the state-labor relationship; (2) the inter-dependent and dynamic characteristics of states and of organized labor; and (3) the creative and diverse ways in which the triad of industrial relations has and will continue to be shaped.

The setback in workers' organization in India's *bidi* and construction industries appears to have been temporary. By the end of the 1970s, as the Indian state continued to absolve employers of responsibility for their workers, informal workers began to show that their increasing vulnerability was unsustainable. In 1979, informal construction workers in

---

25 Although organizational strategies appear consistent across States, I find that the conditions for success or failure vary by state-level economic policy and political leadership. Industry-level variations remain absent in terms of conditions of success. For more on this analysis, see Agarwala 2006.

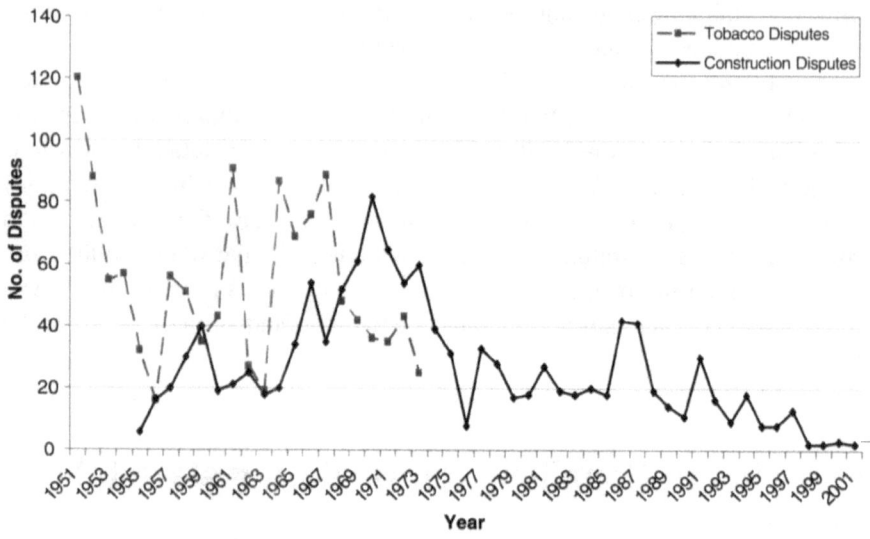

Fig. 2 Number of disputes in *bidi* and construction. Data drawn from Indian Labor Year Book, Ministry of Labor, and Government of India (compiled from multiple issues)

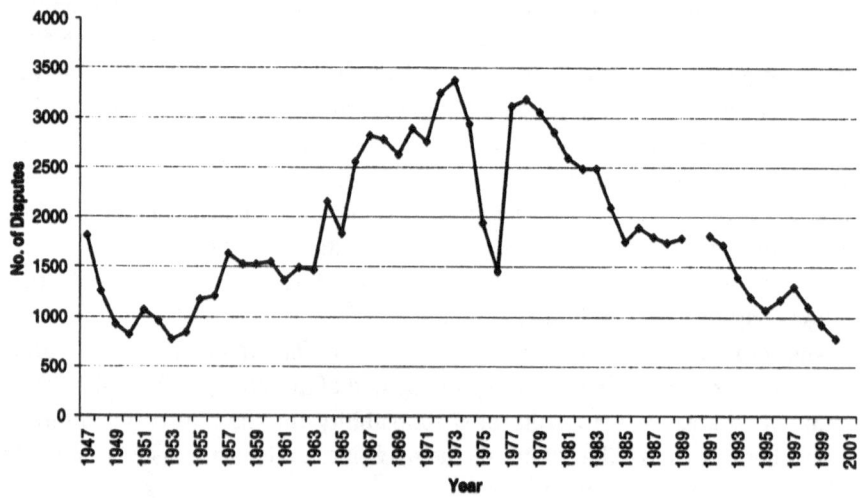

Fig. 3 Number of total disputes (all industries). Data drawn from Indian Labor Year Book, Ministry of Labor, and Government of India (compiled from multiple issues)

Nadu formed the Tamil Nadu Construction Workers Union (TNCWU), which has been heralded in recent media as the forerunner of a reformed informal workers' movement (Manchanda 1993; Reporter 1994; Reporter 1999). By the mid-1980s, informal workers in both industries revived their labor movements, albeit in new terms that could address the state's response to formal workers' demands for employer accountability. The new movement includes the mass labor force of illiterate men and women, and it aims to protect workers *within* their informal employment status, rather than trying to formalize them. As a result, the movement has had to create new institutional structures to overcome the numerous obstacles to organizing informal workers under traditional institutional structures.

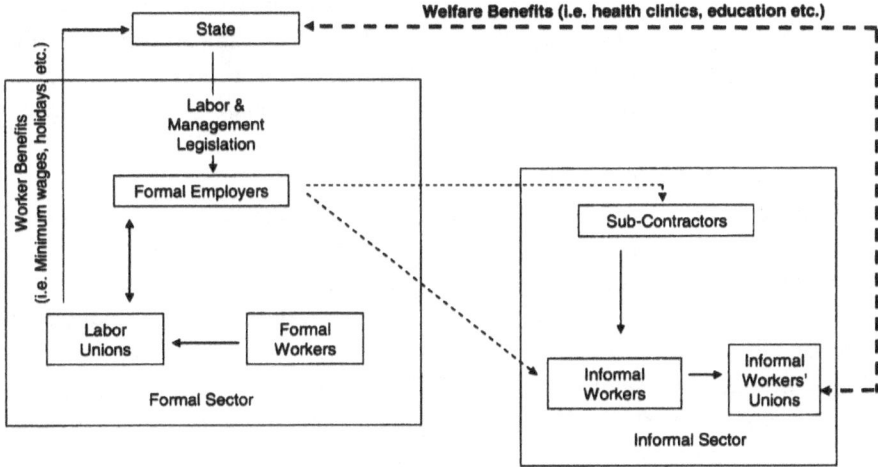

Fig. 4 Reformulated model of state-labor relations

As depicted in Fig. 4, informal workers are indeed organizing into their own unions. Unlike formal workers' unions, however, informal workers are unable to demand that the state hold capital responsible for labor. Rather, organized informal workers are overcoming the employer challenge by holding the state directly responsible for their needs through the concept of *citizenship*. As Charles Tilly (1997: 600) highlights, "Citizenship designates a set of mutually enforceable claims relating categories of person to agents of governments." In the post-war era, scholars highlighted the working class in developed countries as a primary "claim-maker" that successively incorporated civil, political, and, eventually, social rights into a single rhetoric of national citizenship (Hanagan 1997; Marshall 1964). In post-reform India, I find that informal workers are organizing along class lines and using their power as voting citizens to expand their rights and make social welfare claims on the state. To this extent, Indian informal workers are reifying part of the original goal of social democratic labor movements – a social wage that "de-commodifies labor" – by embodying an expanded notion of citizenship.

This alteration in state accountability for labor is expressed as a necessary response to the state's new policies toward capital. As the following testimony eloquently illustrates, even *bidi* organizations that remain tied to left-wing political parties have joined the new approach. Vajeshwari Bital Iravati, a 55-year-old member of Mumbai's *bidi* union, has a typical background for women *bidi* workers in the area. She is a member of the weaver caste. Her family migrated to Maharashtra from the southern state of Andhra Pradesh. Although Vajeshwari grew up in rural Maharashtra, she moved to Mumbai with her husband and in-laws shortly after her marriage 35 years ago. In Mumbai, the men in the family got jobs in the textile mills, while the women continued to roll *bidis* at home. Although the mill work sustained the family for some years, once her husband died, Vajeshwari was responsible for raising their two sons and caring for her elderly in-laws. The mill did not provide any pension.

Vajeshwari joined the *bidi* union shortly after arriving in Mumbai. She learned about the union from the other women on her street with whom she rolled *bidis*. The Mumbai *Bidi* Union is affiliated to the Communist Party of India, so Vajeshwari was raised in the traditional class struggle philosophy. She recalled the early days of the *bidi* struggle, "One time we wanted a bonus like they got in the village. We quickly spread the word to fight the employers, so when the union told us to strike, 2,000 of us stopped working!" Despite her background, Vajeshwari explained why she has had to shift the target of her demands to the state, "Now we always sit outside some parliament building to make sure those fat government officials give us what we need. There is no use in going to the employers. They are all thieves. They don't even admit we work for them. They will just kick us out of our jobs if we ask them for anything. But the government cannot kick us out of the country for making demands!"[26]

Alamele, a 60-year-old construction worker in Chennai explains her focus on the state, "We need to fight with the government for a pension or we will be alone one day. Nobody cares for old women. Employers don't want to hire us and children leave us."[27] Alamele has been the sole income earner in her family since she got married. Her husband had numerous health problems and was unable to work. Ten years after their marriage, he passed away. As a migrant to the city, she had no support from nearby family members. To Alamele, the government is the only source of protection left. When the Tamil Nadu Construction Workers' Union formed, a new

---

26 Interview, May 27, 2003.
27 Interview, August 13, 2003.

party called ADMK[28] had just won the state government elections and, as Union Founder Geeta Ramakrishnan said, "There was an element of hope that the newly elected government would look into our demands more sympathetically."[29]

Because informal workers have shifted their focus directly to the state to avoid footloose capital, they have also had to shift their demands to welfare benefits that the state can ensure, such as health and education, rather than work benefits that rely on an employer, such as minimum wages and job security. Although they also continue to fight for work benefits, organization leaders express frustration with the futility of past efforts, given employers' ability to skirt their legal responsibilities. As Aran Pande, Founder and Head of West Bengal's Independent Construction Union, explains, "Our state [West Bengal] has so many laws for labor, but they are useless and corrupt, even with my good connections. Now, we don't even fight for a minimum wage, because it created so much unemployment here. Instead we fight for our workers to live."[30] In Maharashtra, Vayjanta, General Secretary of NIRMAN, the Mumbai's Construction Workers NGO, explains, "Laborers are not interested in fighting for wages anymore. They are more concerned about human rights issues, such as education, malaria, safe child delivery, and isolation. They don't want to rebel anymore, they want a job."[31]

In virtually all cases, interviewed workers' narrowed their demands to one or two issues, although they lacked basic needs on several fronts. Seventy-two percent of the expressed demands addressed welfare issues, while the remaining 28 % concerned traditional workers' rights issues. In six of the seven organizations, members' demands were consistent within their organization and reflected a campaign that the organization was waging toward the government.[32] For example, in the Mumbai *Bidi* Workers' Union, over 70 % of the interviewees said that their primary need is home-ownership. The Union is in the midst of a massive campaign to hold the state government accountable for their promise to provide all *bidi* workers with housing subsidies under the *Bidi* Welfare Act. Similarly, over 50 % of the interviewees in the Chennai Construction Workers Union said their

---

28 ADMK Stands for Anna Dravida Munnetra Kazhagam. This is a local party in the state of Tamil Nadu, and it is one of the two major parties that have ruled the state since the early 1960s. The other party is DMK (Dravida Munnetra Kazhagam).
29 Interview with Geeta Ramakrishnan, July 9, 2004.
30 Interview, November 16, 2003.
31 Interview, April 16, 2003.
32 In the case of the Calcutta *Bidi* Union, although union leaders stated they were fighting for the implementation of the *Bidi* Welfare Board, most members did not know what the Board was and stated that they needed "everything," when asked what their primary needs were. The reasons for this appeared to be located in leadership style. Further exploration on this is beyond the scope of this article.

primary need is support for the education and marriage of their children. Again, the Union is in the midst of a campaign to force the government to implement these provisions promised under the Construction Welfare Board.

This consistency between organizations' movements and members' responses show that campaigns are being waged by the members, not just the organizational leaders. Members often compare their level of involvement in the new movements to their exclusion from the previous movements. Laxmi Panday Nakka has been a member of the Mumbai *Bidi* Union for 15 years. Like most other *bidi* workers in Mumbai, she is illiterate, a member of the weaver caste, and a migrant. She explains:

> Nowadays, I understand what is happening in the rallies. Before, the big men [union leaders] went inside to talk with employers, and we didn't know what was said. They never taught us how to speak. But now we make Ministers come out and talk to all of us. We speak very softly to them and explain our situation.[33]

Operationalizing a new institutional structure

Although informal workers' ultimate goal of embodying a notion of expanded citizenship mirrors that of early social-democratic labor movements, the institutions they use to attain material welfare benefits from the state deviate from those used by formal European labor, because their political choices and ability to use state machinery differ.

First, informal workers have operationalized their appeals to the state for welfare benefits in the form of tripartite Workers' Welfare Boards. These Boards, which are currently industry-specific, are funded by workers, employers, and the government, and implemented by state governments. In return for their membership fees, workers receive welfare benefits from the Boards. Tables 1 and 2 outline the promised welfare benefits from the Welfare Boards in construction and in *bidi*; note while these benefits are promised under law, they have not yet been received by all members in this study. Because unions have succeeded in reaching informal workers, the government uses unions to certify that Board members are indeed informal workers.[34] Significantly, benefits are extended to workers, *regardless of who their employer is*. The blueprint for informal workers' Welfare

---

33 Mumbai *Bidi* Union, interview, May 30, 2003.
34 Manohar Lai, Director General of Labour Welfare Organisation, interview, June 2, 2003.

Boards came from a model initiated by formal workers in the 1950s (GOI 1952).[35] The early labor welfare laws, however, were viewed by unions as a temporary solution that focused on protecting formal workers at their workplace in areas where labor legislation had not yet extended. As noted by the Ministry of Labor in 1960, welfare provisions were "very slim" among informal contract workers (GOI 1960: 136). In contrast, organized informal workers today channel most of their resources into pressuring state governments to implement the Welfare Boards.[36] These Boards are viewed, not as a temporary solution, but as a new institutional structure that can accommodate informal workers' needs under current economic conditions.

Second, to pressure the government to implement welfare boards, informal workers disrupt the work of political leaders by holding non-violent demonstrations and hunger strikes in front of their offices and during election campaign rallies. During these demonstrations and rallies, organized informal workers no longer appeal to claims of workers' rights and demand the state hold an employer responsible for their livelihoods. Rather, they appeal to citizenship rights by demanding the right to basic needs directly from the state. In return, they offer political leaders their support and their willingness to continue working informally. In other words, informal workers' organizations use the power of their members' votes by *claiming* representation of the mass informal workforce. As a result, independent unions and those tied to left-wing political parties hold all state officials responsible for workers' well-being, regardless of the officials' party affiliation. As a testimony to the success of their message, Jhiru Viruthagiri, Head of Tamil Nadu's Construction Welfare Board, candidly noted, the state's "welfare boards were implemented in an election year. I even had a meeting with senior officers, where they were very open about the importance these boards have in securing votes."[37]

---

[35] The first industry-level labor welfare acts in India were: The Indian Dock Labourer's Act (1934), Mica Mines Labor Welfare Fund Act (1946), and Coal Mines Labor Welfare Fund Act (1947).
[36] Although many are also fighting for a minimum wage, the welfare demands form the bulk of the activity.
[37] Jhiru Viruthagiri, Interview July 2003. Viruthagiri is a Joint Commissioner of Labor in the Tamil State Government.

Table 1 Construction workers' welfare board: contributions and benefits

Contributions	
Employers	0.3 % of cost of building. Required for approval from municipal corporation
Workers	Rs. 25 for registration and Rs. 10 every 2 years for renewal
Government	Contribution for start up and continuation (varies by government)
Benefits to workers (Rs.)	
Accident compensation for worker	100,000 paid to beneficiary
Death of worker	up to 100,000
Loss of limbs, eyes	
Education scholarship for worker's children	
10th grade	1,000
12th grade	1,500
BA, BS, Blaw	1,500; 1,750 if in hostel
English, medicine, veterinarian	2,000; 4,000 if in hostel
Industrial and technical course	1,000; 1,200 if in hostel
Post graduate	2,000; 3,000 if in hostel
Professional post grad training	4,000; 6,000 if in hostel
Marriage	2,000 to child or worker
Maternity leave, abortion, or miscarriage	2,000 to woman worker
Natural death of worker	10,000 to family
Worker's funeral	2.000
Spectacles	250–1,000
Pension	Under consideration

Note: these benefits are promised under the law. Not all have yet been received in the cities under study. (Rs. 39=US$ 1)

Third, informal workers' job insecurity poses a formidable challenge to their participation in traditional strategies that disrupt production through factory-based strikes and violent threats toward employers. Therefore, during their campaigns, informal workers ensure that production continues. Ramakant Patkar, General Secretary of Mumbai *Bidi* Union recalled with great pride a rally he led of 3,500 *bidi* workers in front of the Parliament, "We rolled our *bidis* outside all day. Finally, the Labor Minister and the Housing Minister come out to speak with us. This gave the ladies a lot of confidence. They offered to get us tea, but I warned them not to make these ladies' heads hotter than they already were!"[38] Although leaders of the earlier movements criticize the new approach for being less radical, the members and leaders of the new movements view the welfare-oriented strug-

---

[38] Interview, March 31, 2003.

gle as strong as, and more appealing than, the violent struggles of the past. Many pride themselves for being more attractive to workers than the traditional movements.[39]

Finally, to overcome the challenge of organizing informal workers who do not gather on a shop floor, unions organize members at the neighborhood level. In *bidi*, the home is the workplace. *Bidi* union offices in all three states are located in the slums where most *bidi* workers live, and union leaders invest substantial time visiting each worker's home. In construction, the workplace is oftentimes the home.

Table 2 *Bidi* workers' welfare board: contributions and benefits

Contributions	
Employers	Rs. 2/1,000 *bidis* produced. Collected by
Worker	Department of Custom & Excise
Government	Rs. 100 for registration, Rs. 25/year renewal
Benefits to workers (Rs.)	By item (ex. housing, pension)
Health	
Tuberculosis and cancer	
Kidney failure	100 %
Spectacles	55,000
Child birth	500
Basic treatments	2 child deliveries for woman worker
Education scholarship for worker's children	Free dispensaries
1–7th grade	
8–10th grade	500/year
College	1,000/year
University	3,000/year
Housing–250 ft²	100,000. Must score >70 % on exams (girls
From central government	receive double after 5th grade)
From state government	
Worker's funeral	25,000
Pensions	25,000 (worker pays remaining costs)
	25,000

Note: these benefits are promised under the law. Not all have yet been received in the cities under study. (Rs. 39=US$ 1)

---

39 Although traditional unions have traditionally shunned informal workers, recently their dwindling membership has forced them to increase their interest in partnering with informal workers' movements. At the 2005 annual meeting for CITTJ, one of the largest and oldest union federations in India, for example, leaders made understanding and mobilizing informal workers their top priority for the year.

In Mumbai, for example, contractors bring migrant workers from the village to live on urban construction sites for the duration of a project. The Mumbai Construction NGO enters sites by partnering with municipal corporations to provide workers with on-site childcare centers and health services. Although they gain employers' trust by claiming to offer apolitical social services, they use the day care centers to teach members their welfare rights, while simultaneously fighting for Welfare Boards at the policy level.[40] In West Bengal and Tamil Nadu, where construction workers gather daily at a street corner near their homes in the hopes of getting picked up by a contractor for a day job, members and officials of the construction unions visit the corners to mobilize new members. The West Bengal union then holds fort-nightly "reading circles" in workers' neighborhoods in the evenings. Two literate members teach potential members about the Welfare Boards, so they can all help pressure the state government to implement it.[41] In Tamil Nadu, meetings are often held in various neighborhoods in the evenings; the union office serves as a central focal point where members from different neighborhoods can gather to hold discussions or merely rest.

In 1985, The Tamil Nadu Construction Workers' Union launched a national seminar to extend its movement for a Construction Workers' Welfare Board targeting informally employed workers into all Indian states. For the next 10 years, construction workers' organizations fought against Builders Associations to lobby Chief Ministers, Members of Parliament, and the Prime Ministers of India to pass this bill. In 1989, they submitted a joint petition with 400,000 signatures of construction workers from across the nation demanding the protective legislations. Finally, on August 19, 1996, then-Prime Minister H.D. Deve Gowda enacted the *Building and Other Construction Workers' Welfare Cess Act*, which called on each state to implement its own Construction Workers' Welfare Board.[42] The announcement received substantial media coverage, as it was the first of its kind (Correspondent 2001; Gopinath 1997; Reporter 1994; Reporter 1995; Reporter 1996). To date, Tamil Nadu and Kerala have fully implemented their Boards, and Delhi, Pondicherry, Haryana, Gujarat, and Madhya Pradesh have initiated theirs.

---

[40] The centers are funded by grants attained by NIRMAN, as well as contributions from some employers.

[41] Construction workers in all three states include on-site workers and day job workers who stand at a street corner. For historical reasons the Mumbai NGO targets on-site workers, while the West Bengal and Tamil Nadu unions target the day job workers.

[42] On the same day, the government also enacted The Building and Other Construction Workers' Regulation of Employment and Conditions of Service Act, which catered to the requests of the Builders Association to apply minimal protections on work conditions.

During the same period, *bidi* unions also revived their struggle to pressure state governments to re-implement Welfare Boards for informal *bidi* workers.[43] As a result, the *bidi* cess collection was resumed on May 22, 1987. In addition, the *Bidi* Welfare Fund Act was amended to make the failure to issue worker identity cards to *bidi* workers an offense under the Act. Finally the revised Act made family welfare one of its primary objectives (GOI 1990). By 2002 the *Bidi* Board had provided identity cards to nearly 4 million workers and had built four new hospitals with 160 beds and 210 dispensaries and chest clinics designed especially for *bidi* workers. The hospitals and dispensaries are all located in the heart of the slums and villages, where the majority of *bidi* workers live (GOI 2002). The most publicly lauded success of the *Bidi* Welfare Board has been the housing projects. The state and central governments contribute Rs. 40,000 and each worker contributes Rs. 10,000 toward a one-room kitchen tenement and a courtyard, leased in the woman *bidi* worker's name. In March 2004, the President of India, A.P.J. Abdul Kalam, inaugurated the largest such project of 10,000 homes in Sholapur, Maharashtra. For 4 years, the local workers' organization and a Legislative Assembly Member, Narsayya Adam (member of the Communist Party of India), had pressured the state government to approve the project. It is now completed and exhibited as a model of "public-private partnerships." Chief Executive Officer of the Maharashtra State Housing and Area Development Authority, Uttam Khobragade, wrote, "[This] is a wonderful experiment executed by the collective efforts of the poor" (Pandhe 2002; Singh 2004a, b).

Toward a social legitimacy

India's economic reforms have forced informal workers' organizations to alter their strategies and fight for new institutional structures in order to survive. These strategic and institutional changes have, in turn, had an important impact on reframing the nature of state-labor relations in the current era. Rather than *identifying themselves as antitheses to capital, with the ideal state as a third-party arbiter, informal workers define themselves as worthy citizens, thereby legitimating themselves as primary claim-makers on the state. Such social legitimacy was expressed by almost all the respondents as a means to bypass traditional groupings and to ultimately lend dignity to their discontents.*

---

[43] In 1976, the Government of India passed the *Bidi* Workers Welfare Cess and Fund Act. However, the collection of the cess designed to fund the welfare board was stopped in 1979. Unlike the Construction Boards, the *Bidi* Board is controlled by the Central Government, under the Directorate General of Labor Welfare (DGLW) in the Ministry of Labor.

When informal workers join a welfare board, they receive an official identity card from the government. This card proves state recognition of their work, even in the absence of employer recognition. Forty percent of the respondents in this study who had received a worker identity card said it was one of the most important benefits they had received from their organization, even when they had not yet received any material benefits from the card. On February 10, 2000, 1 month after Tamil Nadu implemented a Welfare Board for 54 unorganized occupations, a leading Indian newspaper reported that activists and trade union leaders expressed, "a general agreement that the most important aspect of the scheme [Board] was that it provided an opportunity for the unorganized sector workers to acquire an identity as toilers/workers" (Correspondent 2000). The importance of the state's acknowledgment of their work status is expressed by workers as a means to social legitimacy, especially when their other identities demote them on the social hierarchy.

Take Jyotsna Bhoya, a member of Calcutta's Communist Construction Union, for example. Jyotsna's parents were construction workers and migrated to West Bengal from the neighboring state of Bihar before she was born. Because her family moved from site to site, and she is a member of the lowest caste in Hindu society, Jyotsna did not attend school and is illiterate. At the age of 13, she was married to a family of sweepers. She is now 28 years old and a mother of four girls; she has no sons. At the age of 17, Jyotsna began working as a construction worker because her husband's income was too small to sustain the growing family. Each day, Jyotsna commutes 4 hours on the train by herself to find work in the city. In order to complete her work shift, she must ride the train before dawn and after sunset. As a young, lower-caste, illiterate, Bihari migrant woman, traveling alone at odd hours, Jyotsna is vulnerable to abuse. Four years ago, a fellow worker convinced her to join the union, because they promised to "empower" her.[44] The most empowering benefit Jyotsna felt she had received from the Union to date has been the identity card. "With this card, I don't feel scared walking home from work at night. If the police stop me, I can show them that I am a construction worker, and not a prostitute or some wasted woman," says Jyotsna.[45]

For Badhrunisa, a member of Chennai's *Bidi* Union, the worker identity card legitimates her as a vital part of modern, urban society. Badhrunisa is 32 years old, illiterate, and Muslim. Badhrunisa was born into a *bidi*-making family and began rolling *bidis* by her mother's side when she was 7 years old. She was married at the age of 20 and gave birth to a daughter the following year. Shortly after her daughter's birth, her husband left her. Today she lives with her mother and her

---

[44] Jyotsna used the word "empower" in English, although she does not speak English.
[45] Interview, December 16, 2003.

12-year-old daughter. Like many of her neighbors, Badhrunisa's most important goal in life is to educate her daughter. Still, however, she relies on her daughter's help in rolling *bidis* after school. Living in an all-female home, Badhrunisa must constantly face the charges that she was a "bad wife" because she could not keep her husband happy or bear any sons; a "bad daughter" because she could not help to keep her father alive; and a "bad mother" because her daughter is still working in "the dirty *bidi* profession". Five years ago, Badhrunisa joined the union because they helped connect her to a new *bidi* contractor. Badhrunisa was adamant that she "did not join the union to fight." The biggest benefit of the Union for Badhrunisa has been the identity card. "This card proves that I am a *good* worker. I show it at the municipal office, when I have to ask for water. I show it when I register my daughter at the school. I show it at the *bidi* workers hospital, so I can get help faster than at the [public] hospital. With this card, everyone knows I work."[46] To Badhrunisa, a government-issued card that proves she is a worker arms her with a legitimate identity that she would otherwise have lost by joining the informal sector. Being a legitimate member of society allows her to meet her basic consumption needs.

Empowering women

In addition to facilitating informal workers' access to welfare benefits and social legitimacy, the state's recognition of their work has empowered women passed their traditional social groupings, such as caste and gender. Over 80 % of the respondents spoke to this point. Within the organization and at meetings women spoke on par with men, and caste delineations faded to the background. *Bidi* organizations, for example, are still led by men who belong to a different caste from that of the members. Yet women spoke forcefully toward male members and leaders.

Anamabai Dararat Yamool, a 90-year-old *bidi* worker in Mumbai, explained, "All I got after all these years of fighting was the title of being a daring person. But I would not be alive today without this title."[47] Anamabai was married at the age of 9, and at the age of 11, she moved with her new husband and in-laws from rural Maharashtra to Mumbai. Like her neighbors, her husband worked in the textile mill while she rolled *bidis* at home. Anamabai learned the trade from her mother-in-law. No one in her family was literate. Although they had enough money to

---

46 Interview, July 14, 2003. Emphasis added.
47 Interview, May 27, 2003.

eat and drink for some years, Anamabai had no security of her own. She had no children, so when her husband died, her in-laws pushed her out of the house. She moved into a one-room home and lived by herself. As a widow with no family, Anamabai was particularly vulnerable. However, she had been an active union member for several years, which has helped her survive.

In another interview, Bappu, the leader of the Chennai *Bidi* Union began chiding women for being uneducated and inactive in the struggles, "Now these women members just want free scholarships. They don't want to fight." Tajunisha, a 38-year-old, Muslim *bidi* roller and member of the union, immediately yelled back in front of the bystanders, "We were there with you fighting for housing, for cards, against the anti-smoking ban! You just don't notice us, and then you tell others you did all the work! You think we are dogs that can't think. We are the ones rolling the *bidis* and cooking and cleaning. You just come in and eat and leave."[48]

Tajunisha wears a *burkha* (Muslim head scarf) and a gown to cover her whenever she is outside. Inside the union office, however, her *burkha* slips from her head, and she does not bother to fix it, despite the presence of men in the room. Tajunisha does not want to participate in the violent struggles that union members engaged in during the 1970s, but she views her current actions as a "strong fight" nonetheless. Tajunisha's mother and husband forbid her to roll *bidis* because they feel it demotes the family. Her husband has a part-time job in a bakery, but "he rarely goes to work. He just drinks and sleeps all day." Therefore, Tajunisha continued to roll *bidis* and collect her own income in stealth. "My *bidi* has been my *Laxmi* [Hindu goddess of wealth]. If it wasn't for my *bidi*, my family would not be alive today," she explained.

Tajunisha studied until the fifth grade and can only sign her name. She is sorry that she is not more educated, but she is proud of what she has done despite this "weakness". She details to me the marches that she has participated in and the newspapers and television cameras that came to cover her. Tajunisha's greatest testimony for her struggles is that none of her three children "even knows how to roll *bidis!*" She exclaims with pride, "I made sure that they are all in school." Since joining the union 5 years ago, she has received an identity card, which has given her children scholarships for the past 2 years, qualified her for a pension account, and allowed her to use the specialized *bidi* hospital in her slum. Tajunisha's membership in an informal workers' union enables her to explicitly contribute to her children's mobility, regardless of her sex or caste.

Tajunisha also uses the union as a source of information. For example, after my interview with Tajunisha, she overheard me asking another interviewee about

---

[48] Interview, July 12, 2003.

bonuses. Tajunisha was not aware that she was eligible for a bonus. After hearing me ask about it, however, she grabbed a fellow union member and neighbor and approached their contractor about bonuses. The contractor denied her any bonus, so she returned to the union office the next day to request help in getting this bonus. Information becomes a powerful resource to union members; it is a medium of exchange to strengthen the tangible benefits represented by the card.

The Tamil Nadu Construction Union has used the union office to create a physical space in which members can bond over their common work experiences and vulnerabilities, despite their diverse gender and caste backgrounds. In the office, they relax after work, vent frustrations about employers and spouses, gossip, and nap. As member, Muniyama, explained, "I have not gotten any monetary benefits from the union. But emotionally, I am more confident. I know my rights. I like coming to meetings here. In this house, I feel like I belong to a group." When a police man once asked her why she is bold enough to participate in a rally, she answered, "I am in the union. The men are striking, so I must too."[49]

Muniyama moved from rural Tamil Nadu to Chennai as a new bride. Her husband was a construction worker and was promised more work in the city. At the time Muniyama did not work. Shortly after their second daughter was born 30 years ago, however, Muniyama's husband died, forcing her to start working. Since then, she has been a construction worker, and she joined the union 20 years ago. Muniyama is provided the strength and support she needs to manage her daily struggles as a woman living alone. For example, Muniyama's most important experience with the Union was when her daughter was kicked out of her husband's home with none of her personal belongings. The union filed a case with the police. "I don't yet know what will happen, but it made me and my daughter very happy."[50] As a union member, Muniyama gains visibility in her society.

Conclusions

Using in-depth interviews of labor leaders and organization members in two industries *(bidi* and construction), this study examines how informal workers are organizing to improve their livelihoods in post-reform India. Contrary to existing assumptions on labor organization, India's informal workers prove that the conditions of informal employment do not preclude a priori workers' organization and interaction with the state. Rather, the recent changes in state regula-

---

49 Chennai Construction Union, July 18, 2003.
50 Interview, July 18, 2003.

tions have forced Indian informal workers to respond by capitalizing on their very working conditions to build a unique collective action effort. As the Indian state attempts to retreat from its earlier role holding employers responsible for workers' well-being, informal workers have held the state directly responsible for the de-commodification of their labor. In doing so, informal workers are challenging long-held assumptions on Indian industrial relations by working around capital's lack of accountability. Through Welfare Boards, informal workers are demanding the state recognizes their work and provides them with welfare benefits, regardless of their employer. Such recognition bestows informal workers with a degree of social legitimacy, thereby dignifying their discontent, empowering women past their traditional groupings, and bolstering their status as claim makers in their society. In return, informal workers agree to engage in economic activities that are not protected by the state or their employer. Such low cost, flexible labor is crucial to the liberalization agenda of both the state and capital. To mobilize unprotected workers, unions organize at the neighborhood level without disrupting production. To attain state attention, informal workers have shifted from a worker's rights rhetoric to one of citizenship rights. Given the growing attention in the recent literature on globalization to the decline of labor mobilization (Western 1995), along-side evidence of states' decreasing capacity to protect their citizens due to their loss of control over capital flows (Castells 1997; Tilly 1995), these findings are surprising, as they show that both the state and labor are exhibiting their continued importance in shaping India's current reform era.

Significantly, this in-depth analysis of the alternative movements emerging among India's informal workers emphasizes (1) the ever-changing *qualitative* nature of state-labor relations, (2) the inter-dependent and dynamic nature of states and labor, and (3) the creative and diverse ways in which the triad of industrial relations has and will continue to be shaped in response to specific historical and political contexts. These conclusions unearth a new set of institutions informal workers are building to rewrite the social contract between state and labor, thereby inspiring a reformulated model of state-labor relations (see Fig. 4).

In addition to improving our understanding of how workers respond to current changes in state policy, the reformulated model yields important implications for future work on informal workers, on collective action, and on democracy. First, the unique relationship that Indian informal workers are building with their government calls for a qualification of the prevailing definition of the informal sector. A more precise definition must acknowledge that informal workers are ensuring that the lack of state regulation and protection of their labor is limited to the conditions of their work and their employer, and does not apply to their welfare at home or in their family. Indian informal workers remain unprotected by state regulations that hold employers accountable for their workforce. However, they have managed to attain some welfare protections and benefits from the state, and they are actively fighting for more.

Second, the strategies that marginalized groups use to express their political voice as state policies erode their material circumstances reveal important insights into the unintended consequences of collective action in the context of neoliberalism. Neoliberal policies are often attributed for undermining the power of labor organization by eclipsing the role of the state in labor protection. However, these very strategies have also empowered informal workers by deeming their flexible labor a crucial peg in the neoliberal project. Indian informal workers are capitalizing on this power, combined with their power as citizens in a democracy, by organizing as a class to secure themselves as direct beneficiaries of the state. Such tactics call on scholars to be more cautious in writing off all class-based politics in the current era of a scriptive-based collective action.

Additionally, neoliberal strategies have succeeded in taking the state out of the detailed planning and control of the economy by blurring the boundaries between the public and private spheres through informal work. Ironically, however, informal workers have used these same strategies to pull the state deeper into directly managing and providing for people's daily lives in the private sphere. In India, informal workers have extended their private expectations, norms, and relations into the public arena by forcing the state to participate in decisions involving their children's education, health-care, marriages, and even personal identity. In doing so, they have reformulated liberal strategies of labor politics that distinguished between the private and public sphere. These findings raise important questions on the future of women's collective action efforts. Feminist movements have long sought a fair balance between state control and state protection in the private sphere. How will this balance be affected as workers force the state to subsidize capital by taking greater responsibly for the reproduction of labor?

Finally, the strategic alterations that informal workers have made to traditional formal labor movements by shifting the focus from worker vs. employer to citizen vs. the state, raises important questions about the future of democracy in India. Economic reforms are increasing the mass population's vulnerability. Yet the nation's political system has enabled the most vulnerable workers to hold the one actor that cannot escape (i.e., the state) responsible for their welfare by forcing the state to acknowledge that they simply cannot live on the below-subsistence wages and unstable work they are currently receiving. While India's liberalization policies have undermined informal workers' rights to make legal claims on employers, India's democracy has armed them with the power of political support and the right to make citizenship claims on the state. On one hand, informal workers are reifying the broader goals of collective interest that European social democracies fought for during the industrialization era. The mechanisms they are using necessarily differ. On the other hand, informal workers' focus on welfare benefits from the state does not address the structural changes needed to ensure social equity. Moreover, informal workers are a long way away from receiving all the welfare benefits that have now been promised by the state. As a result, they invest substantial time and resources into ensuring the sound implementation of the Welfare Boards. This approach opens windows of opportunity for populist political leadership to ascend over progressive, programmatic leadership. Additional research across time and non-democratic countries will be required to test whether this is indeed a new phenomenon or a constancy of democracy.

The informal workers' movement is at a critical juncture in terms of its future growth. On one hand, the movement could grow to shape the state's role in workers' lives across all sectors of the economy. On the other hand, the movement could regress into a traditional patron-client pattern where the state extends benefits to workers in an ad hoc manner. Further research into informal workers' movements in a liberalization context is essential to understanding the differences in organizational structures and the challenges that emerge in the implementation of state benefits for workers.

Acknowledgments The research for this article was funded by a Fulbright-Hays Foundation Doctoral Dissertation Research Abroad Fellowship and a Dissertation Research Grant from the Program for Urbanization and Migration, Princeton University. I wish to thank (listed in alphabetical Order): David Bensman, Fred Block, Vivek Chibber, Dan Clawson, Patricia Fernandez-Kelly, Ron Herring, Atul Kholi, Ching Kwan Lee, Alejandro Portes, Andrew Schrank, Gay Seidman, Marta Tienda, and *Theory and Society* reviewers for their extremely insightful comments on earlier drafts.

References

Agarwala, R. (2006). *From work to welfare: Informal workers' organizations and the state in India*. Doctoral Dissertation, Department of Sociology, Princeton University.

Ahluwalia, M. S. (2002). *Report of the task force on employment opportunities*. New Delhi: Planning Commission.

Andrews, E. (2005). *New Zealand named best nation for business*. Washington: New York Times.

Arandarenko, M. (2001). Waiting for the workers: Explaining labor quiescence in Serbia. In S. Crowley, & D. Ost (Eds.) *Workers after workers' states: Labor and politics in post-communist Eastern Europe*. Lanham, MD: Rowman and Littlefield.

Badie, B., & Birnbaum, P. (1983). *The sociology of the state*. Chicago and London: University of Chicago Press.

Baran, P. (1957). *The political economy of growth*. New York: Monthly Review.

Beneria, L., & Roldan, M. (1987). *The crossroads of class & gender: Industrial homework, subcontracting, and household dynamics in Mexico City*. Chicago: University of Chicago Press.

Benton, L. (1990). *Invisible factories: The informal economy and industrial development in Spain*. Albany: State University of New York Press.

Block, F. (1994). The roles of the state in the economy. In N. J. Smelser, & R. Swedberg (Eds.) *The handbook of economic sociology*, pp. 691–711. Princeton: Princeton University Press.

Block, F. (2001). Introduction. In K. Polanyi (Ed.) *The great transformation*. Boston: Beacon.

Carr, M., Chen, M., & Jhabvala R. (Eds.) (1996). *Speaking out*. New Delhi: Vistaar Publications.

Castells, M. (1997). *The Information age, vol 2: The power of identity*. Oxford: Blackwell.

Chakrabarti, D. (1998). *Report on organisation of construction workers federation of India*. Calcutta: Construction Workers Federation of India.

Chase-Dunn, C., & Rubinson, R. (1977). Toward a structural perspective on the world-system. *Politics and Society, 7*, 453–476.

Chauhan, Y. (2001). *History and struggles of Beedi workers in India*. New Delhi: AITUC and ILO.

Chibber, V. (2003). *Locked in place: State-building and late industrialization in India*. Princeton: Princeton University Press.

Chowdhury, S. R. (2003). Old classes and new spaces: urban poverty, unorganized labour and new unions. *Economic and Political Weekly*.

Collier, R. B., & Collier, D. (1979). Inducements versus constraints: Disaggregating "Corporatism". *American Political Science Review, 73*, 967–986.

Collier, R. B., & Collier, D. (1991). *Shaping the political arena: Critical junctures, the labor movement, and regime dynamics in Latin America*. Princeton: Princeton University Press.

Collier, R. B., & Mahoney, J. (1997). Adding collective actors to collective outcomes: Labor and recent democratization in South America and Southern Europe. *Comparative Politics, 29*, 285–303.

Correspondent, Special (2000). Call for Changes in Scheme for Unorganised Labour. In Hindu, p. H50. Madras.

Correspondent, Special (2001). Construction Workers Demand Implementation of Welfare Measures. In Hindu, p. H51. Madras.

Cross, J. (1998). *Informal politics: Street vendors and the state in Mexico City*. Stanford: Stanford University Press.

Crowley, S., & Ost, D. (Eds.) (2001). *Workers after workers' states: Labor and politics in post-communist Eastern Europe*. Lanham, MD: Rowman and Littlefield.

De Janvry, A., & Garramon, C. (1977). Laws of motion of capital in the center-periphery structure. *Review of Radical Political Economics, 9*, 29–38.

De Soto, H. (1989). *The other path: The informal revolution*. New York: Harper and Row.

Deyo, F. (1989). Labor and development policy in East Asia. *Annals of the American Academy of Political and Social Science, 505*, 152–161.

Fine, J. (2006). *Worker centers: Organizing communities at the edge of the dream*. Ithaca: Cornell University Press.

Frank, A. G. (1969). *Latin America: Underdevelopment or revolution. Essays on the development of underdevelopment and the immediate enemy*. New York: Monthly Review.
Girija, P. L. T., Ramakrishnan, G., & Ramakrishnan, S. (1988). *A study of Chitals: Women construction labour in the City of Madras*. Madras: Institute for the Study of Women.
GOI (1952). *Indian labour year book*. New Delhi: Ministry of Labour and Rehabilitation, Government of India.
GOI (1960). *Indian labour year book*. New Delhi: Ministry of Labour and Rehabilitation, Government of India.
GOI (1970). *Indian labour year book*. New Delhi: Ministry of Labour and Rehabilitation, Government of India.
GOI (1990). *Indian labour year book*. New Delhi: Ministry of Labour and Rehabilitation, Government of India.
GOI (2002). Directorate general labor welfare report. Edited by Ministry of Labor: Government of India.
Gopinath (1997). Welfare of construction workers: Legal measures. In Hindu, p. H51. Madras.
Grasmuck, S., & Espinal, R. (2000). Market success or female autonomy? Income, ideology, and empowerment among microentrepreneurs in the Dominican Republic. *Gender and Society, 14*, 231255.
Gugler, J. (1991). Employment in The City. In A. Gilbert, & J. Gugler (Eds.) *Cities, poverty, and development: Urbanization in the third world*. Oxford: Oxford University Press.
Gupta, S. P. (2002). *Report of the special group on targeting ten million employment opportunities per year over the 10th plan period*. New Delhi: Planning Commission.
Hanagan, M. (1997). Recasting citizenship: Introduction. *Theory and Society, 26*, 449–474.
Harris, J., & Todaro, M. (1970). Migration, unemployment and development: A two sector analysis. *American Economic Review, 40*, 126–142.
Harvey, D. (1990). *The condition of post-modemity*. Cambridge: Blackwell.
Held, D., McGrew, A., Goldblatt, D., & Perraton, J. (1999). *Global transformations: Politics, economics and culture*. Stanford: Stanford University Press.
Heller, P. (1999). *The labor of development: Workers and the transformation of capitalism in Kerala, India*. Ithaca: Cornell University Press.
Heller, P. (2000). Degrees of democracy: Some comparative lessons from India. *World Politics, 52*, 484–519.
Hirschman, A. O. (1977). *The passions and the interests: Political arguments for capitalism before its triumph*. Princeton: Princeton University Press.
Horowitz, D. L. (1991). *A democratic South Africa: Constitutional engineering in a divided society*. Berkeley: University of California Press.
Huntington, S. (1968). *Political order in changing societies*. New Haven: Yale University Press.
Hyman, R. (1992). Trade unions and the disaggregation for the working class. In M. Regini (Ed.) *The future of labour movements*. Newbury Park: Sage.
ILO (2004). Bureau of Statistics.
Isaac, T. M., Thomas, F., Richard, W., & Raghavan, P. (1998). *Democracy at work in an Indian industrial cooperative*. Ithaca: Cornell University Press.
Katznelson, I., & Zolberg, A. R. (Eds.) (1986). *Working-class formation: Nineteenth-century patterns in Western Europe and the United States*. Princeton: Princeton University Press.
Kohli, A. (2006). Politics of economic growth in India. *Economic and Political Weekly*. pp. 1251–1259, 1361–1370.

Krueger, A. O. (1990). Government failures in development. *The Journal of Economic Perspectives*, 4, 923.
Kulshreshtha, A. C., & Singh, G. (1999). Gross Domestic Product and Employment in the Informal Sector of the Indian Economy. *Indian Journal of Labour Economics*, 42, 217–230.
Kundu, A., & Sharma, A. N. (Eds.) (2001). *Informal sector in India: Perspectives and policies*. New Delhi: Institute for Human Development and Institute of Applied Manpower Research.
Kuznets, S. (1955). Economic growth and income inequality. *American Economic Review*, 45, 1–26.
Lee, C. K. (1999). From organized dependence to disorganized despotism: Changing labour regimes in Chinese factories. *China Quarterly*, 157, 44–71.
Lenin, V. I. (1939). *Imperialism, the highest stage of capitalism*. New York: International.
Lewis, W. A. (1955). *The theory of economic growth*. London: Allen & Unwin.
Luxemburg, R. (1951). *The accumulation of capital*. London: Routledge and Kegan Paul.
Macharia, K. (1997). *Social and political dynamics of the informal economy in African cities: Nairobi and Harare*. Oxford: University Press of America.
Mahadevia, D. (1998). Informalisation of employment and incidence of poverty in Ahmedabad. *Indian Journal of Labour Economics*, 41, 515–530.
Manchanda, R. (1993). *Building the builders movement*. In Telegraph, p. H51. Calcutta.
Marshall, T. H. (1964). *Class, citizenship, and social development: Essays*. Garden City, NY: Doubleday.
Marx, K. (1906). *Capital: A critique of political economy*. Chicago: Kerr.
Milkman, R. (2006). *L.A. story: Immigrant workers and the future of the U.S. Labor Movement*. New York: Russell Sage Foundation.
Moore, B. (1966). *Social origins of dictatorship and democracy: Lord and peasant in the making of the modern world*. Boston: Beacon.
NCL (2002). *Report of the 2nd National Commission on Labour*. New Delhi: Ministry of Labour, Government of India.
NSSO (2001). *Employment and unemployment situation in India, 1999–2000*. Calcutta: National Sample Survey Organisation (NSSO), Government of India.
Oberai, A. S., & Chadha, G. K. (Eds.) (2001). *Job creation in urban informal sector in India: Issues and policy options*. New Delhi: International Labour Organisation (ILO).
Pandhe, A. (2002). Mass housing scheme for bidi workers: The Sholapur experience – the first of its kind in Asia. in *Maharashtra Infrastructure Summit, 2002*, edited by Maharashtra Economic Development Corporation. Maharashtra, India: M. E. D. Corporation.
Polanyi, K. (2001). *The great transformation: The political and economic origins of our time*. Boston: Beacon. First printed in 1944.
Portes, A. (1994). The informal economy and its paradoxes. In N. Smelser, & R. Swedberg (Eds.) *Handbook of economic sociology* (pp. 426–449). Princeton: Princeton University Press.
Portes, A., Castells, M., & Benton, L. A. (1989). *The informal economy: Studies in advanced and less developed countries*. Baltimore: Johns Hopkins University Press.
Portes, A., & Schauffler, R. (1993). Competing perspectives on the Latin American informal sector. *Population and Development Review*, 19, 33–60.
Przeworski, A. (1991). *Democracy and the market: Political and economic reforms in Latin America and Eastern Europe*. New York: Cambridge University Press.
Przeworski, A., & Wallerstein, M. (1982). The structure of class conflict in democratic capitalist societies. *American Political Science Review*, 76, 215–238.
Punekar, S. D. (1948). *Trade Unionism in India*. Bombay: New Book Company.

Ramaswamy, E. A. (1988). *Worker consciousness and trade union response.* New Delhi: Oxford University Press.
Reagan, R. (1981). Inaugural Address, as US President.
Reporter, Staff (1994). *Representation for workers in new board sought.* In Hindu, p. H51, Madras.
Reporter, Staff (1995). *Construction workers demand central act.* In Hindu, p. H51, Madras.
Reporter, Staff (1996). *Mandatory registration of construction workers sought.* In Hindu, p. H51, Madras.
Reporter, Staff (1999). *A better deal for construction workers.* In Hindu, p. H51, Madras.
Rostow, W. W. (1960). *The stages of economic growth: A non-communist Manifesto.* Cambridge: Cambridge University Press.
Rudolph, L. I., & Rudolph, S. H. (1987). *In pursuit of Lakshmi: The political economy of the Indian State.* Chicago: University of Chicago Press.
Rueschemeyer, D., Stephens, E. H., & Stephens, J. D. (1992). *Capitalist development and democracy.* Chicago: University of Chicago Press.
Sabel, C. F., & Stark, D. (1982). Planning, politics, and shop-floor power: Hidden forms of bargaining in Soviet-imposed state-socialist societies. *Politics & Society, II,* 397–438.
Samant, S. R. (1998). *Employers Guide to Labour Laws.* Mumbai: Labour Law Agency.
Sanyal, B. (1991). Organizing the self-employed: The politics of the urban informal sector. *International Labour Review, 130,* 39–56.
Sassen, S. (1994). The informal economy: Between new developments and old regulations. *Yale Law Journal, 103,* 2289–2304.
Satpathy, A. (2004). *Size, composition and characteristics of informal sector in India. In National Labor Institute Research Studies Series.* New Delhi: V.V. Giri National Labour Institute.
Schmitter, P. C. (1974). Still in the century of corporatism? In F. B. Pike, & T. Stritch (Eds.) *The new corporatism.* South Bend: University of Notre Dame Press.
Sharma, A. N., & Antony, P. (2001). "Women Workers in the Unorganized Sector: The More the Merrier?" New Delhi: Institute for Human Development.
Silver, B. J. (2003). *Forces of labor: Workers' movements and globalization since 1870.* Cambridge: Cambridge University Press.
Singer, H. (1997). The golden age of the Keynesian consensus – the pendulum swings back. *World Development, 25,* 293–295.
Singh, A. (2004a). Solapur housing project was a big challenge. pp. 9 in *Times News Network.* Bombay.
Singh, A. (2004b). Women bidi workers to get dream homes. in *Times News Network.* Bombay.
Stark, D., & Bruszt, L. (1998). *Post-socialist pathways: Transforming politics and property in East Central Europe.* Cambridge: Cambridge University Press.
Stiglitz, J. (2003). *Globalization and its discontents.* New York: Norton.
Sundaram, K. (2001). The employment-unemployment situation in India in the 1990s: Some results from the NSS 55th Round Survey (July 99–June 2000). *Economic and Political Weekly, 34,* 931–940.
Swenson, P A. (2002). *Capitalists against markets: The making of labor markets and welfare States in the United States and Sweden.* Oxford: Oxford University Press.
Teeple, G. (2000). *Globalization and the decline of social reform.* Aurora: Garamond.
Thompson, E. P. (1966). *The making of the English working class.* New York: Vintage.
Tilly, C. (1978). *From mobilization to revolution.* Reading: Addison-Wesley.

Tilly, C. (1995). Globalisation threatens labor's rights. *International Labor and Working Class History, 47,* 1–23.

Tilly, C. (1997). *A primer on citizenship.* Theory and Society, Special Issue on Recasting Citizenship, 26, *599–602.*

Unni, J. (1999). *Urban informal sector: Size and Income Generation Processes in Gujarat* (p.87). Ahmedabad: Gujarat Institute of Development Research & Self-employed Women's Association.

Vaid, K. N. (1997). *Contract labor in the construction industry.* Mumbai: Publication Bureau, National Institute of Construction Management and Research.

Vaid, K. N. (Ed.) (1999). *Women in construction.* Mumbai: NICMAR Publications Bureau.

Voss, K. (1993). *The making of American exceptionalism: The knights of labor and class formation in the nineteenth Century.* Ithaca: Cornell University Press.

Western, B. (1995). A comparative study of working-class disorganization: Union decline in eighteen advanced capitalist countries. *American Sociological Review, 60,* 179–201.

Williamson, J. (1993). Democracy and the Washington consensus. *World Development, 21,* 1329–1336.

World Bank (1995). *World development report 1995: Workers in an integrating world.* New York: Oxford University Press.

Zolberg, A. R. (1995). Working-class dissolution. *International Labor and Working Class History, 47,* 28–38.

About authors

Rina Agarwala
Department of Sociology
University of Copenhagen
ra@soc.ku.dk

Gopalan Balachandran
Graduate Institute of International and Development Studies
gopalan.balachandran@graduatein-stitute.ch

Philip Bonner
History Research Group
University of the Witwatersrand, Johannesburg
philip.bonner@wits.ac.za

Sidney Chalhoub
Department of History
Harvard University
chalhoub@fas.harvard.edu

Michael Denning
American Studies
Yale University
michael.denning@yale.edu

Andreas Eckert
Department of Asian and African Studies / International Research Center Work and Human Life Cycle in Global History
Humboldt University of Berlin
andreas.eckert@asa.hu-berlin.de

Jonathan Hyslop
Africana & Latin American Studies
Colgate University
jhyslop@colgate.edu

Alex Lichtenstein
Department of History
Indiana University Bloomington
lichtens@indiana.edu

Marcel van der Linden
International Institute of Social History (IISH), Amsterdam
University of Amsterdam
mvl@iisg.nl

Alf Lüdtke
Historical Anthropology
University of Erfurt
alf.luedtke@uni-erfurt.de

Prabhu P. Mohapatra
Department of History
University of Delhi
prabhuayan@gmail.comi

Gerd Spittler
Social Anthropology Unit
University of Bayreuth
Gerd.Spittler@uni-bayreuth.de

Alessandro Stanziani
Centre de Recherches Historiques
Ecole des hautes études en sciences sociales (EHESS)
alessandro.stanziani@iehess.fr

Christian G. De Vito
School of History
University of Leicester
cdv8@leicester.ac.uk

Lucien van der Walt
Department of Sociology and Industrial Sociology
Rhodes University
l.vanderwalt@ru.ac.za

Kathie Weeks
Program in Gender, Sexuality, and Feminist Studies
Duke University
kweeks@duke.edu

www.ingramcontent.com/pod-product-compliance
Lightning Source LLC
Chambersburg PA
CBHW030431300426
44112CB00009B/950